BOOK 1

ALFRED'S

Group Piano

FOR ADULTS

An Innovative Method with Optional Compact Discs and General MIDI Disks for Enhanced Practice and Performance

E. L. Lancaster • Kenon D. Renfrow

Alfred

Alfred Publishing Co., Inc.
16380 Roscoe Blvd.
Van Nuys, CA 91406

Lancaster, E. L.
Alfred's group piano for adults : an innovative method with optional compact discs and general MIDI disks for enhanced practice and performance / E. L. Lancaster, Kenon D. Renfrow.
v. of music.
Includes index.
ISBN 0-88284-653-1 (v. 1)
1. Piano—Methods—Group instruction. I. Renfrow, Kenon D. II. Title.
MT222.L256 1995

Cover art: *Impression III (Concert). 1911.*
Wassily Kandinsky
Städtische Galerie im Lenbachhaus, Munich, Germany

Book production: Tom Gerou, Greg Plumblee, Linda Lusk
Art direction: Ted Engelbart • Cover/book design: Susan H. Hartman

Foreword

Alfred's Group Piano for Adults, Book 1, is designed for non-keyboard music majors with little or no keyboard experience. It also may be used successfully by non-music majors or independent teachers seeking creative ways to develop functional skills in their adult students.

Most music educators agree that the piano is indispensable for all musicians. Piano study helps students gain a better understanding of music theory as theoretical concepts are applied to the keyboard. Many music majors who have had no previous piano experience find the first piano classes challenging. Experience has proven that with the proper approach and consistent practice, anyone can grasp the skills necessary to function and perform at the keyboard.

This text is easy to use. It contains 30 units, each designed to be covered in one week, thus filling two semesters or three quarters of study. The title page of each unit contains the objectives for the unit and a space to record assignments for the week. Measures are numbered in all examples (repertoire, reading, harmonization, improvisation) to promote ease of use in the classroom.

The reading approach is eclectic, combining the best elements of intervallic and multi-key reading. Reading exercises are designed to promote movement over the entire keyboard while maintaining the advantages of playing in familiar positions. Reading examples are a mixture of standard repertoire and newly composed pieces.

Suggestions for counting are given but the approach used is left to the discretion of the teacher. Rhythms and note values are introduced systematically and specially designed rhythm reading exercises promote rhythmic security.

The student begins to play music immediately. Each unit has at least one repertoire piece that may be used for performance or study. A section of supplementary repertoire is contained in the back of the book for those students who need additional music or for teachers who like a wider choice of music for students. The supplementary repertoire was chosen to represent a variety of levels and can be used throughout the book.

Each unit contains a balance of new information with materials that reinforce concepts presented in previous units. Written review worksheets, designed to be submitted to the teacher for feedback, appear periodically throughout the text.

Theory, technique, sight-reading, repertoire, harmonization, improvisation and ensemble activities are taught thoroughly and consistently throughout the text. Two-hand accompaniments and multiple-line ensembles help students develop skills in accompanying and score reading. Four-part ensembles often are created from analysis of repertoire.

Technique is developed in a systematic way throughout the entire book. Repertoire, harmonization melodies, technical exercises and sight-reading examples are carefully fingered to aid the student in developing good technique. Harmonization skills are developed using single tones, open fifths, full chords and various accompaniment styles. Harmonization examples use a mixture of Roman numerals, letter symbols and melodies with no symbols given.

This is the first group piano text to be fully supported by Compact Discs and Standard MIDI File (SMF) disks. Each example in the text that contains an accompaniment is identified by an icon that shows the disk number and TRACK number for the example: 🔊 **1-1 (35)** The first number after the icon denotes the CD/SMF disk number. The second number is the TRACK number on the CD and the Type 0 MIDI file on the SMF disk. The third number (in parentheses) is the TRACK number of the Type 1 MIDI file on the SMF disk. (See MIDI disk documentation for more information on MIDI file types.) Accompaniments range from simple drum patterns to full orchestrations. These accompaniments add musical interest and motivate students to complete assignments both in the classroom and in the practice room.

A Teacher's Handbook for the text serves as an aid in curriculum development and daily lesson planning. The handbook contains suggested daily lesson plans for the entire year, suggested assignments following each lesson plan, teaching tips for each unit, suggested examinations for the entire year and answer keys for all harmonization exercises and review worksheets. It also suggests ways to successfully integrate keyboard and computer technology into the curriculum.

Upon completion of this book, students will have a strong grasp of functional skills, keyboard technique and musical styles, and will be ready to begin *Alfred's Group Piano for Adults, Book 2.*

Table of Contents

Unit 1

Keyboard Basics

Objectives

Upon completion of this unit the student will be able to:

1. Name, find and play all keys on the keyboard.
2. Improvise black-key melodies as the teacher plays an accompaniment.
3. Apply basic musical concepts of rhythm, notation, terminology and symbols to performance at the keyboard.
4. Read and perform melodies written on the grand staff.
5. Identify and play whole steps, half steps and the chromatic scale on the keyboard.

Assignments

Week of ________

Write your assignments for the week in the space below.

How to Sit at the Keyboard

Sit tall! Leaning slightly forward, let your arms hang loosely from the shoulders with your elbows slightly higher than the keys. The bench must face the piano squarely. Position your knees slightly under the keyboard, with your feet flat on the floor. The right foot may be slightly forward.

Hand Position

Curve your fingers when you play, as though you have a bubble in your hand.

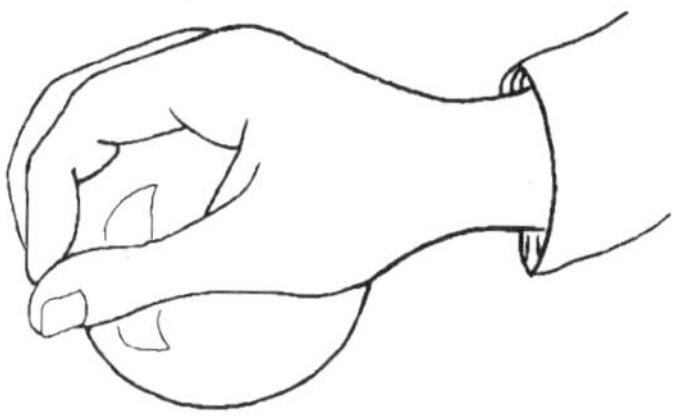

Curved fingers bring the thumb into the proper playing position and provide an arch that allows the thumb to pass under the fingers or the fingers to cross over the thumb.

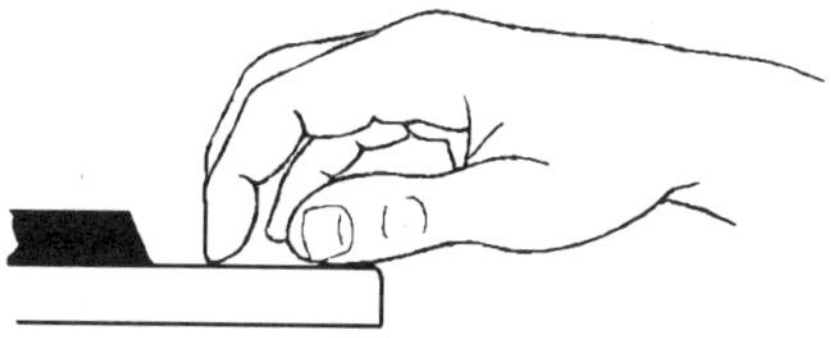

Finger Numbers

The fingers of the left hand (LH) and the right hand (RH) are numbered as shown. The thumb is the first finger of each hand.

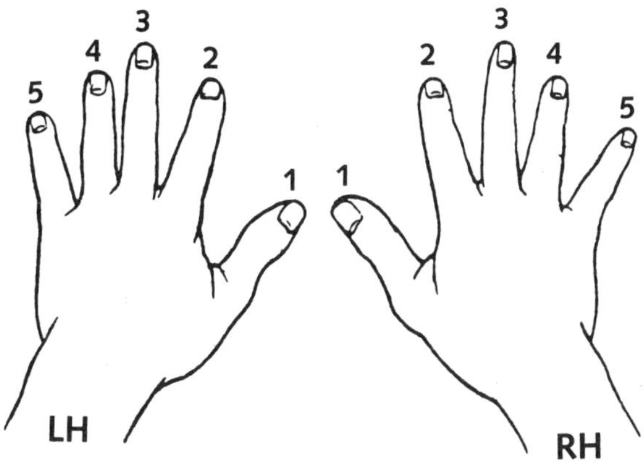

Basic Note Values

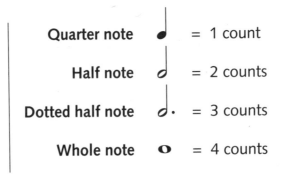

Quarter note = 1 count

Half note = 2 counts

Dotted half note = 3 counts

Whole note = 4 counts

Clap (or tap) the following rhythm. Clap once for each note, counting aloud. Notice how the bar lines divide the music into measures of equal duration.

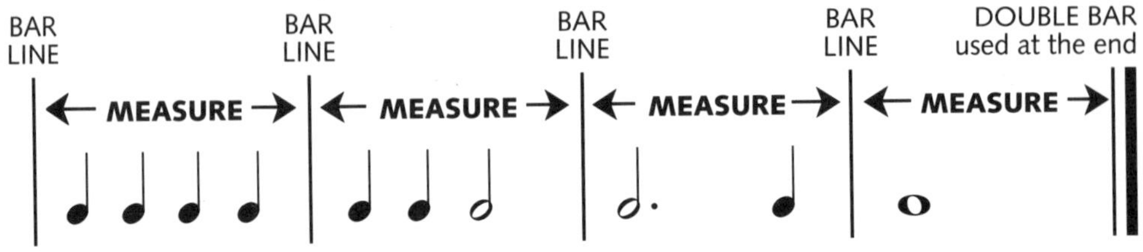

Rhythm Reading

Tap the following rhythms with the indicated hands and finger numbers.

1-1 (35) → Track number of Type 1 MIDI file on SMF disk

Track number on CD or Type 0 MIDI file on SMF disk

CD / SMF Disk Number

Hands separately:

1-1 (35)

1. RH

1-2 (36)

2. LH

Hands together:

1-3 (37)

3. RH / LH

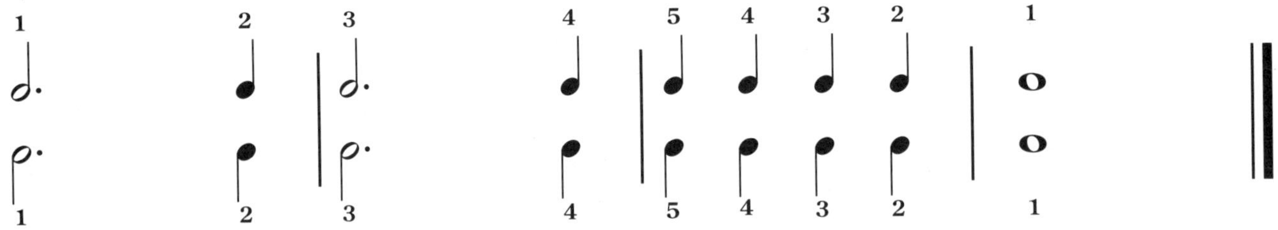

1-4 (38)

4. RH / LH

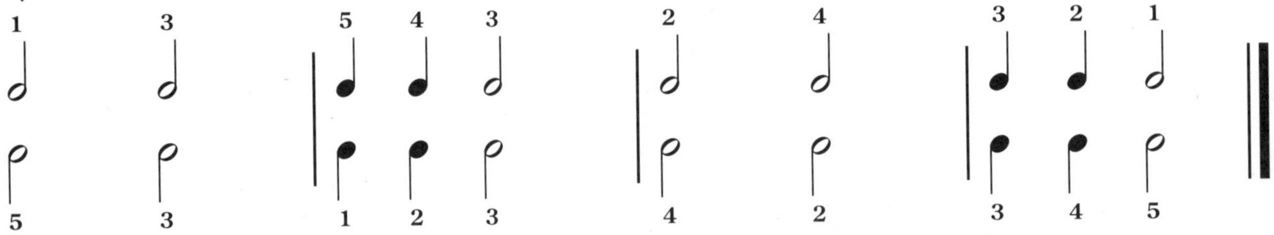

The Keyboard

The keyboard is made up of white keys and black keys. The black keys are in groups of twos and threes. On the keyboard, down is to the left, and up is to the right. As you move left, the tones sound lower. As you move right, the tones sound higher.

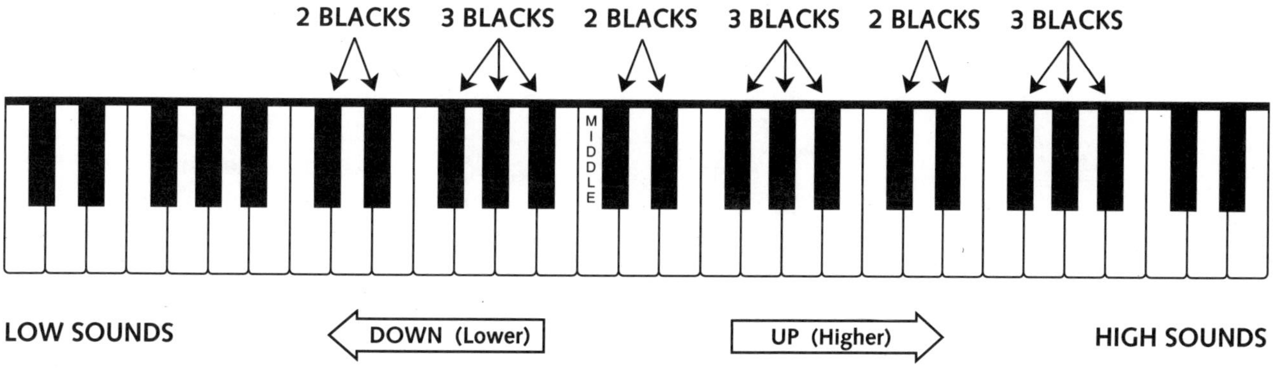

Two-Black-Key Groups

LH

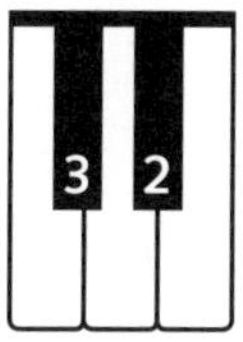

1. Using LH 2 3, begin at the middle and play all the 2-black-key groups going down the keyboard (both keys at once).

RH

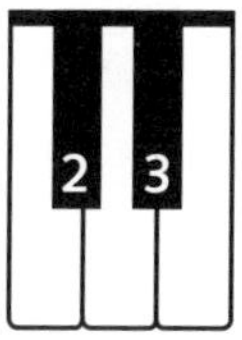

2. Using RH 2 3, begin at the middle and play all the 2-black-key groups going up the keyboard (both keys at once).

3. With RH 2 3, begin at the middle and play all the 2-black-key groups going up the keyboard, using the indicated rhythm and finger numbers (one key at a time).

1-5 (39)

RH

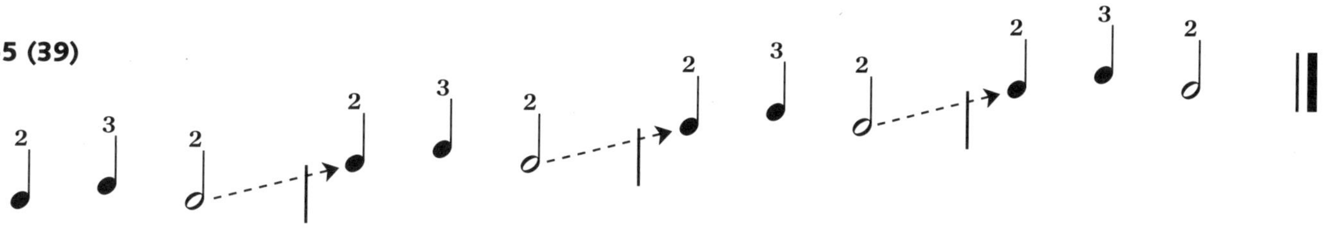

4. With LH 2 3, begin at the middle and play all the 2-black-key groups going down the keyboard, using the indicated rhythm and finger numbers (one key at a time).

1-6 (40)

LH

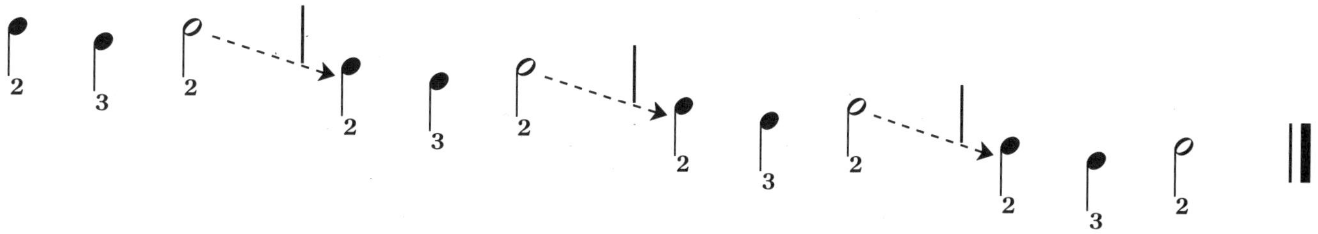

Three-Black-Key Groups

LH

1. Using LH 2 3 4, begin at the middle and play all the 3-black-key groups going down the keyboard (all 3 keys at once).

RH

2. Using RH 2 3 4, begin at the middle and play all the 3-black-key groups going up the keyboard (all 3 keys at once).

3. With RH 2 3 4, begin at the middle and play all the 3-black-key groups going up the keyboard, using the indicated rhythm and finger numbers (one key at a time).

1-7 (41)

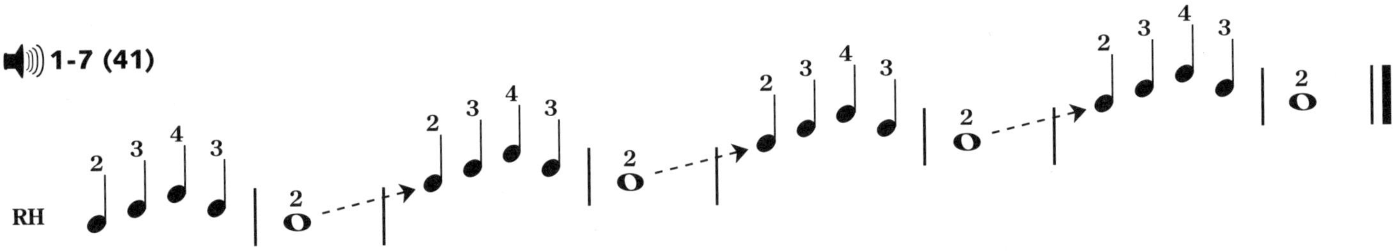

4. With LH 2 3 4, begin at the middle and play all the 3-black-key groups going down the keyboard, using the indicated rhythm and finger numbers (one key at a time).

1-8 (42)

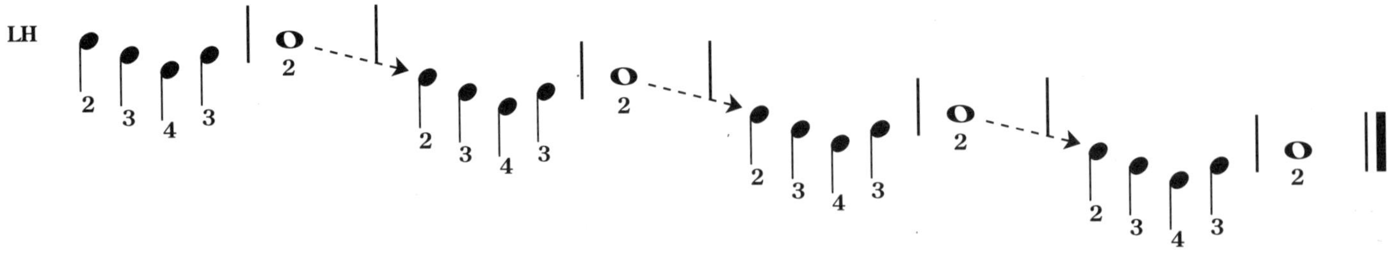

Black-Key Improvisation

Improvise an 8-measure melody using the given black-key position as the teacher plays each accompaniment. Listen to the 4-measure introduction to establish the tempo, mood and style before beginning the melody.

1. Begin and end your melody on the indicated key (↓):

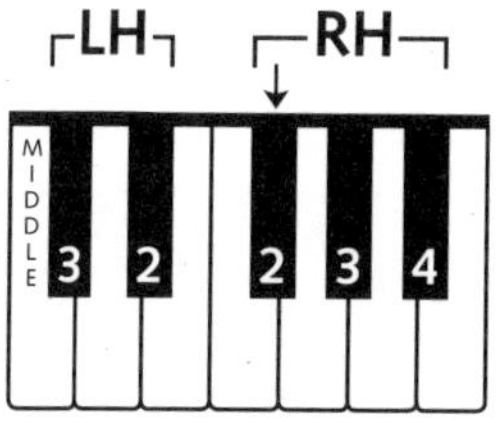

1-9 (43)

TEACHER ACCOMPANIMENT

Lively (♩=144)
Introduction
Student improvisation begins

2. Begin and end your melody on the indicated key (↓):

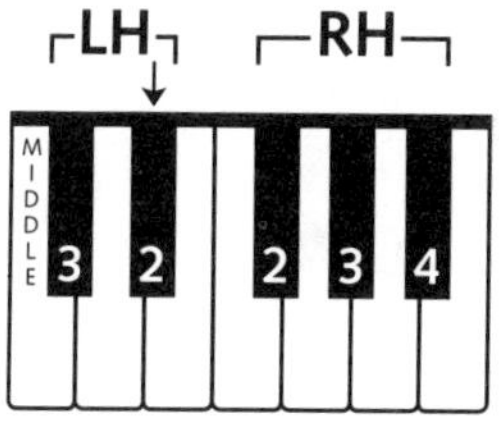

1-10 (44)

TEACHER ACCOMPANIMENT

Andante (♩=104)
Introduction
Student improvisation begins

Naming White Keys

Piano keys are named for the first seven letters of the alphabet. The key names are A B C D E F G, used over and over! The lowest key on the piano is A. The C nearest the middle of the piano is called middle C. The highest key on the piano is C. Going up the keyboard, the notes sound higher and higher. While most acoustic pianos have 88 keys, some digital keyboards may have fewer.

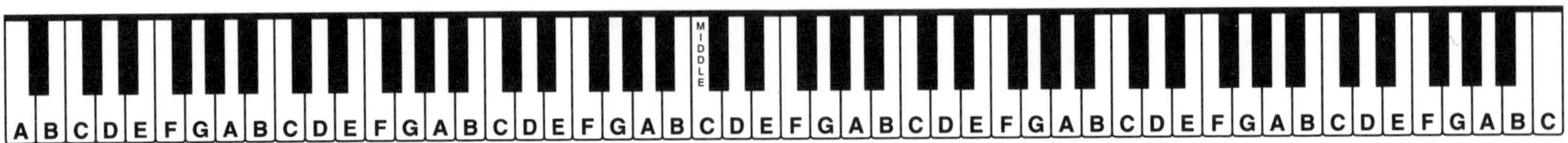

LOW Middle C HIGH

Beginning at the low end and moving *up* the keyboard, play and name every white key beginning with the bottom **A,** using the indicated rhythm. Use LH 3 for keys below the middle of the keyboard. Use RH 3 for keys above the middle of the keyboard.

1-11 (45)

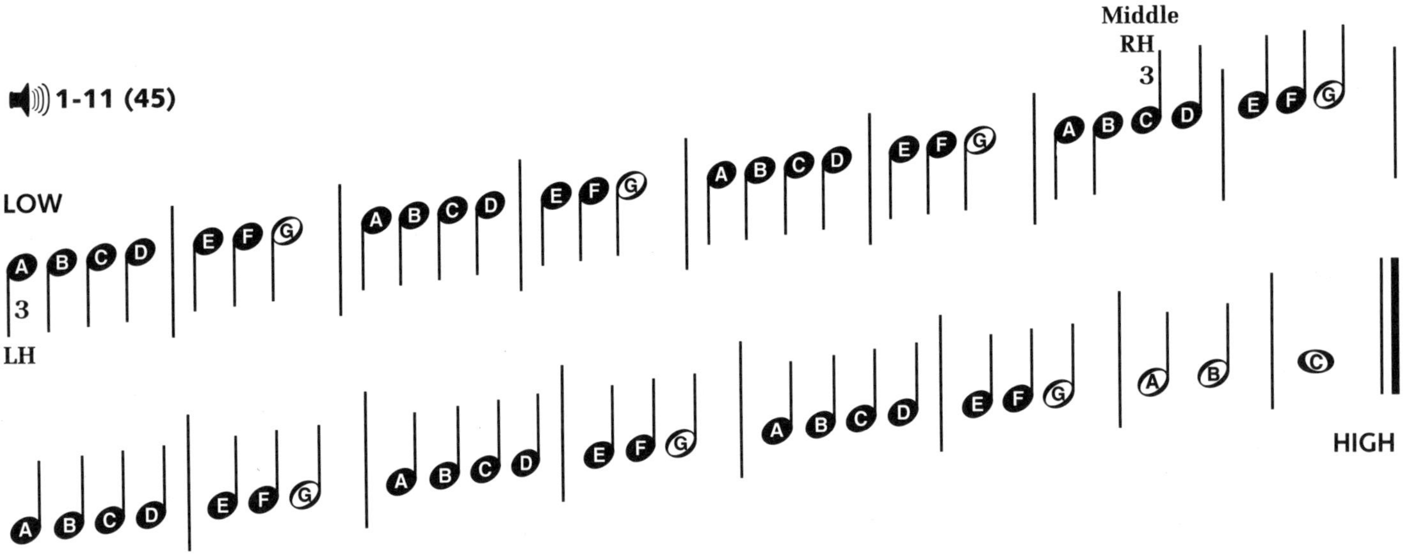

Play all the **A**s on your piano.

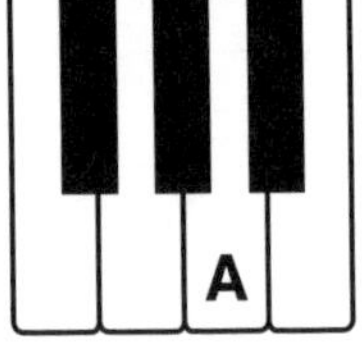

Beginning at the low end and moving *up* the keyboard, play every **A**, using ♩♩𝅗𝅥 on each key. Say the name of each key aloud as you play. Use LH 3 for keys below middle C on the keyboard. Use RH 3 for middle C and keys above middle C on the keyboard. Repeat this exercise for **B, C, D, E, F** and **G.**

Play all the **B**s.

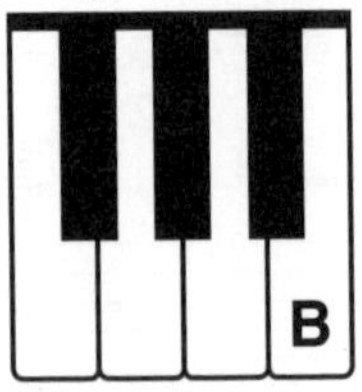

Play all the **C**s.

Play all the **D**s.

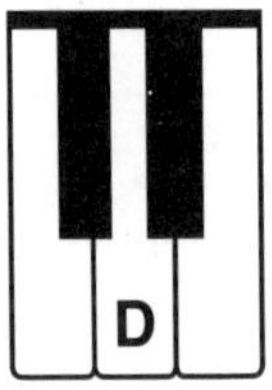

Play all the **E**s.

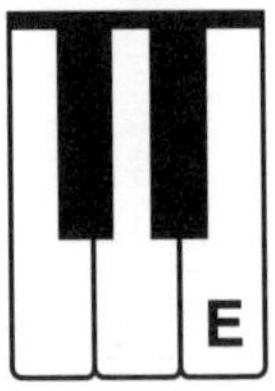

Play all the **F**s.

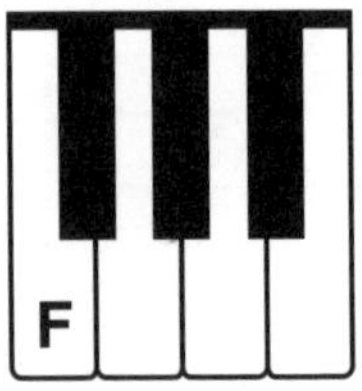

Play all the **G**s.

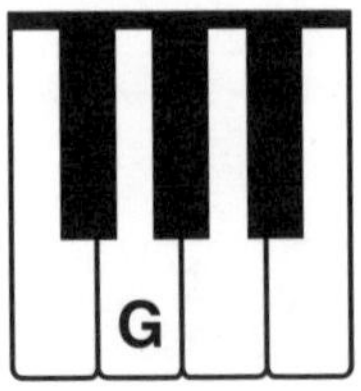

Octave

An **octave** is the distance from one key on the keyboard to the next key (lower or higher) with the same letter name.

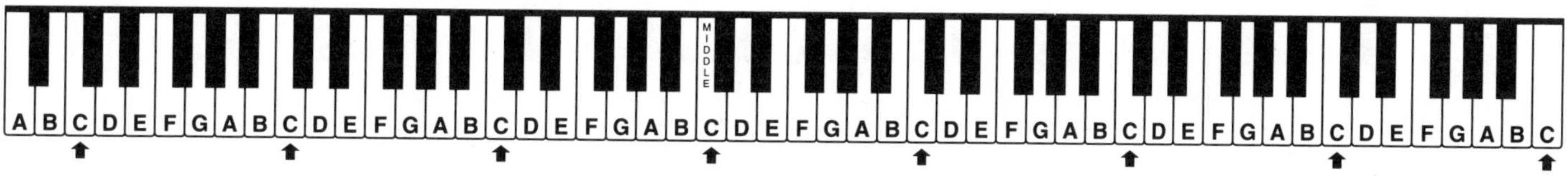

C-D-E Groups

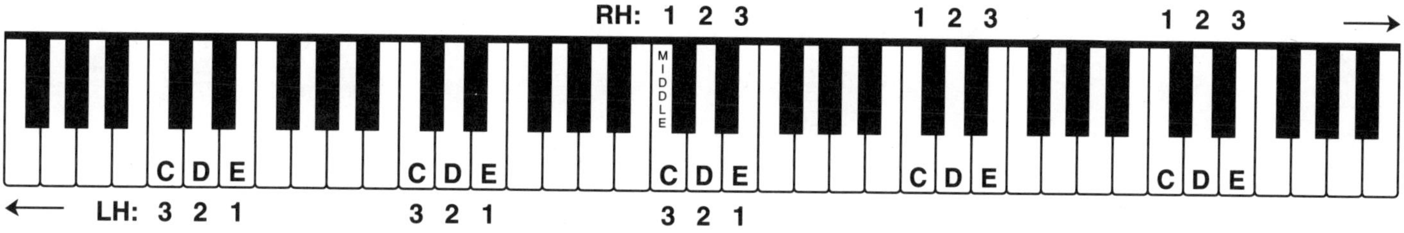

With RH 1 2 3, begin on middle **C** and play all of the **C-D-E** groups going *up* the keyboard, using the indicated rhythm and finger numbers.

1-12 (46)

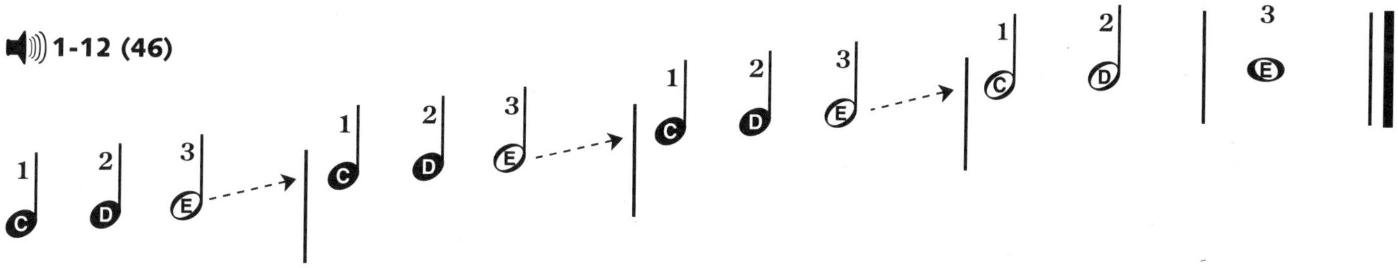

With LH 1 2 3, begin on the **E** above middle **C** and play all of the **E-D-C** groups going *down* the keyboard, using the indicated rhythm and finger numbers.

1-13 (47)

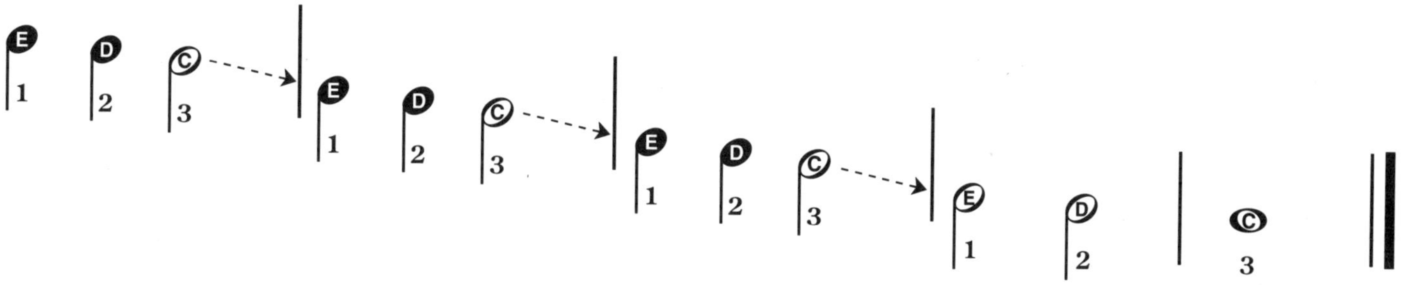

F-G-A-B Groups

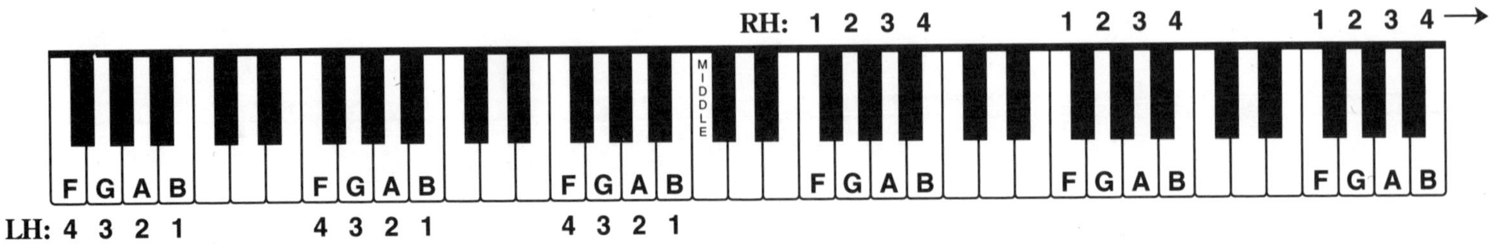

With RH 1 2 3 4, begin on the **F** above middle **C** and play all of the **F-G-A-B** groups going *up* the keyboard using the indicated rhythm and finger numbers.

1-14 (48)

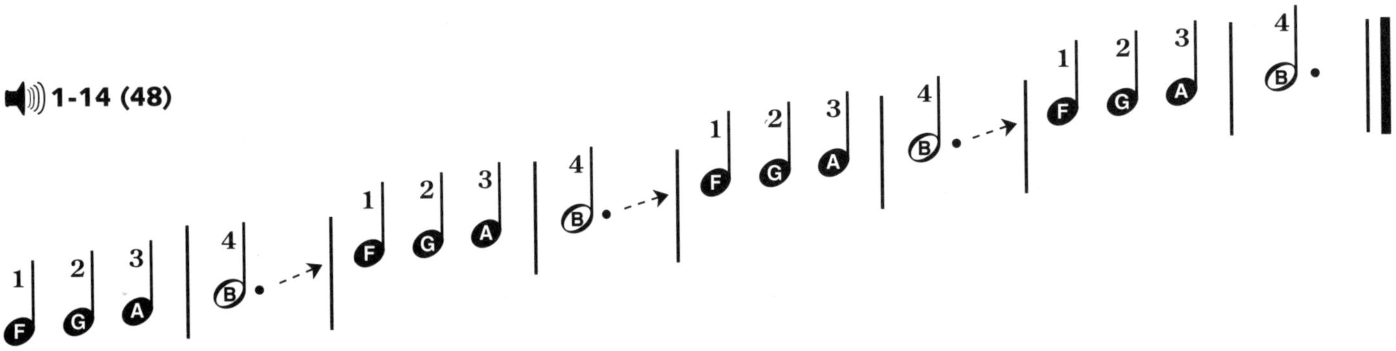

With LH 1 2 3 4, begin on the **B** below middle **C** and play all of the **B-A-G-F** groups going *down* the keyboard using the indicated rhythm and finger numbers.

1-15 (49)

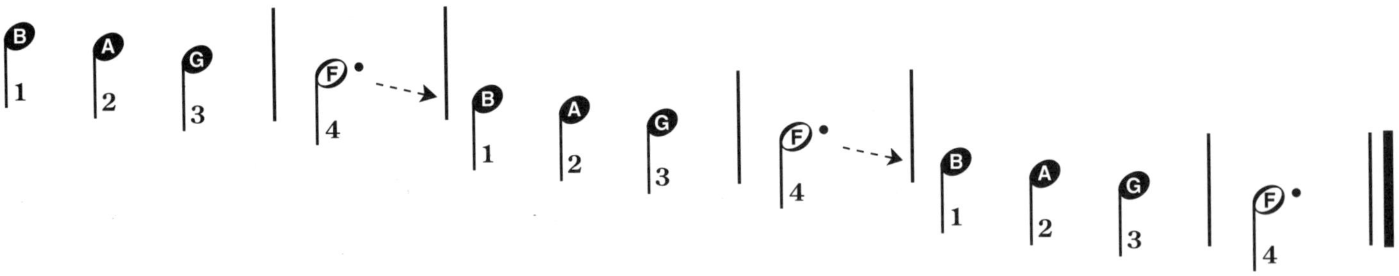

Dynamic Signs

Dynamic signs tell how loudly or softly to play. Common dynamic signs include:

- ***p*** *(piano)* = soft
- ***mf*** *(mezzo forte)* = moderately loud
- ***f*** *(forte)* = loud

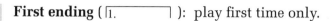

First ending (1.): play first time only.

Second ending (2.): play second time only.

Repeat sign (:‖): repeat from the beginning.

Solo Repertoire

starting key: **RH**

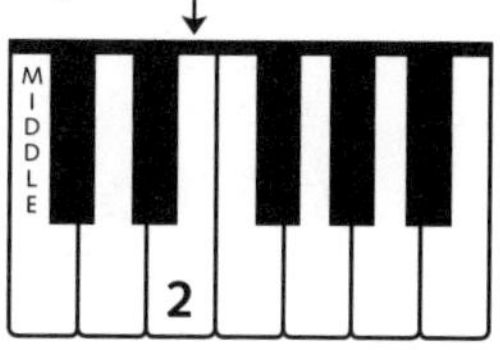

SUMMER NIGHT

1-16 (50)

Flowing (♩=96)

Kenon D. Renfrow

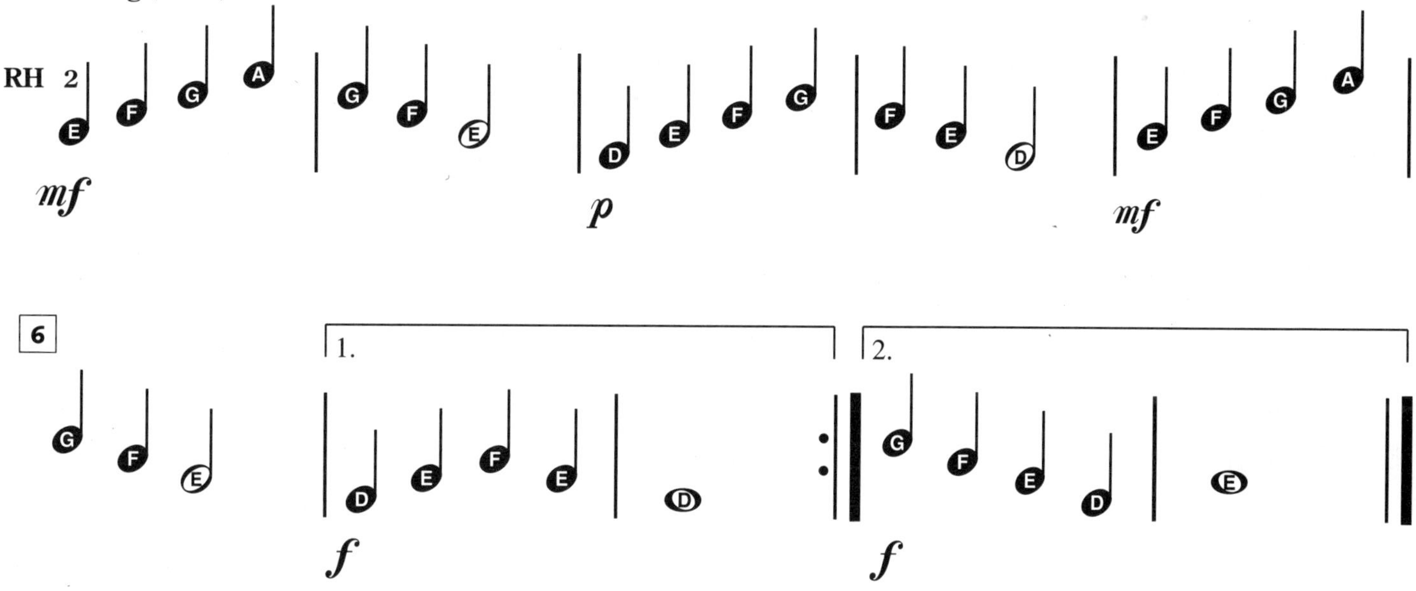

TEACHER ACCOMPANIMENT

Sharp, Flat and Natural Signs

The **sharp sign** (♯) before a note means play the next key to the *right*, whether black or white. The **flat sign** (♭) before a note means play the next key to the *left*, whether black or white.

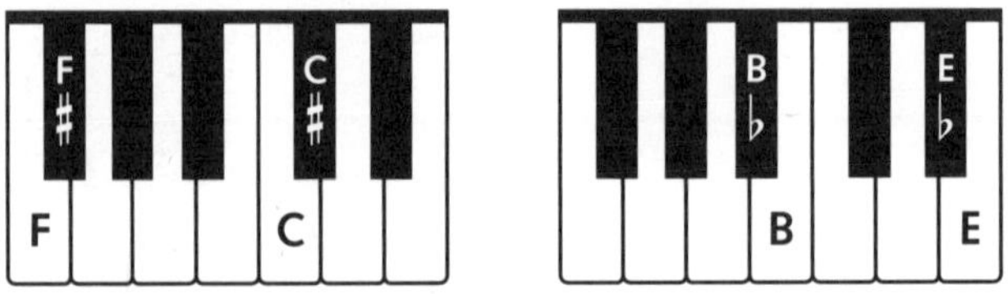

When a sharp or a flat appears before a note, it applies to that note for the rest of the measure. The **natural sign** (♮) cancels a sharp or flat. A note after a natural sign is always a white key!

Half Steps

A **half step** is the distance from any key to the very next key above or below it (black or white)—there is no key between.

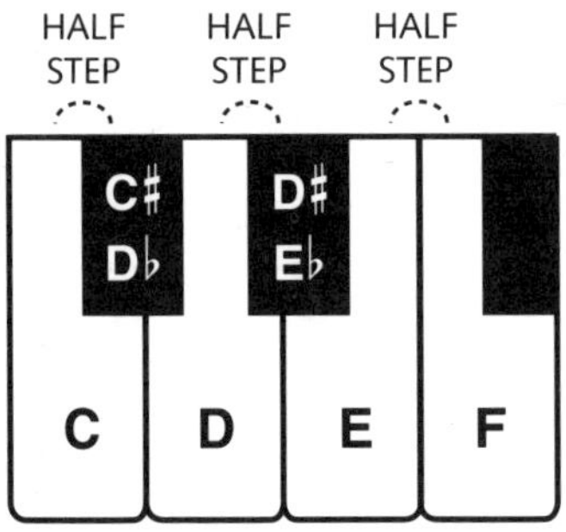

The Chromatic Scale

The **chromatic scale** is made up entirely of half steps. It goes up and down, using every key, black and white. It may begin on any key.

The fingering rules are:

- Use 3 on each black key.
- Use 1 on each white key, except when two white keys are together (no black key between), then use 1 2 or 2 1.

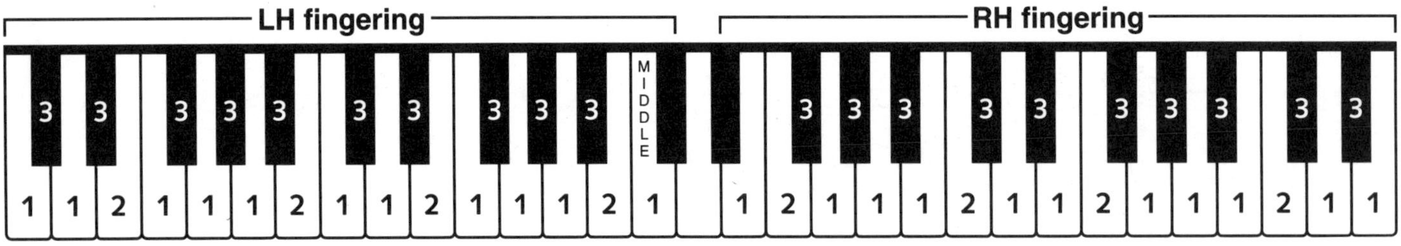

Playing the Chromatic Scale

1. Looking at the keyboard above, play the chromatic scale with the LH. Begin on middle C and go down for two octaves and then go up again.
2. Looking at the keyboard above, play the chromatic scale with the RH. Begin on E above middle C and go up for two octaves and then go down again.
3. By combining steps 1 and 2 above, play the chromatic scale hands together. Notice that each hand plays the same finger at the same time.

Whole Steps

A **whole step** is equal to two half steps. Skip one key (black or white).

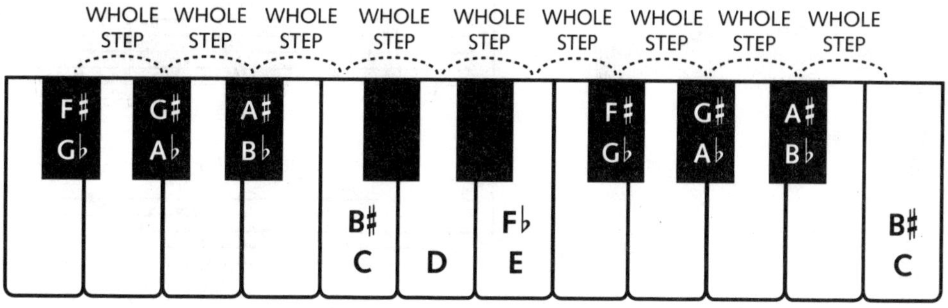

Building Five-Finger Patterns of Whole Steps

1. Begin on the given key and build an ascending five-finger pattern using only whole steps. Write the names of the keys in the blanks. Do not skip any letters.

C ______ ______ ______ ______♯ ______♯

E ______♯ ______♯ ______♯ ______♯

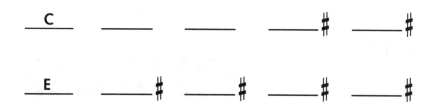

Play each pattern up and down with:

1. RH fingers 1 2 3 4 5
2. LH fingers 5 4 3 2 1 (an octave lower)
3. Hands together (an octave apart)

2. Begin on the given key and build a descending five-finger pattern using only whole steps. Write the names of the keys in the blanks. Do not skip any letters. Read and play from right to left.

______♭ ______♭ ______♭ ______ D

______♭ ______♭ ______ ______ E

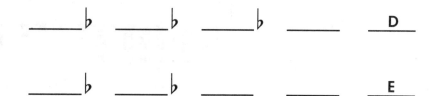

Play each pattern down and up with:

1. RH fingers 5 4 3 2 1
2. LH fingers 1 2 3 4 5 (an octave lower)
3. Hands together (an octave apart)

The Staff

Music is written on a **staff** of 5 lines and 4 spaces. Some notes are written on lines and some are written in spaces.

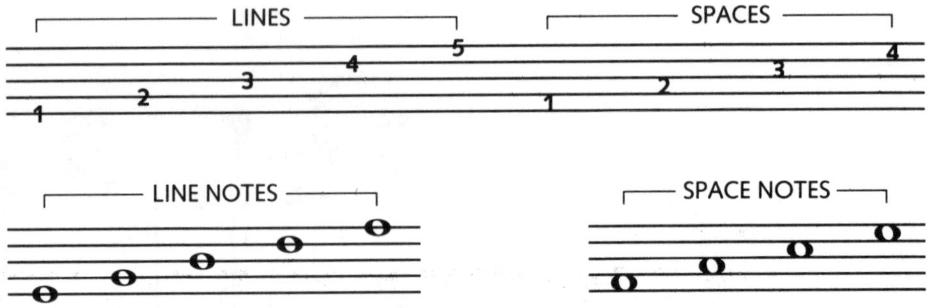

The Treble Clef Sign

The **treble clef sign** locates the G above the middle of the keyboard. This sign came from the letter G.

By moving up or down from this G, you can name any note on the treble staff.

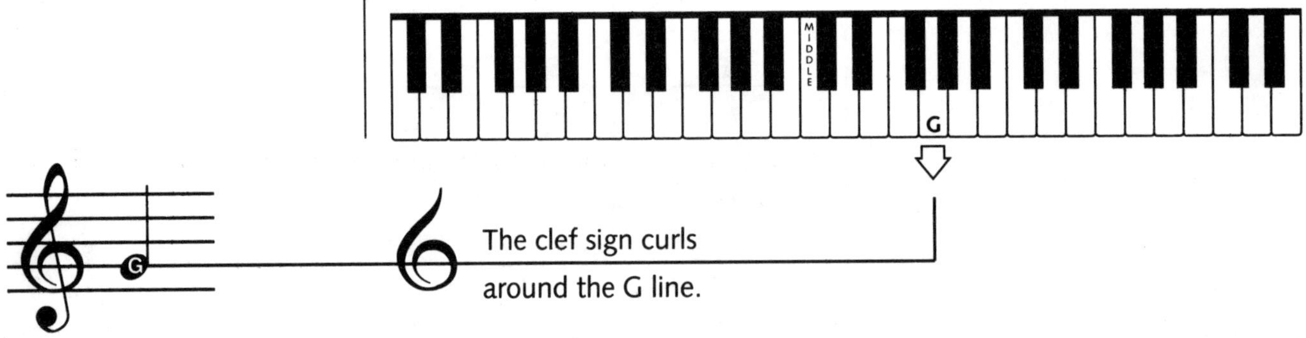

The Bass Clef Sign

The **bass clef sign** locates the F below the middle of the keyboard. This sign came from the letter F.

By moving up or down from this F, you can name any note on the bass staff.

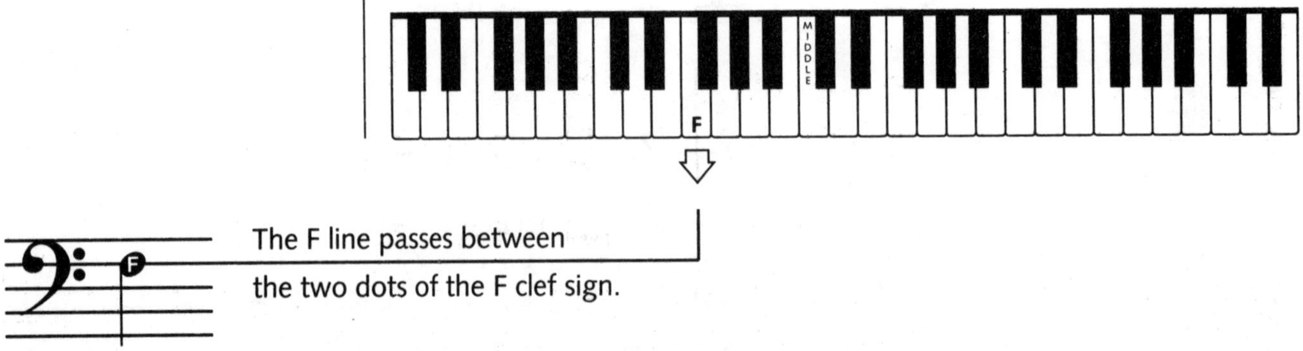

The Grand Staff

The bass staff and the treble staff are joined together by a **brace** to make the **grand staff.** A **leger line** is used between the two staves for middle C. Leger lines are also used above and below the grand staff to extend its range.

The notes with arrows are landmarks or guideposts. Learn to identify and find them quickly on the keyboard, as they assist in reading the notes surrounding them.

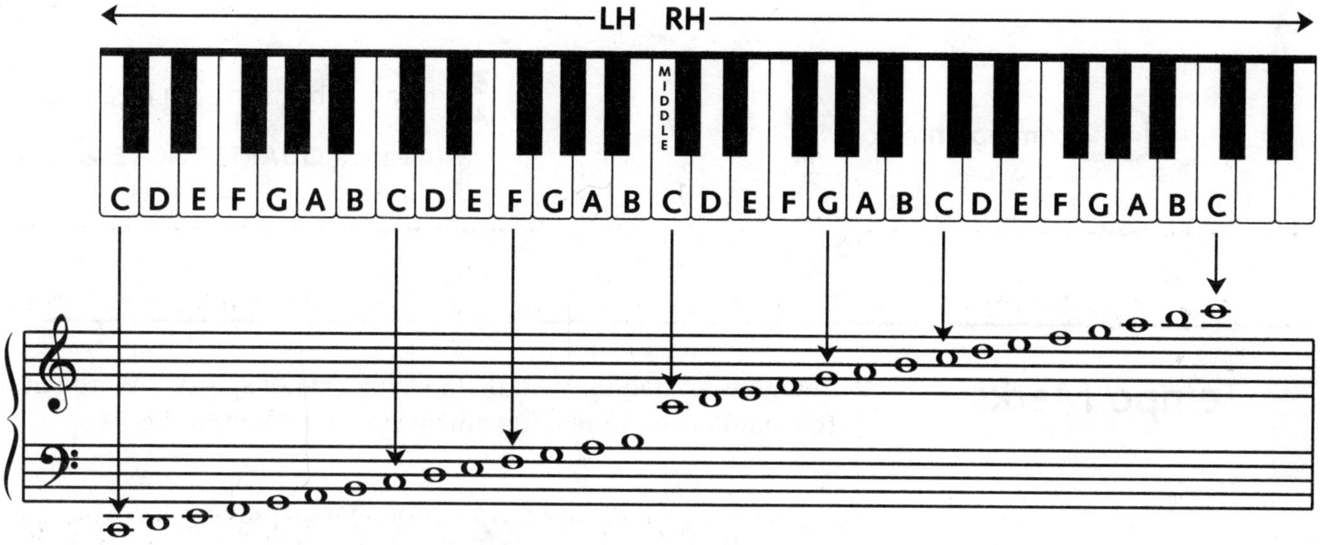

Name and play the following treble clef notes, using the indicated RH finger.

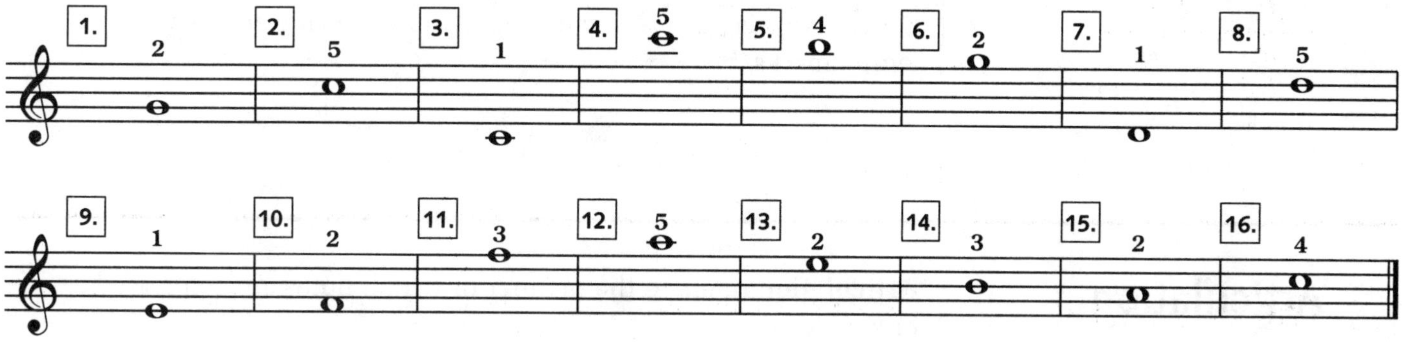

Name and play the following bass clef notes, using the indicated LH finger.

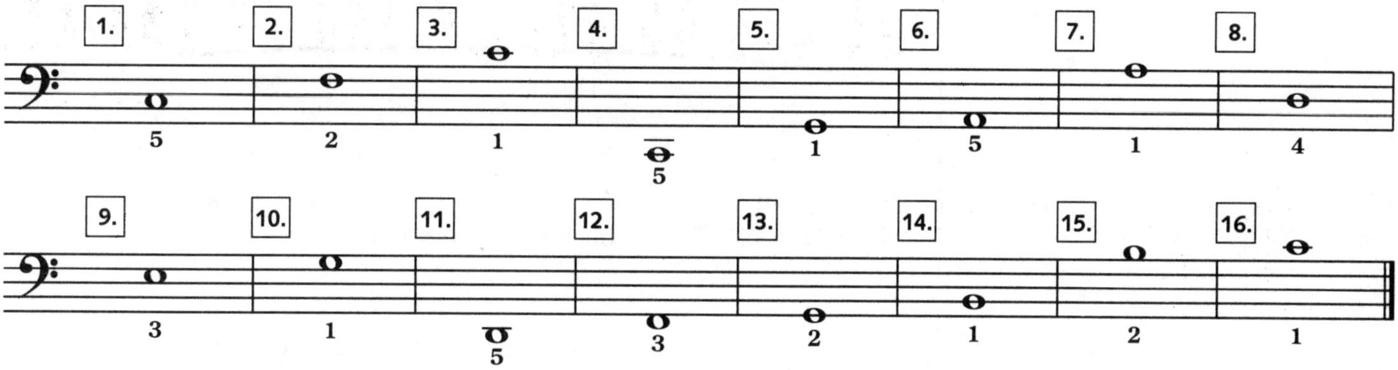

Time Signatures

Music has numbers at the beginning called a **time signature.**

4 means 4 beats to each measure.
4 means a **QUARTER NOTE** ♩ gets 1 beat.

3 means 3 beats to each measure.
4 means a **QUARTER NOTE** ♩ gets 1 beat.

C = **common time** or $\frac{4}{4}$

2 means 2 beats to each measure.
4 means a **QUARTER NOTE** ♩ gets 1 beat.

Tempo Marks

Tempo is an Italian word that means "rate of speed." Words indicating the tempo used in playing music are called **tempo marks.**

Some of the most important tempo marks are:

Allegro	=	Quickly, happily
Moderato	=	Moderately
Andante	=	Moving along (The word actually means "walking.")
Adagio	=	Slowly

English words such as *lively, happily* and *flowing* are also used as tempo marks.

Articulation

Articulation refers to the manner in which notes are connected or separated.

A **slur** is a curved line over or under notes on *different* lines or spaces. Slurs mean play **legato** (smoothly connected).

Slurs often divide the music into phrases. A **phrase** is a musical thought or sentence.

The dot over or under the notes indicates the **staccato** touch. Make these notes very short!

When there are no articulation marks over or under notes, they are generally played **non legato** (disconnected but not staccato).

Reading Treble-Clef Melodies

The melodies that follow utilize the musical concepts presented in this unit. Use the indicated tempos, dynamics and articulation as you play these exercises with the RH.

Use the following practice directions:

1. Clap and count aloud.
2. Play and count aloud.
3. Play and say note names.

1-17 (51)

Moderato

1.

Count: 1 1 1 1 1 1 1 2 1 1 1 1 1 2 3 4
or: 1 2 3 4 1 2 3 4 1 2 3 4 1 2 3 4

1-18 (52)

Adagio

2.

Count: 1 2 1 2 1 1 1 2
or: 1 2 3 4 1 2 3 4

1-19 (53)

Allegro

3.

Count: 1 1 1 2
or: 1 2 1 2

1-20 (54)

Happily

4.

Count: 1 1 1 2
or: 1 2 1 2

1-21 (55)

Andante

5.

Count: 1 2 3 1 2 3 1 2 1
or: 1 2 3 1 2 3 1 2 3

1-22 (56)

Moderato

6.

Count: 1 2 1 1 2 1
or: 1 2 3 1 2 3

Reading Bass-Clef Melodies

Use the indicated tempos, dynamics and articulation as you play these exercises with the LH.

Use the following practice directions:

1. Clap and count aloud.
2. Play and count aloud.
3. Play and say note names.

1-23 (57)

Andante

1.

Count: 1 1 1 1 1 1 1 2
or: 1 2 3 4 1 2 3 4

1-24 (58)

Adagio

2.

Count: 1 2 1 2 1 1 1 2
or: 1 2 3 4 1 2 3 4

1-25 (59)

Lively

3.

Count: 1 1 1 1
or: 1 2 1 2

1-26 (60)

Moderato

4.

Count: 1 2 1 2 1 1
or: 1 2 1 2 1 2

1-27 (61)

Flowing

5.

Count: 1 2 3 1 2 3 1 2 1
or: 1 2 3 1 2 3 1 2 3

1-28 (62)

Allegro

6.

Count: 1 1 1 1 1 1
or: 1 2 3 1 2 3

Rests

Rests are signs for silence.

Quarter rest (𝄽) means rest for the value of a quarter note.
Half rest (▬) means rest for the value of a half note.
Whole rest (▬) means rest for the value of a whole note or any whole measure.

Reading on the Grand Staff

Use the indicated tempos, dynamics and articulation as you play these exercises.

Use the following practice directions:

1. Clap and count aloud.
2. Play and count aloud.
3. Play and say note names.

1-29 (63)

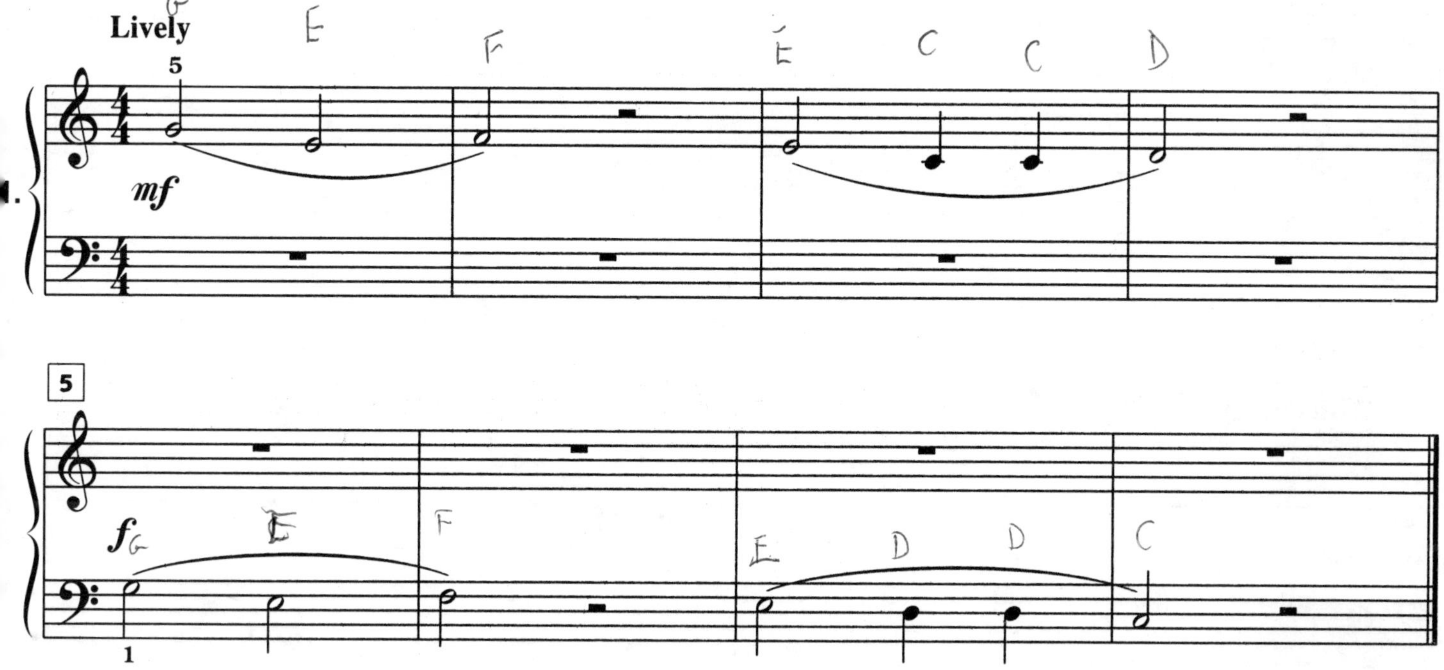

1-30 (64)

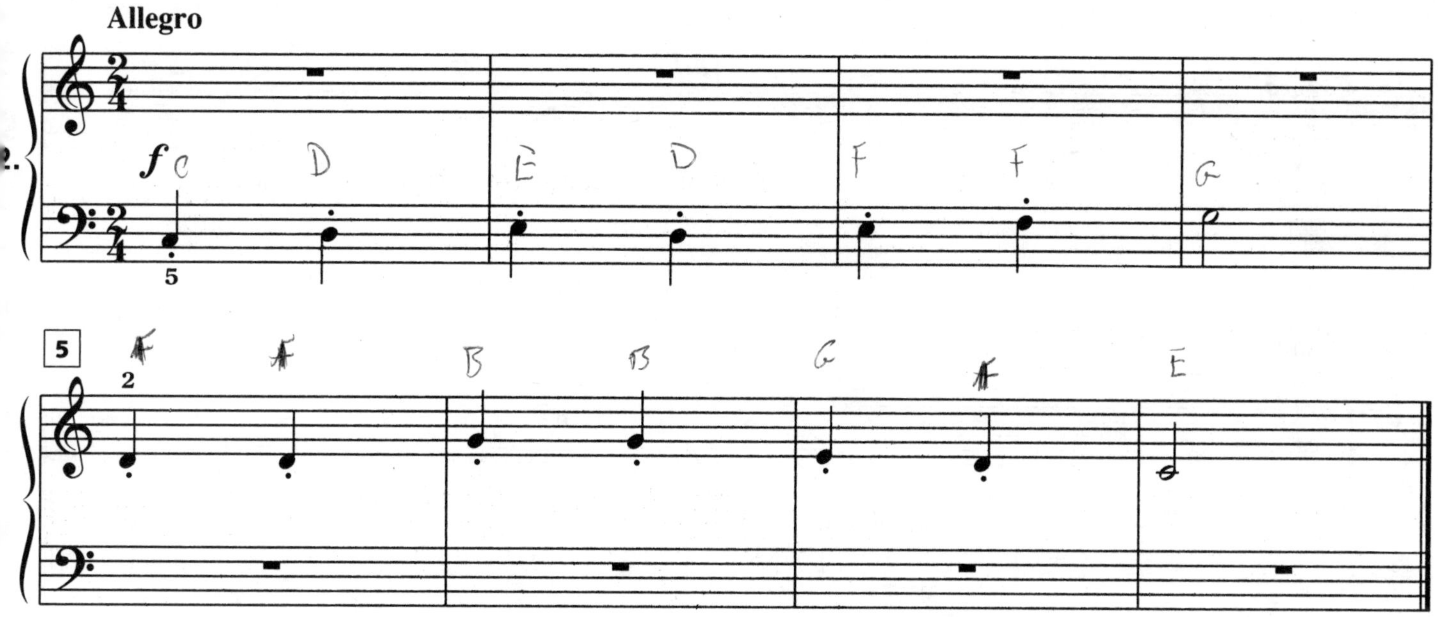

Reading on the Grand Staff (continued)

1-31 (65)

3.

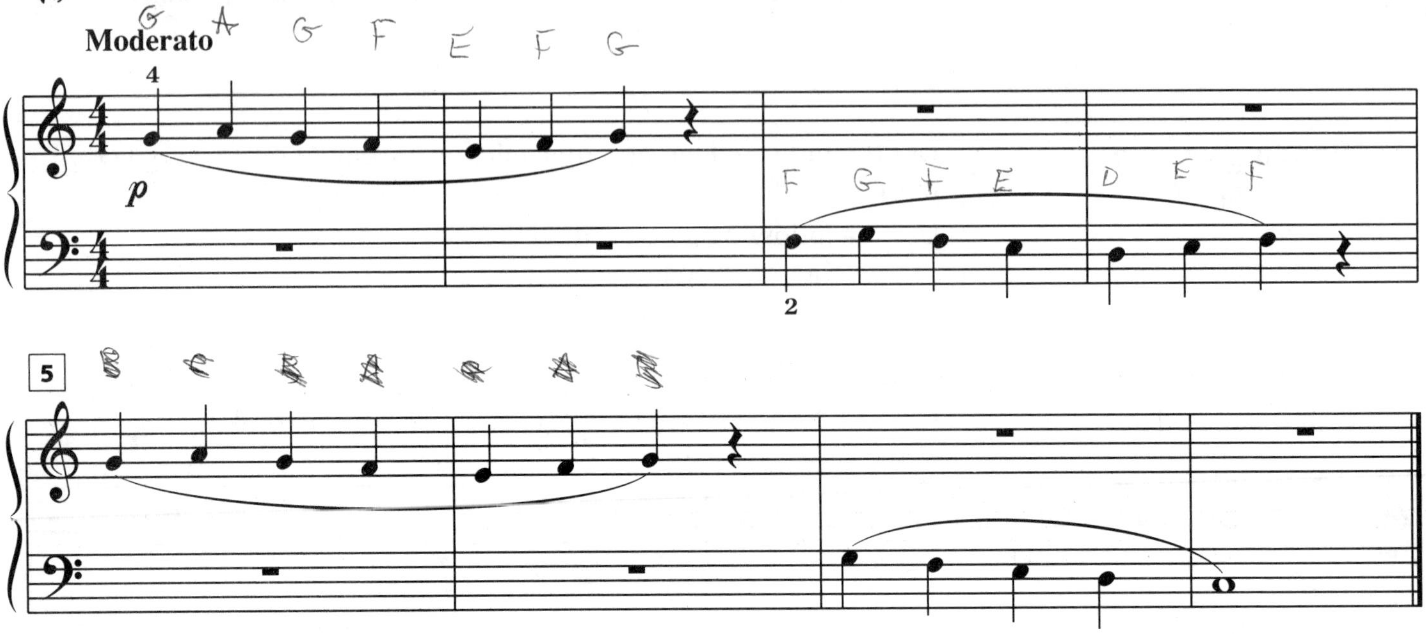

1-32 (66)

4.

1-33 (67)

5.

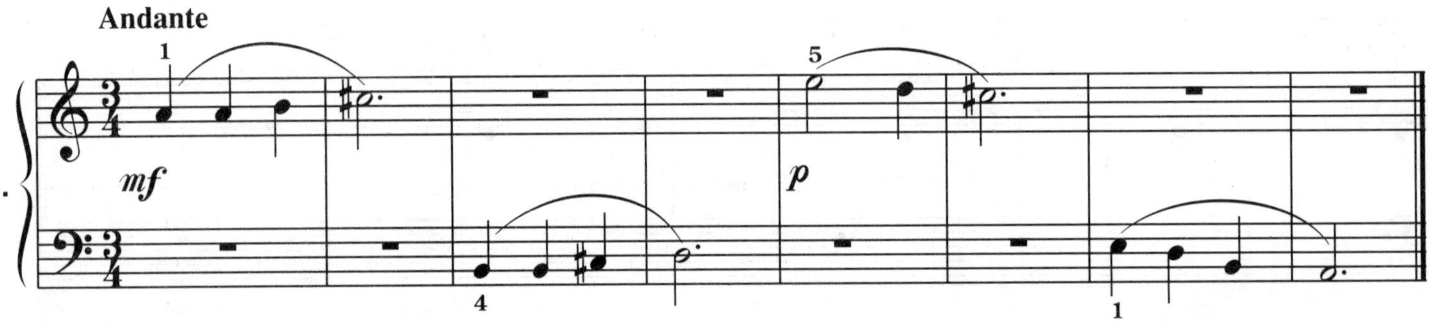

1-34 (68)

6. 

Intervals

Distances between tones are measured in **intervals,** called 2nds, 3rds, 4ths, 5ths, etc.

- The distance from any white key to the next white key, up or down, is called a 2nd.
- When you skip a white key, the interval is a 3rd.
- When you skip two white keys, the interval is a 4th.
- When you skip three white keys, the interval is a 5th.

Melodic Intervals

Notes played separately make a melody. The intervals between these notes are called **melodic intervals.**

Listen to the sound of each interval as you play these melodic 2nds, 3rds, 4ths and 5ths.

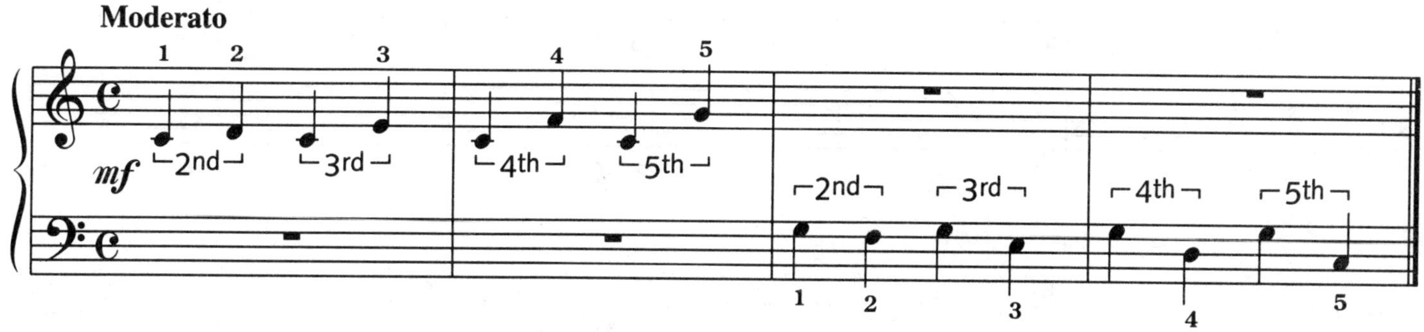

▶ Now play these intervals beginning on G in the RH and beginning on D in the LH. Playing music in a different key from the original is called **transposition.**

Harmonic Intervals

Notes played together make harmony. The intervals between these notes are called **harmonic intervals.**

Listen to the sound of each interval as you play these harmonic 2nds, 3rds, 4ths and 5ths.

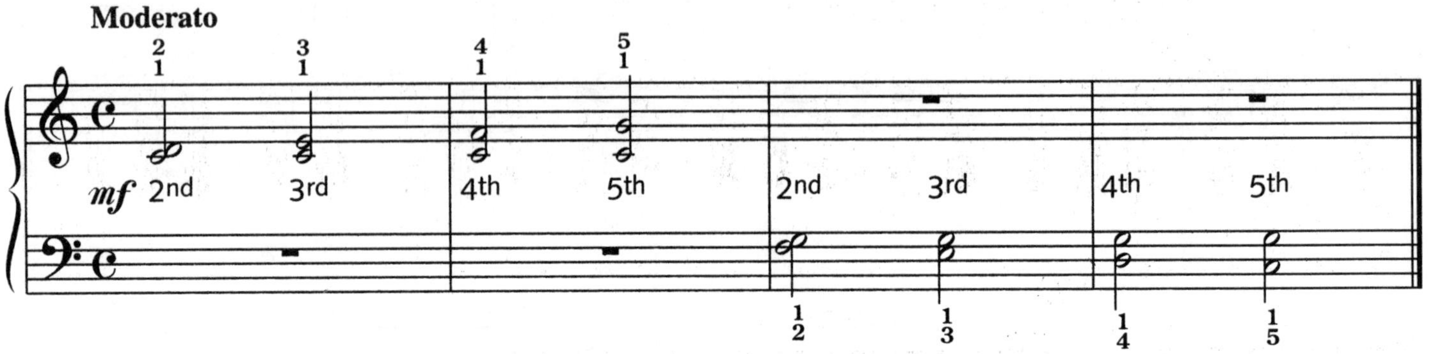

▶ Now play these intervals beginning on G in the RH and beginning on D in the LH.

Playing Melodic and Harmonic Intervals

Name and play the following intervals.

Unit 1 Review Worksheet

Name ______________________ *Date* ______________________

1. Write the letter name on each key marked X.

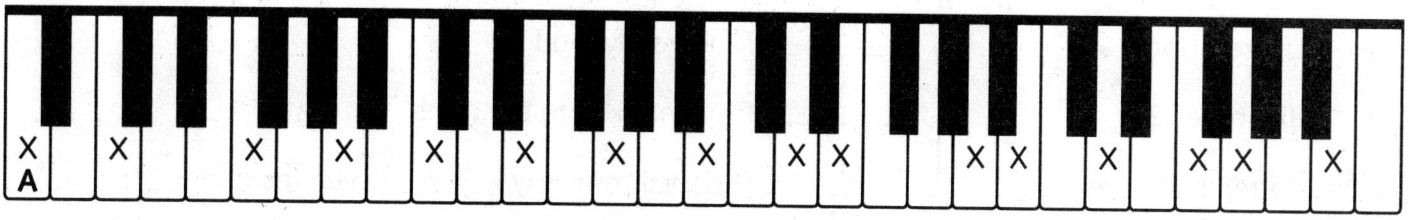

2. Write a half note below the given note to make the indicated *melodic* interval. Notes *on* or *above* the middle line have stems pointing down. Notes *below* the middle line have stems pointing up. Write the name of each note in the square below it.

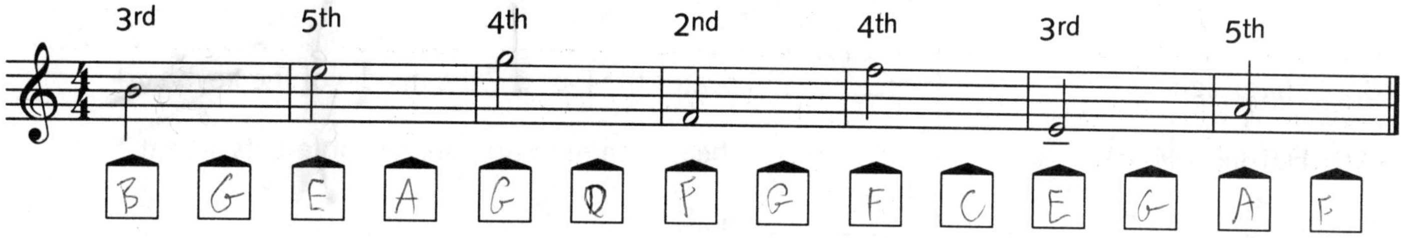

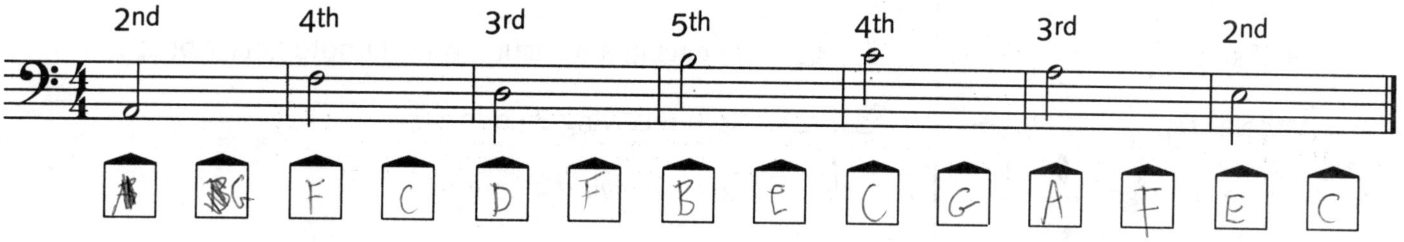

3. Write a whole note above the given note to make the indicated *harmonic* interval. Write the names of the notes in the squares. Write the name of the lower note in the lower square; the name of the higher note in the higher square.

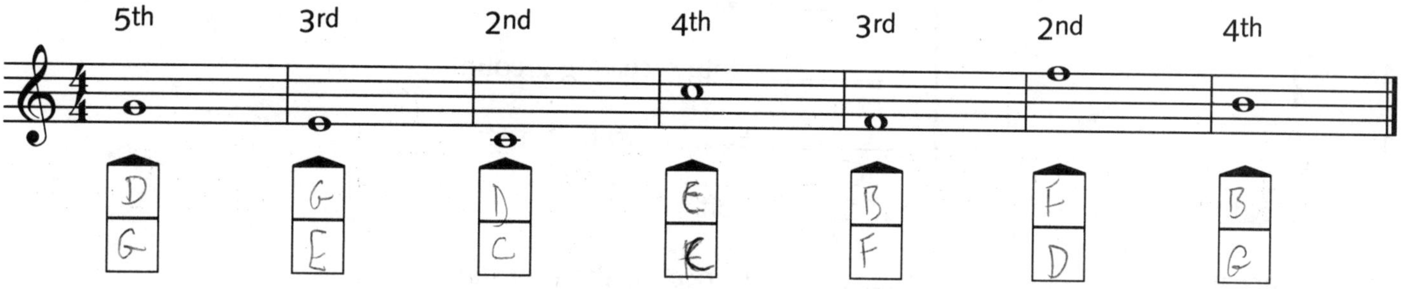

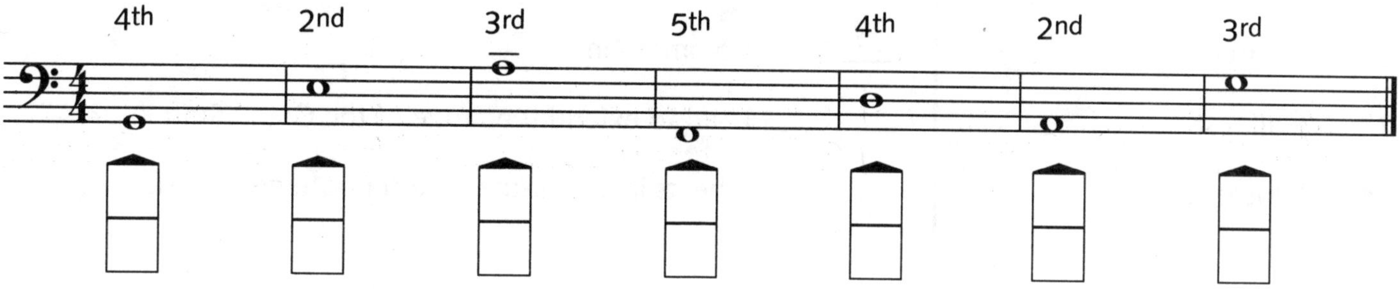

4. Write the numbers from column A in the appropriate blanks in column B to match each item with its best description.

Column A		Column B	
1.	Quarter note 𝅘𝅥	6	Moderately loud
2.	Half note 𝅗𝅥	8	Play next key to the right
3.	Dotted half note 𝅗𝅥.	11	Distance from any key to the very next key
4.	Whole note 𝅝	20	Smoothly connected
5.	Piano *p*	21	Very short
6.	Mezzo forte *mf*	13	Locates the G above the middle of the keyboard
7.	Forte *f*	24	𝄻
8.	Sharp sign ♯	14	Locates the F below the middle of the keyboard
9.	Flat sign ♭	16	2 beats in a measure, quarter note gets 1 beat
10.	Natural sign ♮	7	Loud
11.	Half step	17	3 beats in a measure, quarter note gets 1 beat
12.	Whole step	3	Note receiving 3 counts
13.	Treble clef sign 𝄞	4	Note receiving 4 counts
14.	Bass clef sign 𝄢	9	Play next key to the left
15.	Leger line	22	𝄽
16.	2/4	1	Note receiving 1 count
17.	3/4	23	𝄼
18.	4/4	2	Note receiving 2 counts
19.	𝄴	12	Equals two half steps
20.	Legato	5	Soft
21.	Staccato	10	Cancels a sharp or flat
22.	Quarter rest	19	Common time
23.	Half rest	15	Used to extend the range of the Grand Staff
24.	Whole rest	18	4 beats in a measure, quarter note gets 1 beat

Unit 2

More Keyboard Basics

Objectives

Upon completion of this unit the student will be able to:

1. Perform solo repertoire from Grand Staff notation.
2. Apply additional musical concepts to performance at the keyboard.
3. Identify key signatures in major keys.
4. Harmonize melodies with fifths as an accompaniment.

Assignments

Week of ________

Write your assignments for the week in the space below.

Eighth Notes, Eighth Rests, and Dotted Quarter Notes

Two **eighth notes** (♫) are played in the time of one quarter note.

When eighth notes appear singly, they look like this: ♪ or ♪

Single eighth notes are often used with **eighth rests.** ♪ 𝄾

A dot increases the length of a note by one half its value.
A **dotted quarter note** is equal to a quarter note plus an eighth note.

♩	+	♪	=	♩.
1 count		1/2 count		1-1/2 counts

In $\frac{2}{4}$, $\frac{3}{4}$, or $\frac{4}{4}$ time, the dotted quarter note is almost always followed by an eighth note. ♩. ♪

New Time Signature

$\frac{6}{8}$ 6 beats to each measure. 8 eighth note gets 1 beat.

♪ eighth note or 𝄾 eighth rest = 1 count

♩ quarter note or 𝄽 quarter rest = 2 counts

♩. dotted quarter note or 𝄽 𝄾 rests = 3 counts

𝅗𝅥. dotted half note = 6 counts

For a whole measure of silence, a whole rest (𝄻) is used.

In $\frac{6}{8}$ time, the ♩. is often felt as the pulse, with two large beats per measure.

New Dynamic Signs

mp (mezzo piano)	=	moderately soft
pp (pianissimo)	=	very soft
ff (fortissimo)	=	very loud

crescendo (cresc.) (gradually louder)

diminuendo (dim.) or **decrescendo (decresc.)** (gradually softer)

Key Signatures

Sharps or flats that follow the clef signs are called the **key signature.** The key signature indicates the notes that are to be sharped or flatted throughout the piece and aids in identifying the key in which the piece is written.

Sharps appear in the following order in the key signature:

The name of a sharp major key can be determined by moving up a half step from the last sharp.

This is the key signature for the **key of B major.** A half step up from A♯ is B.

Flats appear in the following order in the key signature:

The order of flats is reversed from the order of sharps in key signatures.

The name of a flat major key can be determined by the name of the next-to-last flat.

This is the key signature for the **key of A♭ major.** The next-to-last flat is A♭.

Two major key signatures cannot be determined using the above rules:

- C major—no sharps or flats
- F major—one flat (B♭)

Rhythm Reading

Tap the following rhythm patterns using RH for notes with stems going up and LH for notes with stems going down. Tap hands separately first, and then hands together, always counting aloud.

2-1 (43)

Count: 1 & 2 & 3 & 4 &

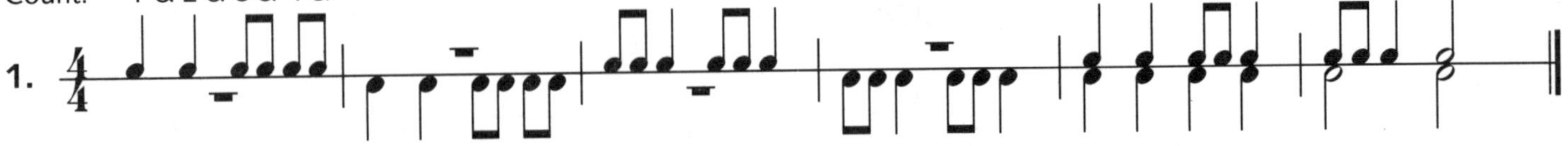

2-2 (44)

Count: 1 & 2 & 3 &

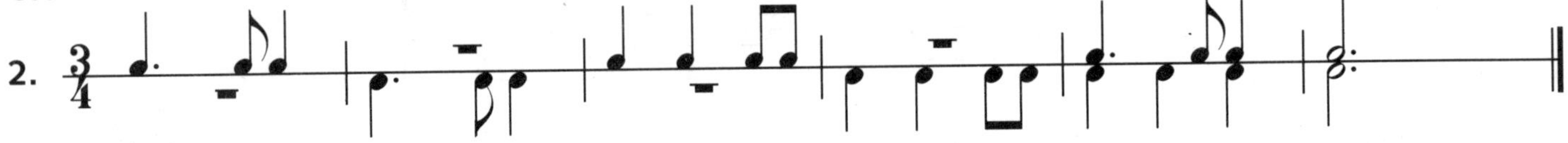

2-3 (45)

Count: 1 2 3 4 5 6

2-4 (46)

Count: 1 2 3 4 5 6

Technique

Play the following exercises that increase finger dexterity and aid in moving up and down the keyboard.

2-5 (47)

Moderato

Continue upward beginning on white keys until...

2-6 (48)

Moderato

2-7 (49)

Moderato

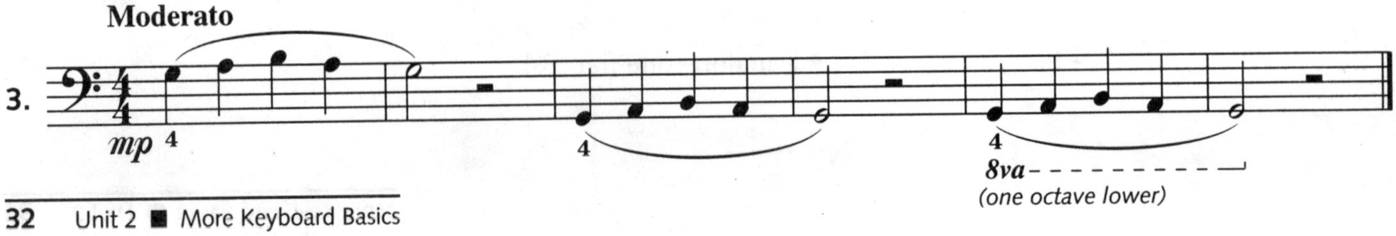

Ritardando (rit. or **ritard.)** means gradually slowing.

MINIATURE WALTZ

2-8 (50)

E. L. Lancaster
Kenon D. Renfrow

Moderato

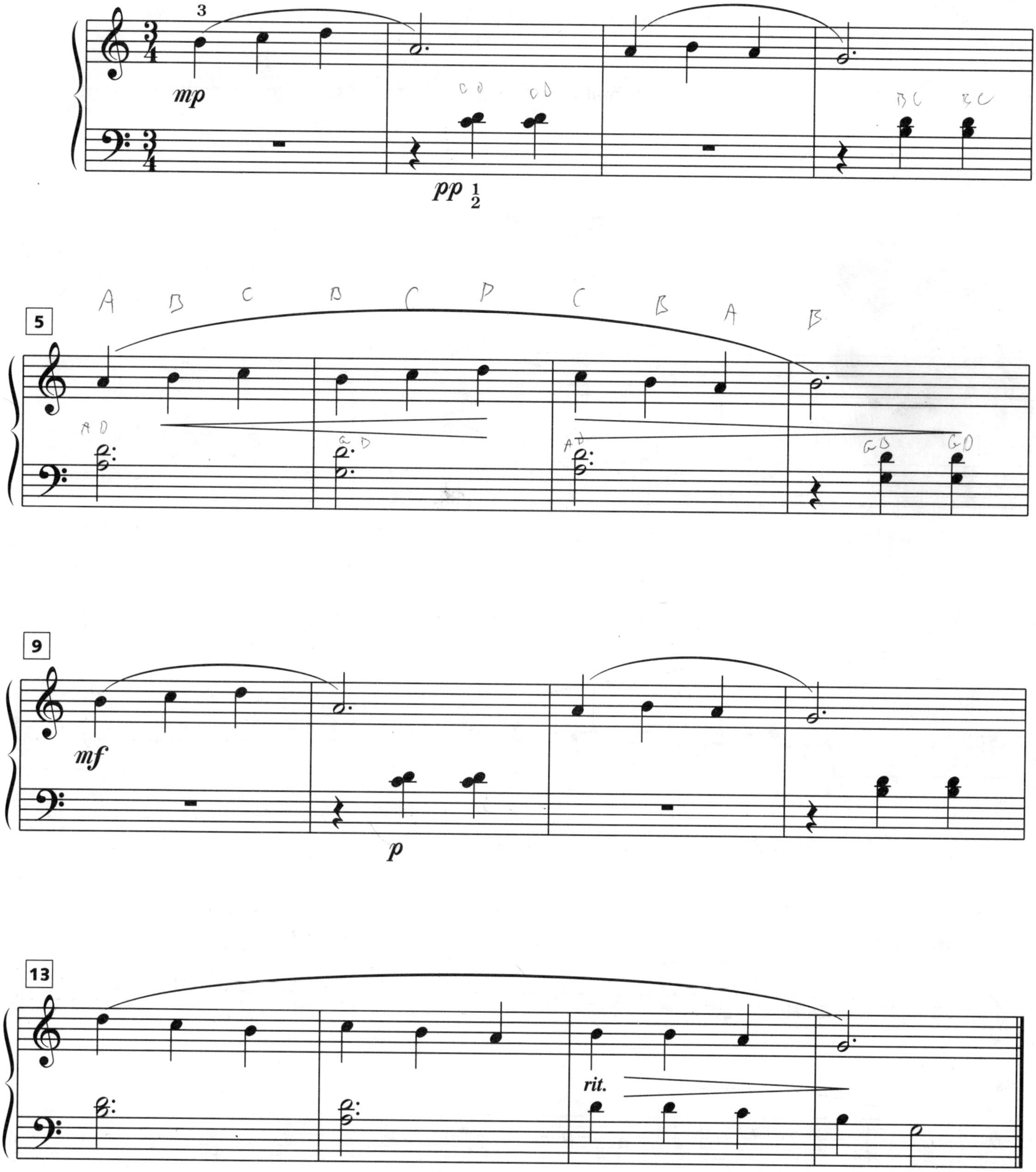

Reading

Identify the key of each example. Use the indicated tempo, dynamics and articulation as you play these exercises.

Use the following practice directions:

1. Clap and count aloud.
2. Play and count aloud.
3. Play and say note names.

A **tenuto** mark (–) means to hold the note for its full value.

When notes on the same line or space are joined by a curved line, we call them **tied notes** (𝅗𝅥‿𝅗𝅥). The key is held down for the *combined* values of both notes.

A **fermata** sign (𝄐) means to hold the note under the sign longer than its value.

First Piece

Dmitri Kabalevsky (1904–1987)
Op. 89, No. 1

2-9 (51)

Andante

1.

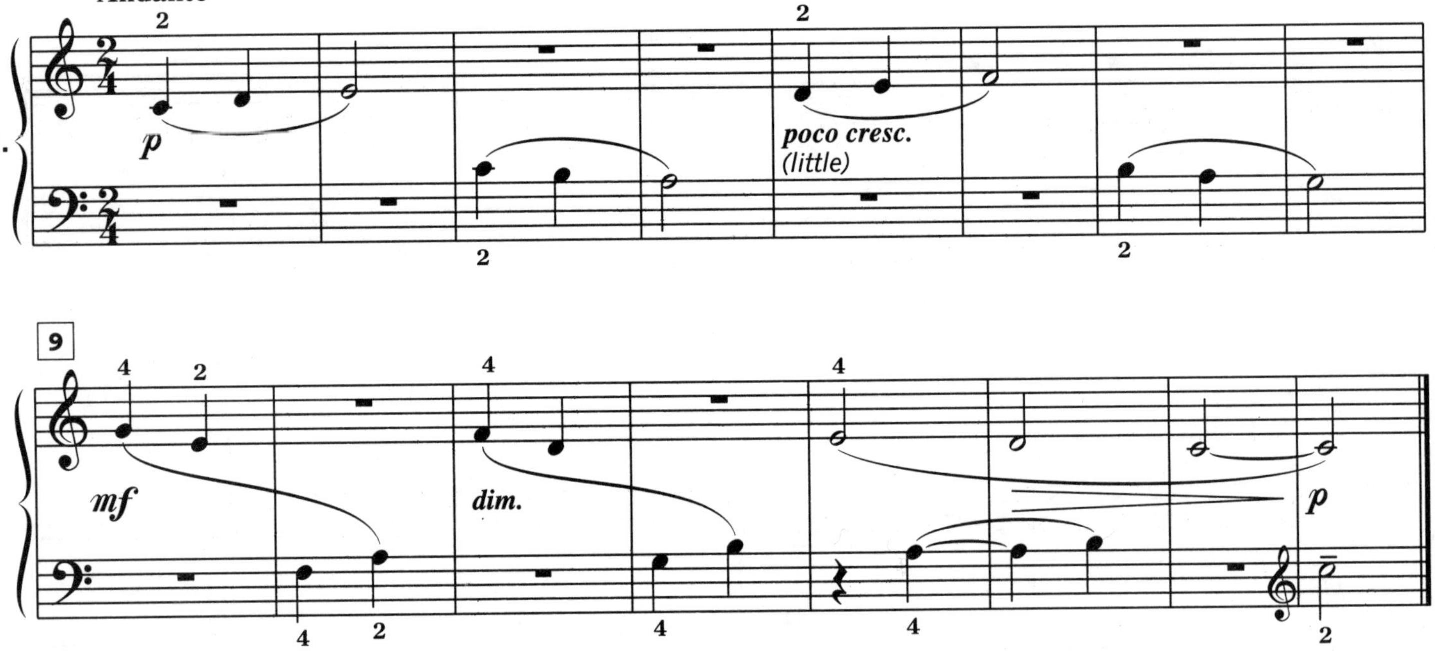

2-10 (52)

Maestoso *(majestically)*

2.

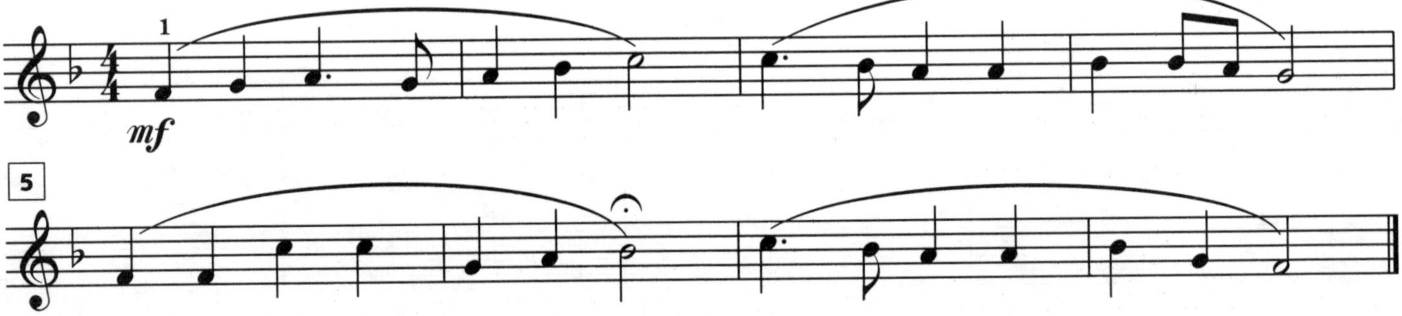

2-11 (53)

2-12 (54)

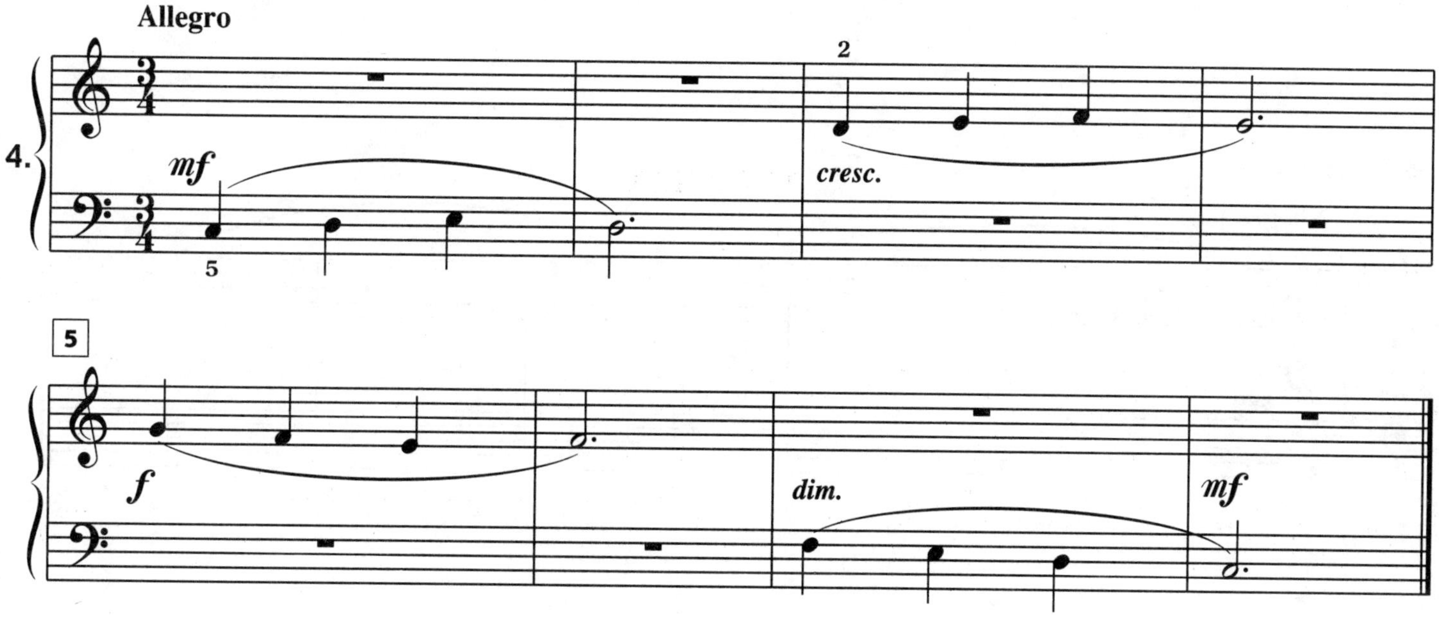

2-13 (55)

2-14 (56)

Harmonization

Harmonize each of the melodies below by playing the harmonic 5th (used in measure 1) on the first beat of every measure.

2-15 (57)

2-16 (58)

2-17 (59)

2-18 (60)

Unit 2

Review Worksheet

Name ______________________ *Date* ______________________

1. Write the 7 sharps as they appear in key signatures on the Grand Staff.

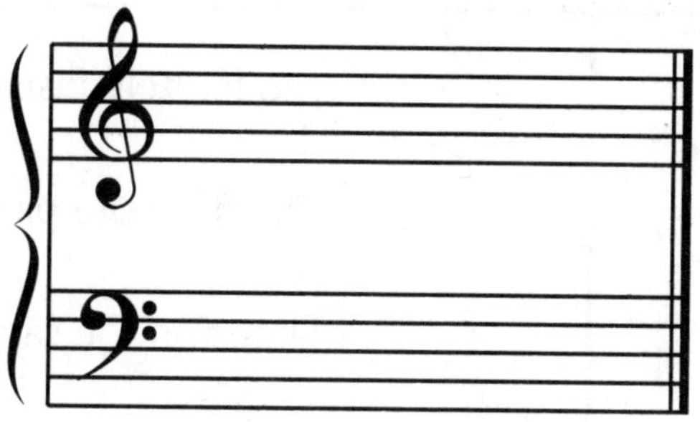

2. Write the 7 flats as they appear in key signatures on the Grand Staff.

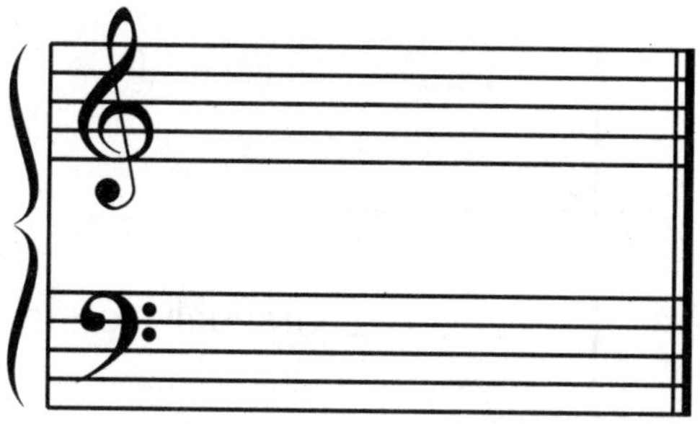

3. Identify each major sharp key signature by writing its name on the line.

E ___ C# ___ D ___ A ___ G ___ F# ___ B ___

4. Identify each major flat key signature by writing its name on the line.

Ab ___ Gb ___ Bb ___ Db ___ Eb ___ Cb ___ F ___

5. Write the numbers from column A in the appropriate blanks in column B to match each item with its best description.

Column A	Column B
1. Tied Notes	16 Moderately fast
2. ♫	5 Quarter note plus an eighth note
3. Eighth rest	1 Notes on the same line or space joined by a curved line
4. $\frac{6}{8}$	14 One octave lower
5. Dotted quarter note ♩.	2 Two eighth notes
6. Mezzo piano *mp*	15 Majestically
7. Pianissimo *pp*	19 Slow
8. Fortissimo *ff*	9 Gradually louder
9. Crescendo (<)	17 Little
10. Diminuendo (>) or Decrescendo	8 Very loud
11. rit.	4 6 beats in a measure, eighth note gets 1 beat
12. *8va*- - - - - -┐	3 𝄾
13. Repeat sign	20 In a singing style
14. *8va*- - - - - -┘	6 Moderately soft
15. Maestoso	18 Hold the note longer than its value
16. Allegretto	10 Gradually softer
17. poco	21 Very slow
18. Fermata 𝄐	13 :‖
19. Lento	12 One octave higher
20. Cantabile	7 Very soft
21. Largo	11 Gradually slowing

Unit 3

Major Five-Finger Patterns Beginning on White Keys

Objectives

Upon completion of this unit the student will be able to:

1. Play major five-finger patterns and major triads beginning on any white key.
2. Perform solo repertoire that utilizes major five-finger patterns.
3. Sight-read and transpose melodies in major five-finger patterns.
4. Harmonize major melodies with tonic and dominant tones as an accompaniment.
5. Improvise melodies in major five-finger patterns as the teacher plays an accompaniment.
6. Perform duet repertoire with a partner.

Assignments

Week of ________

Write your assignments for the week in the space below.

Memorize

Major Five-Finger Patterns

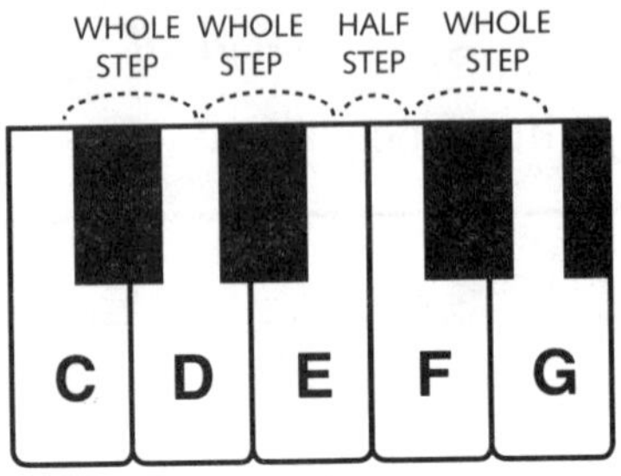

A major five-finger pattern is a series of five notes having the pattern: *whole step, whole step, half step, whole step.*

The first note of the pattern is the tonic (**I**). The fifth note of the pattern is the dominant (**V**).

LH five-finger patterns are fingered 5 4 3 2 1.
RH five-finger patterns are fingered 1 2 3 4 5.

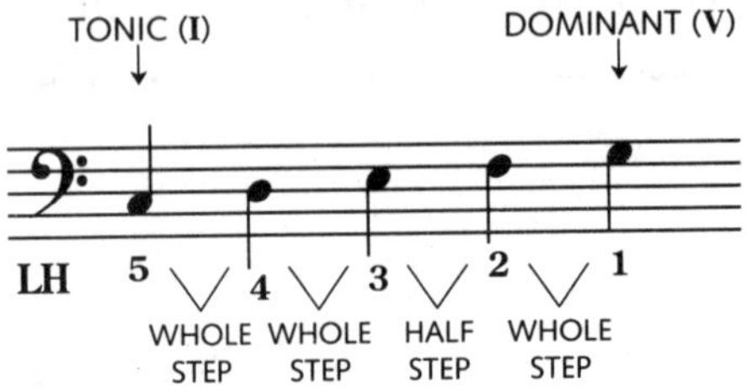

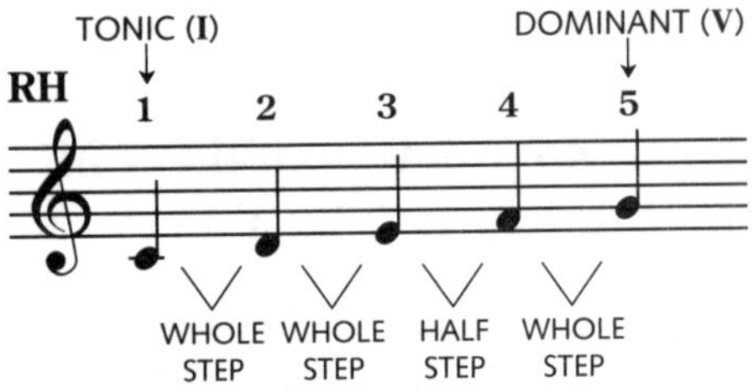

■ **Written Exercise:**
Write letter names on the correct keys to form each major five-finger pattern.

Example:

C Major

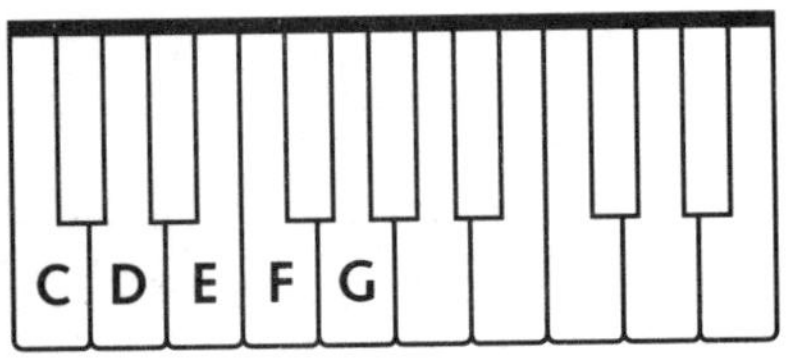

D Major

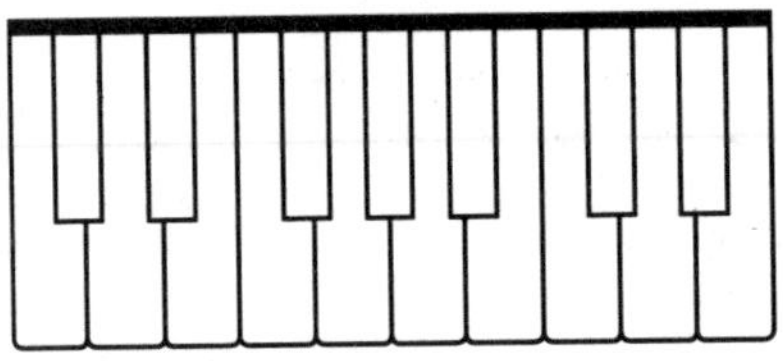

G Major

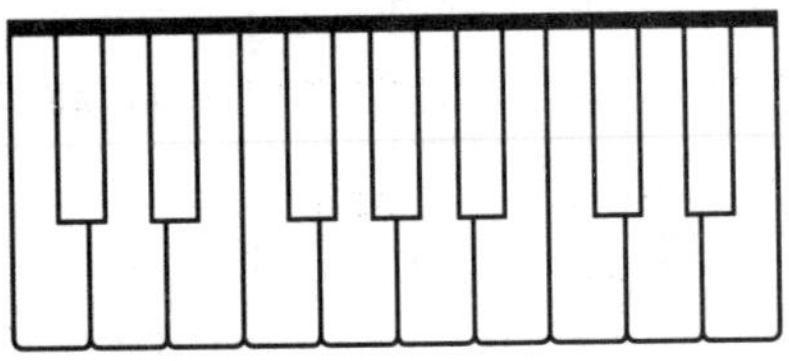

E Major

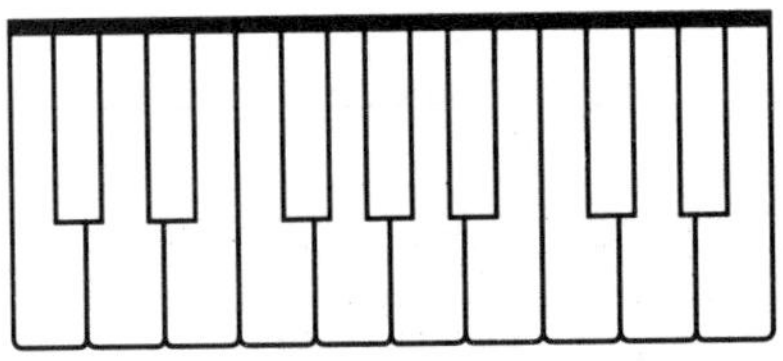

A Major

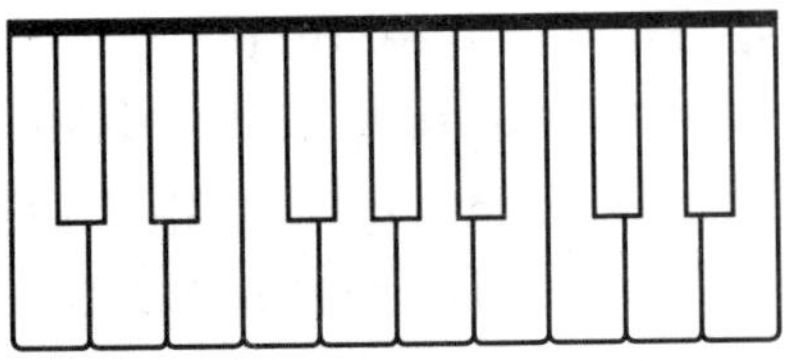

F Major

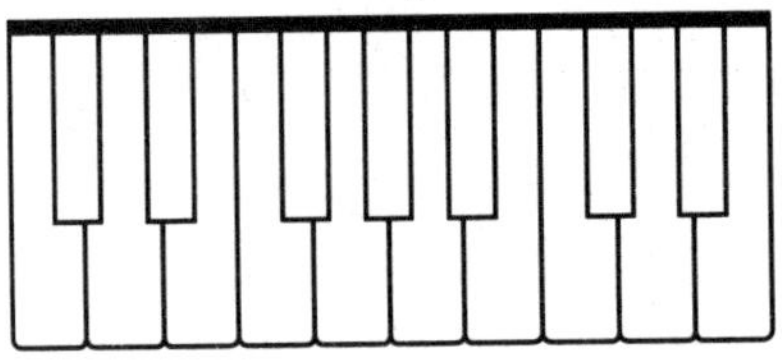

B Major

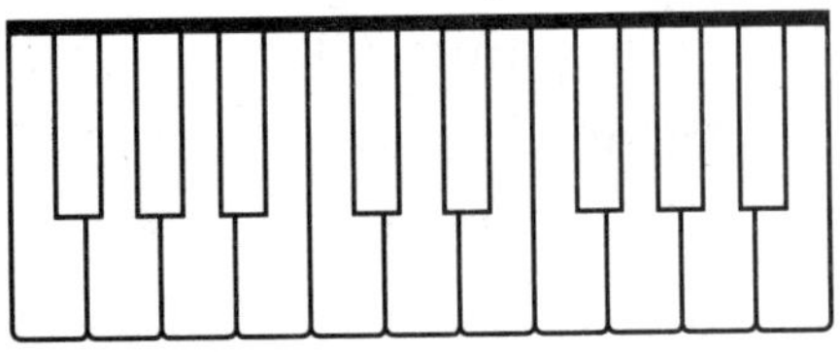

Playing Major Five-Finger Patterns

Play the following exercise that uses major five-finger patterns.

2-19 (61)

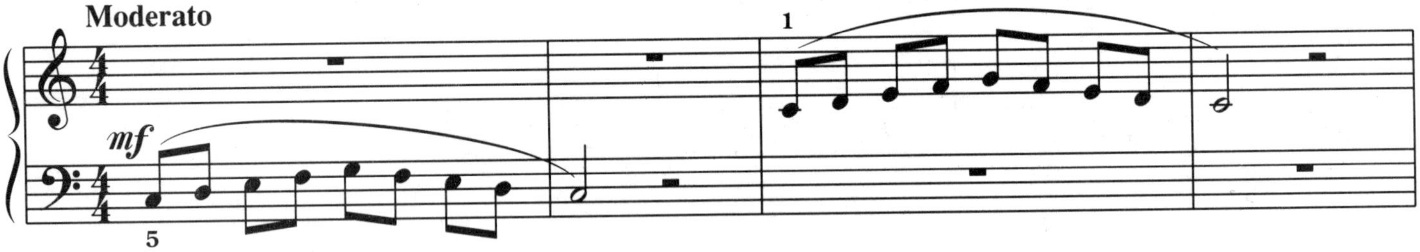

Continue upward beginning on white keys until...

Major Triads (Chords)

A **triad** is a three-note chord. The three notes of a triad are the root (1), the third (3), and the fifth (5). The **root** is the note from which the triad gets its name. The root of a C triad is C. Triads in root position (with the root at the bottom) always look like this:

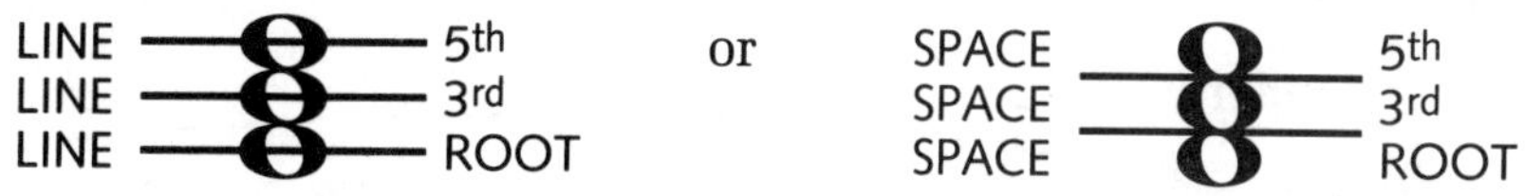

LH chords are fingered 5 3 1. RH chords are fingered 1 3 5.

Playing Major Five-Finger Patterns and Chords

Play the following exercises that use major five-finger patterns and chords.

2-20 (62)

2-21 (63)

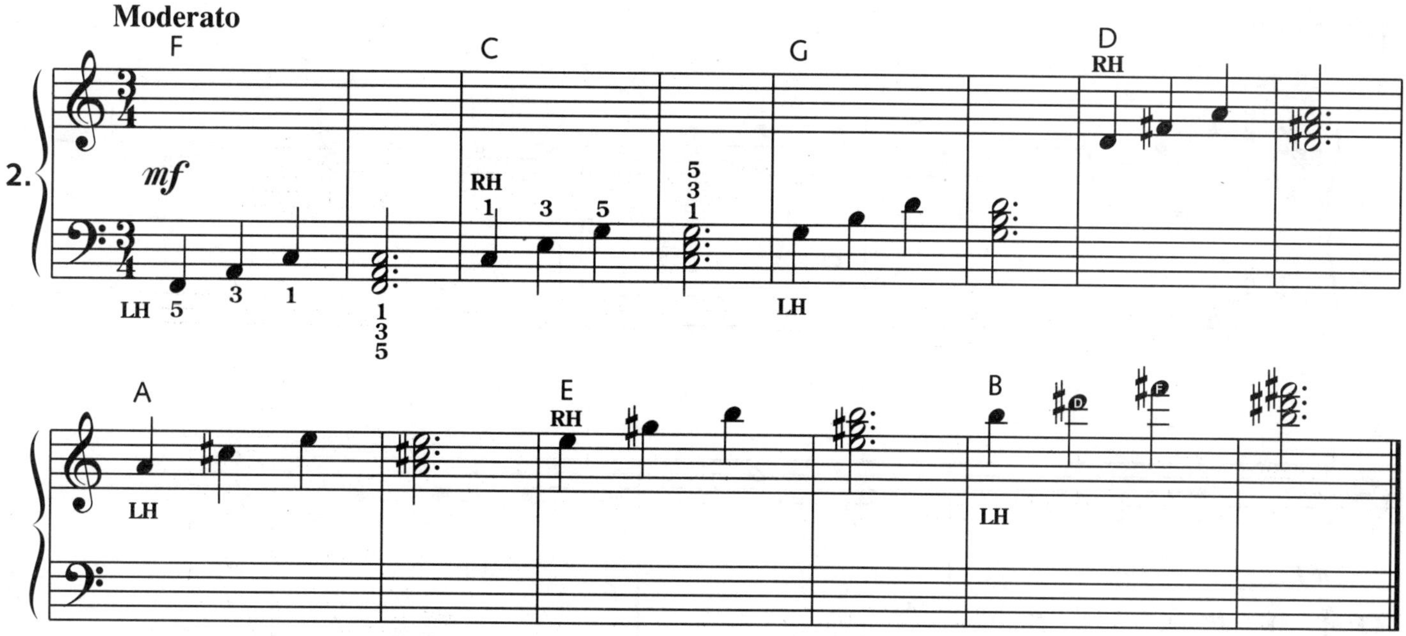

Solo Repertoire

Study
(The First Term at the Piano)

2-22 (64)

Béla Bartók
(1881–1945)

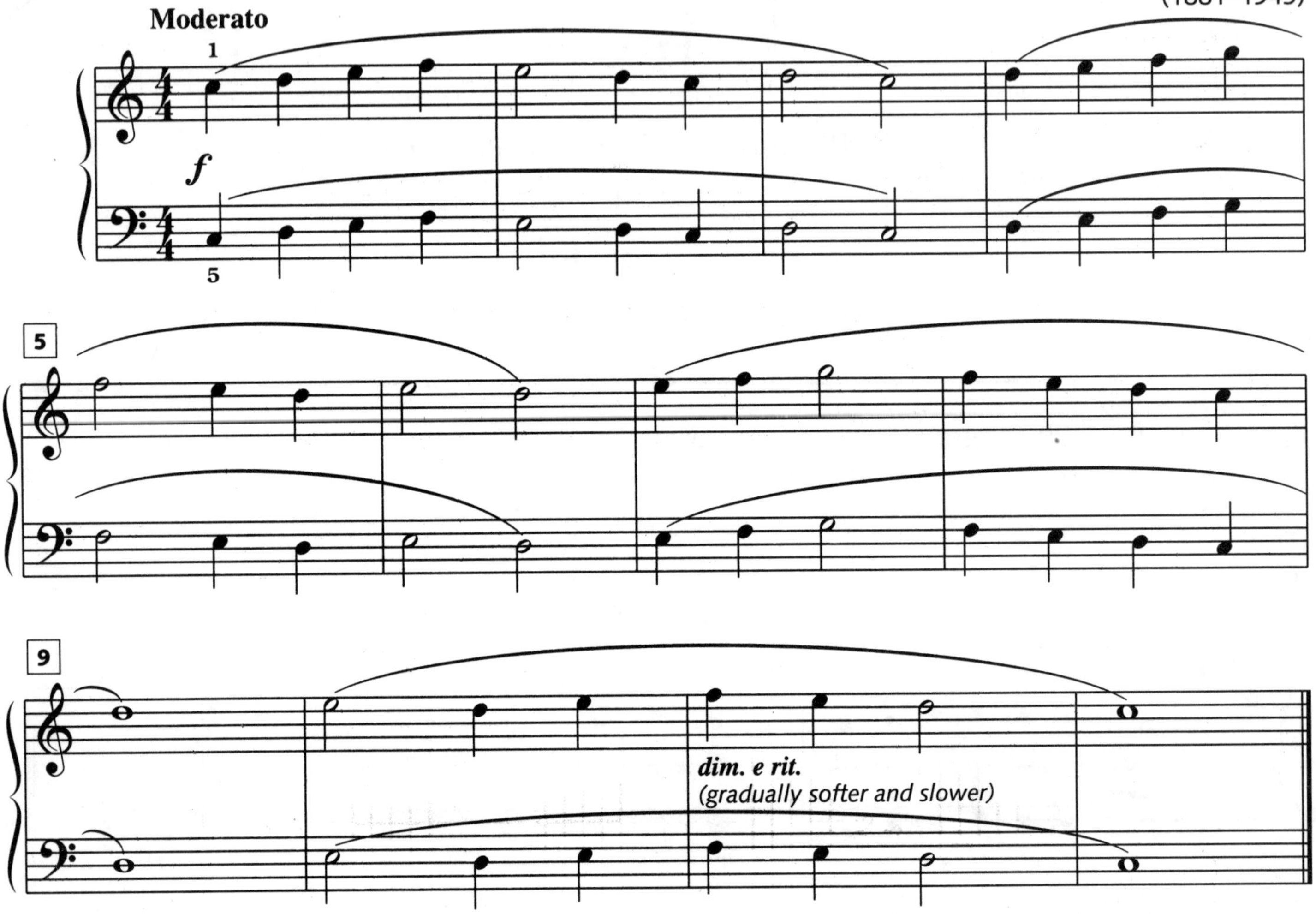

March

2-23 (65)

Daniel Gottlob Türk
(1756–1813)

Bright Lights Boogie

🔊 2-24 (66)

Gayle Kowalchyk
E. L. Lancaster

TEACHER ACCOMPANIMENT: *(Student plays 1 octave higher)*

New Time Signature

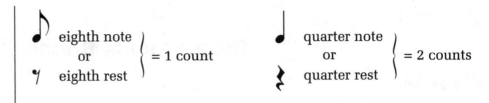

$\frac{3}{8}$ — 3 beats to each measure. Eighth note gets 1 beat.

♪ eighth note or 𝄾 eighth rest = 1 count

♩ quarter note or 𝄽 quarter rest = 2 counts

♩. dotted quarter note or 𝄽 𝄾 rests = 3 counts

In $\frac{3}{8}$ time the ♩. is often felt as the pulse, with one large beat per measure.

Rhythm Reading

Tap the following rhythm patterns using RH for notes with stems going up and LH for notes with stems going down. Tap hands separately first, and the hands together, always counting aloud.

2-25 (67)

1.
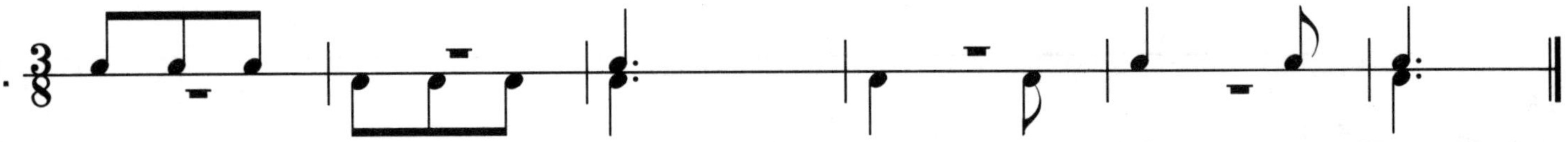

Count: 1 2 3 … 1 2 3

2-26 (68)

2.
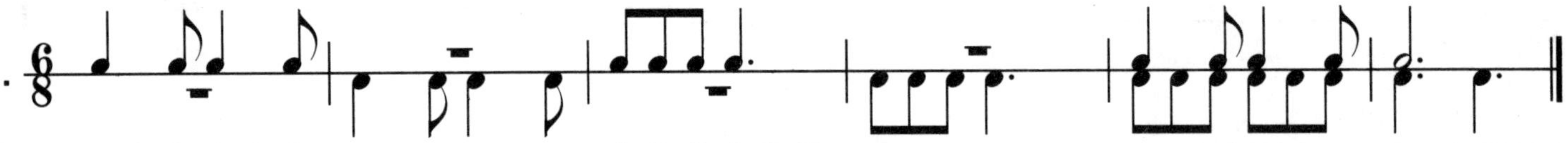

Count: 1 2 3 4 5 6 … 1 2 3 4 5 6

2-27 (69)

3.
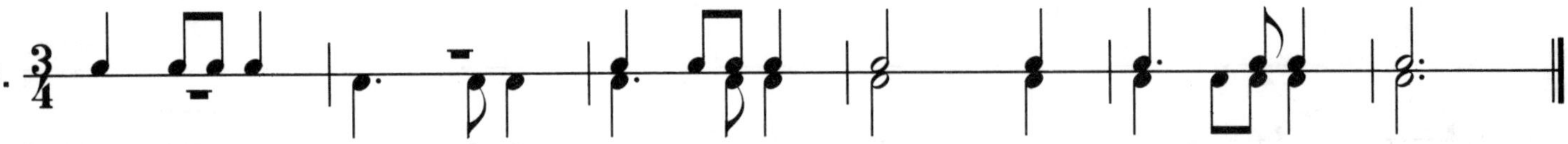

Count: 1 2 & 3 … 1 & 2 & 3

2-28 (70)

4.
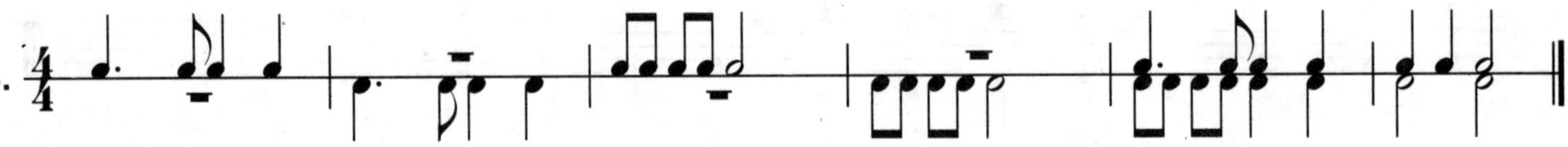

Count: 1 & 2 & 3 4 … 1 & 2 & 3 4

Technique

2-29 (71)

Transpose means to perform at a pitch other than the original. Each pitch must be raised or lowered by precisely the same interval, resulting in a change of key.

2-30 (72)

▶ Transpose to D major and E major.

2-31 (73)

▶ Transpose to G major and A major.

Reading

Identify the key of each example. Use the indicated tempo, dynamics and articulation as you play these exercises.

Use the following practice directions:

1. Clap and count aloud.
2. Play hands separately and count aloud.
3. Play hands separately and say note names.
4. Play hands together and count aloud.

An **accent sign** (>) over or under a note means play that note louder.

THE TRUMPETER AND THE ECHO

Dmitri Kabalevsky (1904–1987)
Op. 89, No. 15

2-32 (74)

Marcato *(marked, stressed)*

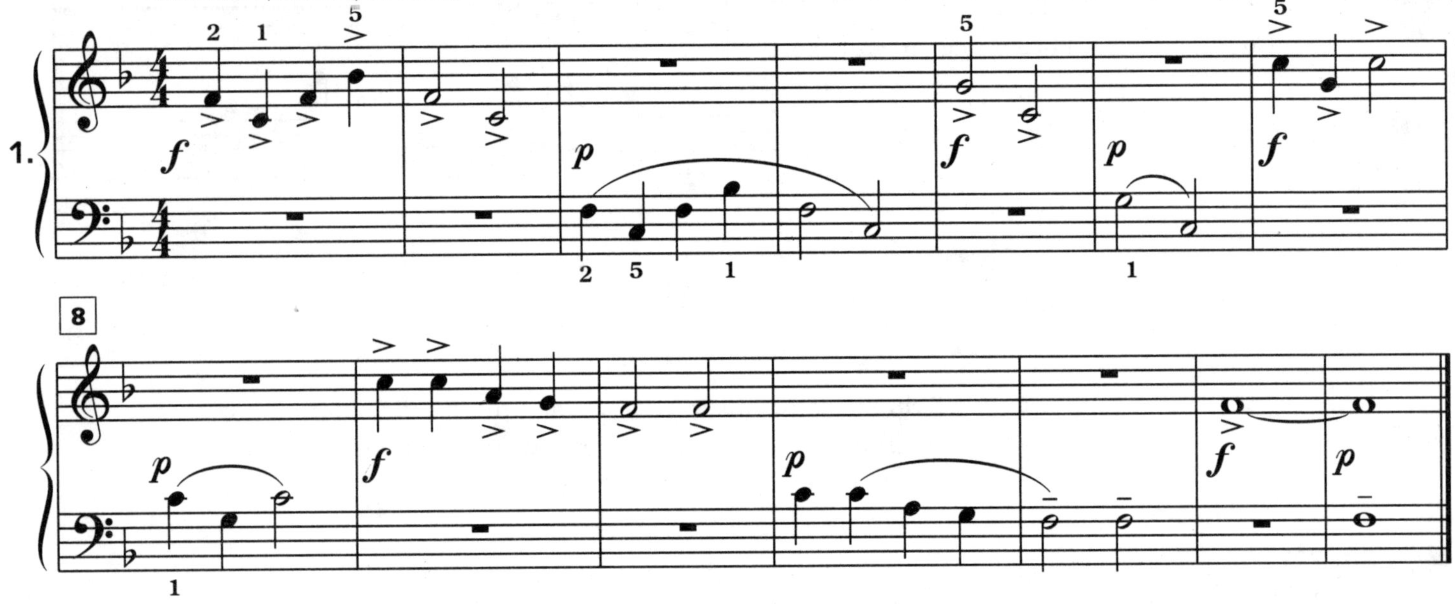

2-33 (75)

Moderato

▶ Transpose to G major.

2-34 (76)

▶ Transpose to C major.

2-35 (77)

▶ Transpose to D major.

Harmonization

Harmonize each of the melodies by playing tonic (**I**) or dominant (**V**) on the first beat of every measure.

- Use tonic when most of the melody notes are 1, 3 and 5.
- Use dominant when most of the melody notes are 2, 4 and 5.
- Begin and end each harmonization using tonic.

Dominant almost always precedes tonic at the end of the piece.

2-36 (78)

▶ Transpose to E major.

2-37 (79)

▶ Transpose to F major.

2-38 (80)

▶ Transpose to G major.

2-39 (81)

▶ Transpose to C major.

Duet Repertoire

Waltz

from The Children's Musical Friend

Secondo—Teacher

2-40 (82)

Heinrich Wohlfahrt (1797–1883)
Op. 87, No. 39

WALTZ

FROM THE CHILDREN'S MUSICAL FRIEND

Primo—Student

> ***D. C. (da capo) al Fine*** means repeat from the beginning and play to ***Fine*** (the end).

🔊 **2-40 (82)**

Heinrich Wohlfahrt (1797–1883)
Op. 87, No. 39

Tranquillo *(tranquil)*

RH one octave higher than written throughout

LH two octaves higher than written throughout

Five-Finger Improvisation

Improvise an 8-measure melody using notes from the indicated five-finger pattern as the teacher plays each accompaniment. Listen to the 4-measure introduction to establish the tempo, mood and style before beginning the melody.

1. Using a RH D major five-finger pattern, begin and end your melody on the D above middle C.

2-41 (83)

TEACHER ACCOMPANIMENT

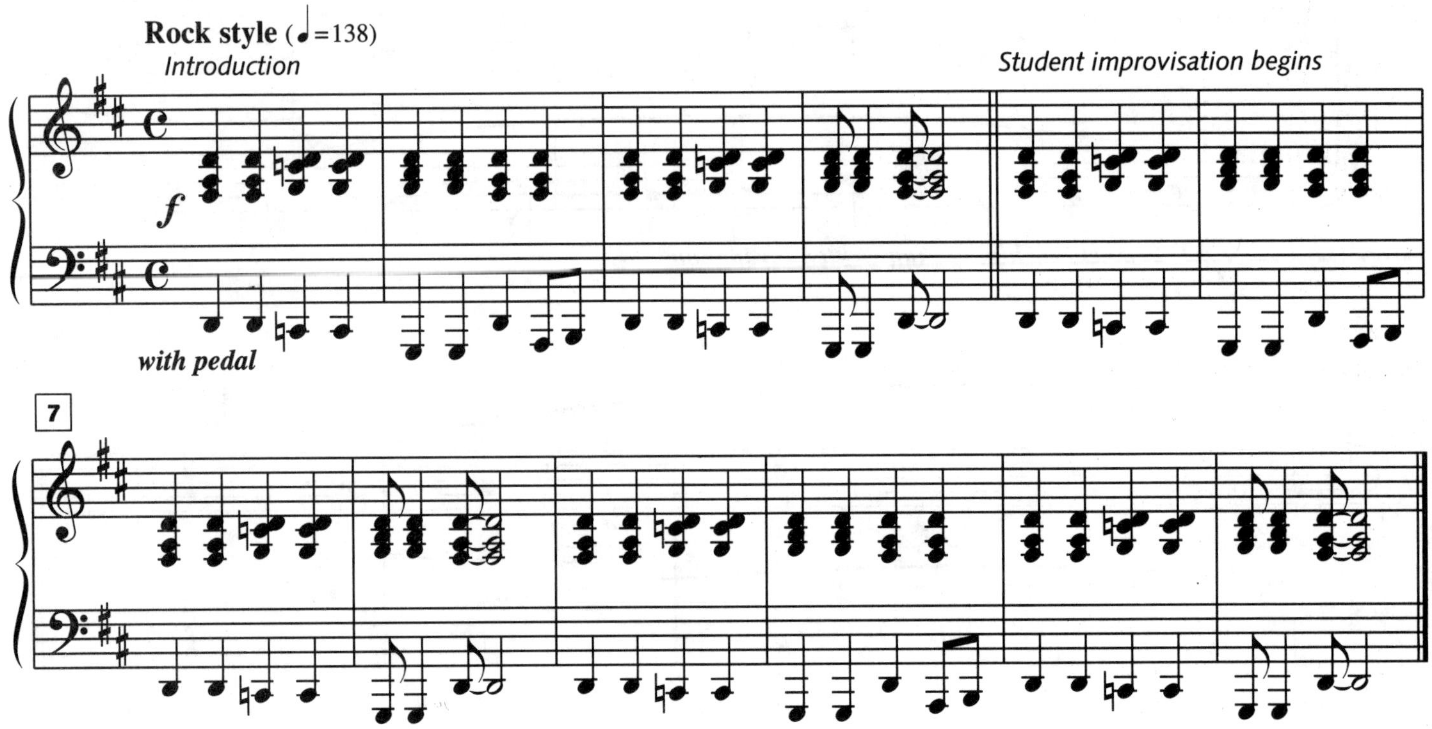

2. Using a RH F major five-finger pattern, begin and end your melody on the F above middle C.

2-42 (84)

TEACHER ACCOMPANIMENT

Playing Major Five-Finger Patterns and Chords

Play the following exercises that use major five-finger patterns and chords beginning on black keys.

3-2 (42)

1. 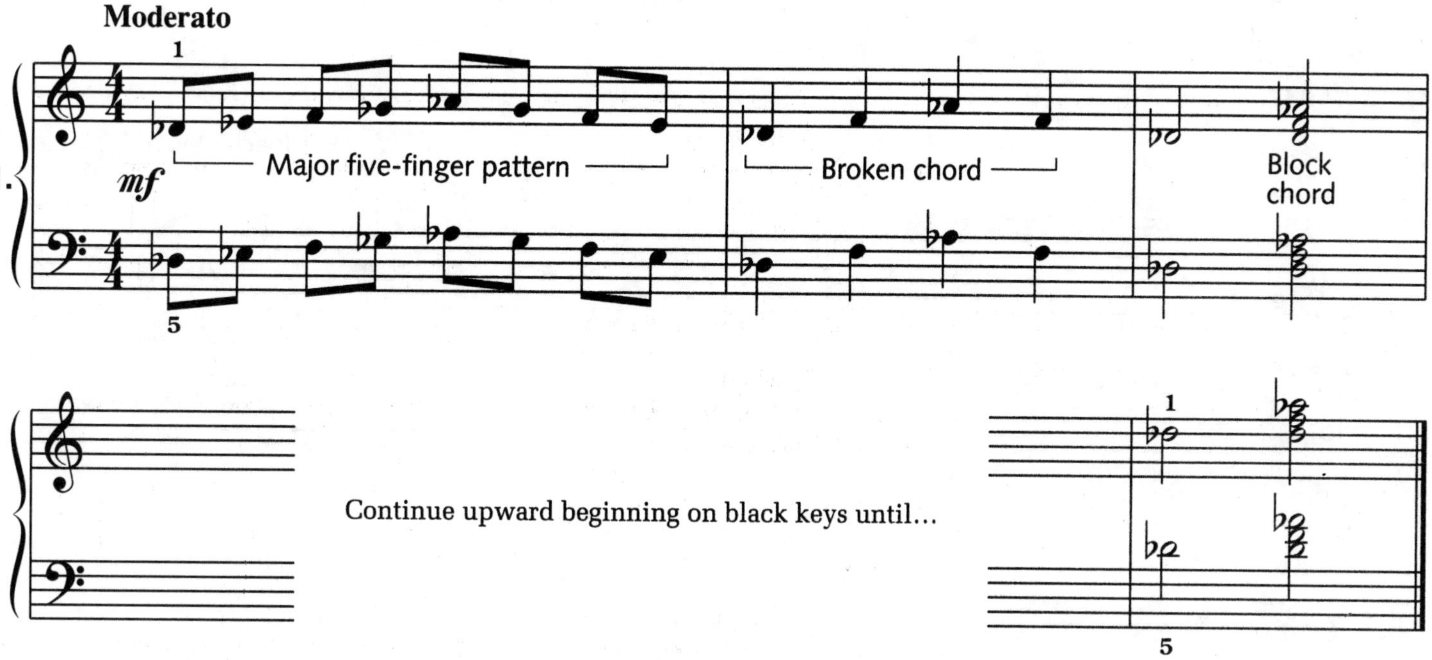

3-3 (43)

2. 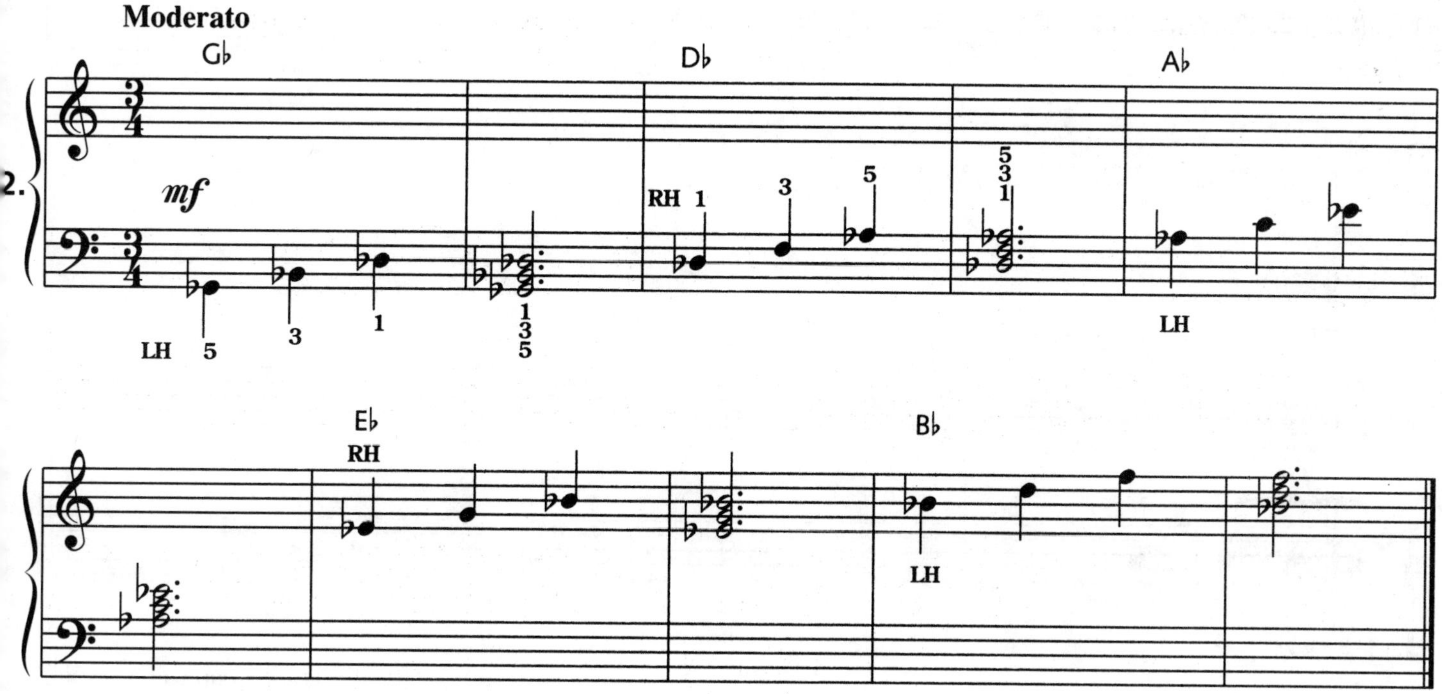

Solo Repertoire

DANCE

3-4 (44)

Joachim van der Hofe
(c. 1612)

Moderato

▶ Transpose to G♭ major.

Echoes of Scotland

3-5 (45)

Lively

2nd time RH 8va

E. L. Lancaster
Kenon D. Renfrow

Rhythm Reading

Tap the following rhythm patterns using RH for notes with stems going up and LH for notes with stems going down. Tap hands separately first, and then hands together, always counting aloud.

3-6 (46)

1. 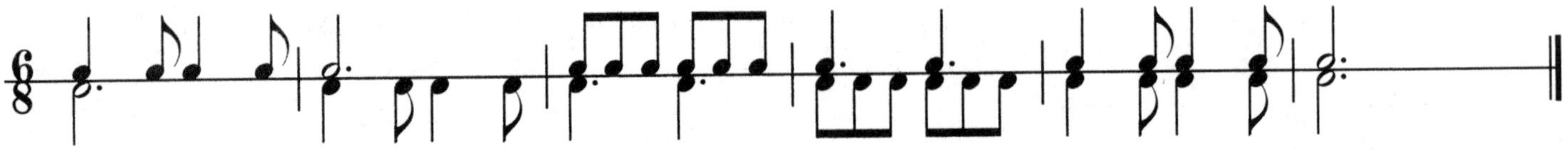

3-7 (47)

2. 

3-8 (48)

3. 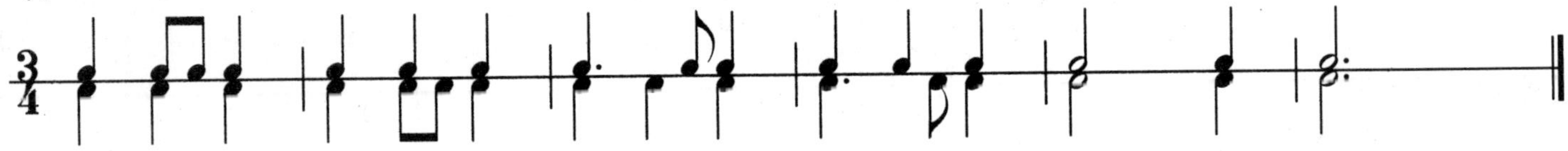

3-9 (49)

4. 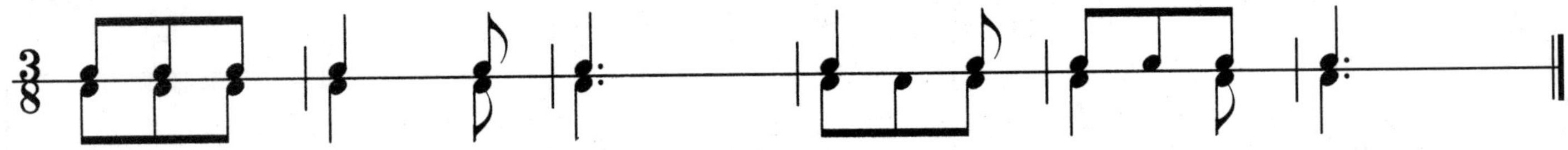

Technique

3-10 (50)

Moderato

1. 

3-11 (51)

Andante

2. 

▶ Transpose to E♭ major and G♭ major.

3-12 (52)

Andante

3. 

▶ Transpose to A♭ major and B♭ major.

Reading

Identify the key of each example. Use the indicated tempo, dynamics and articulation as you play these exercises.

Use the following practice directions:

1. Clap and count aloud.
2. Play hands separately and count aloud.
3. Play hands separately and say note names.
4. Play hands together and count aloud.

3-13 (53)

Moderato

1.

3-14 (54)

Andante

2.

▶ Transpose to D♭ major.

3-15 (55)

Allegro

3.

▶ Transpose to A♭ major.

3-16 (56)

Adagio

4.

▶ Transpose to B♭ major.

Harmonization

Harmonize each of the melodies by playing tonic (**I**) or dominant (**V**) on the first beat of every measure.

- Use tonic when most of the melody notes are 1, 3 and 5.
- Use dominant when most of the melody notes are 2, 4 and 5.
- Begin and end each harmonization using tonic.

Dominant almost always precedes tonic at the end of a piece.

3-17 (57)

▶ Transpose to B♭ major.

3-18 (58)

▶ Transpose to D♭ major.

3-19 (59)

3.

▶ Transpose to E♭ major.

3-20 (60)

4.

▶ Transpose to A♭ major.

Ensemble Repertoire

Forty-Finger Ensemble

Part 1

3-21 (61)

E. L. Lancaster

Lively

Part 2

3-21 (61)

E. L. Lancaster

Lively

Part 3

3-21 (61)

Lively

Both hands one octave higher than written throughout

E. L. Lancaster

Part 4

3-21 (61)

Lively

Both hands two octaves lower than written throughout

E. L. Lancaster

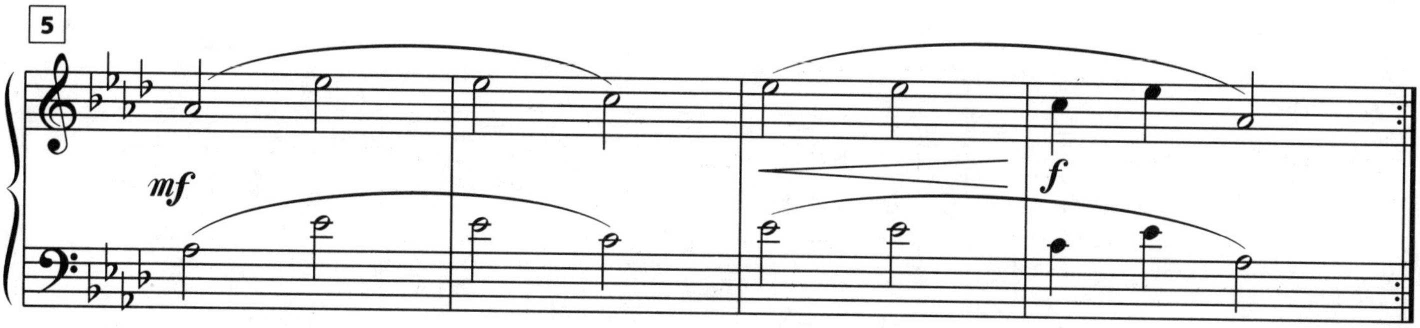

Five-Finger Improvisation

Improvise an 8-measure melody using notes from the indicated five-finger pattern as the teacher plays each accompaniment. Listen to the 4-measure introduction to establish the tempo, mood and style before beginning the melody.

1. Using a RH E♭ major five-finger pattern, begin and end your melody on the E♭ above middle C.

🔊 3-22 (62)

TEACHER ACCOMPANIMENT

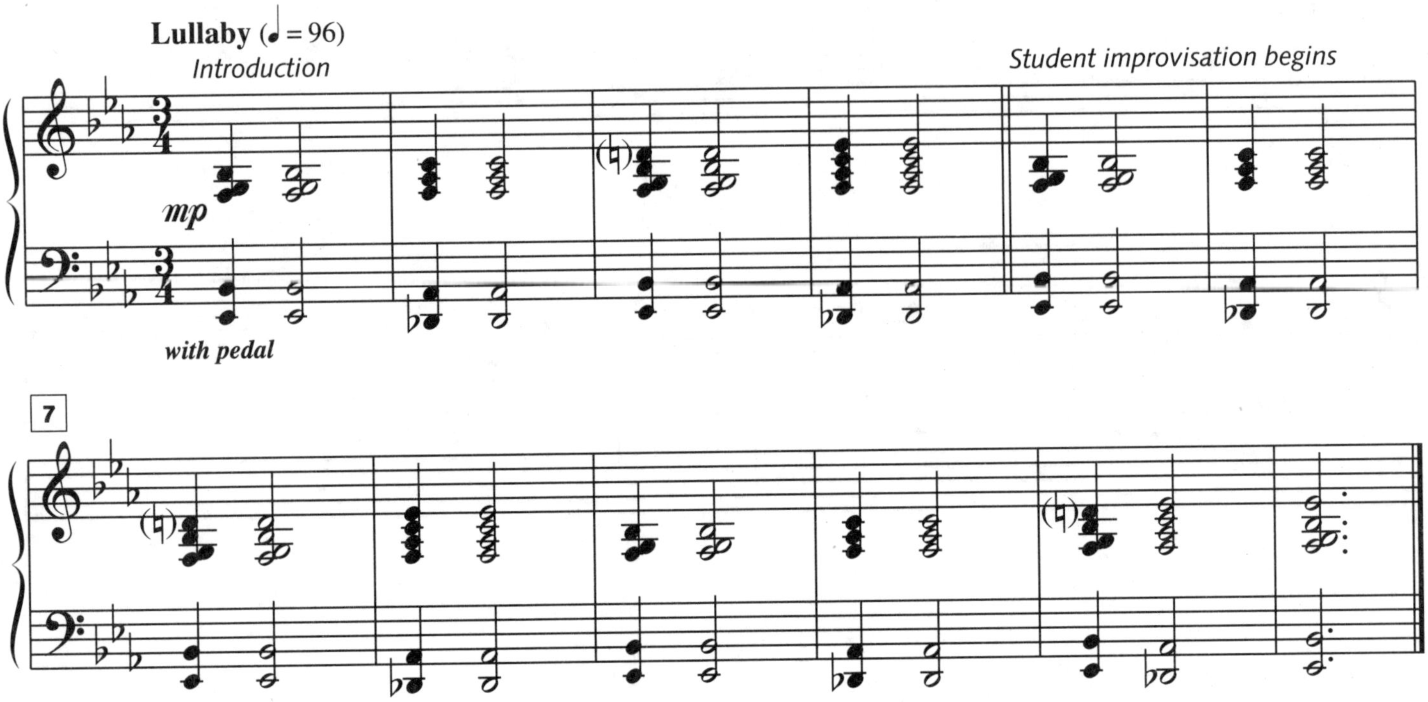

2. Using a RH G♭ major five-finger pattern, begin and end your melody on the G♭ above middle C.

🔊 3-23 (63)

TEACHER ACCOMPANIMENT

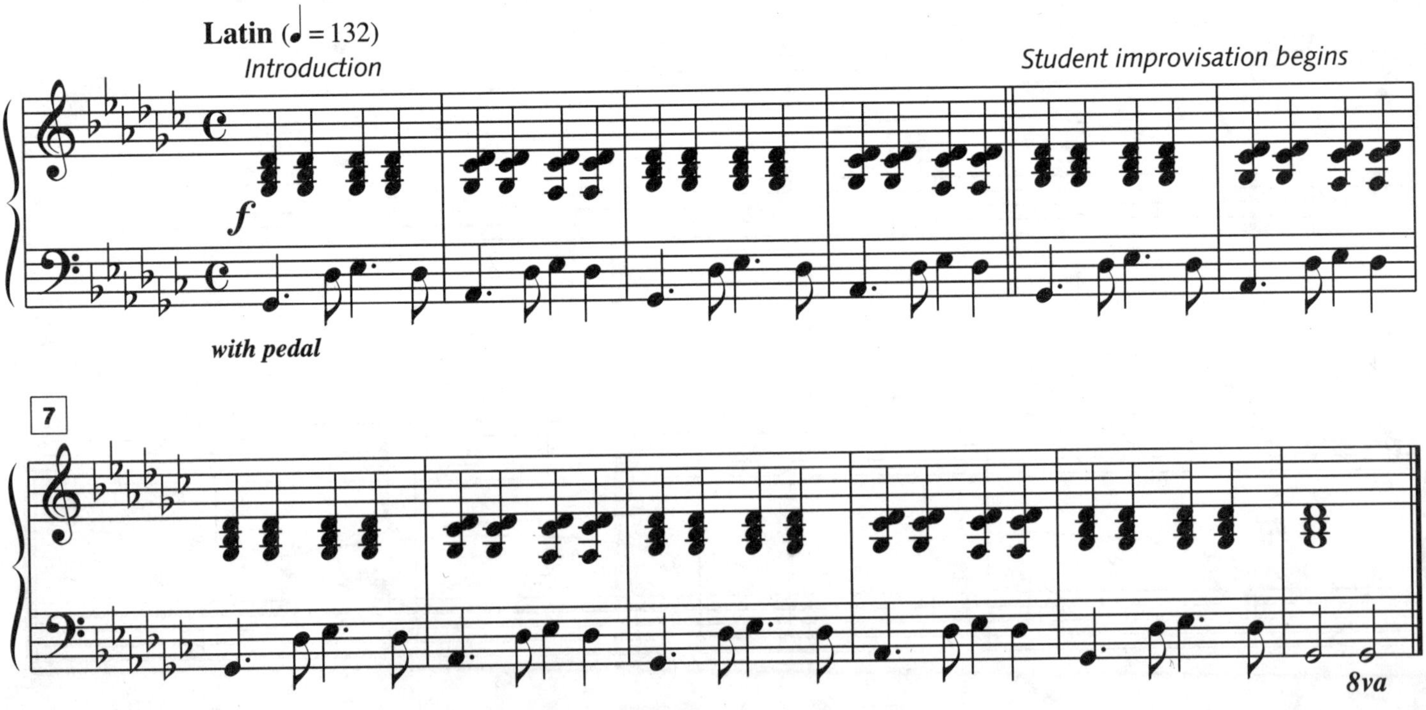

Playing Major Chords

Play the following exercises that use major chords with alternating hands:

3-24 (64)

Moderato

3-25 (65)

Moderato

Playing Major Five-Finger Patterns and Broken Chords

Play the following exercise that uses major five-finger patterns and broken chords:

3-26 (66)

Moderato

Sixteenth Notes

When a sixteenth note is written alone it has two flags. When written in pairs or groups of four, they are joined with two beams.

Four sixteenth notes are played in the time of one quarter note:

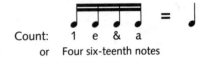

Count: 1 e & a
or Four six-teenth notes

Rhythm Reading

Tap the following rhythm patterns using RH for notes with stems going up and LH for notes with stems going down. Tap hands separately first, and then hands together, always counting aloud.

3-27 (67)

3-28 (68)

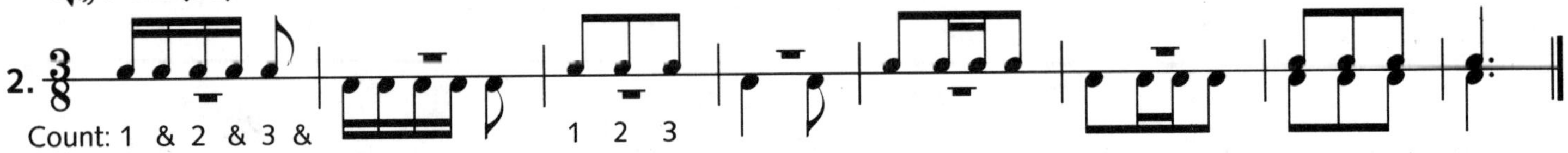

3-29 (69)

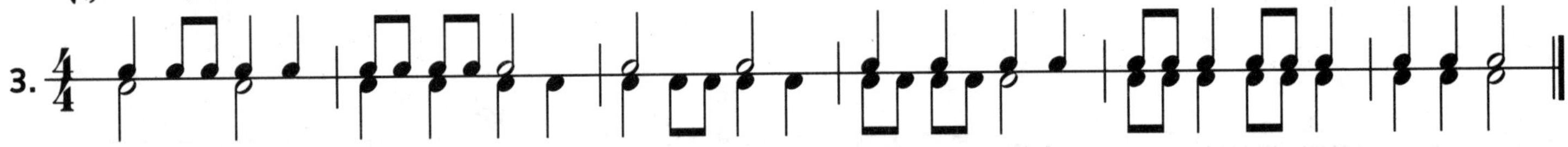

Technique

3-30 (70)

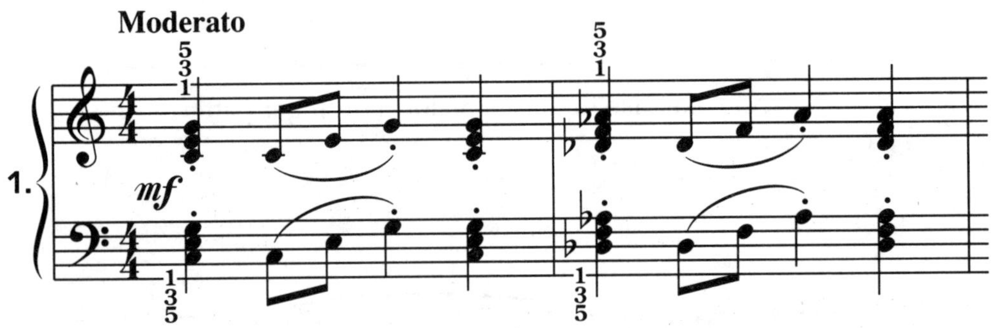

Continue upward by half steps until. . .

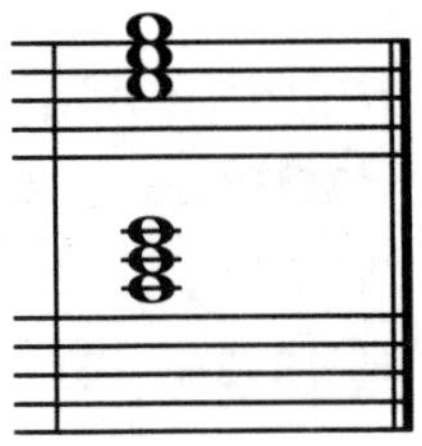

3-31 (71)

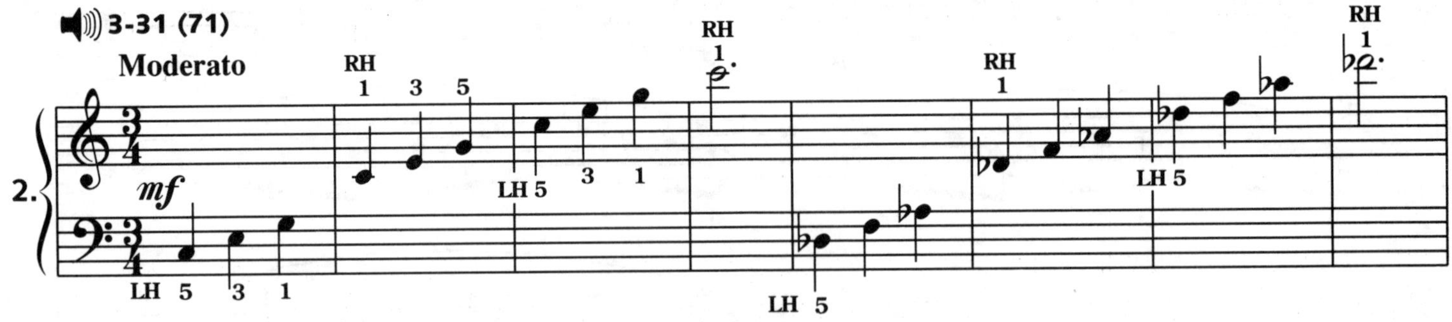

Continue upward by half steps until. . .

Solo Repertoire

A Little Joke

3-32 (72)

Dmitri Kabalevsky (1904–1987)
Op. 39, No. 6

Scherzando *(Playful)*

Reading

Identify the key of each example. Use the indicated tempo, dynamics and articulation as you play these exercises.

Use the following practice directions:

1. Tap RH and count aloud; then LH.
2. Play hands separately and count aloud.
3. Tap hands together and count aloud.
4. Play hands together and count aloud.

3-33 (73)

The Break

Dmitri Kabalevsky (1904–1987)
Op. 89, No. 4

3-34 (74)

▶ Transpose to E♭ major.

3-35 (75)

3.

▶ Transpose to G major.

3-36 (76)

4.

▶ Transpose to C major.

Harmonization

Harmonize each of the melodies by playing the indicated root-position chord. In measures where no chords are indicated, the last chord from the previous measure is repeated on beat one.

3-37 (77)

Lively

3-38 (78)

Andante

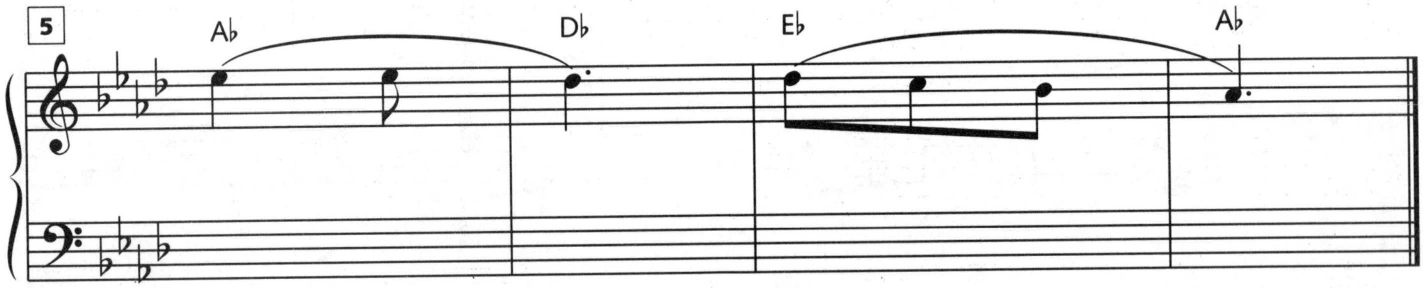

Harmonization with Two-Hand Accompaniment

Using the indicated chords, create a two-hand accompaniment for the following melody by continuing the pattern given in the first three measures.

3-39 (79)

Ensemble Repertoire

Play the four-part ensemble using the indicated chords to complete parts 3 and 4.

Part 1: Melody
Part 2: Countermelody (one octave higher than written throughout)
Part 3: Two-hand accompaniment
Part 4: Roots of chords (one octave lower than written throughout)

BARCAROLLE

3-40 (80)

E. L. Lancaster

Flowing

Unit 6

Minor Five-Finger Patterns Beginning on White Keys

Objectives

Upon completion of this unit the student will be able to:

1. Play minor five-finger patterns and minor triads beginning on any white key.
2. Perform solo repertoire that utilizes minor five-finger patterns.
3. Sight-read and transpose melodies in minor five-finger patterns.
4. Harmonize minor melodies with tonic and dominant tones as an accompaniment.
5. Improvise melodies in minor five-finger patterns as the teacher plays an accompaniment.
6. Perform duet repertoire with a partner.

Assignments

Week of ________

Write your assignments for the week in the space below.

Minor Five-Finger Patterns

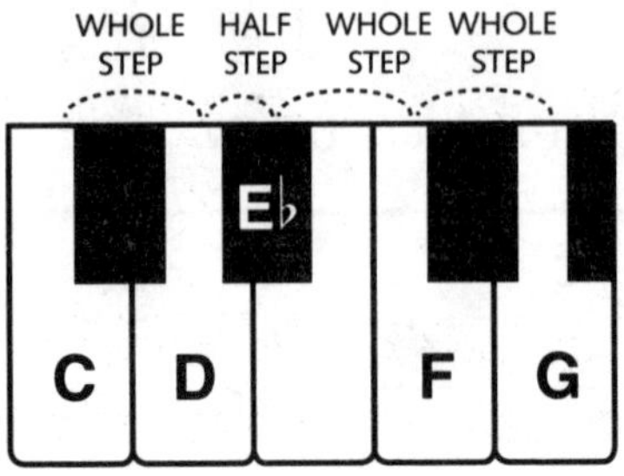

A minor five-finger pattern is a series of five notes having a pattern of *whole step, half step, whole step, whole step.*

The first note of the pattern is the tonic (**i**). The fifth note of the pattern is the dominant (**V**).

LH five-finger patterns are fingered 5 4 3 2 1.
RH five-finger patterns are fingered 1 2 3 4 5.

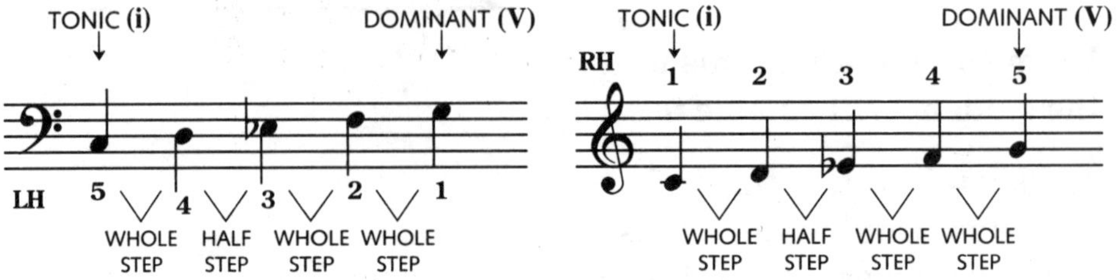

■ **Written Exercise:**
Write letter names on the correct keys to form each minor five-finger pattern.

Example:

C Minor

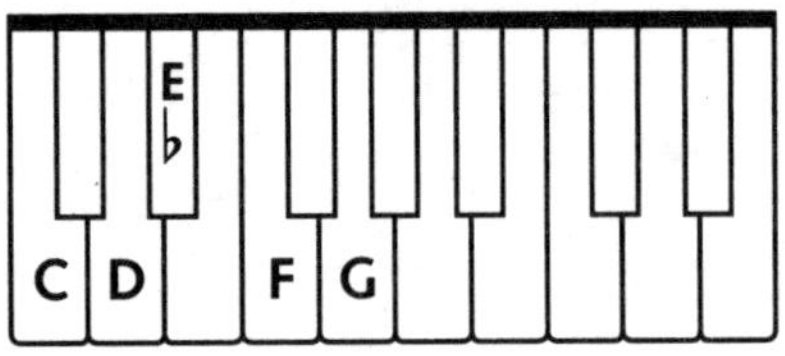

D Minor

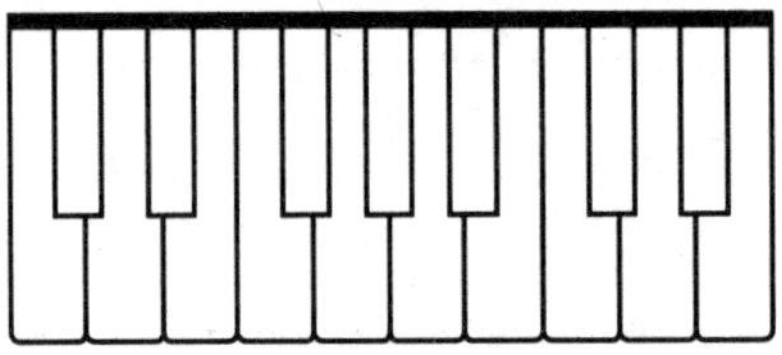

G Minor

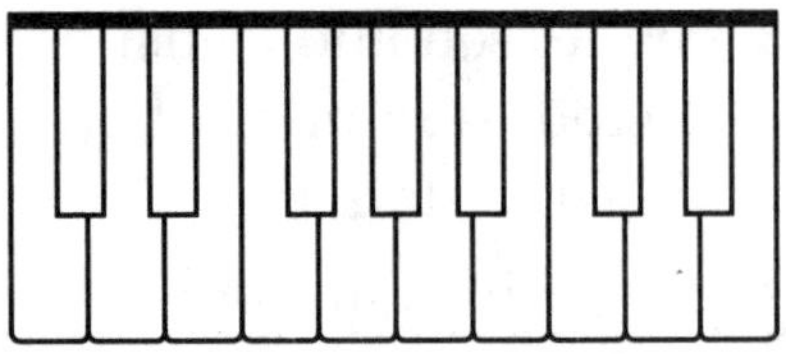

E Minor

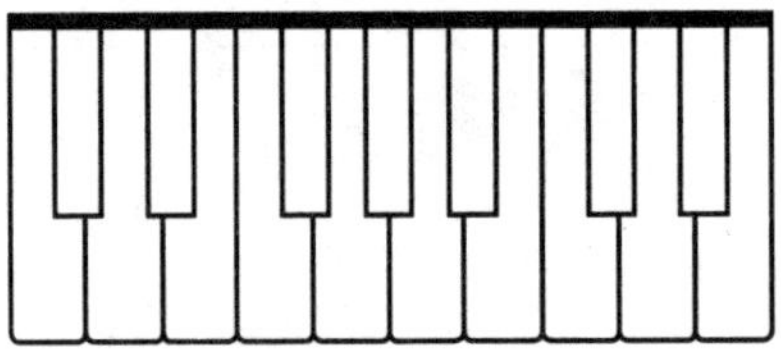

A Minor

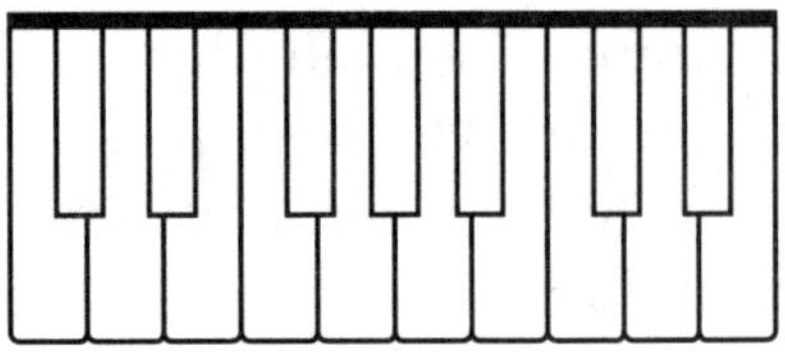

F Minor

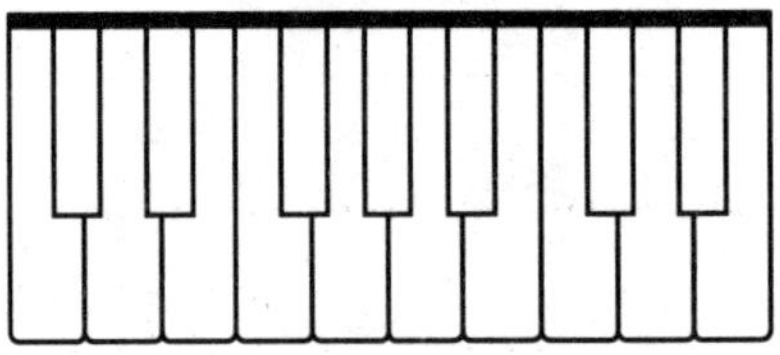

B Minor

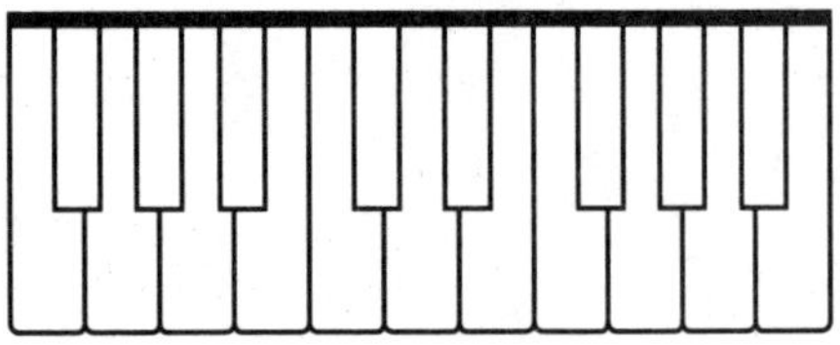

Major and Minor Five-Finger Patterns

Major five-finger patterns become minor five-finger patterns when the middle note is lowered a half step.

Major Five-Finger Pattern:

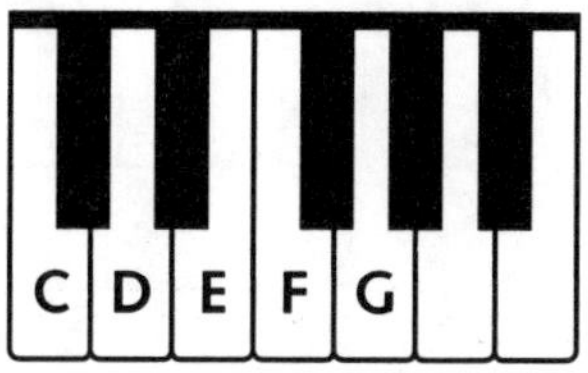

Minor Five-Finger Pattern:

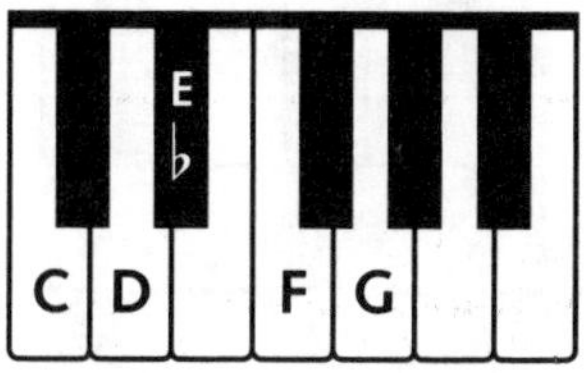

Playing Major and Minor Five-Finger Patterns

Play the following exercise that uses major and minor five-finger patterns.

4-1 (42)

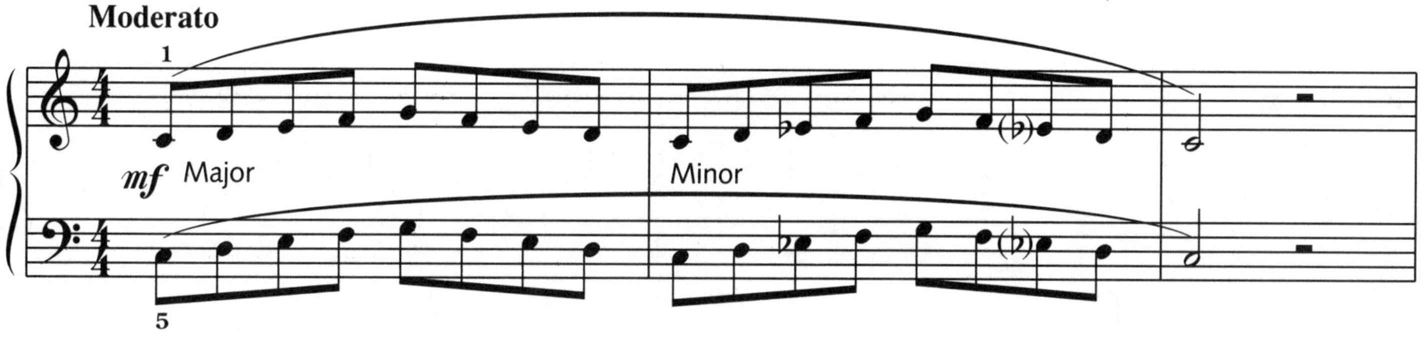

Minor Chords

Major chords become minor chords when the middle note is lowered a half step.

Major Chord

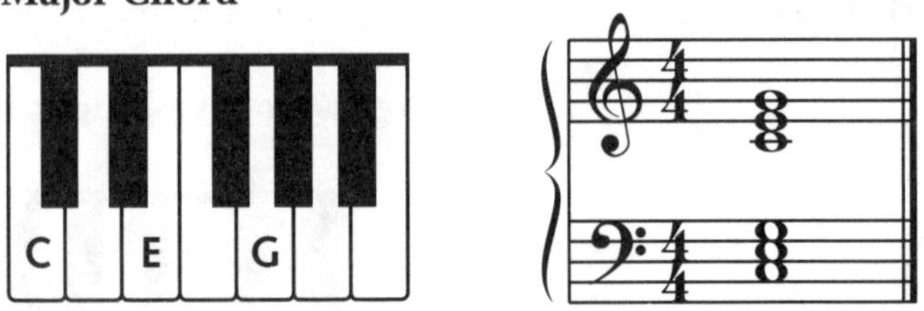

Minor Chord

Playing Minor Five-Finger Patterns and Chords

Play the following exercises that use minor five-finger patterns and chords.

4-2 (43)

Moderato

4-3 (44)

Moderato

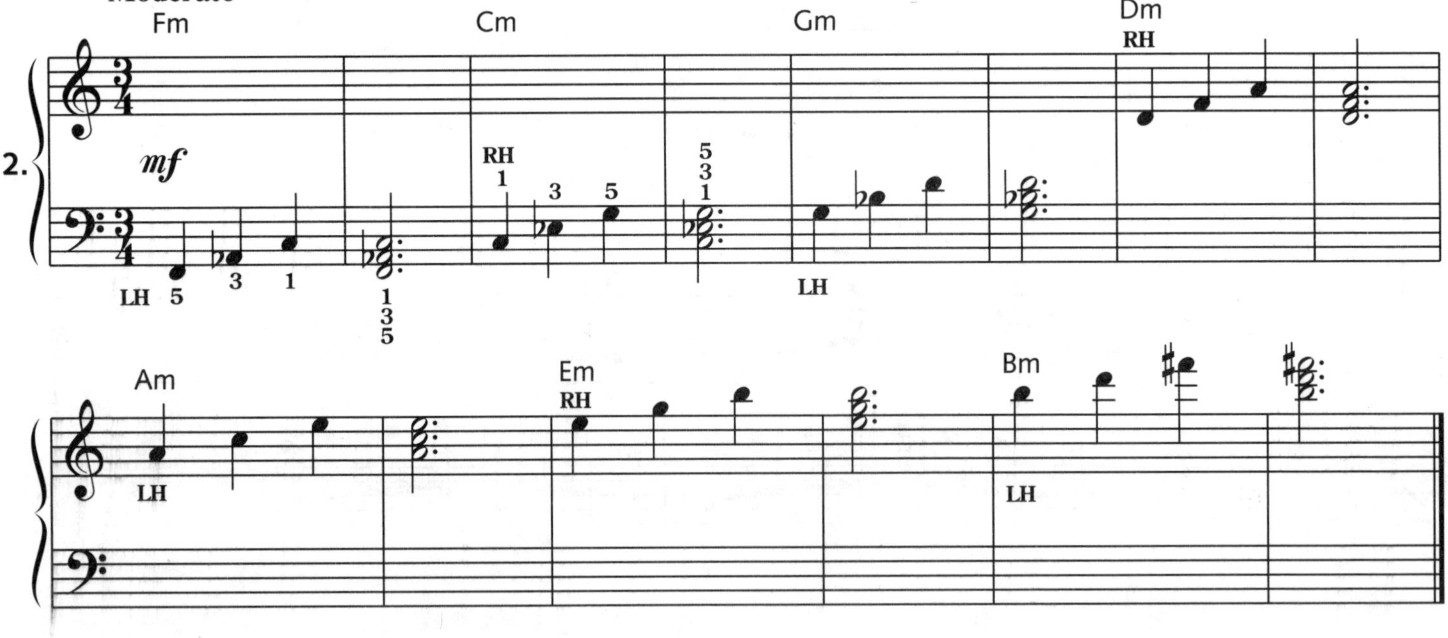

Relative Minor Keys

Every major key has a **relative minor key** that shares the *same key signature.* The name of the relative minor can be found by moving down (left) three half steps from the name of the major key. Always skip two keys and one alphabet letter.

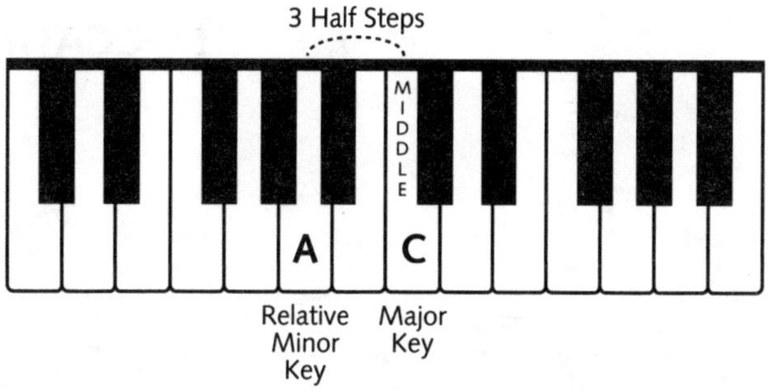

■ **Written Exercise:**
Write the name of each major key in the blank in the middle column. Write the name of its relative minor in the blank in the right column.

	Key Signature	Major Key	Minor Key
1.	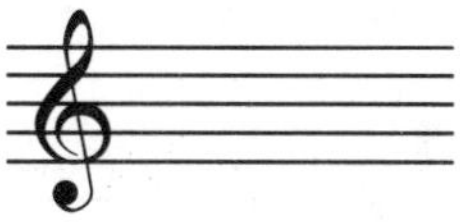	C	A
2.		______	______
3.	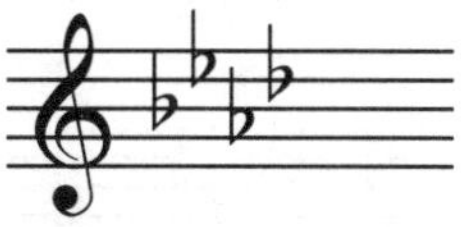	______	______
4.		______	______
5.	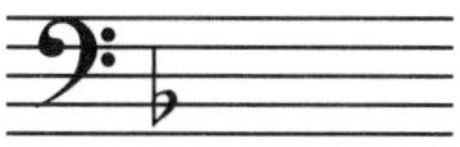	______	______
6.	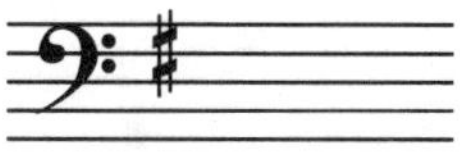	______	______
7.		______	______

Solo Repertoire

𝄵 This time signature is **alla breve,** sometimes called "cut time." This indicates $\frac{2}{2}$ time. Count *one* for each half note, etc.

TOCCATINA

4-4 (45)

E. L. Lancaster

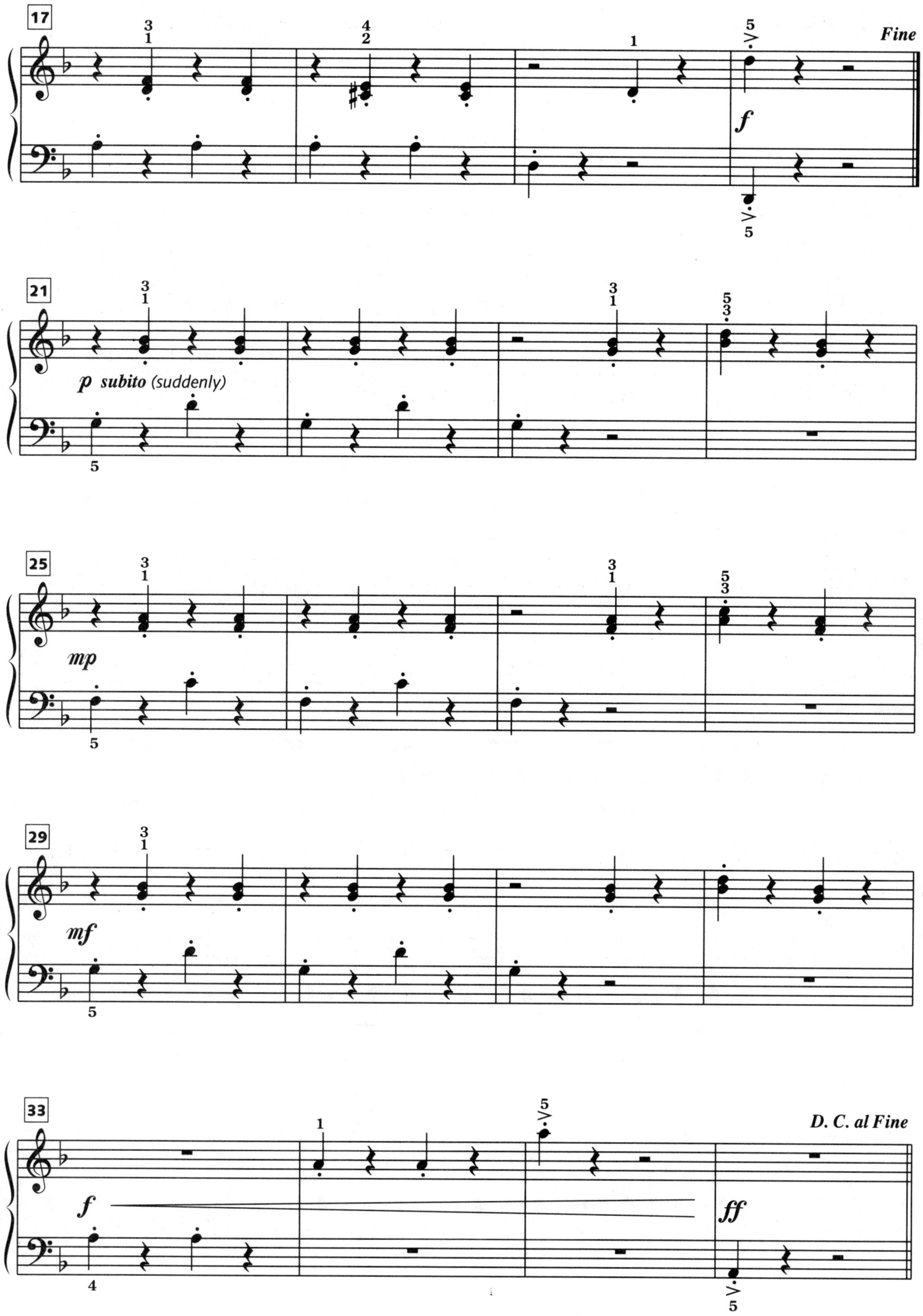
17
Fine
f
21
p subito (suddenly)
25
mp
29
mf
33
D. C. al Fine
f
ff

Eighth-Note Triplets

When three notes are grouped together with a figure "3" above or below the notes, the group is called a **triplet.** The three notes of an eighth-note triplet group equal one quarter note.

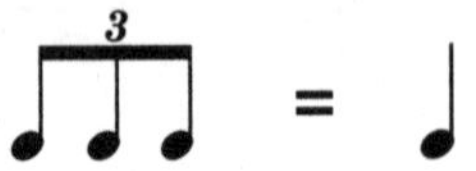

When a piece contains triplets, count "trip-a-let" or "1-and-a."

Rhythm Reading

Tap the following rhythm patterns using RH for notes with stems going up and LH for notes with stems going down. Tap hands separately first, and then hands together, always counting aloud.

Some pieces begin with an **incomplete measure.** The first measure in Exercise 1 below has only one count. The three missing counts are found in the last measure.

4-5 (46)

1. 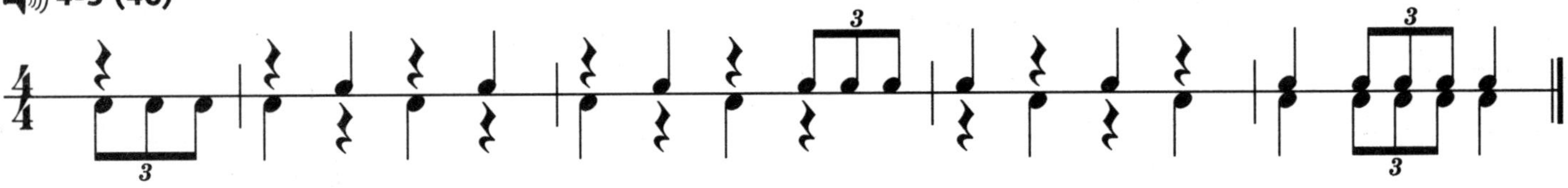

Count: Trip - a - let 1 2 3 4

4-6 (47)

2. 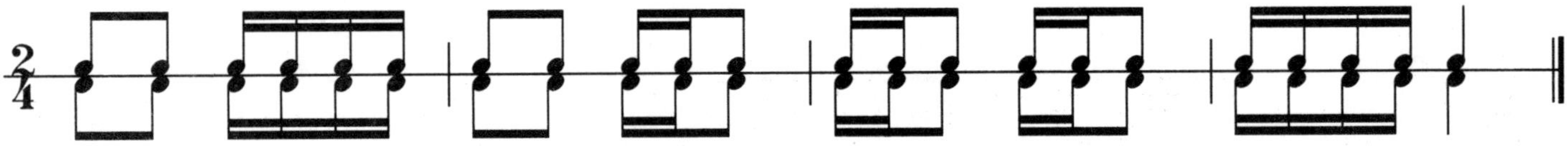

4-7 (48)

3. 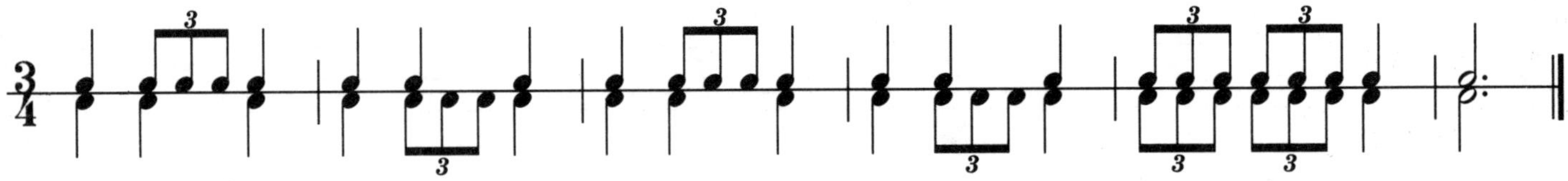

4-8 (49)

4. 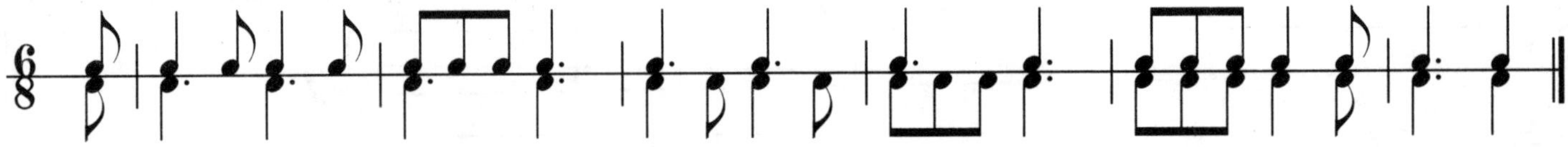

Technique

4-9 (50)

Moderato

1. 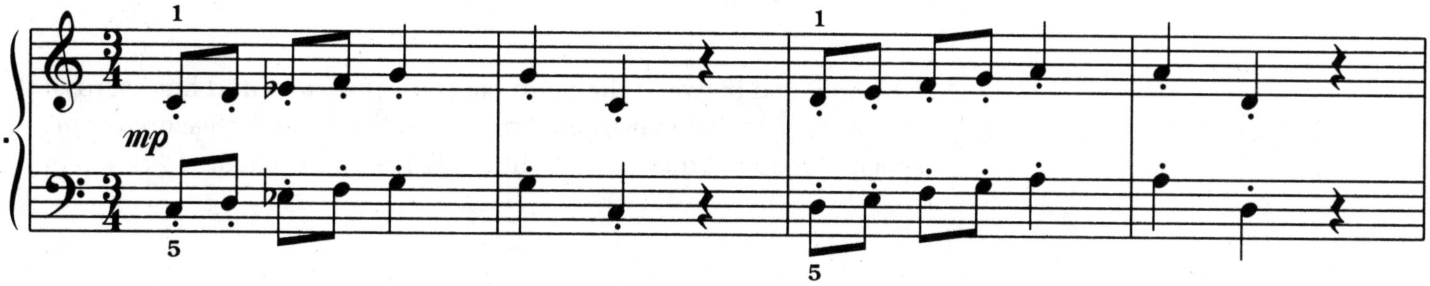

Continue upward
beginning on white keys until...

4-10 (51)

Andante

2. 

▶ Transpose to D minor and E minor.

4-11 (52)

Andante

3. 

▶ Transpose to G minor and A minor.

Reading

Identify the key of each example. Use the indicated tempo, dynamics and articulation as you play these exercises.

Use the following practice directions:

1. Tap RH and count aloud; then LH.
2. Play hands separately and count aloud.
3. Tap hands together and count aloud.
4. Play hands together and count aloud.

Notes played between the main beats of a measure and held across the beat are called **syncopated notes.** In the second measure of this piece, the dotted quarter note in the RH is syncopated.

4-12 (53)

Animato *(animated, lively)*

1.

▶ Transpose to D minor.

4-13 (54)

Relaxed

2.

▶ Transpose to C minor.

4-14 (55)

▶ Transpose to G minor.

4-15 (56)

▶ Transpose to D minor.

Harmonization

Harmonize each of the melodies by playing tonic (**i**) or dominant (**V**) on the first beat of every measure.

- Use tonic when most of the melody notes are 1, 3 and 5.
- Use dominant when most of the melody notes are 2, 4 and 5.
- Begin and end each harmonization using tonic.

Dominant almost always precedes tonic at the end of the piece.

4-16 (57)

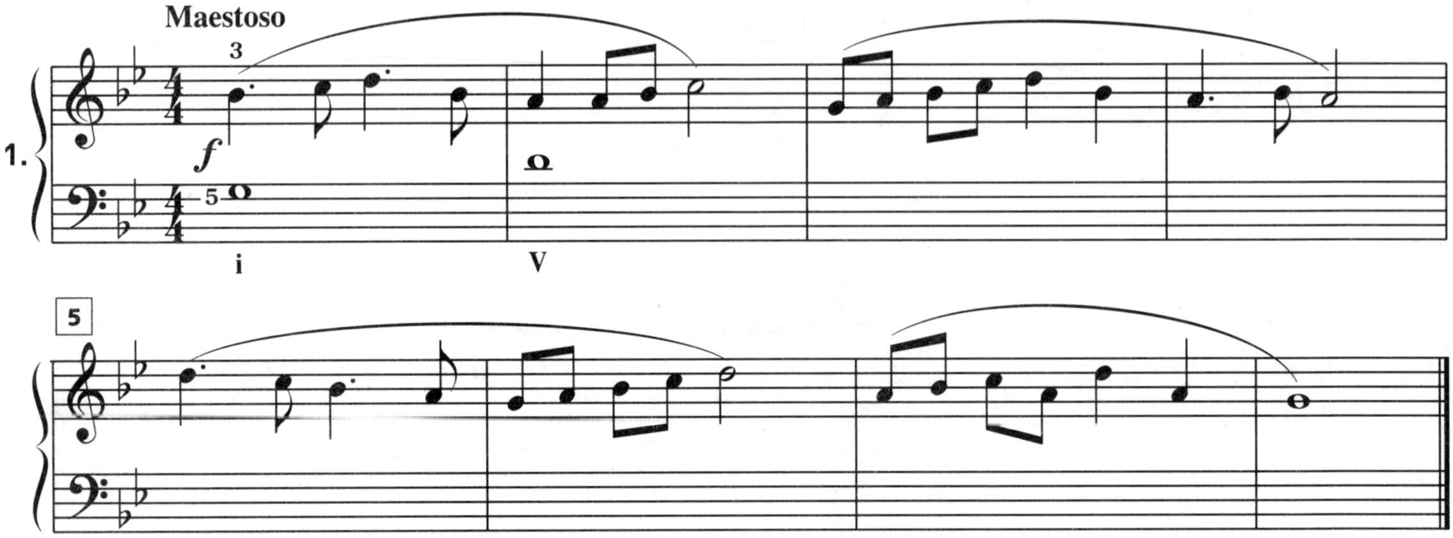

▶ Transpose to A minor.

4-17 (58)

▶ Transpose to D minor.

4-18 (59)

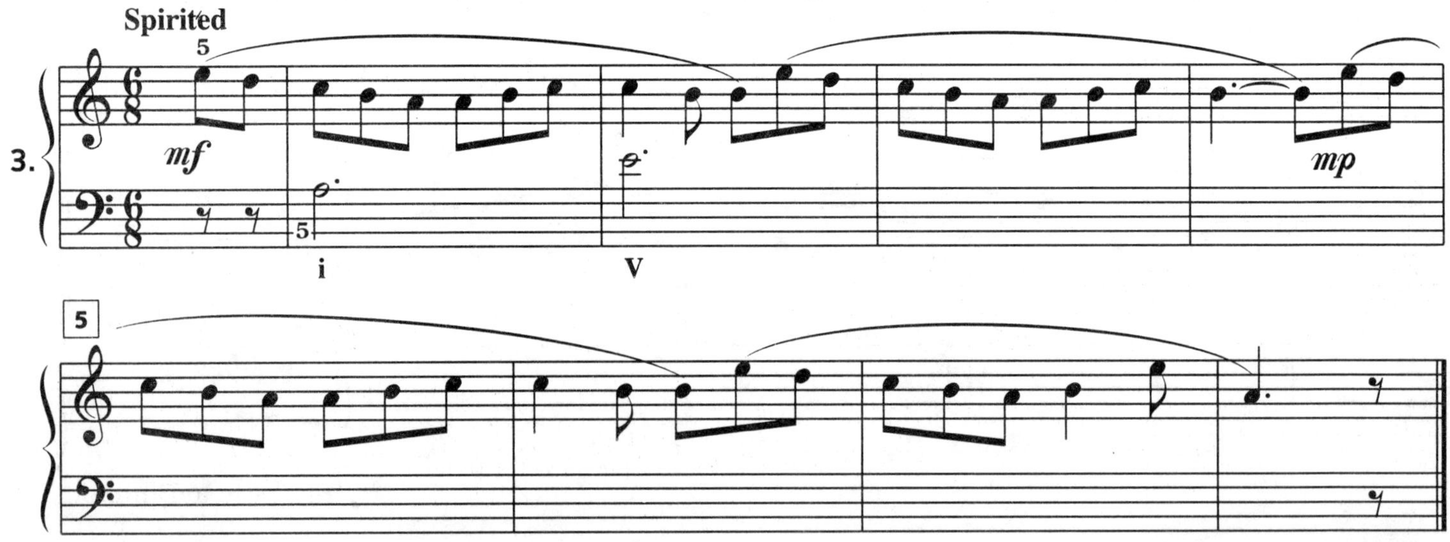

▶ Transpose to C minor.

Five-Finger Improvisation

Improvise an 8-measure melody using notes from the indicated five-finger pattern as the teacher plays each accompaniment. Listen to the 4-measure introduction to establish the tempo, mood and style before beginning the melody.

1. Using a RH D minor five-finger pattern, begin and end your melody on the D above middle C.

4-19 (60)

TEACHER ACCOMPANIMENT

2. Using a RH G minor five-finger pattern, begin and end your melody on the G above middle C.

4-20 (61)

TEACHER ACCOMPANIMENT

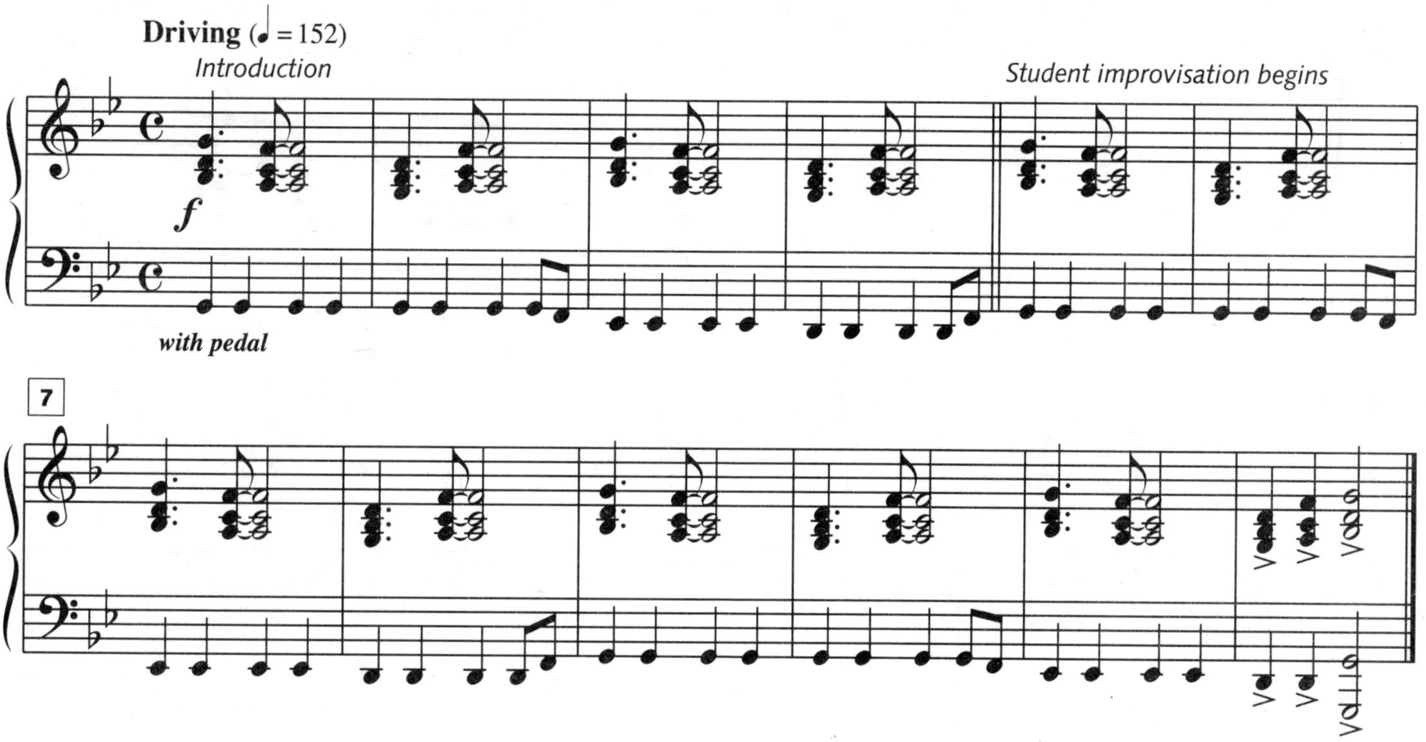

Prelude

from The Children's Musical Friend

Secondo—Teacher

Heinrich Wohlfahrt (1797–1883)
Op. 87, No. 2

4-21 (62)

PRELUDE

FROM THE CHILDREN'S MUSICAL FRIEND

Primo—Student

4-21 (62)

Heinrich Wohlfahrt (1797–1883)
Op. 87, No. 2

Unit 7

Minor Five-Finger Patterns Beginning on Black Keys

Objectives

Upon completion of this unit the student will be able to:

1. Play minor five-finger patterns and minor triads beginning on any black key.
2. Perform solo repertoire that utilizes minor five-finger patterns.
3. Sight-read and transpose melodies in minor five-finger patterns.
4. Harmonize minor melodies with tonic and dominant tones as an accompaniment.
5. Improvise melodies in minor five-finger patterns as the teacher plays an accompaniment.
6. Create four-part ensembles from chord symbols.

Assignments

Week of ________

Write your assignments for the week in the space below.

Minor Five-Finger Patterns

Review

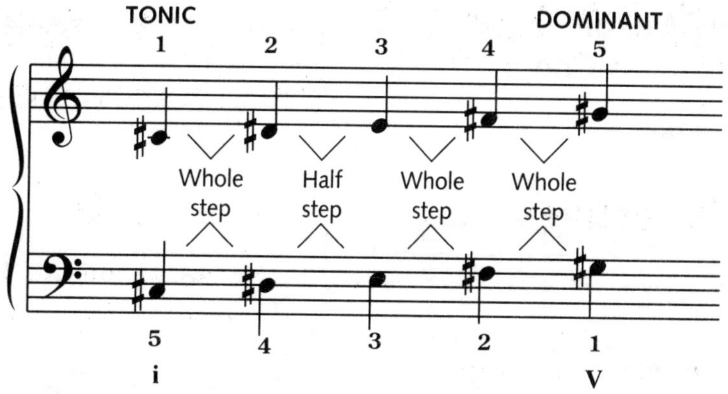

■ **Written Exercise:**

Write letter names on the correct keys to form each minor five-finger pattern.

C♯ minor

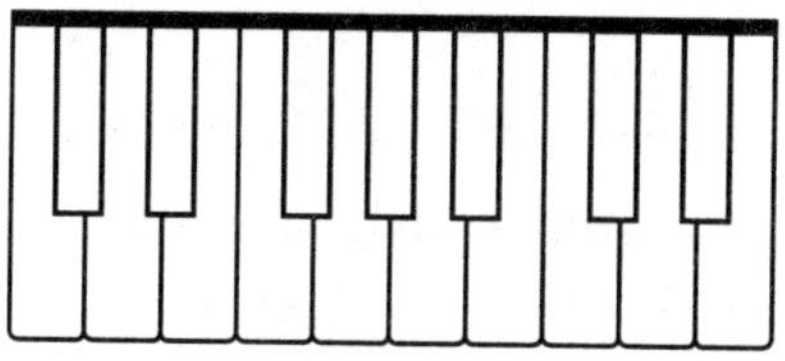

D♯ minor

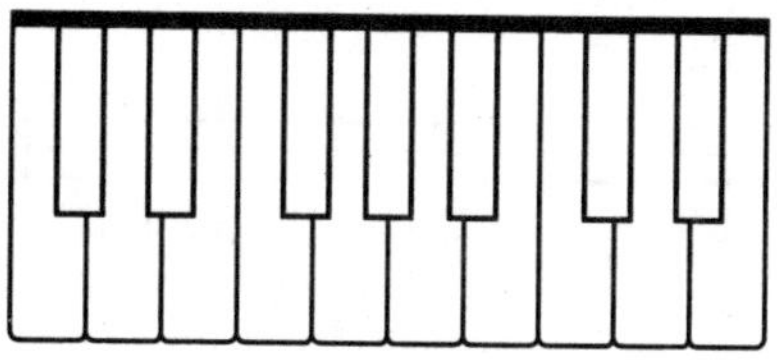

E♭ minor

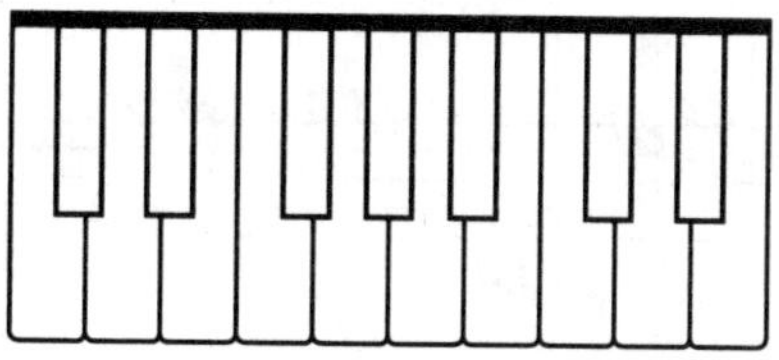

F♯ minor

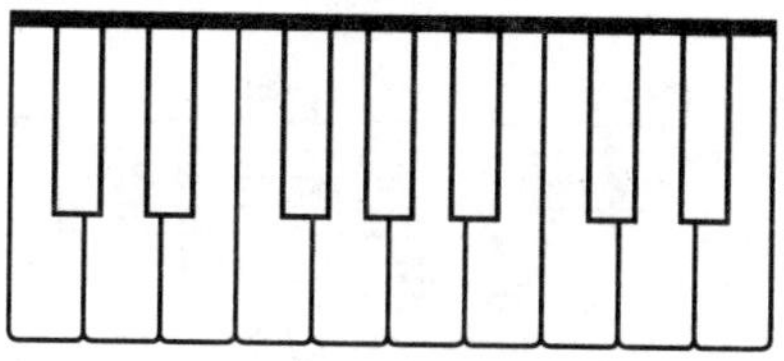

G♯ minor

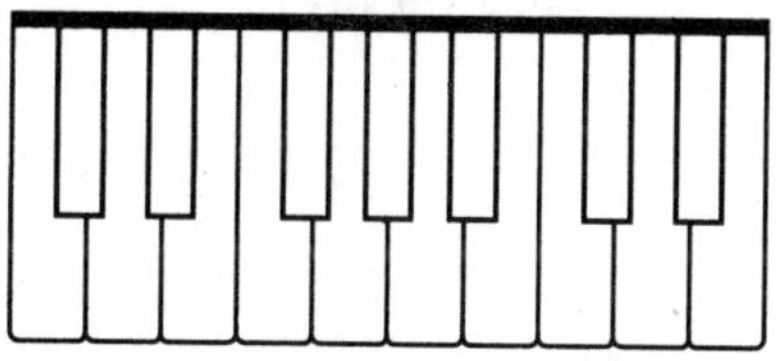

A♭ minor

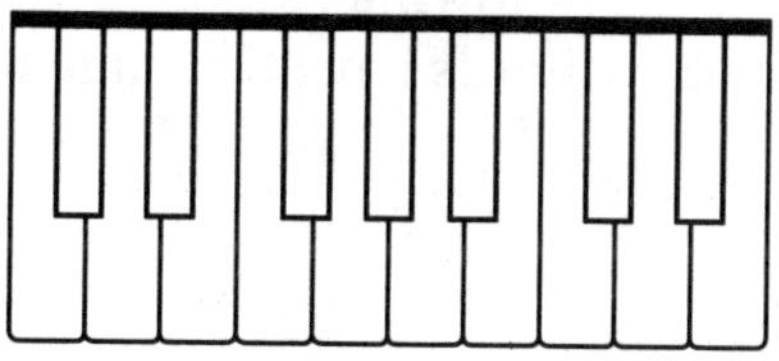

B♭ minor

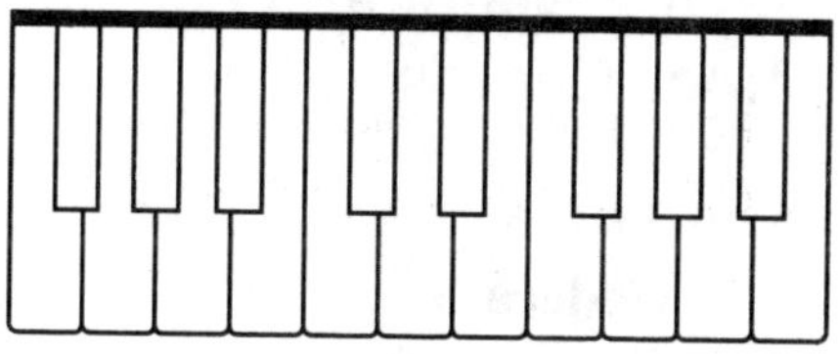

Playing Minor Five-Finger Patterns

Play the following exercise that uses minor five-finger patterns beginning on black keys.

4-22 (63)

Moderato

Continue upward beginning on black keys until. . .

Playing Minor Five-Finger Patterns and Chords

Play the following exercises that use minor five-finger patterns and chords beginning on black keys.

4-23 (64)

4-24 (65)

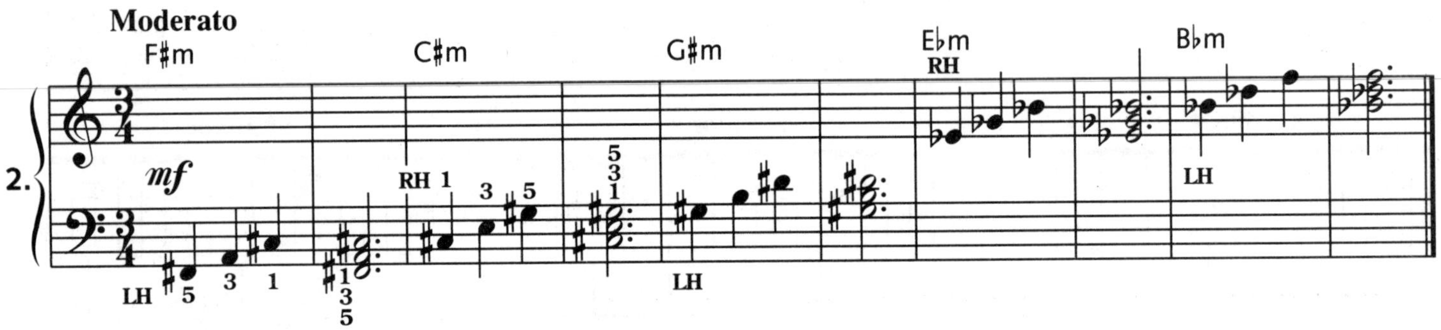

Playing Major and Parallel Minor Chords

Play the following exercises that use major and parallel minor chords. Parallel chords have the same root.

4-25 (66)

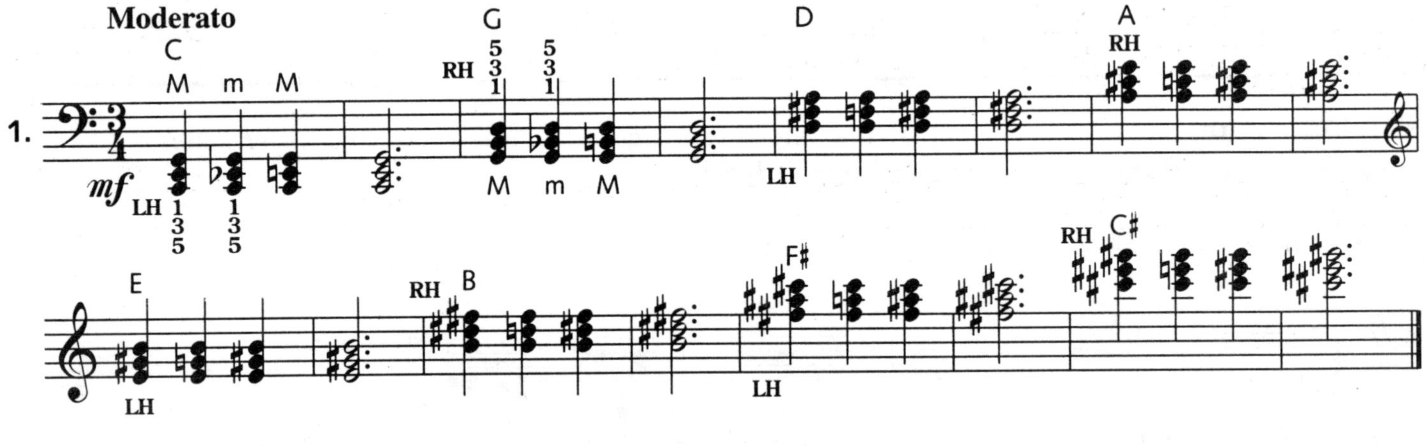

4-26 (67)

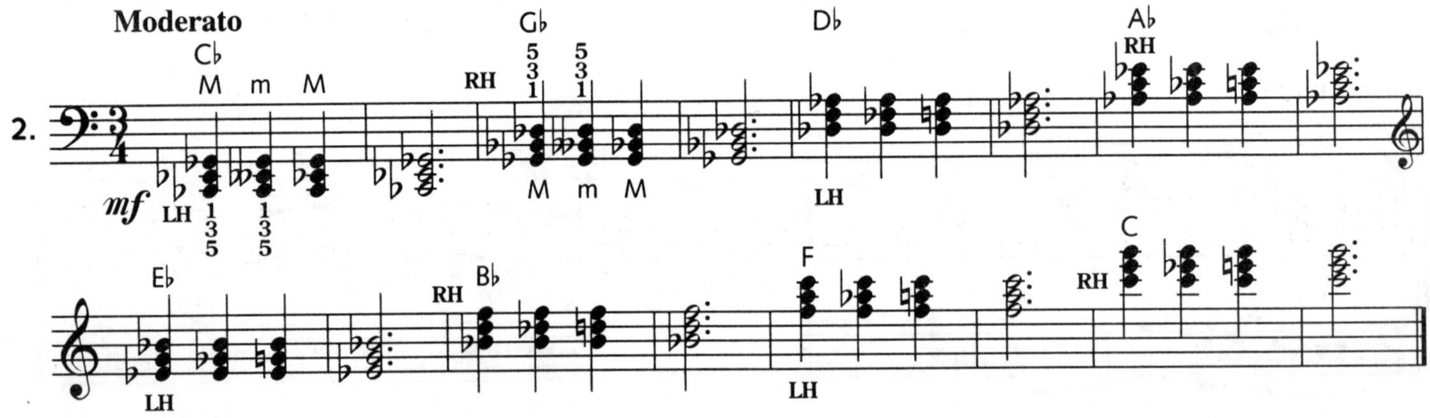

Playing Major and Relative Minor Five-Finger Patterns

Play the following exercise that uses major and relative minor five-finger patterns.

4-27 (68)

Moderato

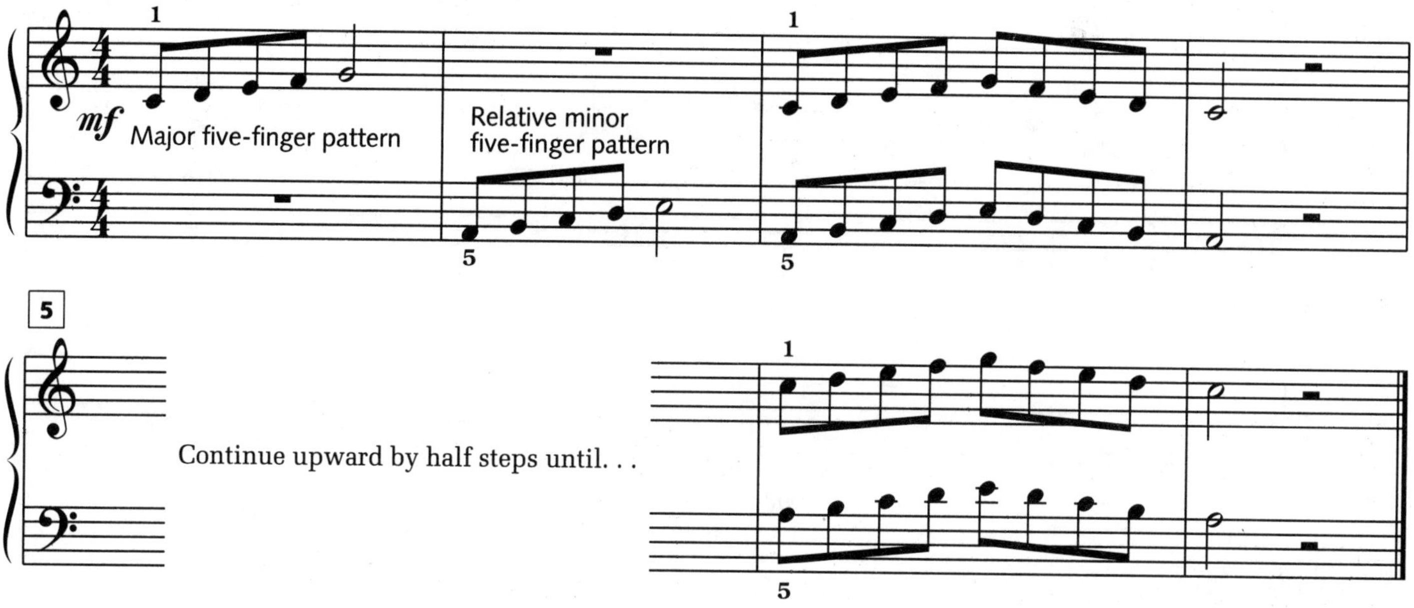

Technique

4-28 (69)

Moderato

1.

4-29 (70)

Andante

2.

▶ Transpose to E♭ minor and F♯ minor.

4-30 (71)

Andante

3.

▶ Transpose to G♯ minor and B♭ minor.

Solo Repertoire

LITTLE PRELUDE

4-31 (72)

Flowing

E. L. Lancaster

Reading

Identify the key of each example. Use the indicated tempo, dynamics and articulation as you play these exercises.

Use the following practice directions:

1. Tap RH and count aloud; then LH.
2. Play hands separately and count aloud.
3. Tap hands together and count aloud.
4. Play hands together and count aloud.

4-32 (73)

Andante

▶ Transpose to G♯ minor.

4-33 (74)

Allegretto

2.

▶ Transpose to B minor.

4-34 (75)

Moderato

3.

▶ Transpose to C minor.

4-35 (76)

Relaxed

4.

▶ Transpose to C♯ minor.

Harmonization

Harmonize each of the melodies by playing tonic (**i**) or dominant (**V**) on the first beat of every measure.

- Use tonic when most of the melody notes are 1, 3 and 5.
- Use dominant when most of the melody notes are 2, 4 and 5.
- Begin and end each harmonization using tonic.

Dominant almost always precedes tonic at the end of the piece.

4-36 (77)

▶ Transpose to F minor.

4-37 (78)

▶ Transpose to D minor.

4-38 (79)

▶ Transpose to F♯ minor.

Five-Finger Improvisation

Improvise an 8-measure melody using notes from the indicated five-finger pattern as the teacher plays each accompaniment. Listen to the 4-measure introduction to establish the tempo, mood and style before beginning the melody.

4-39 (80)

TEACHER ACCOMPANIMENT

1. Using a RH A♭ minor five-finger pattern, begin and end your melody on the A♭ above middle C.

4-40 (81)

TEACHER ACCOMPANIMENT

2. Using a RH C♯ minor five-finger pattern, begin and end your melody on the C♯ above middle C.

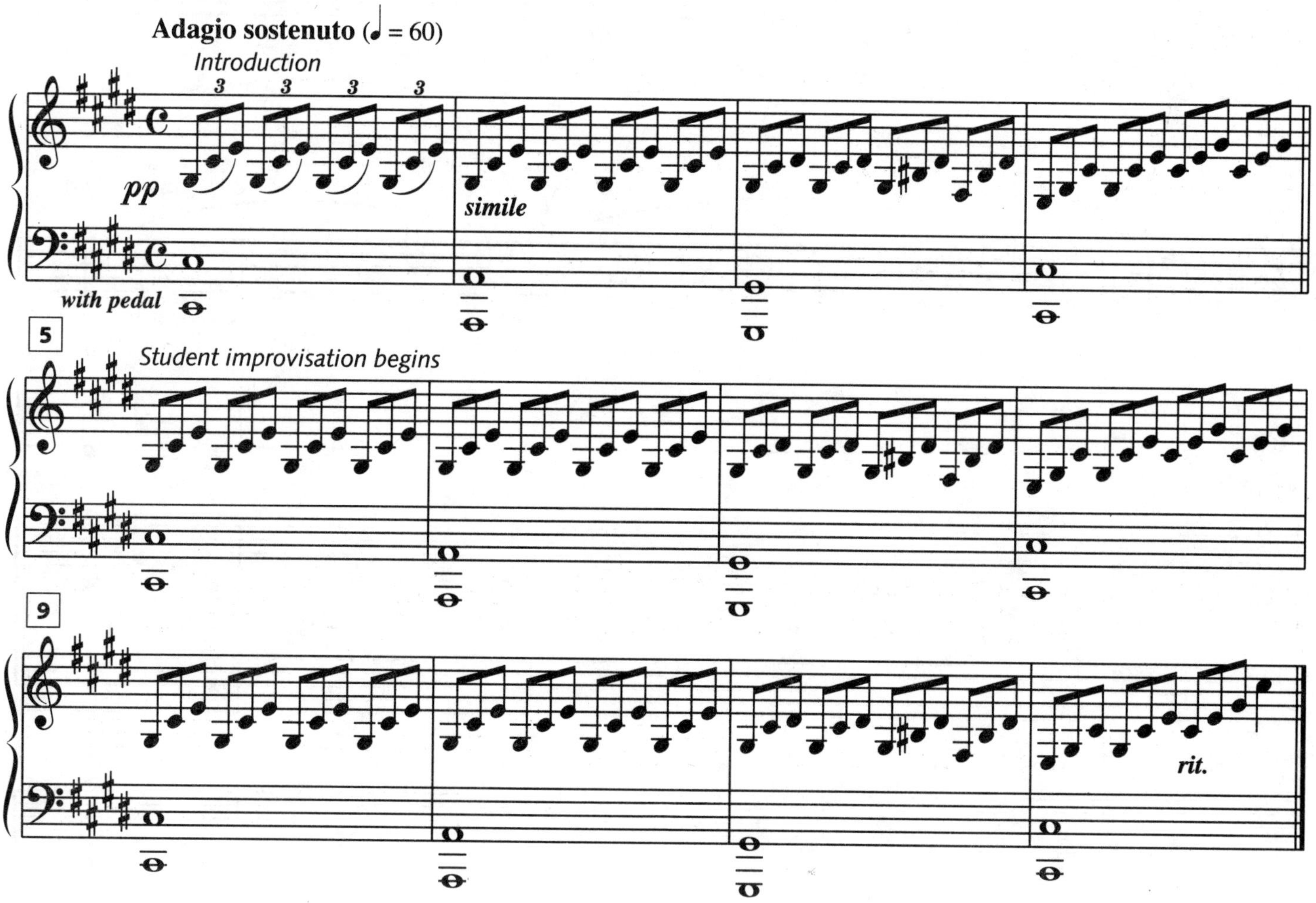

Ensemble Repertoire

Play the four-part ensemble using the indicated chords to complete parts 2, 3 and 4.

Part 1: Melody
Part 2: Broken chords (one octave higher than written throughout)
Part 3: Two-hand accompaniment
Part 4: Roots of chords

4-41 (82)

ERIE CANAL

Review Worksheet

Name ____________________ *Date* ____________________

1. Begin on each given key and build an ascending minor five-finger pattern. Write the names of the keys in the blanks.

B	___	___	___	___
F	___	___	___	___
E♭	___	___	___	___
C♯	___	___	___	___

2. Identify each minor five-finger pattern from its black-white key sequence. Write the name of the five-finger pattern in the blank.

W	B	W	W	W	___
B	B	W	W	B	___
B	W	B	B	B	___
W	W	B	B	W	___

3. Identify each minor triad by writing its name on the line.

___ ___ ___ ___ ___ ___ ___

4. Identify the minor chords from their black-white key sequence. Write the names of the chords in the blanks.

B	**W**	**B**	______	______	______
W	**B**	**W**	______	______	______
W	**W**	**W**	______	______	______

5. Draw a line to connect the minor key on the left with its corresponding key signature on the right.

F minor	
B minor	
D♯ minor	
E♭ minor	
E minor	
G minor	

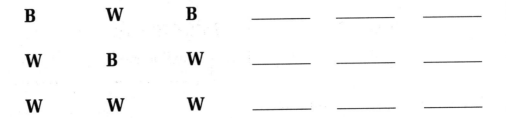

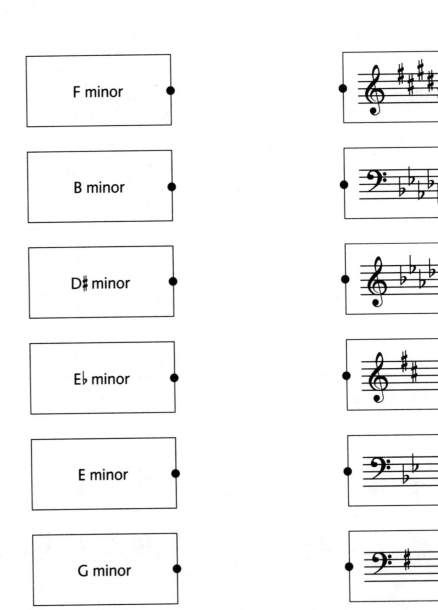

Unit 8

Chord Qualities

Objectives

Upon completion of this unit the student will be able to:

1. Play major, minor, augmented and diminished chords beginning on any key.
2. Perform solo and ensemble repertoire that uses various chord qualities.
3. Sight-read melodies with various chord qualities as an accompaniment.
4. Create two-hand accompaniments from chord symbols.
5. Create ensemble parts to accompany solo repertoire.

Assignments

Week of ________

Write your assignments for the week in the space below.

Augmented Chords

A major chord becomes **augmented** when the fifth is raised a half step. A plus sign (+) indicates an augmented chord.

C Major Chord

C

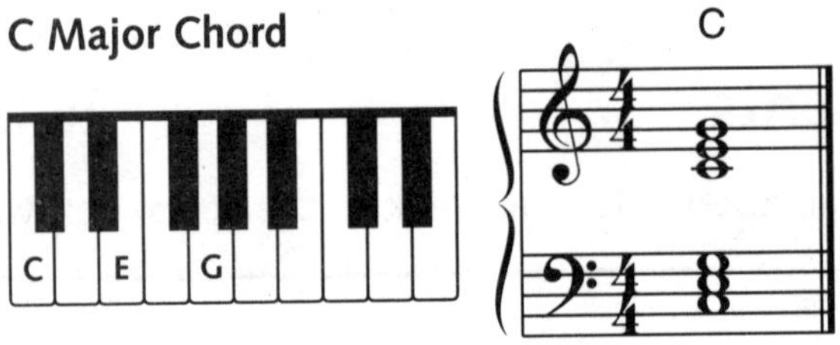

C Augmented Chord

C+

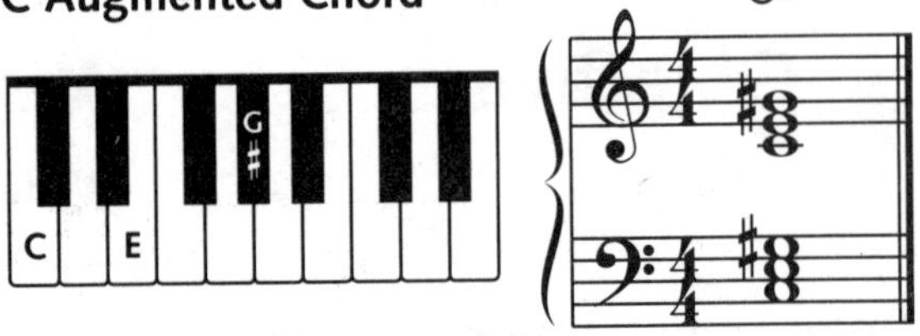

Playing Major and Augmented Chords

Play the following exercise that uses major (M) and augmented (A) chords.

🔊 5-1 (30)

Continue upward by half steps until. . .

Diminished Chords

A minor chord becomes **diminished** when the fifth is lowered a half step. A small circle (°) indicates a diminished chord.

C Minor Chord

Cm

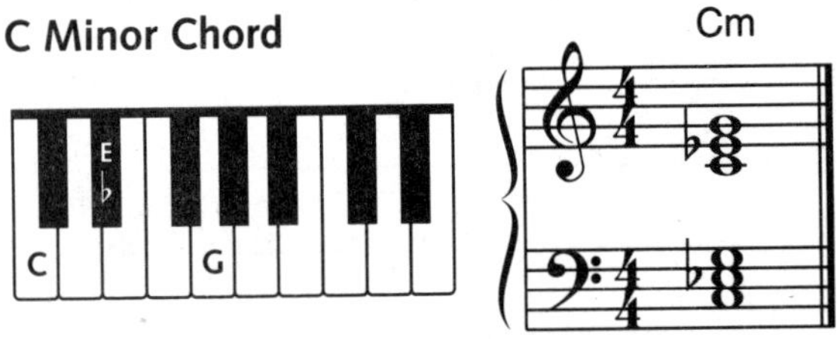

C Diminished Chord

C dim. or C°

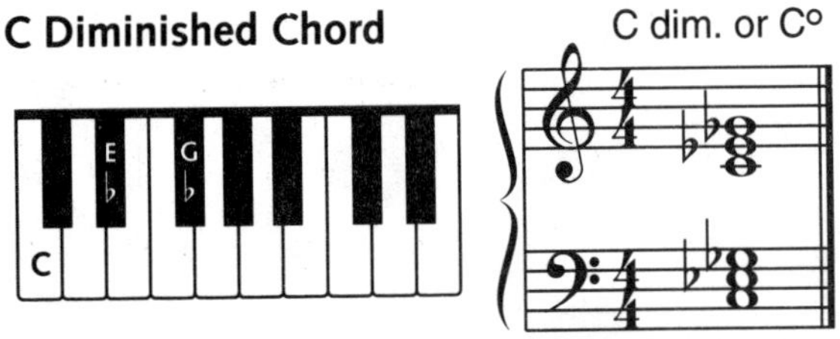

Playing Minor and Diminished Chords

Play the following exercise that uses minor (m) and diminished (d) chords.

A **double flat (𝄫)** lowers a flatted note another half step, or a natural note one whole step.

🔊 5-2 (31)

Continue upward by half steps until. . .

Playing Major, Augmented, Minor and Diminished Chords

Play the following exercise that uses major (M), augmented (A), minor (m) and diminished (d) chords.

A **double sharp** (×) raises a sharped note another half step, or a natural note one whole step.

5-3 (32)

Continue downward by half steps until. . .

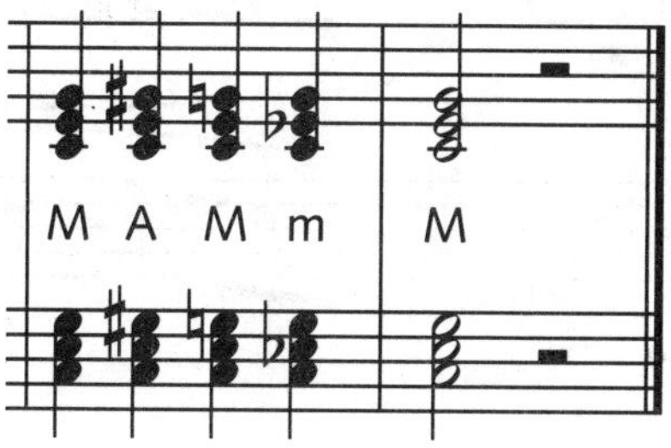

The Dotted Eighth Note

A dotted eighth note has the same value as an eighth note tied to a sixteenth note.

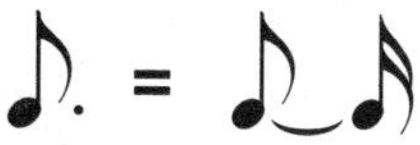

Rhythm Reading

Tap the following rhythm patterns using RH for notes with stems going up and LH for notes with stems going down. Tap hands separately first, and then hands together, always counting aloud.

5-4 (33)

1. 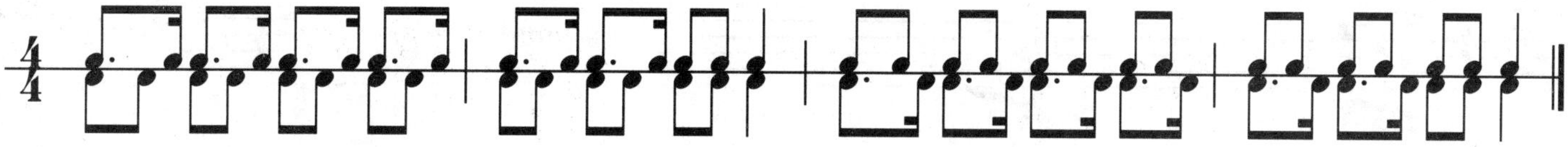

5-5 (34)

2. 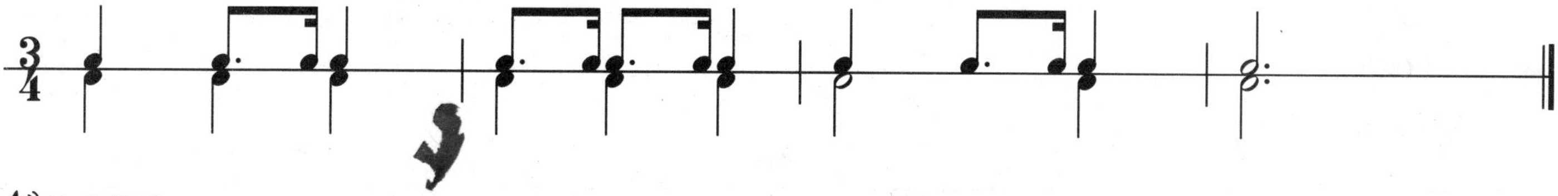

5-6 (35)

3. 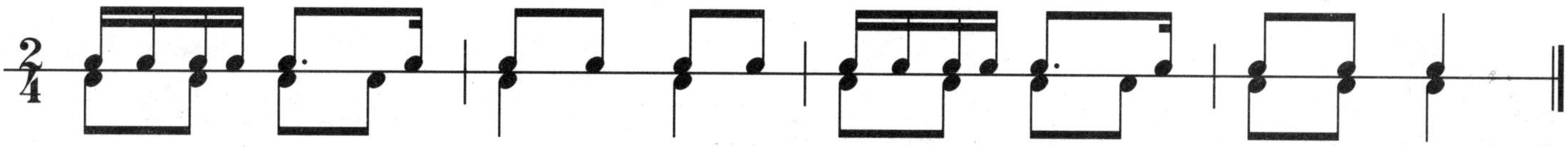

5-7 (36)

4. 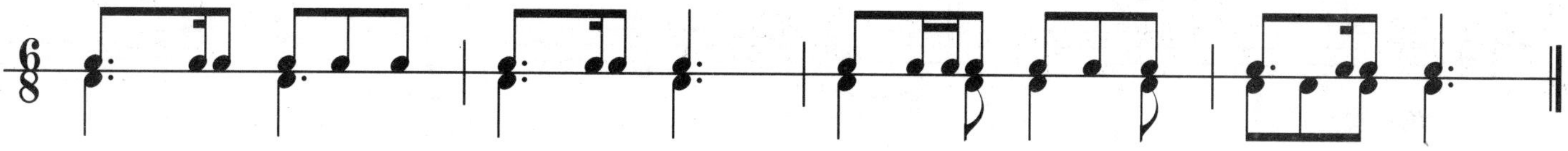

Technique

5-8 (37)

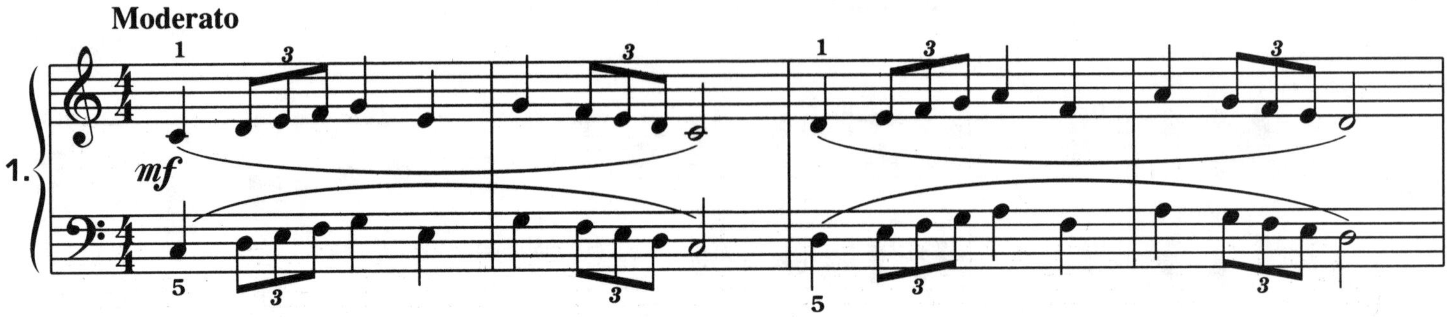

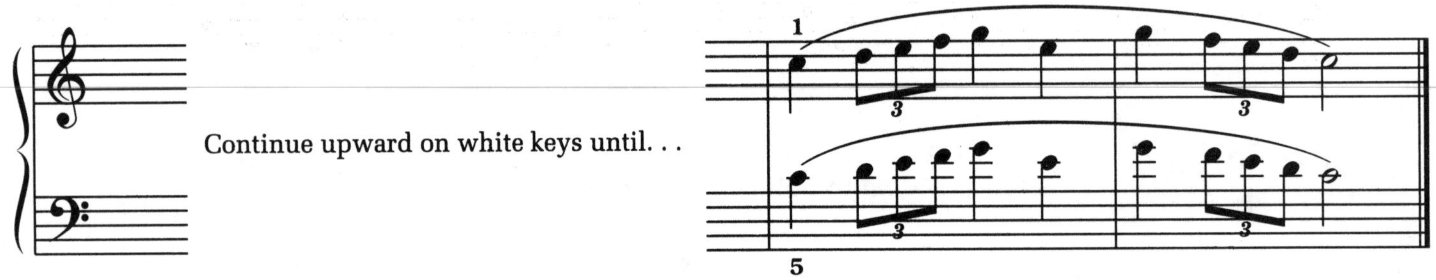

5-9 (38)

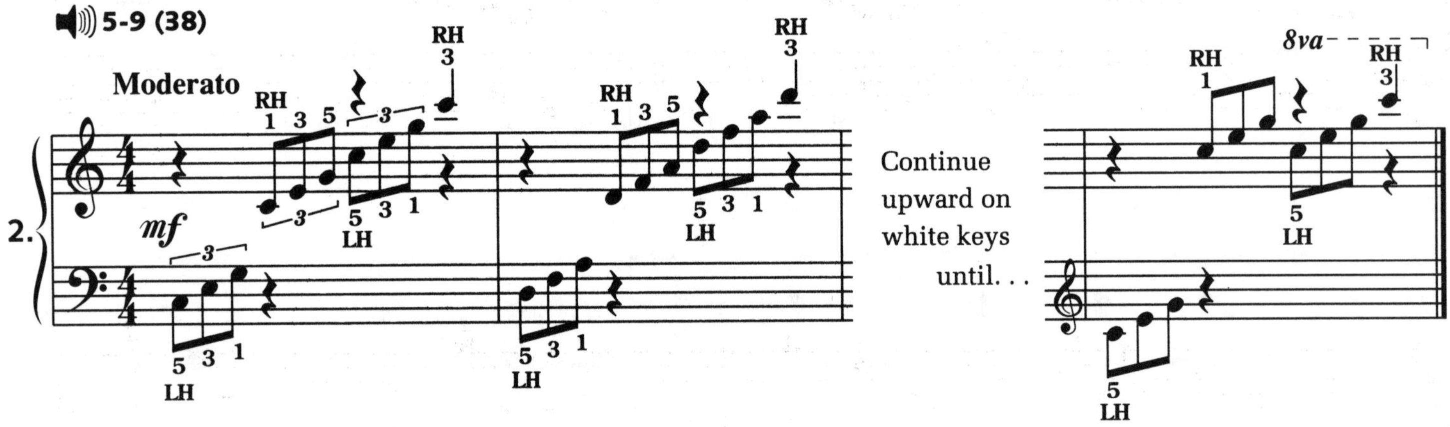

5-10 (39)

▶ Transpose to E♭ and F.

5-11 (40)

▶ Transpose to F♯ and D.

Solo Repertoire

SCHERZO

5-12 (41)

Dmitri Kabalevsky (1904–1987)
Op. 39, No. 12

Vivo, giocoso *(lively, humorous)*

Ensemble Repertoire

Play the four-part ensemble using the indicated chords to complete parts 2, 3 and 4.

Part 1: Kabalevsky *Scherzo* (page 107)
Part 2: Broken and block chords (play one octave higher than written throughout)
Part 3: Broken chords
Part 4: Roots of chords

5-13 (42)

Reading

Identify the key of each example. Use the indicated tempo, dynamics and articulation as you play these exercises.

Use the following practice directions:

1. Tap RH and count aloud; then LH.
2. Play hands separately and count aloud.
3. Tap hands together and count aloud.
4. Play hands together and count aloud.

5-14 (43)

5-15 (44)

Reading (continued)

5-16 (45)

Harmonization with Two-Hand Accompaniment

Using the indicated chords, create a two-hand accompaniment for the melody by continuing the pattern given in the first two measures.

5-17 (46)

Unit 9

Major Scales

Objectives

Upon completion of this unit the student will be able to:

1. Play major scales in tetrachord position.
2. Play exercises that utilize intervals up to an octave.
3. Use the damper pedal in performance.
4. Perform solo repertoire that uses intervals up to an octave.
5. Sight-read melodies with intervals of 5ths, 6ths, 7ths and 8ths (octaves) as accompaniment.

Assignments

Week of ________

Write your assignments for the week in the space below.

Tetrachords and the Major Scale

A **tetrachord** is a series of four notes having a pattern of *whole step, whole step, half step.*

LH tetrachords are fingered 5 4 3 2.
RH tetrachords are fingered 2 3 4 5.

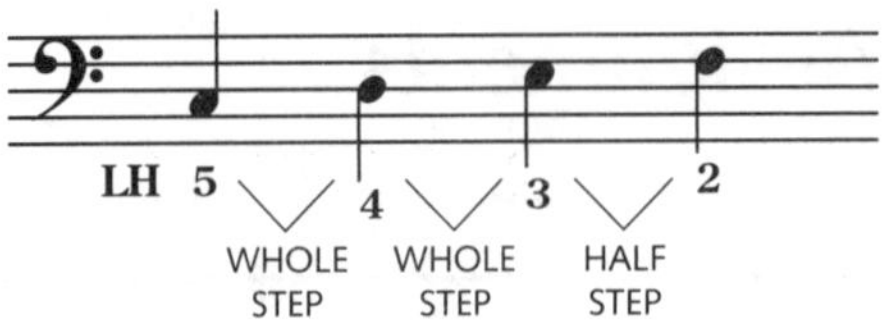

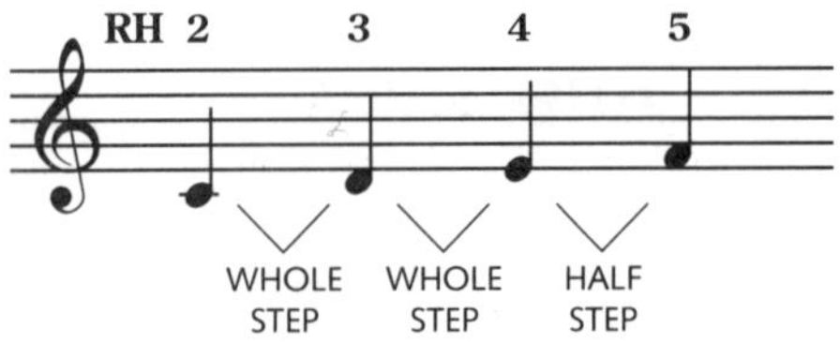

The **major scale** is made of two tetrachords joined by a whole step. Each scale begins and ends on a note of the same name as the scale, called the **key note.** Any major scale can be formed by following this sequence of whole and half steps: W W H W W W H.

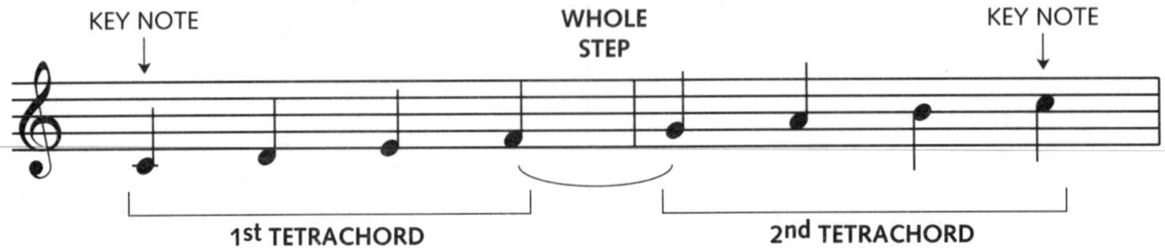

■ **Written exercise:**

Write letter names on the correct keys to form each major scale. Then play using tetrachord position.

Example:

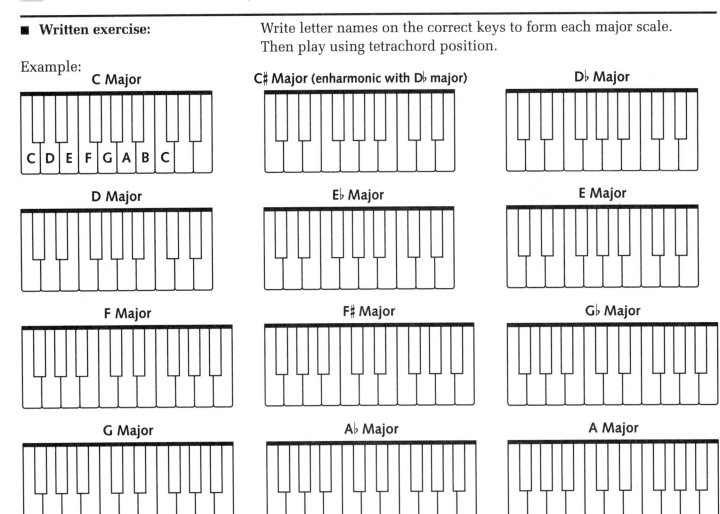

C Major

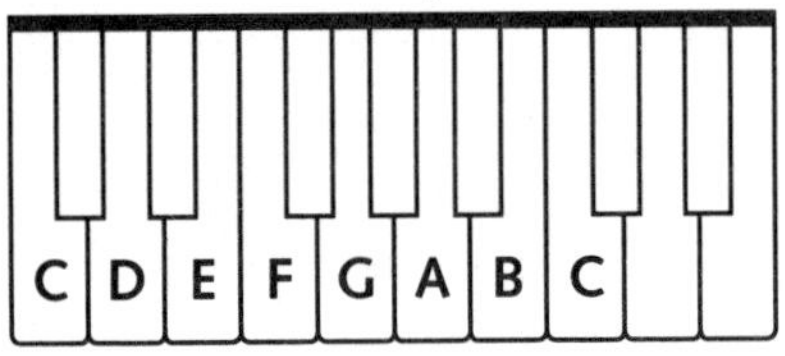

C♯ Major (enharmonic with D♭ major)

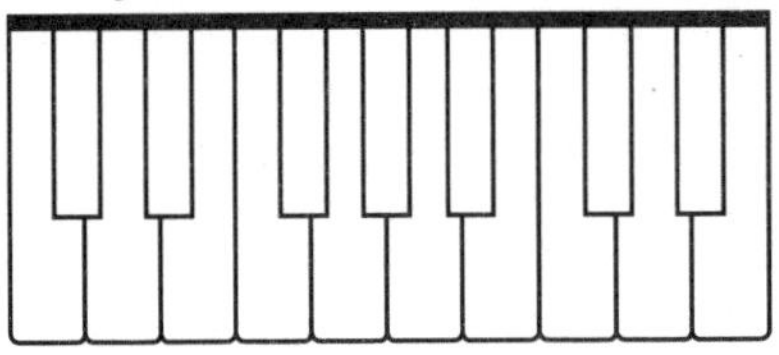

D♭ Major

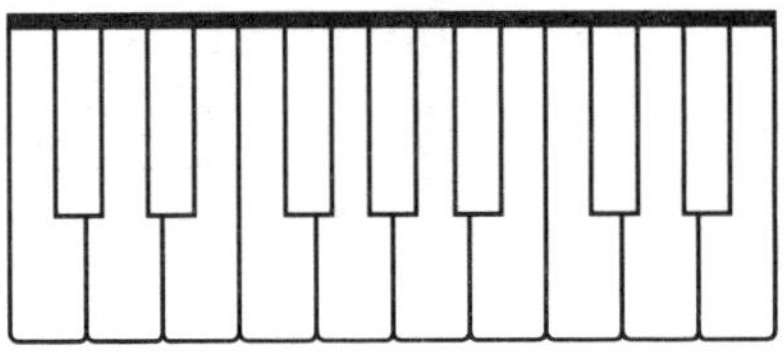

D Major

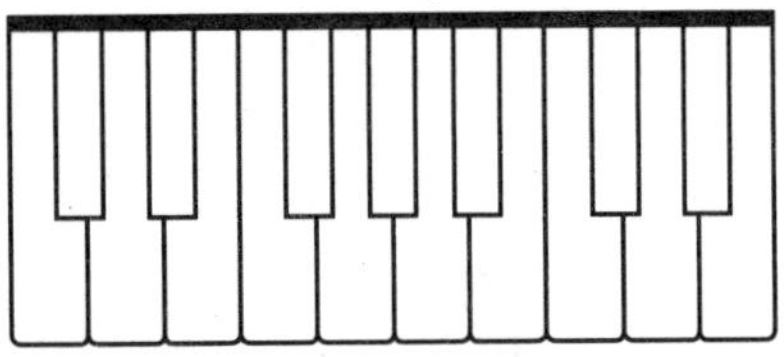

E♭ Major

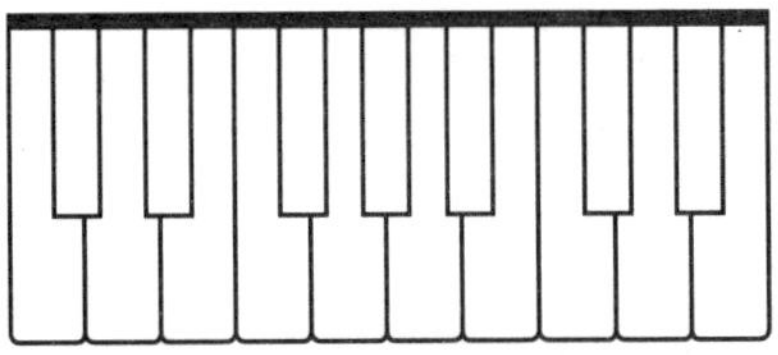

E Major

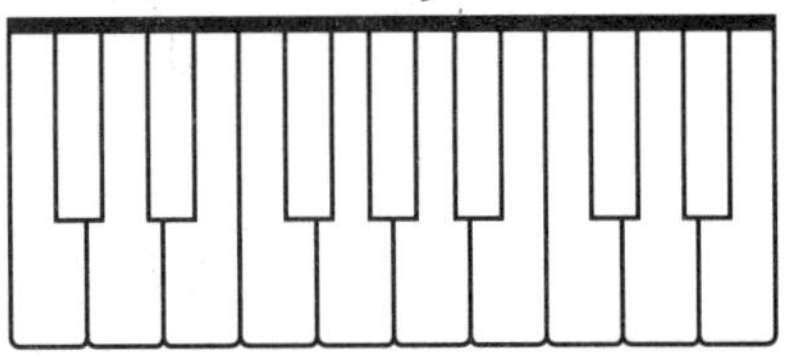

F Major

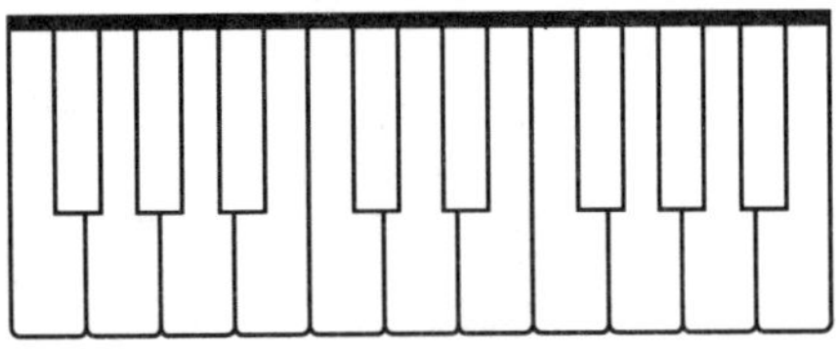

F♯ Major

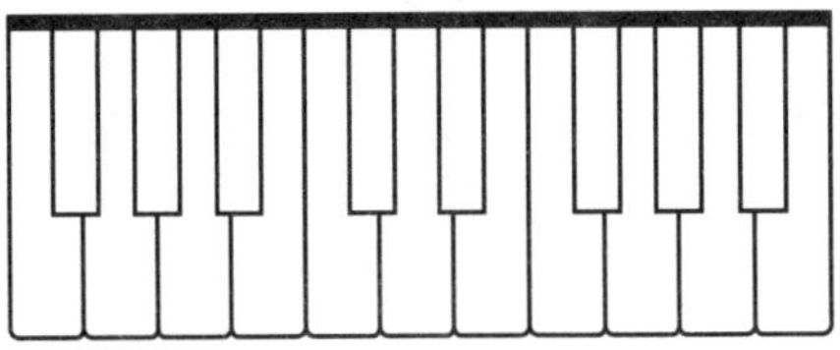

G♭ Major

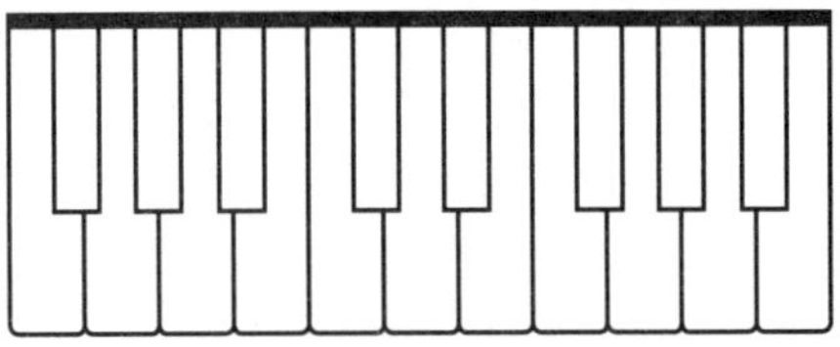

G Major

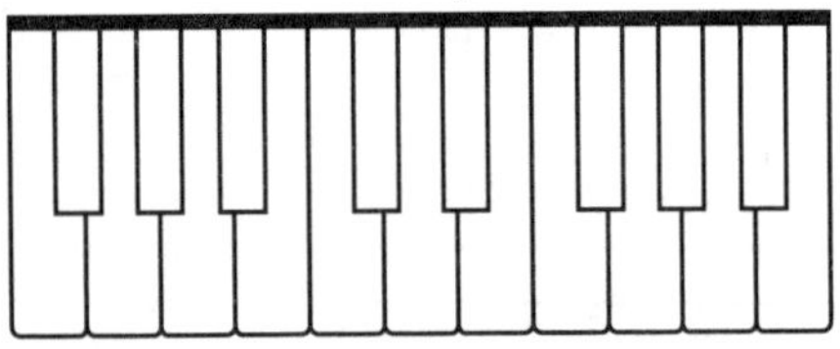

A♭ Major

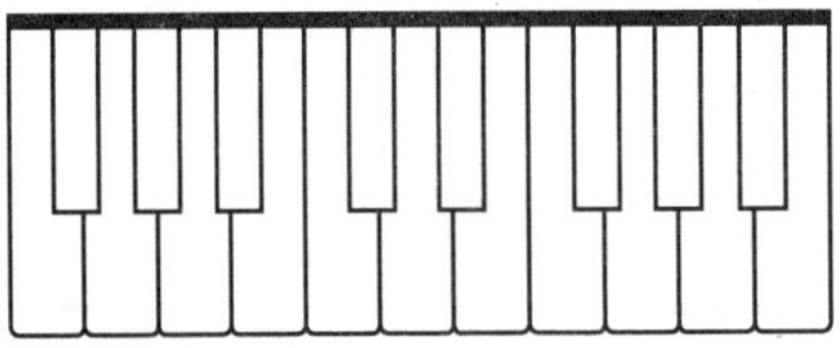

A Major

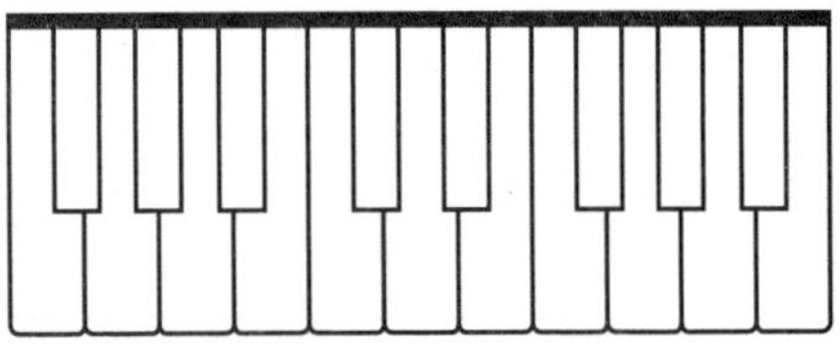

B♭ Major

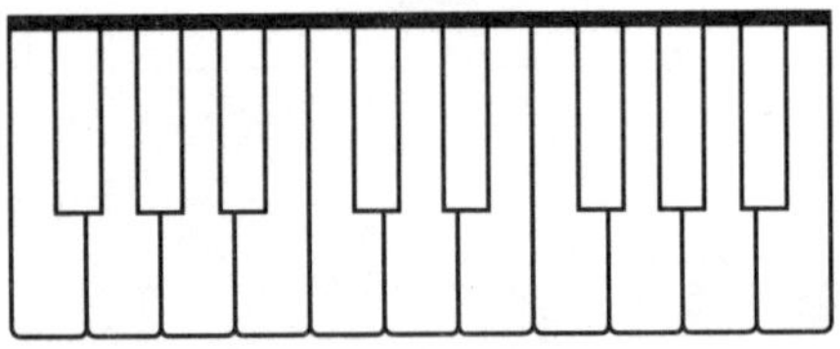

B Major

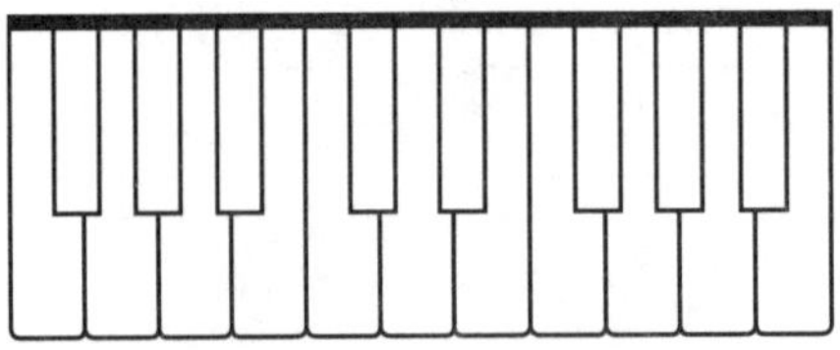

C♭ Major (enharmonic with B major)

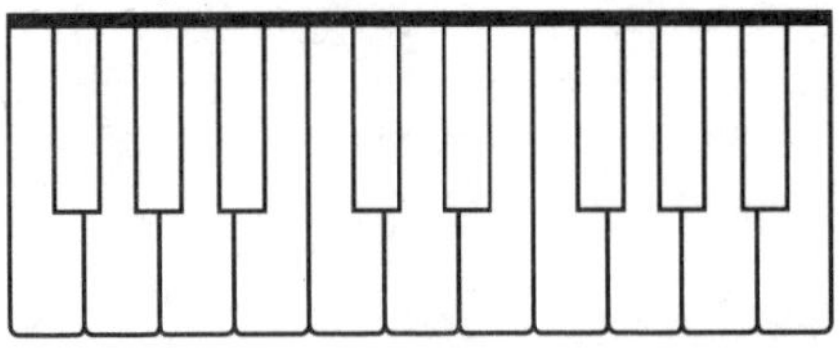

Playing Tetrachord Scales in Sharp Keys

Play the following major scales in tetrachord position while the teacher plays an accompaniment.

5-18 (47)

Playing Tetrachord Scales in Sharp Keys (continued)

41 **E Major**

51 **B Major**

61 **F♯ Major**

71 **C♯ Major**

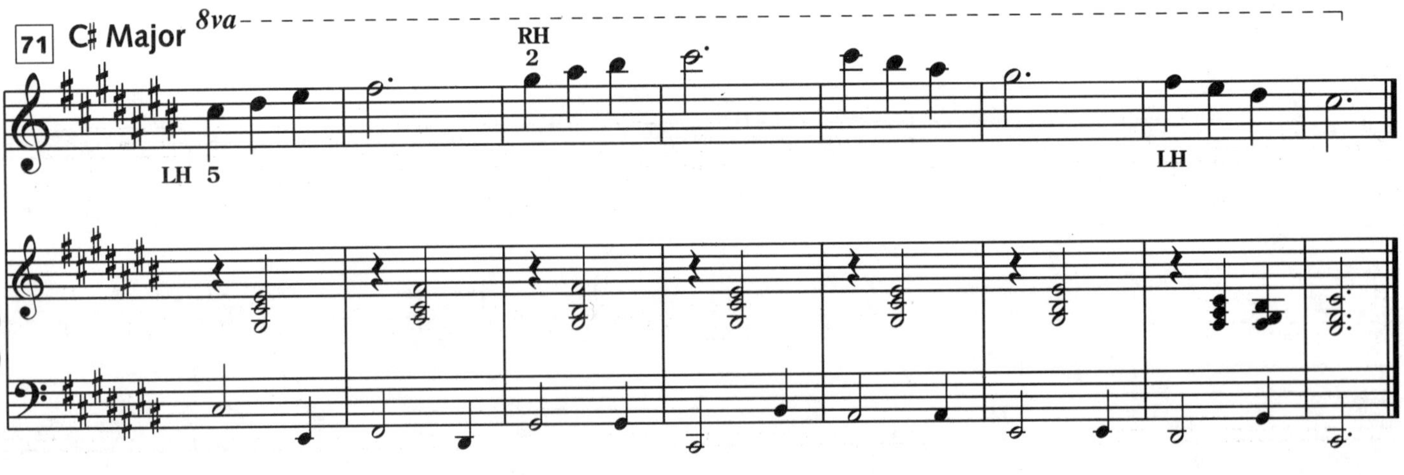

Playing Tetrachord Scales in Flat Keys

Play the following major scales in tetrachord position while the teacher plays an accompaniment.

5-19 (48) **Moderate waltz tempo**

C♭ Major

11 G♭ Major

21 D♭ Major

31 A♭ Major

Playing Tetrachord Scales in Flat Keys (continued)

41 E♭ Major

51 B♭ Major

F Major

61

71 C Major

Intervals of 6ths, 7ths and 8ths (octaves)

When you skip four white keys, the interval is a 6th.
6ths are written line-space or space-line.

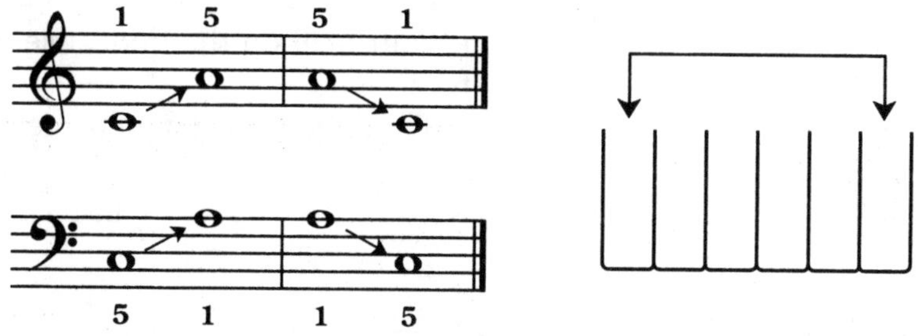

When you skip five white keys, the interval is a 7th.
7ths are written line-line or space-space.

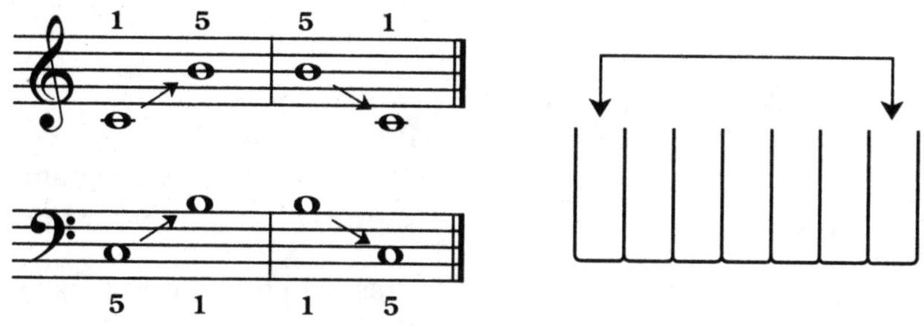

When you skip six white keys, the interval is an 8th (octave).
Octaves are written line-space or space-line.

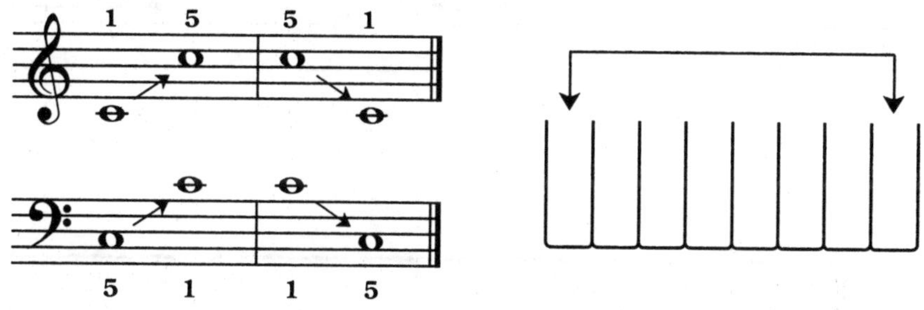

Play the following exercises that use intervals.

5-20 (49)

Moderato

1. 

▶ Transpose to G major and D major.

5-20 (49)

Moderato

2. 

▶ Transpose to F major and B♭ major.

The Damper Pedal

The right pedal is called the **damper pedal.** When you hold the damper pedal down, any tone you play continues after you release the key. The right foot is used on the damper pedal. Always keep your heel on the floor; use your ankle like a hinge.

This sign shows when the damper pedal is to be used:

It means:

PEDAL DOWN ↓ —— HOLD PEDAL —— ↑ PEDAL UP

Practice the following pedal exercise using intervals of 5ths, 6ths and 7ths. Notice how the damper pedal causes the tones to continue to sound, even after your hands have released the keys.

Press the pedal down as you play each group of notes. Hold it down through the rests.

Overlapping Pedal

The following sign is used to indicate **overlapping pedal.**

PLAY

PEDAL DOWN ⋀ PEDAL DOWN

↑

At this point, the pedal comes up,
and it goes down again immediately!

Practice the following exercise. As you play each interval, let the pedal up and press it down again immediately. The pedal must come up exactly at the instant the notes come down, as if the pedal "comes up to meet the hand!" Careful listening is the key to successful pedaling.

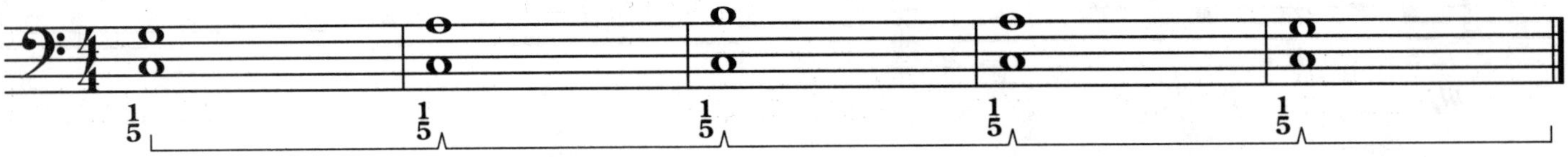

Technique

5-21 (50)

Moderato

1.

Continue upward on white keys until. . .

5-21 (50)

Moderato

2.

Continue upward on white keys until. . .

5-22 (51)

Allegretto

3.

Continue upward on white keys until. . .

5-22 (51)

Allegretto

4.

Continue upward on white keys until. . .

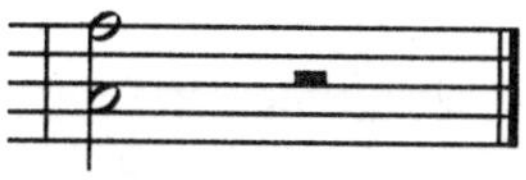

5-23 (52)

Allegretto

5.

Continue upward on white keys until. . .

5-23 (52)

Allegretto

6.

Continue upward on white keys until. . .

5-24 (53)

Moderato

7.

Continue upward on white keys until. . .

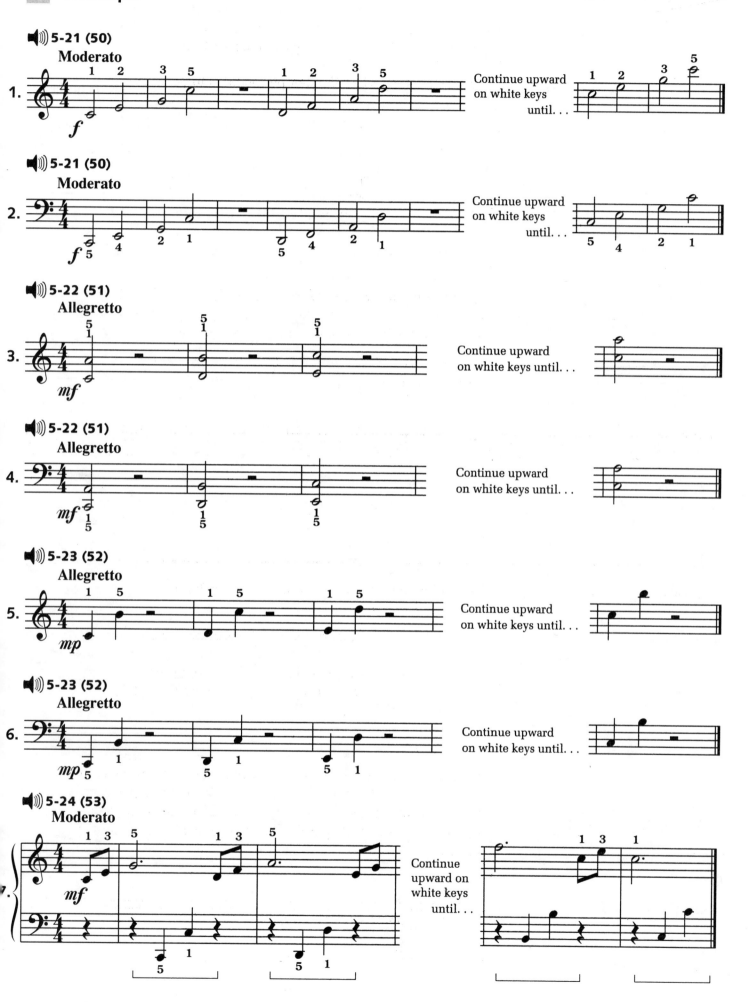

Solo Repertoire

Etude I

5-25 (54)

Slowly, with feeling

Paul Sheftel

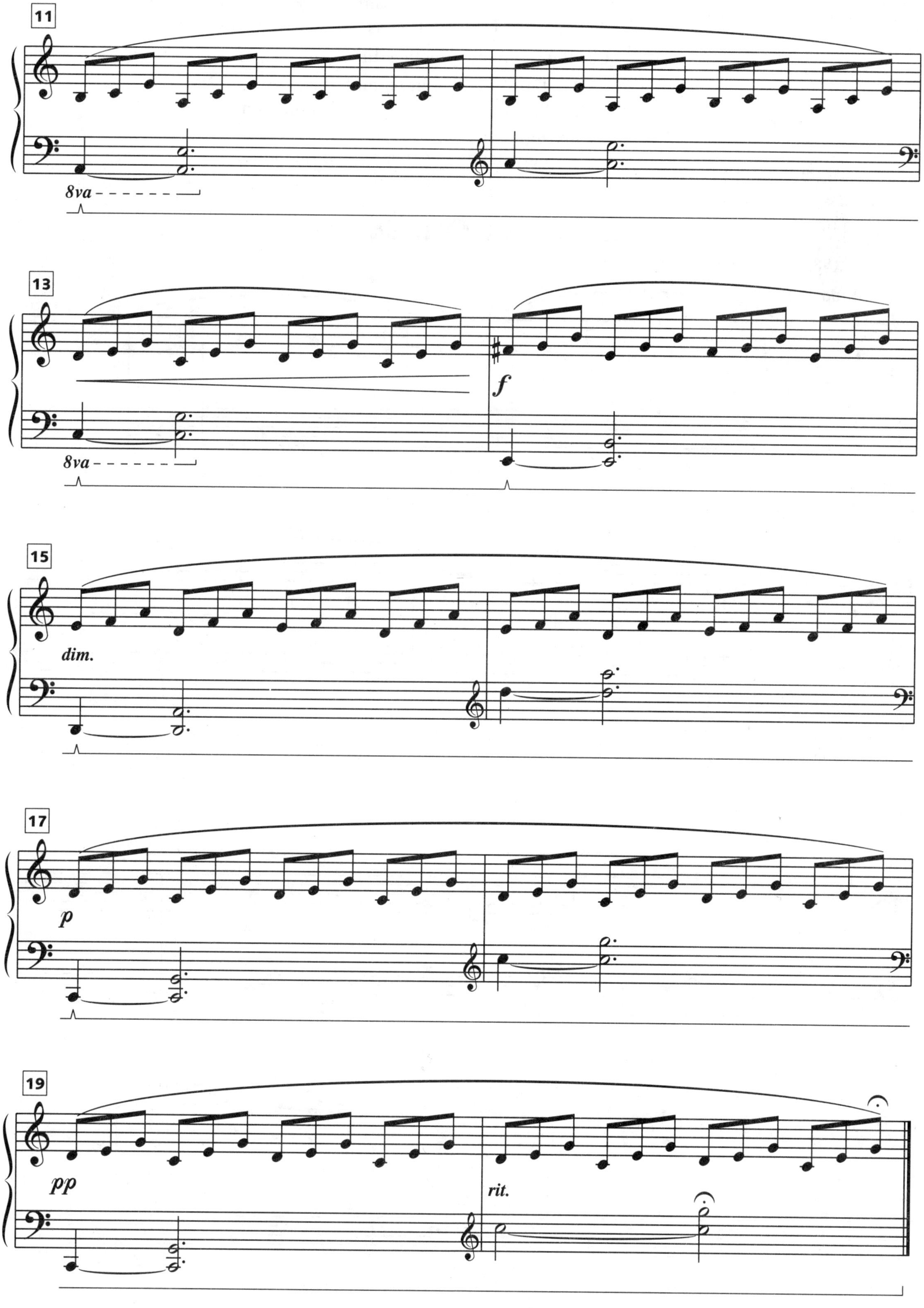
11
8va
13
8va
f
15
dim.
17
p
19
pp
rit.

Reading

Identify the key of each example. Use the indicated tempo, dynamics and articulation as you play these exercises.

Use the following practice directions:

1. Tap RH and count aloud; then LH.
2. Play hands separately and count aloud.
3. Tap hands together and count aloud.
4. Play hands together and count aloud.

ON TOP OF OLD SMOKY

5-26 (55)

United States

5-27 (56)

5-28 (57)

Harmonization with Two-Hand Accompaniment

Using the indicated chords, create a two-hand accompaniment for the melody by continuing the pattern given in the first two measures.

5-29 (58)

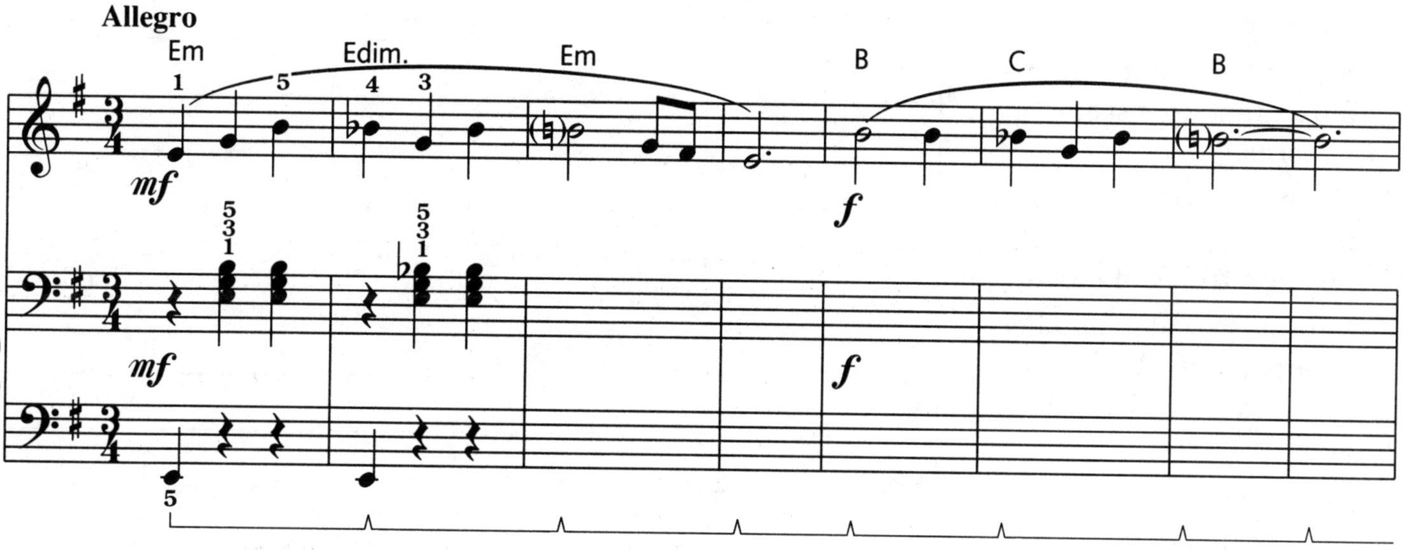

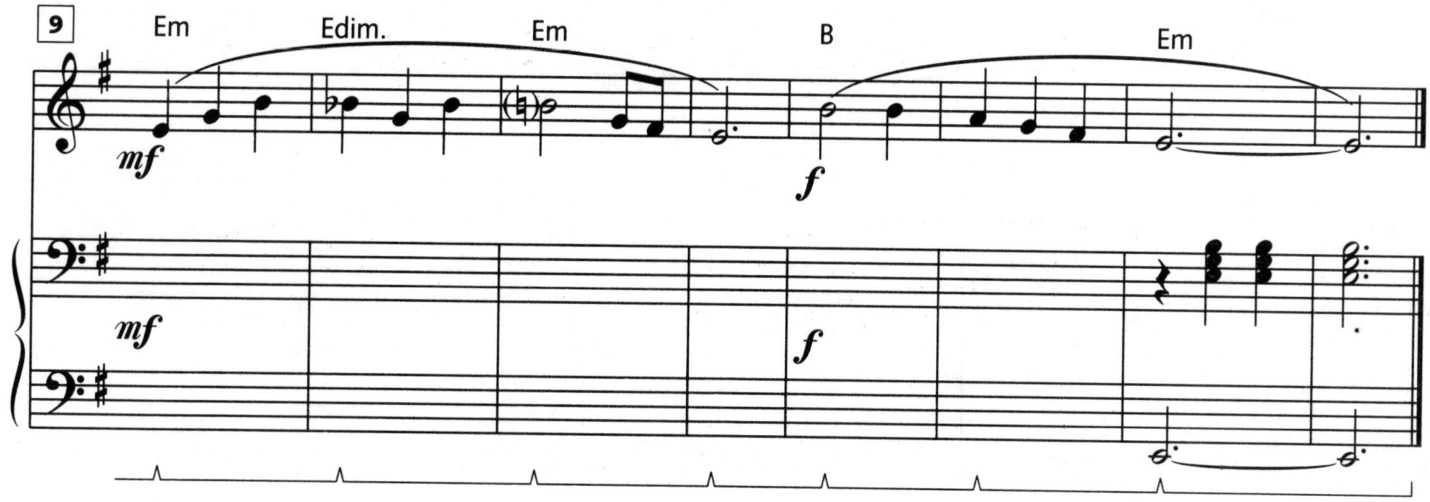

Unit 10

Triads of the Key

Objectives

Upon completion of this unit the student will be able to:

1. Build a triad on any note of the scale.
2. Play major scales and arpeggios beginning on white keys using traditional fingerings.
3. Perform solo repertoire that uses scale and arpeggio patterns.
4. Sight-read and transpose music that uses scale patterns.
5. Harmonize melodies with roots of chords and root-position triads of the key.
6. Improvise scale melodies over roots of chords and root-position triads of the key.

Assignments

Week of ________

Write your assignments for the week in the space below.

Playing Triads of the Key

Triads may be built on any note of any scale. The sharps or flats in the key signature must be used when playing these triads. Triads of the key are identified by Roman numerals. These triads built on each scale degree are called **diatonic.**

6-1 (49)

Play triads of the key in C major.

1. 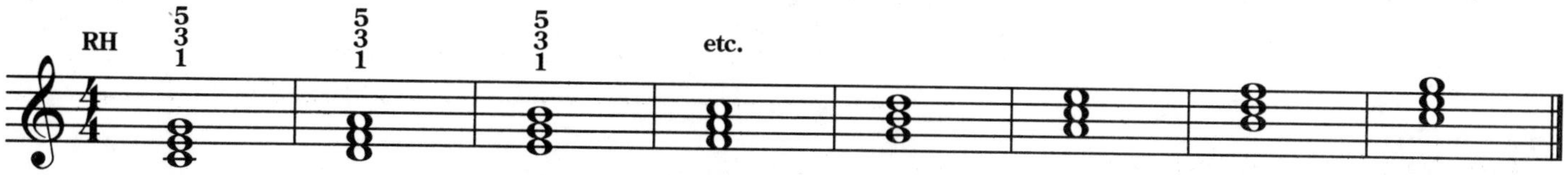

I	ii	iii	IV	V	vi	vii°	I
Major Tonic	Minor Supertonic	Minor Mediant	Major Subdominant	Major Dominant	Minor Submediant	Diminished Leading tone	Major Tonic

6-1 (49)

2. 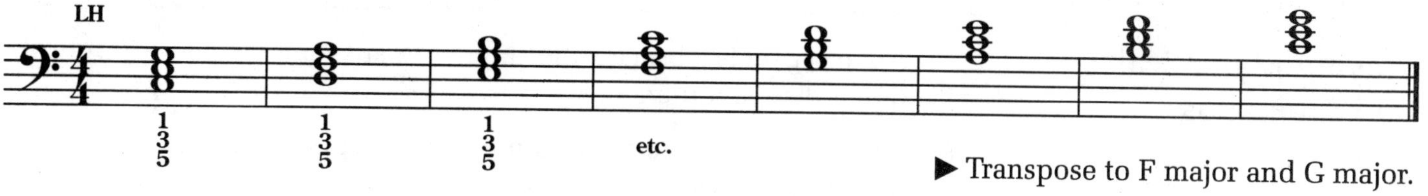

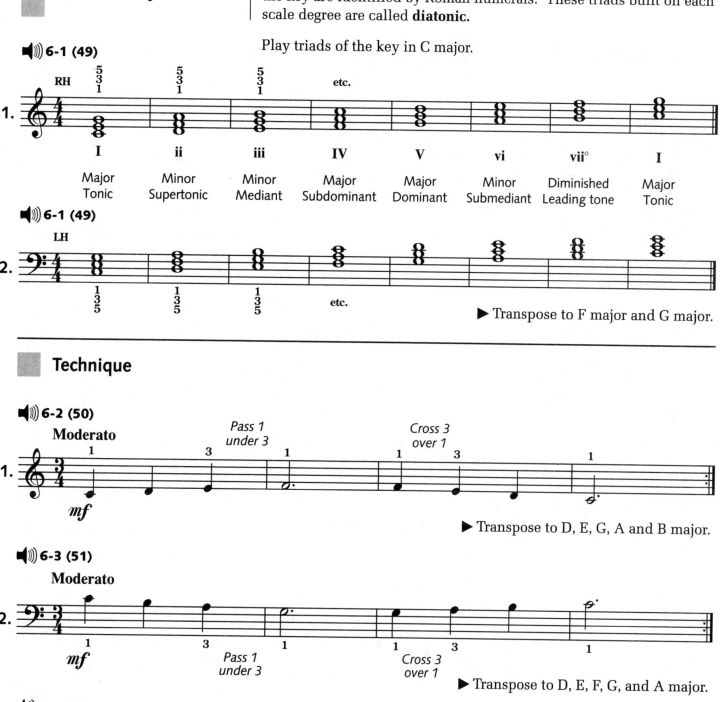

▶ Transpose to F major and G major.

Technique

6-2 (50)

1. 

▶ Transpose to D, E, G, A and B major.

6-3 (51)

2. 

▶ Transpose to D, E, F, G, and A major.

6-4 (52)

3. 

Continue upward on white keys until...

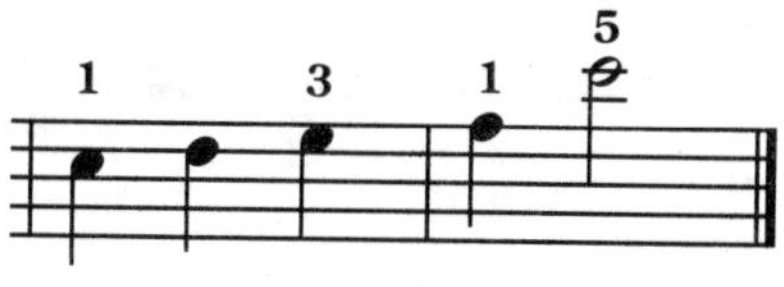

6-5 (53)

4. 

Continue downward on white keys until...

Technique (continued)

6-6 (54)

5. 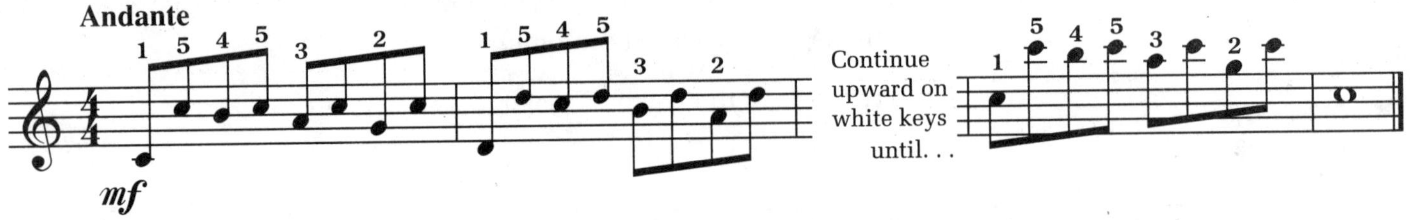

6-6 (54)

6. 

Playing Major Scales and Arpeggios

An **arpeggio** is a broken chord; pitches are sounded successively rather than simultaneously.

Build each scale in tetrachord position, then practice hands separately:

1. The blocked scale as written.
2. The scale as written.
3. The arpeggio as written.

C Major

1. 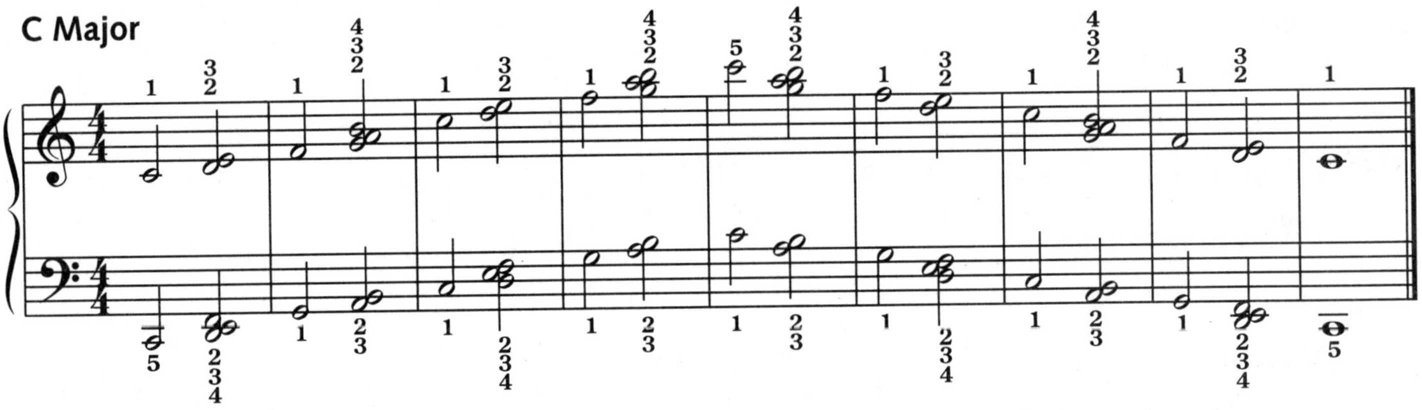

6-7 (55)

2. 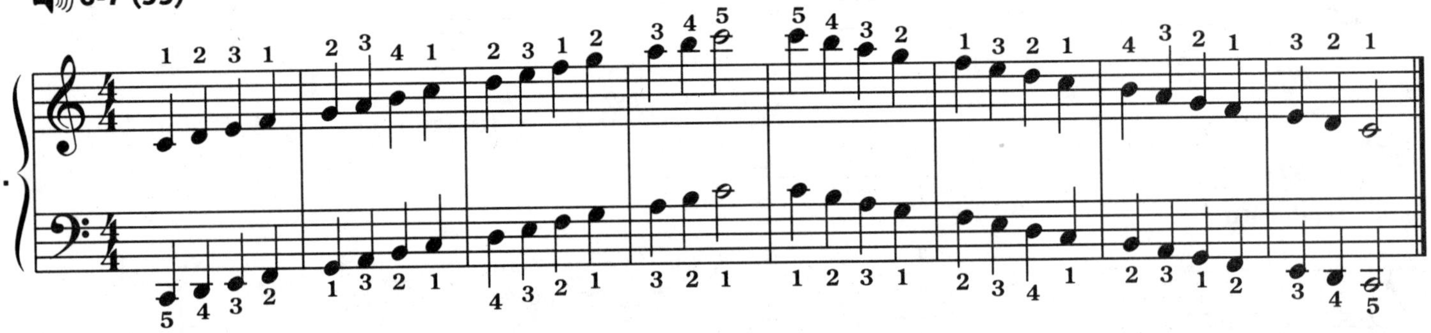

6-8 (56)

3. 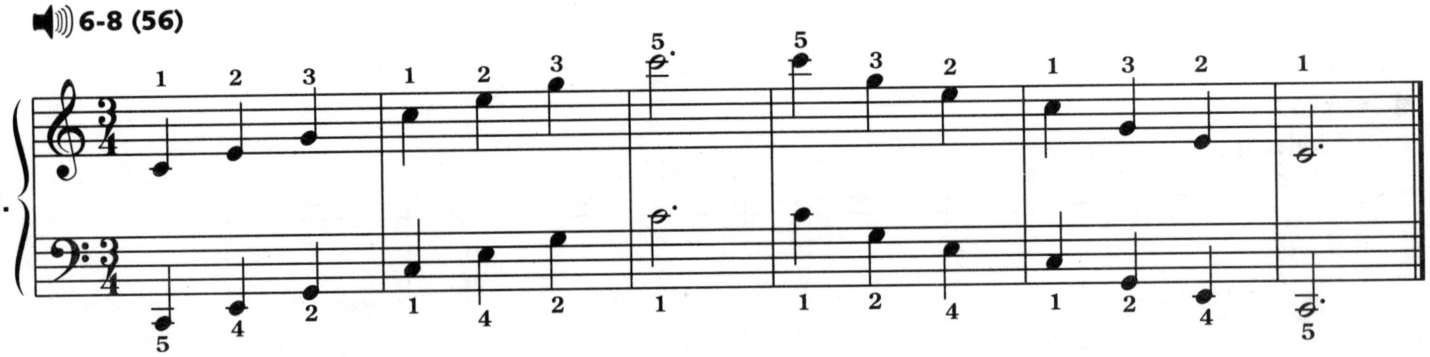

G Major

1.
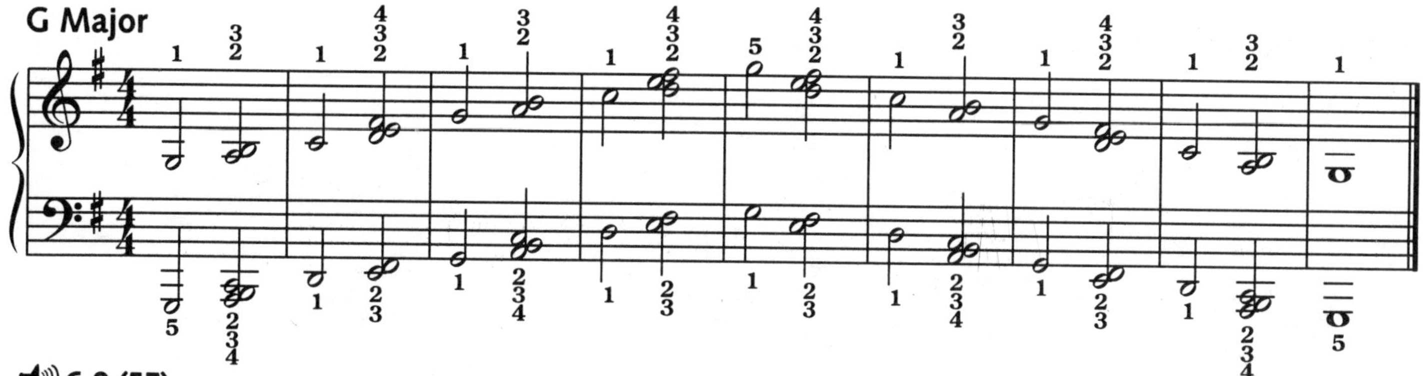

6-9 (57)

2.

6-10 (58)

3.

D Major

1.
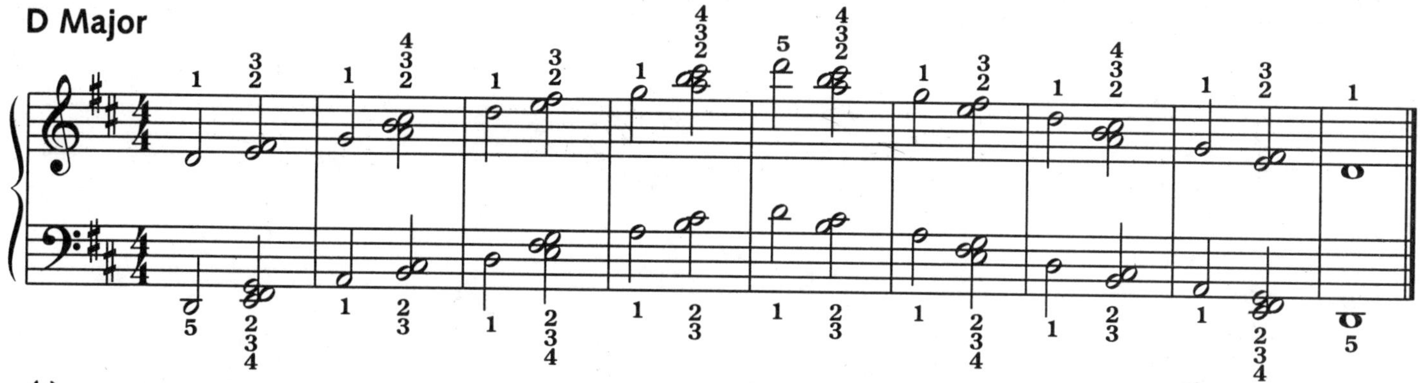

6-11 (59)

2.

6-12 (60)

3.
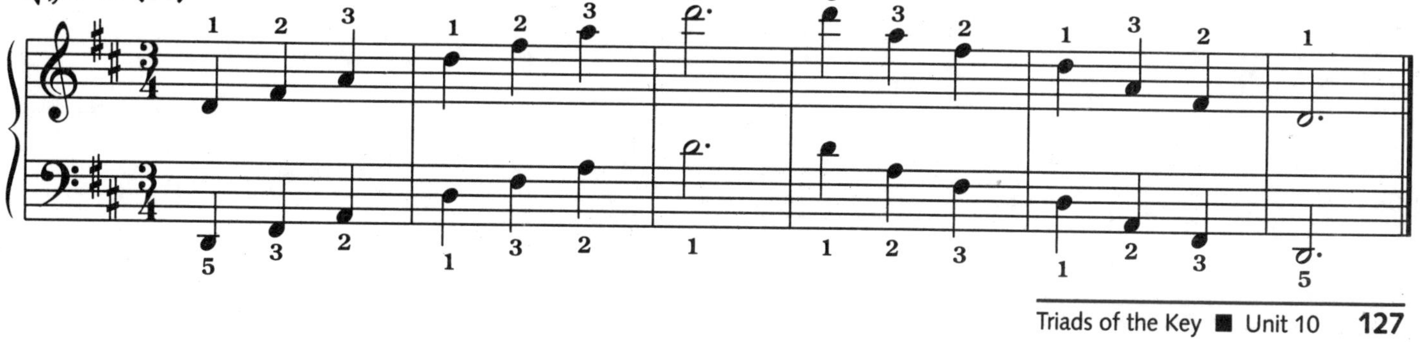

Playing Major Scales and Arpeggios (continued)

A Major

1.

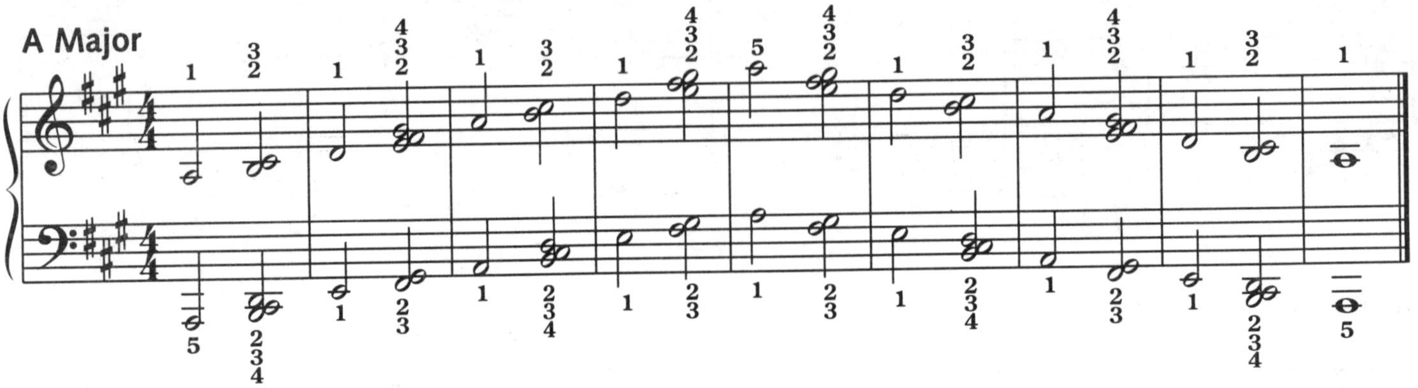

6-13 (61)

2.

6-14 (62)

3.

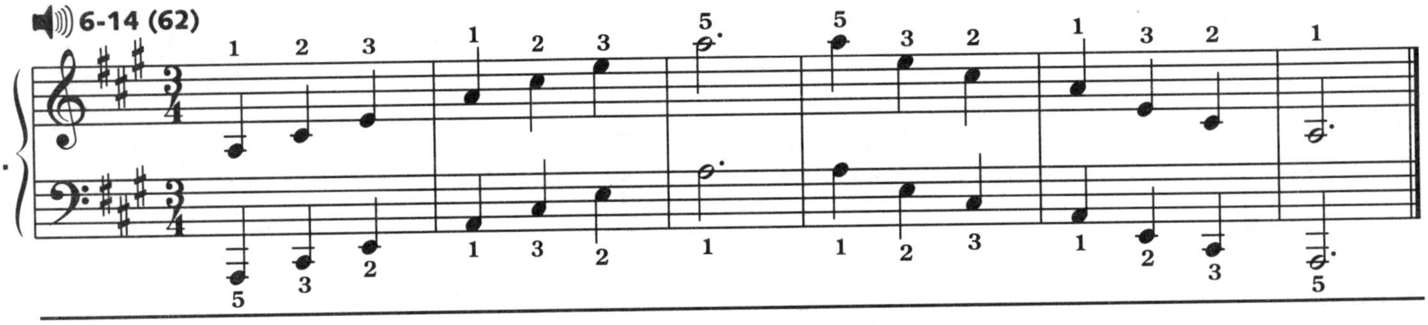

E Major

1.

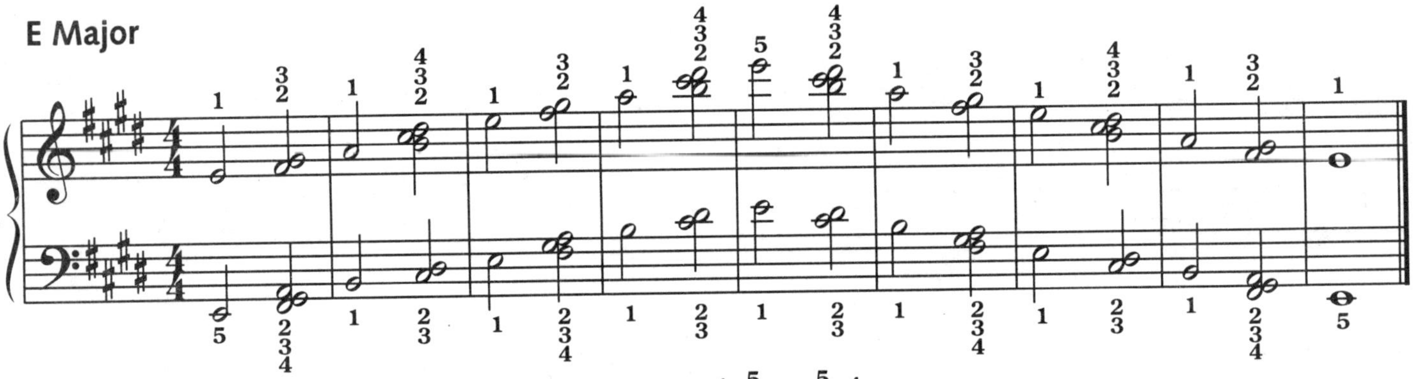

6-15 (63)

2.

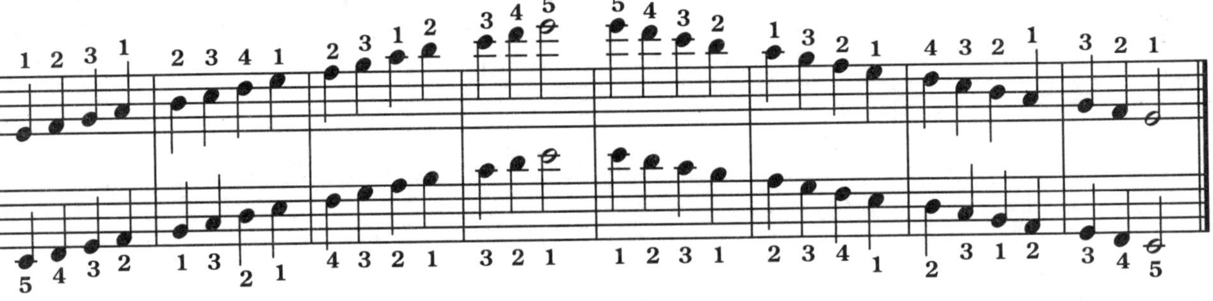

6-16 (64)

3.

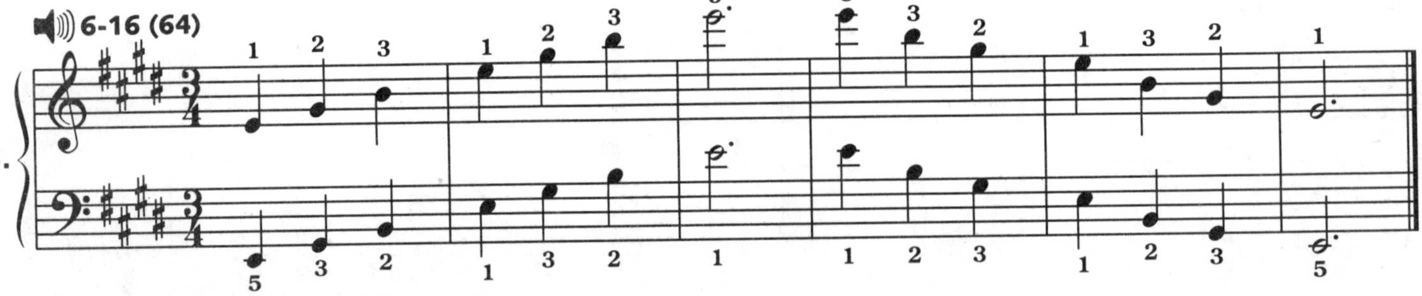

B Major

1.
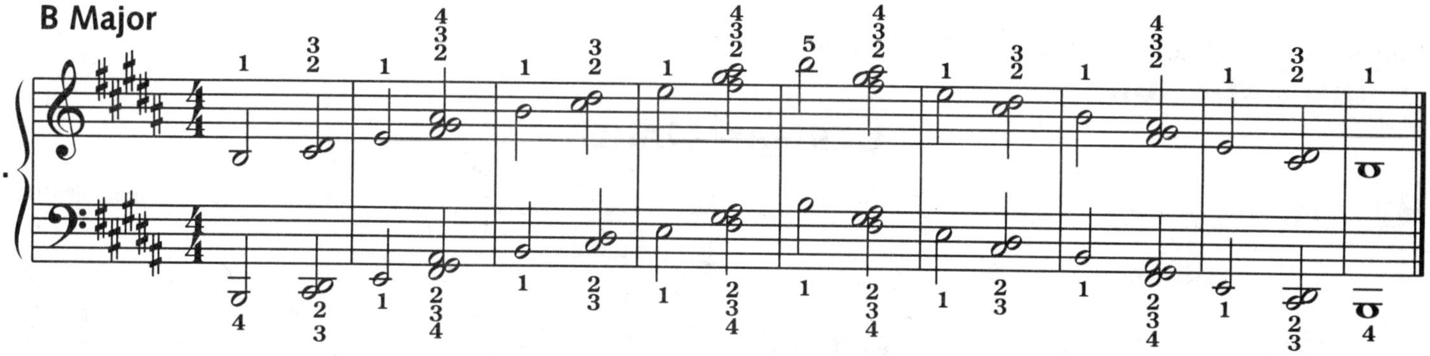

🔊 6-17 (65)

2.

🔊 6-18 (66)

3.

F Major

1.
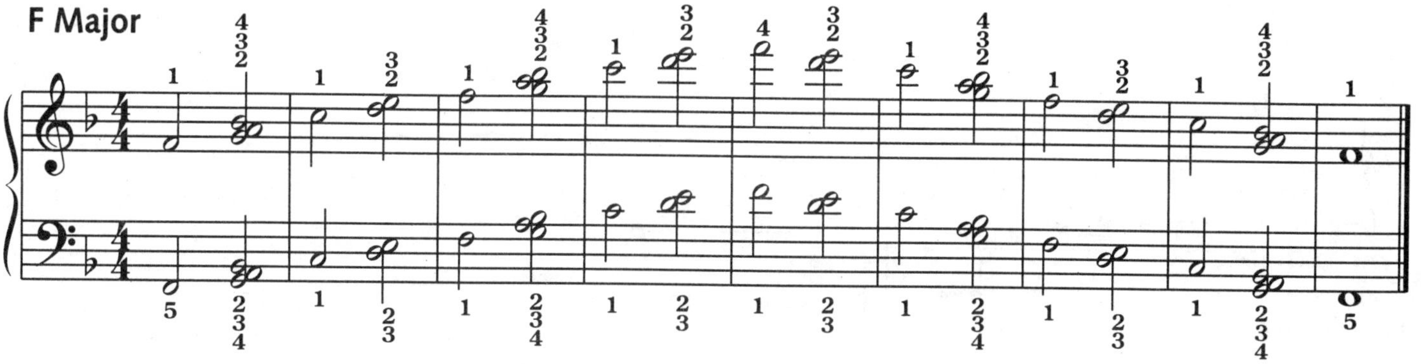

🔊 6-19 (67)

2.

🔊 6-20 (68)

3.

Solo Repertoire

German Dance

6-21 (69)

Ludwig van Beethoven
(1770–1827)

Reading

Identify the key of each example. Use the indicated tempo, dynamics and articulation as you play these exercises.

Use the following practice directions:

1. Tap RH and count aloud; then LH.
2. Play hands separately and count aloud.
3. Tap hands together and count aloud.
4. Play hands together and count aloud.

THE SCALE LADDER

6-22 (70)

Allegro non troppo *(quickly, but not too much)*

Daniel Gottlob Türk
(1756–1813)

1.

6-23 (71)

Moderato

2.

Reading (continued)

6-24 (72)

▶ Transpose to F major.

6-25 (73)

▶ Transpose to A major.

Harmonization

Harmonize each melody below in two ways:

- Using the root of the indicated triads.
- Using the indicated root position triads.

6-26 (74)

1.

▶ Transpose to A major.

6-27 (75)

2.

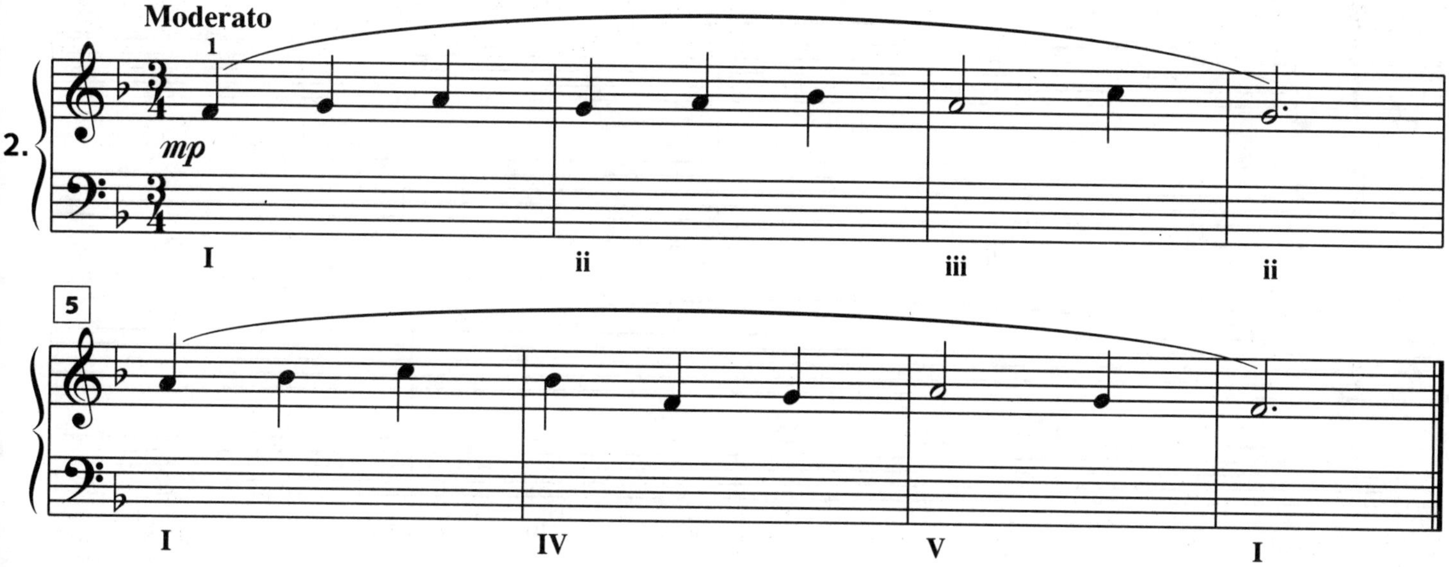

▶ Transpose to E major.

6-28 (76)

3.

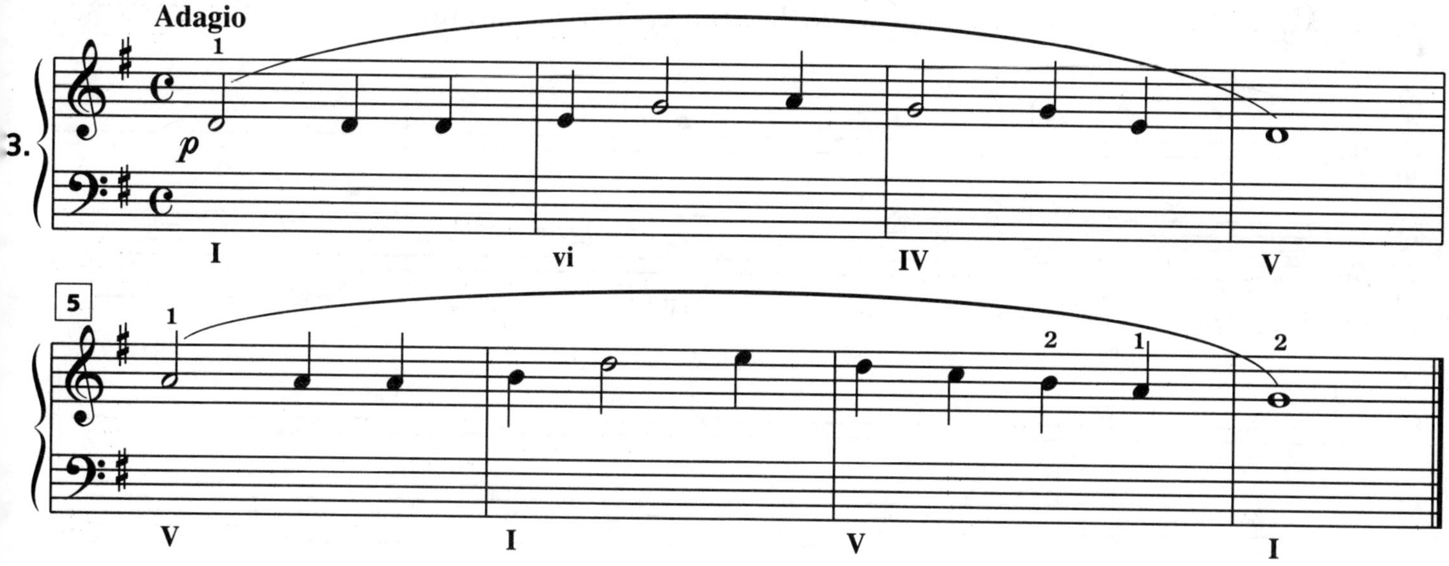

▶ Transpose to C major.

Improvisation from Chord Symbols

Improvise a RH melody for the chord progression below while the LH plays the root of the indicated chords. Begin and end each phrase with the given notes. Notate your favorite improvisation.

6-29 (77)

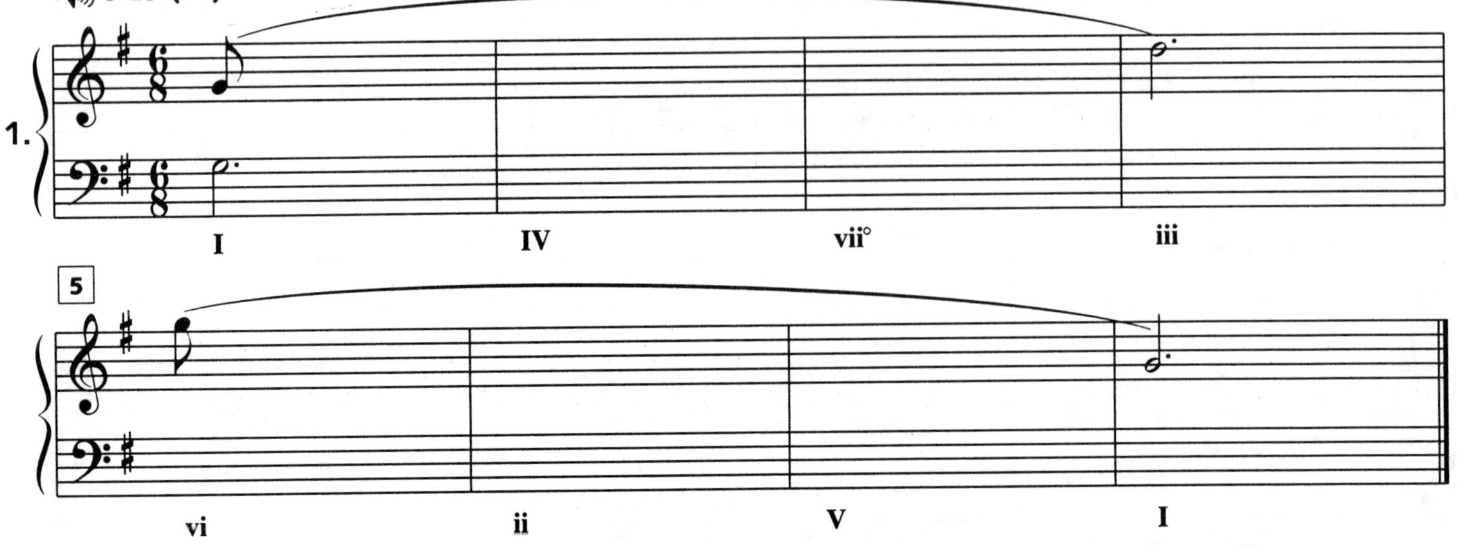

Improvise a RH melody for the chord progression below while the LH plays the indicated root-position triads. Begin and end each phrase with the given notes. Notate your favorite improvisation.

6-30 (78)

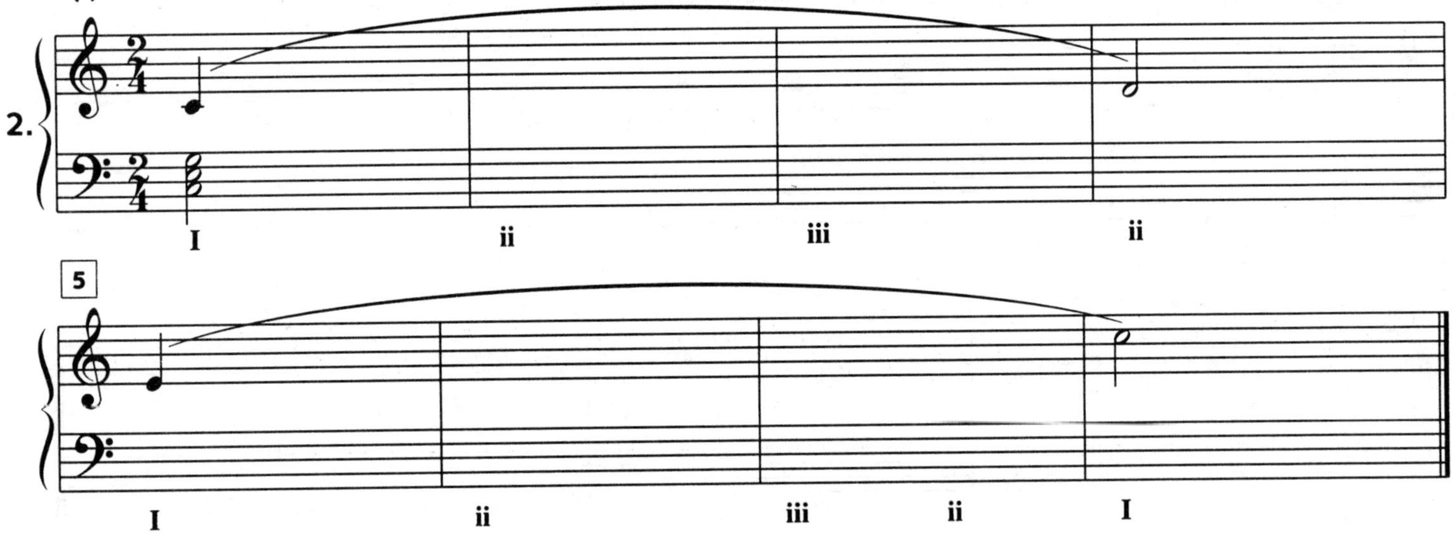

Continue the RH melodic **sequence** (a short musical motive stated successively, beginning on different pitches) for the chord progression below while the LH plays the root-position chords.

6-31 (79)

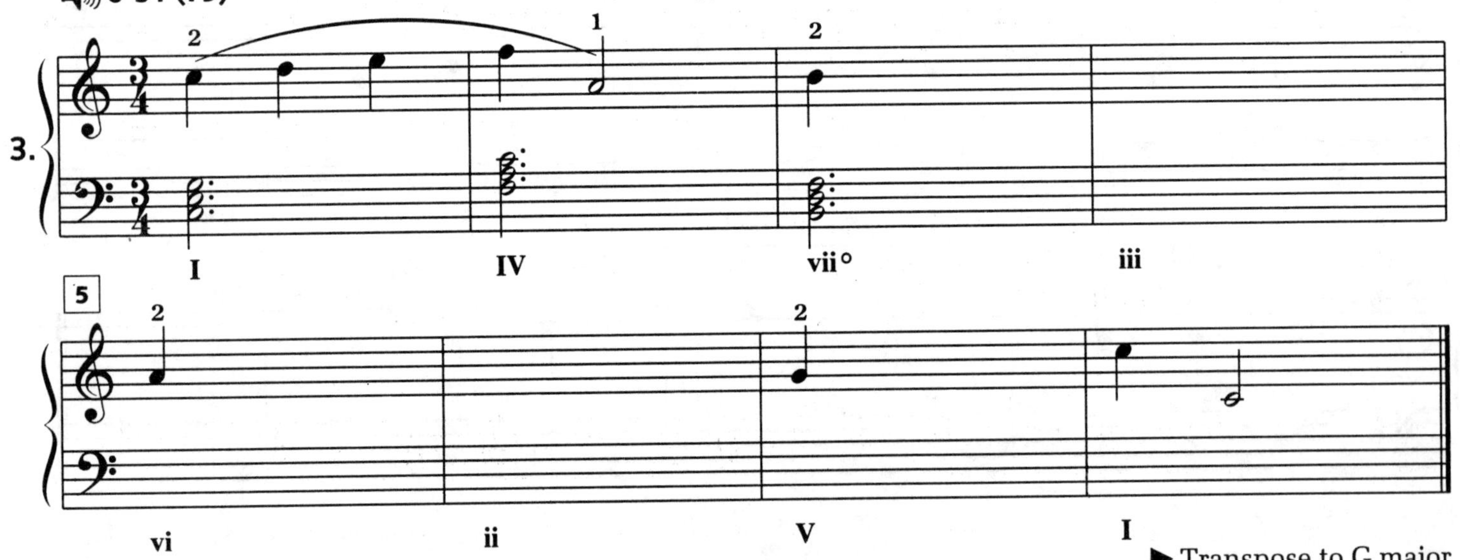

▶ Transpose to G major.

Unit 10 **Review Worksheet**

Name ______________________ *Date* ____________________

1. Identify each major scale below by writing its name on the indicated line. Write the correct RH fingering on the line above the staff and the correct LH fingering on the line below the staff.

___ **major scale**

___ **major scale**

___ **major scale**

___ **major scale**

2. Identify each major key by writing its name on the line above the staff. Write the Roman numeral name for the given triad in that key on the line below the staff.

3. Identify each major key signature below by writing its name on the indicated line. Following the key signature, write the notes for that major scale on the staff, using whole notes. Write the sharps or flats from the key signature in front of the appropriate notes.

_____ **major**

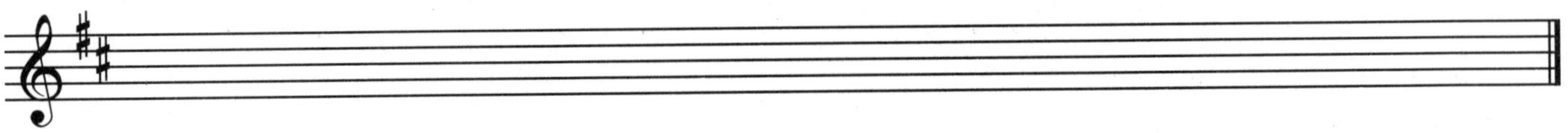

_____ **major**

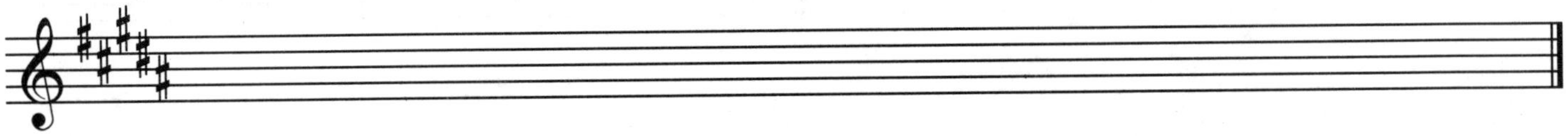

_____ **major**

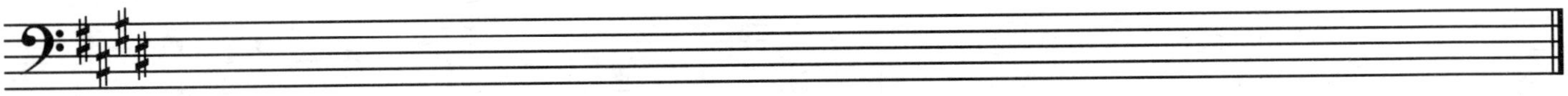

_____ **major**

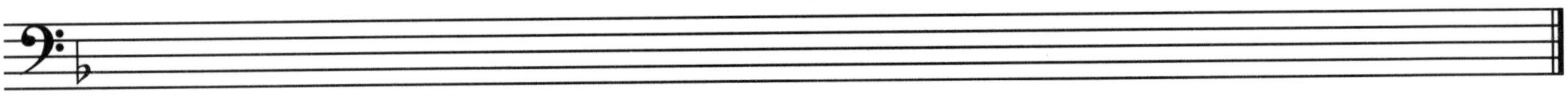

4. Identify each major key by writing its name on the line above the staff. Using whole notes on the staff, write the triad indicated by each Roman numeral.

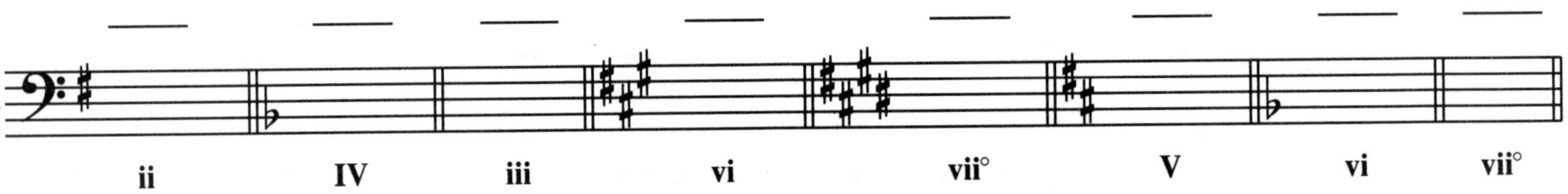

Unit 11

Chord Inversions

Objectives

Upon completion of this unit the student will be able to:

1. Play triads in root position, first inversion and second inversion.
2. Perform solo repertoire that uses triads and inversions.
3. Sight-read music that uses triads and inversions.
4. Harmonize melodies with triads and inversions.
6. Improvise melodies over triads and inversions.

Assignments

Week of ________

Write your assignments for the week in the space below.

Triads: First Inversion

When the root of the chord is moved to the top and the third becomes the lowest note of the triad, it is said to be in the **first inversion.**

C E G becomes E G C

The root is always the top note of the interval of a 4th.

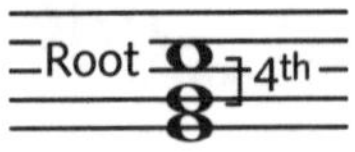

Play the following first-inversion triads in the key of C with RH, using 1 2 5 on each triad. Repeat with LH one octave lower, using 5 3 1 on each triad.

6-32 (80)

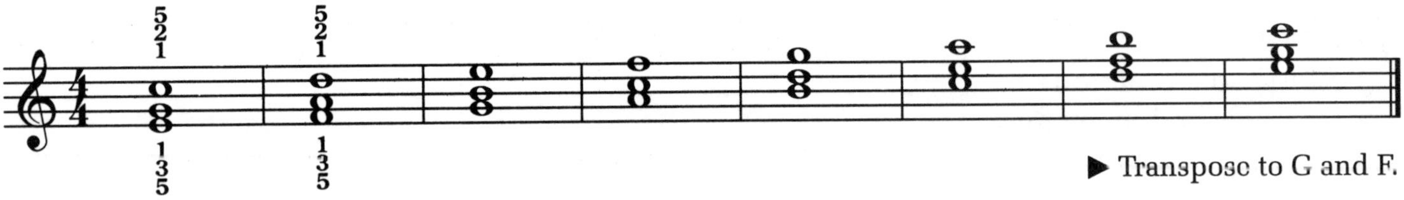

▶ Transpose to G and F.

Play with RH, using the indicated fingering. Repeat with LH one octave lower, using 5 3 1 on each triad.

6-33 (81)

Triads: Second Inversion

Any first-inversion triad may be inverted again by moving the lowest note to the top. All letter names are the same, but the root is in the middle and the fifth is the lowest note of the triad. This is called the **second inversion.**

E G C becomes G C E

The root is always the top note of the interval of a 4th.

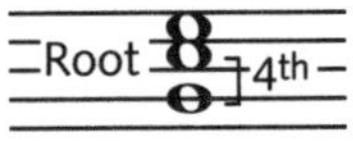

Play the following second-inversion triads in the key of C with LH, using 5 2 1 on each triad. Repeat with RH one octave higher, using 1 3 5 on each triad.

6-34 (82)

▶ Transpose to G and F.

Triads: in All Positions

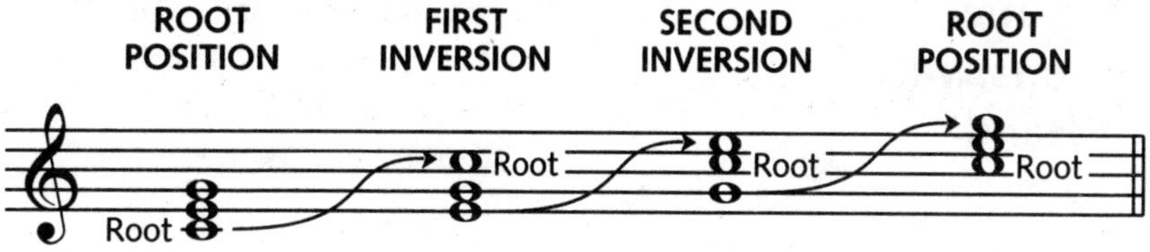

Play the following:

6-35 (83)

1.

▶ Transpose to G and F.

6-35 (83)

2.

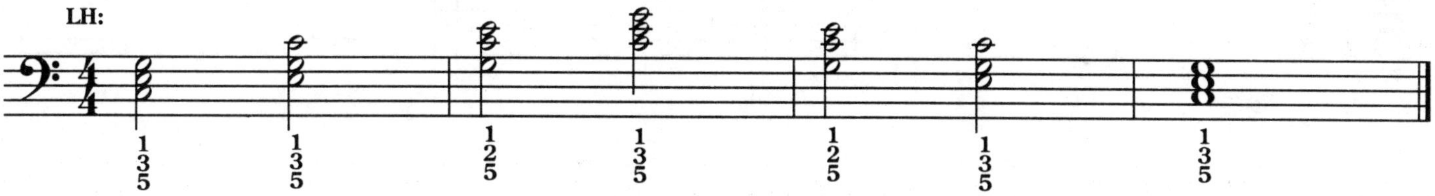

▶ Transpose to G and F.

Naming Triads and Inversions

Roman numerals identify the scale degrees on which triads are built within a key.

Numbers to the right of the Roman numerals indicate the intervals between the lowest note and each of the other notes of the chord.

In the first inversion, the number 3 is usually omitted.

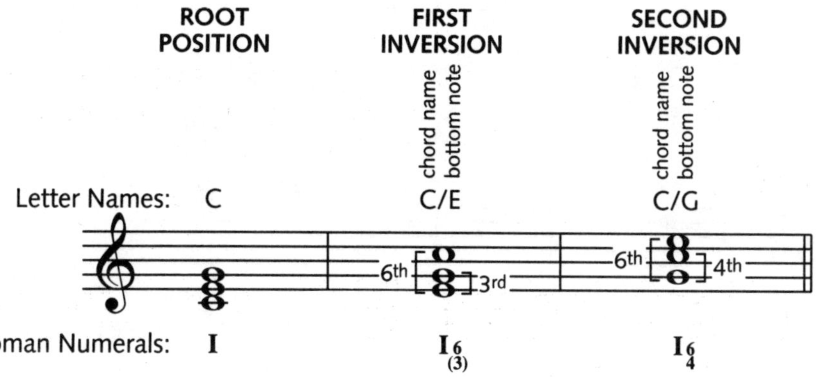

Playing Triads and Inversions with the Right Hand

Play these diatonic triads and inversions in the key of C major.

6-36 (84)

Playing Triads and Inversions with the Left Hand

Play these diatonic triads and inversions in the key of C major.

6-36 (84)

Technique

6-37 (85)

Moderato

1.

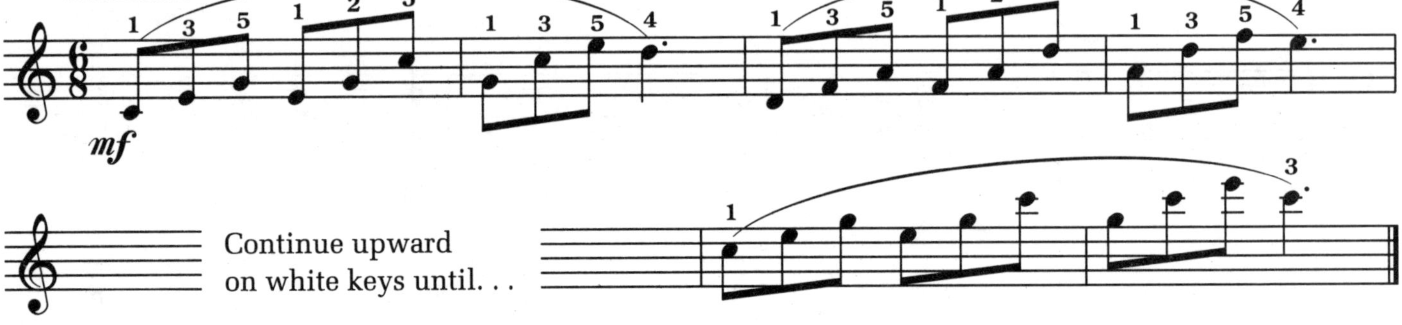

6-37 (85)

Moderato

2.

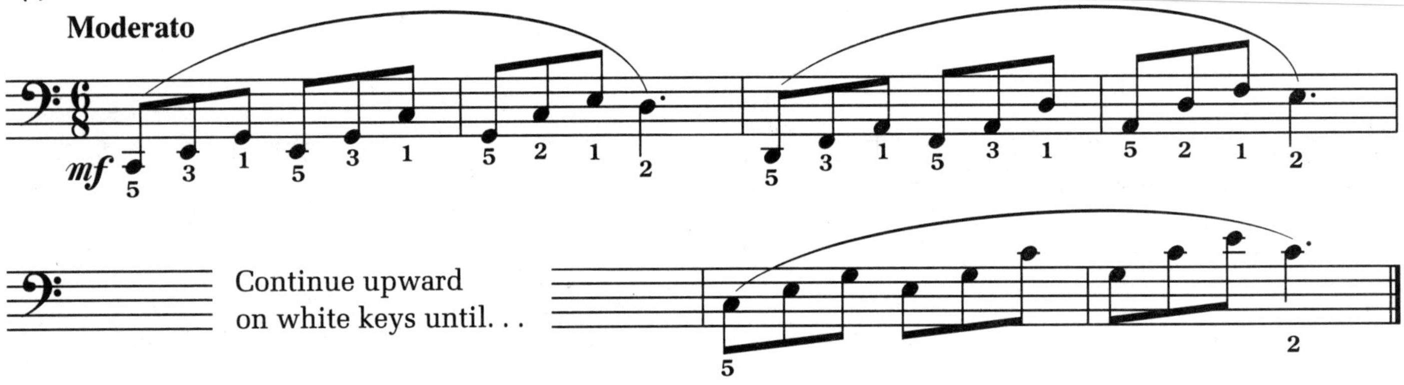

6-38 (86)

Allegretto

3.

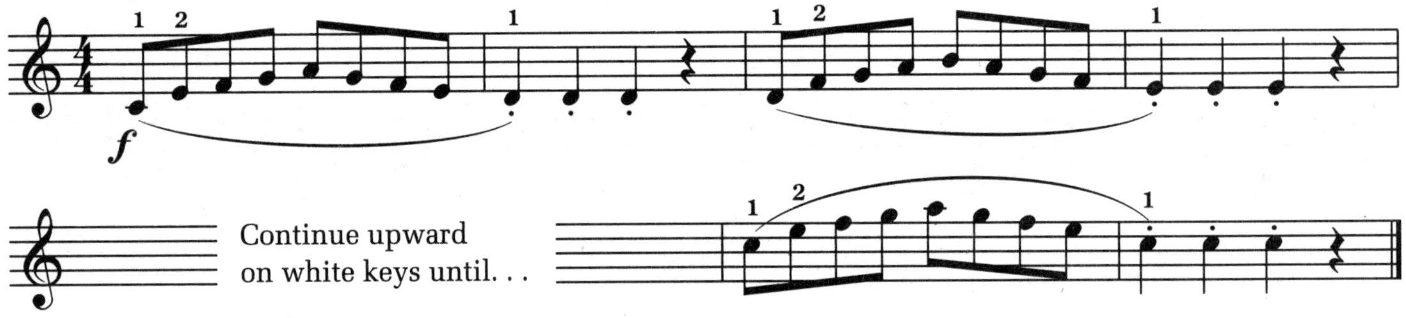

6-39 (87)

Allegretto

4.

Solo Repertoire

Simile as used in this piece means to continue pedal in the same way.

Etude

6-40 (88)

Cornelius Gurlitt
(1820–1901)

Reading

Identify the key of each example. Use the indicated tempo, dynamics and articulation as you play these exercises.

Use the following practice directions:

1. Tap RH and count aloud; then LH.
2. Play hands separately and count aloud.
3. Tap hands together and count aloud.
4. Play hands together and count aloud.

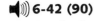

6-41 (89)

Alla marcia *(in march style)*

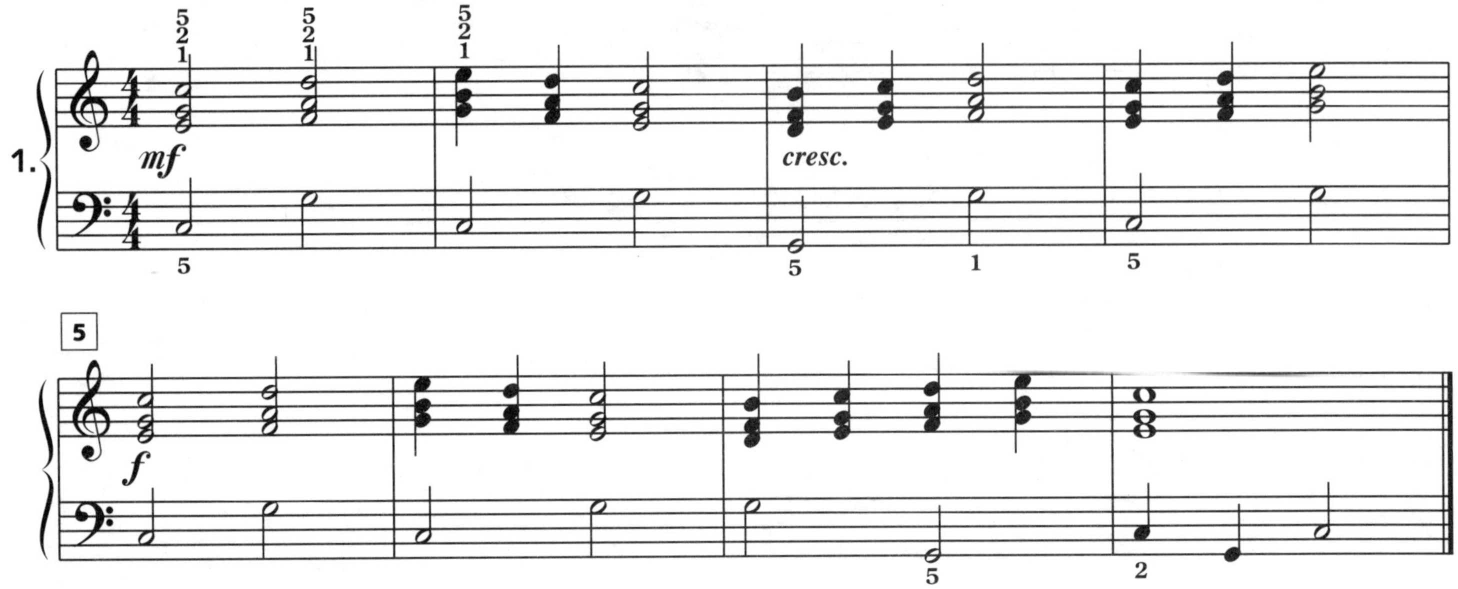

6-42 (90)

Andante

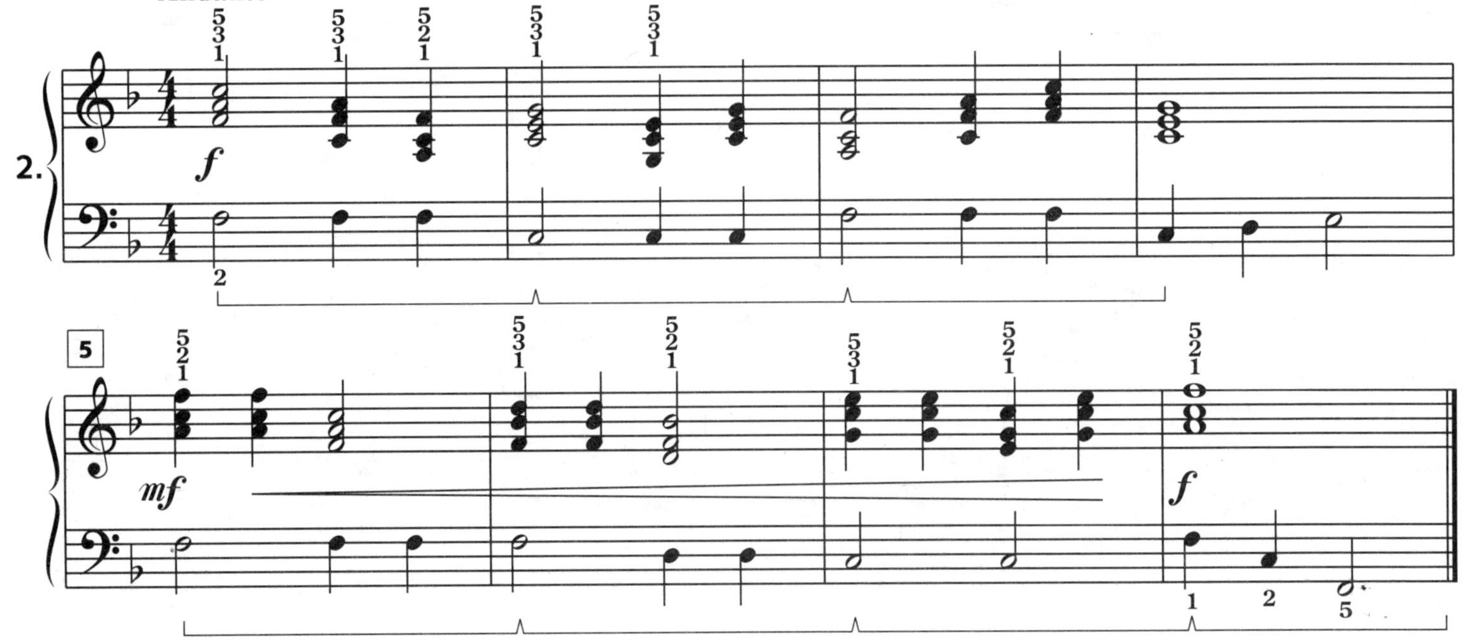

6-43 (91)

Moderato

Harmonization

Harmonize the following melody using the bottom note of each triad and inversion.

6-44 (92)

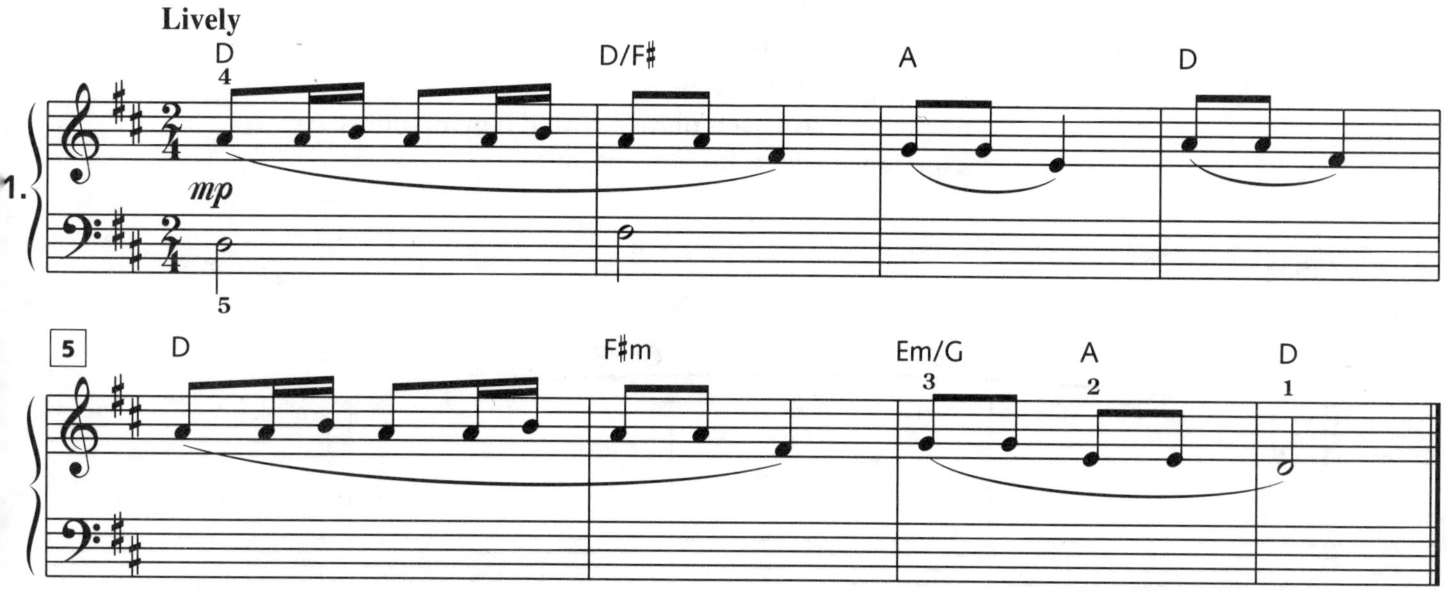

Harmonize the following melodies using the indicated triads and their inversions.

Tempo di Menuetto

(from Sonata in G)

6-45 (93)

Ludwig van Beethoven (1770–1827)
Op. 49, No. 2

6-46 (94)

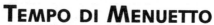

Improvisation from Chord Symbols

Improvise a right-hand melody for each of the chord progressions below in two ways:

- While the left hand plays the bottom note of each indicated triad.
- While the left hand plays the indicated triads and their inversions.

Begin and end each phrase with the given notes.
Notate your favorite improvisation.

6-47 (95)

1.

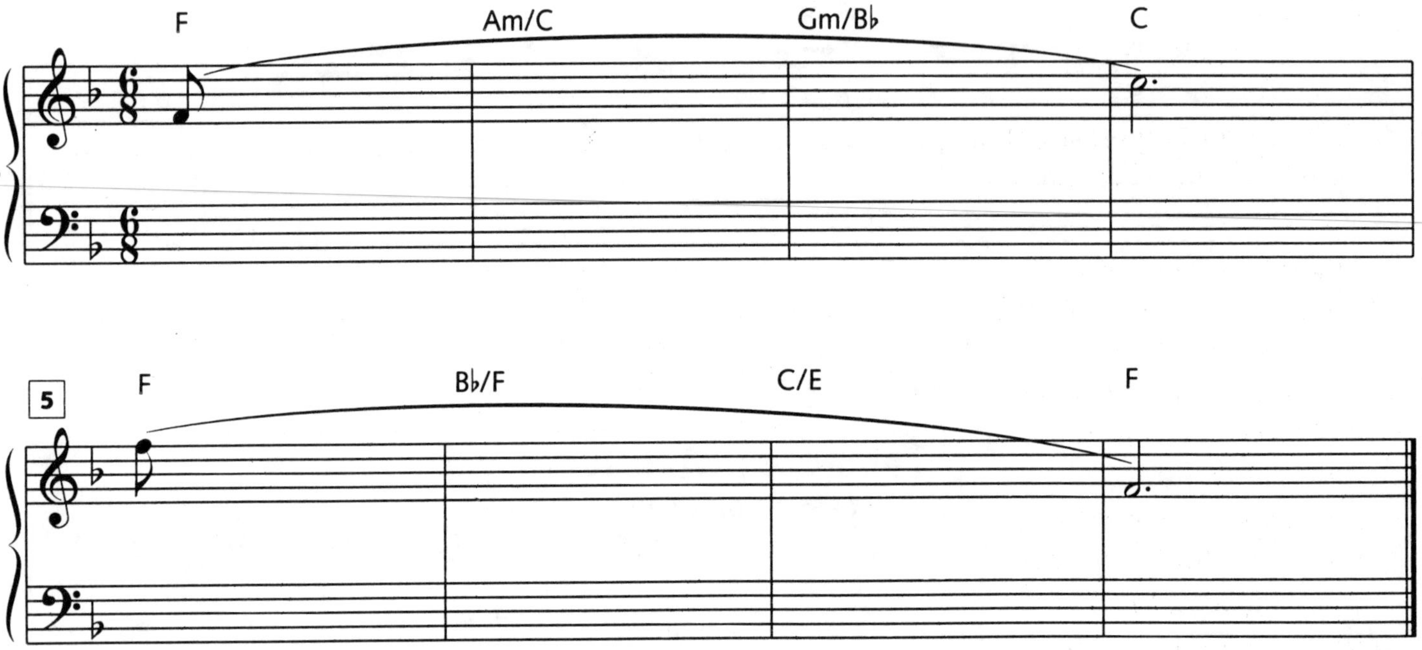

6-48 (96)

2.

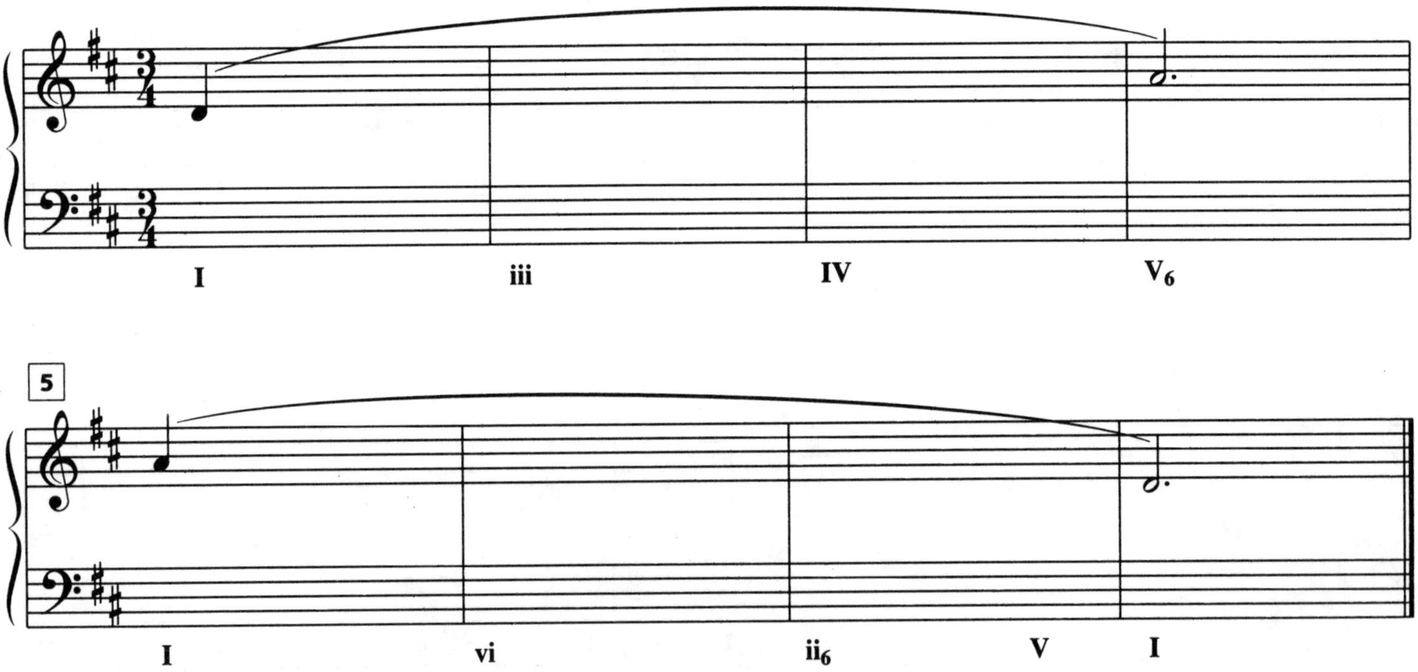

Unit 12

The Dominant and Dominant Seventh Chords

Objectives

Upon completion of this unit the student will be able to:

1. Play I–V^6_3–I and I–V^6_5–I chord progressions in all major keys.
2. Perform solo repertoire that uses tonic and dominant harmonies.
3. Sight-read and transpose music that uses tonic and dominant chords.
4. Harmonize and transpose melodies with tonic and dominant chords.
5. Improvise melodies over tonic and dominant chords.
6. Create two-hand accompaniments from Roman numerals.

Assignments

Week of ________

Write your assignments for the week in the space below.

Tonic and Dominant

In the key of C, the **I** chord (tonic) is the C triad.
The **V** chord (dominant) is the G triad.

To make chord progressions easier to play and sound better, the **V** chord may be played in first inversion by moving the two top notes down an octave.

Playing the I–$V_{\substack{6\\(3)}}$–I Progression

Play the following chord progression:

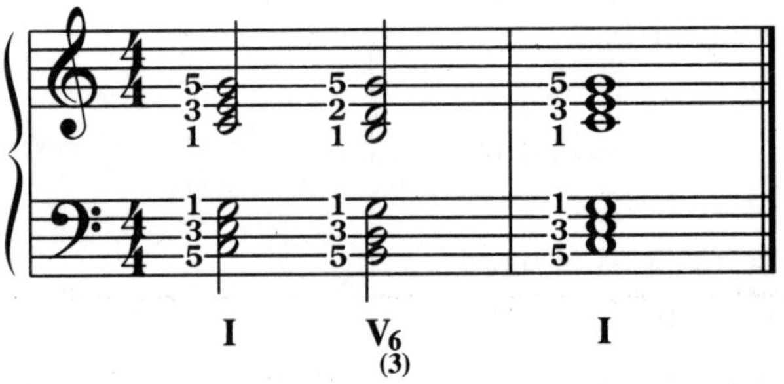

▶ Transpose to all major keys.

The V7 Chord

In many pieces a **V7** chord is used instead of a **V** triad. To make a **V7** chord, a note an interval of a 7th above the root is added to the **V** triad.

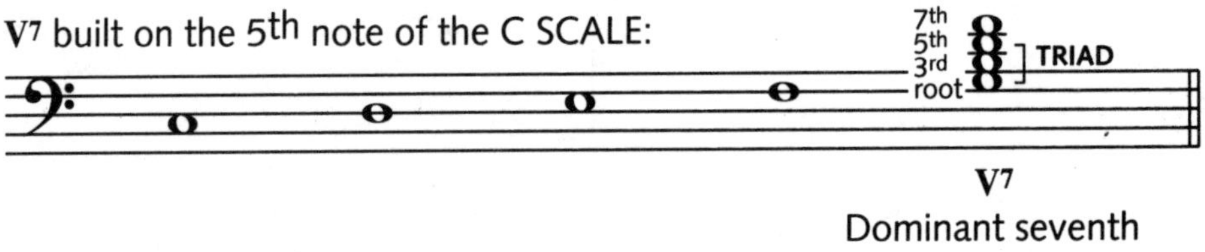

To make a smoother and easier progression:

- The 5th (D) is omitted.
- The 3rd (B) and 7th (F) are moved down an octave.

When a 7th chord is not in root position, the root is always the *upper* note of the interval of a 2nd!

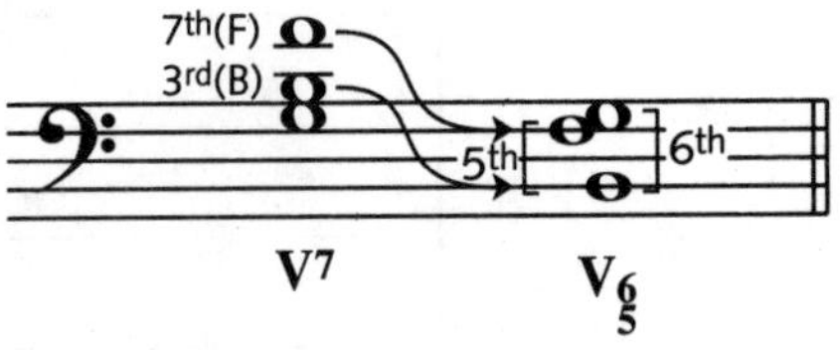

Playing the I–V^6_5–I Chord Progression

Use the steps that follow to play the **I–V^6_5–I** chord progression exercise:

1. Top note remains the same
2. Middle note moves *up* a half step
3. Bottom note moves *down* a half step.

7-1 (35)

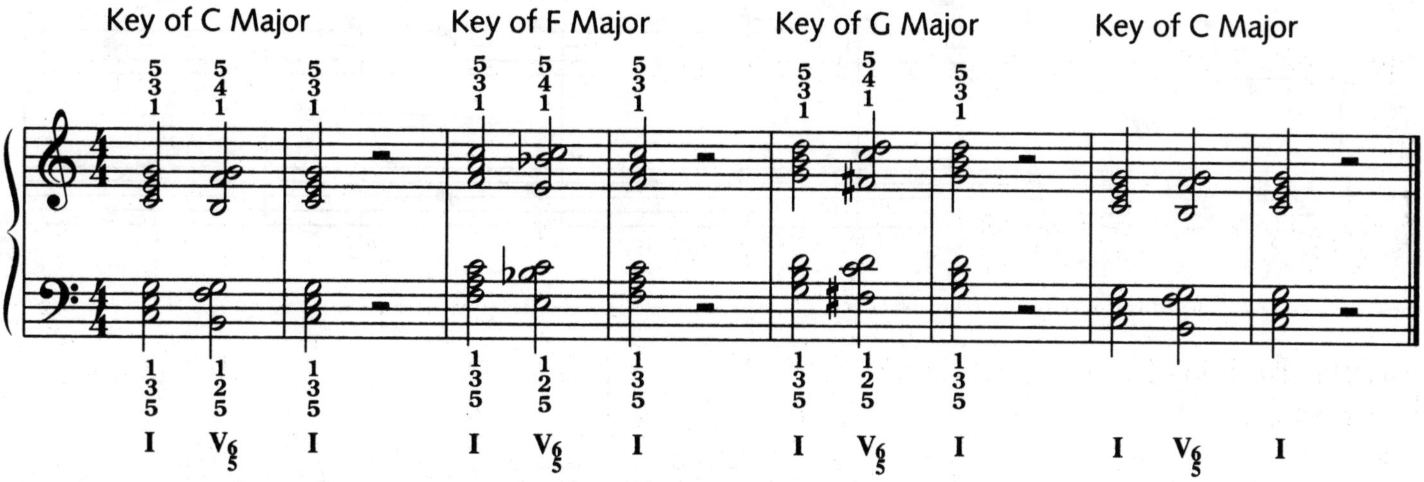

Practice the above exercise in the following major keys:

7-2 (36) 1. D G A D

7-3 (37) 2. E A B E

7-4 (38) 3. D♭ G♭ A♭ D♭

7-5 (39) 4. E♭ A♭ B♭ E♭

Solo Repertoire

German Dance

7-6 (40)

Franz Joseph Haydn
(1732–1809)

Reading

Identify the key of each example. Use the indicated tempo, dynamics and articulation as you play these exercises.

Use the following practice directions:

1. Tap RH and count aloud; then LH.
2. Play hands separately and count aloud.
3. Tap hands together and count aloud.
4. Play hands together and count aloud.

ALLEGRETTO

7-7 (41)

Cornelius Gurlitt (1820–1901)
Op. 117, No. 5

Allegretto

▶ Transpose to G major.

DANCE

7-8 (42)

Carl Czerny (1791–1857)
Op. 823, No. 11

Moderato

▶ Transpose to D major.

Block Chords and Broken Chords

Chords are often used as follows:

- **Block chords** (all notes together)

- **Broken chords** (one note at a time)

Reading (continued)

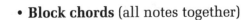

🔊 **7-9 (43)**

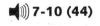

3.

▶ Transpose to B♭ major.

🔊 **7-10 (44)**

4.

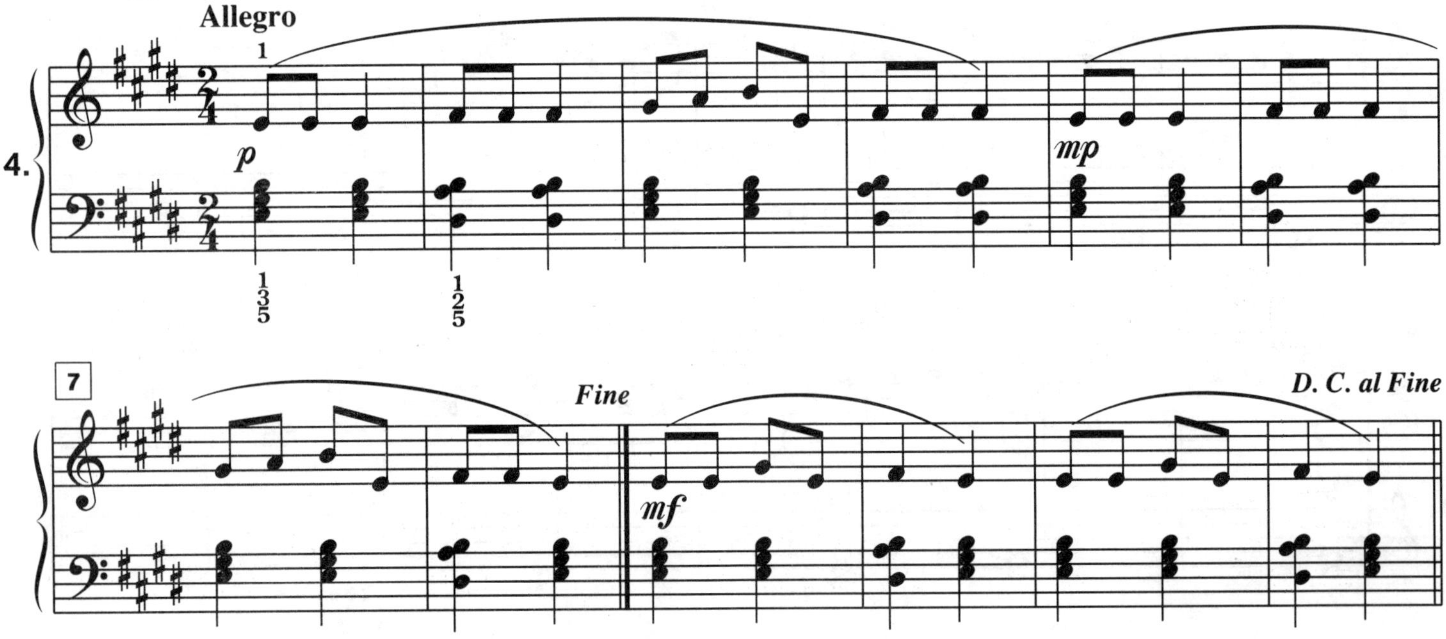

▶ Transpose to F major.

Harmonization Using Tonic and Dominant Chords

Rules for harmonization:

1. Analyze the melody notes to determine which chords to use for each measure.
2. When the melody notes in a measure consist primarily of scale tones 1, 3 and 5, the tonic chord is generally used.
3. When the melody notes in a measure consist primarily of scale tones 2, 4, 5 and 7, the dominant chord is generally used.
4. Most harmonizations begin and end on tonic.
5. The ear should always be the final guide in determining which chord to use.

Using tonic (**I**) and dominant (**V7** or $\mathbf{V^6_5}$) chords, harmonize the following melodies with block or broken chords as indicated. Write the letter name of each chord on the line above the staff and the Roman numeral name of each chord on the line below the staff.

1. Broken Chord Accompaniment

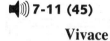

7-11 (45)

Du, du liegst mir im Herzen

Vivace

Germany

▶ Transpose to E major.

2. Block Chord Accompaniment

La Cucaracha

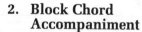

7-12 (46)

Moderato

Mexico

▶ Transpose to A major.

Harmonization Using Tonic and Dominant Chords (continued)

3. **Block Chord Accompaniment**

Boala Boala

7-13 (47)

A. M. Hirsch

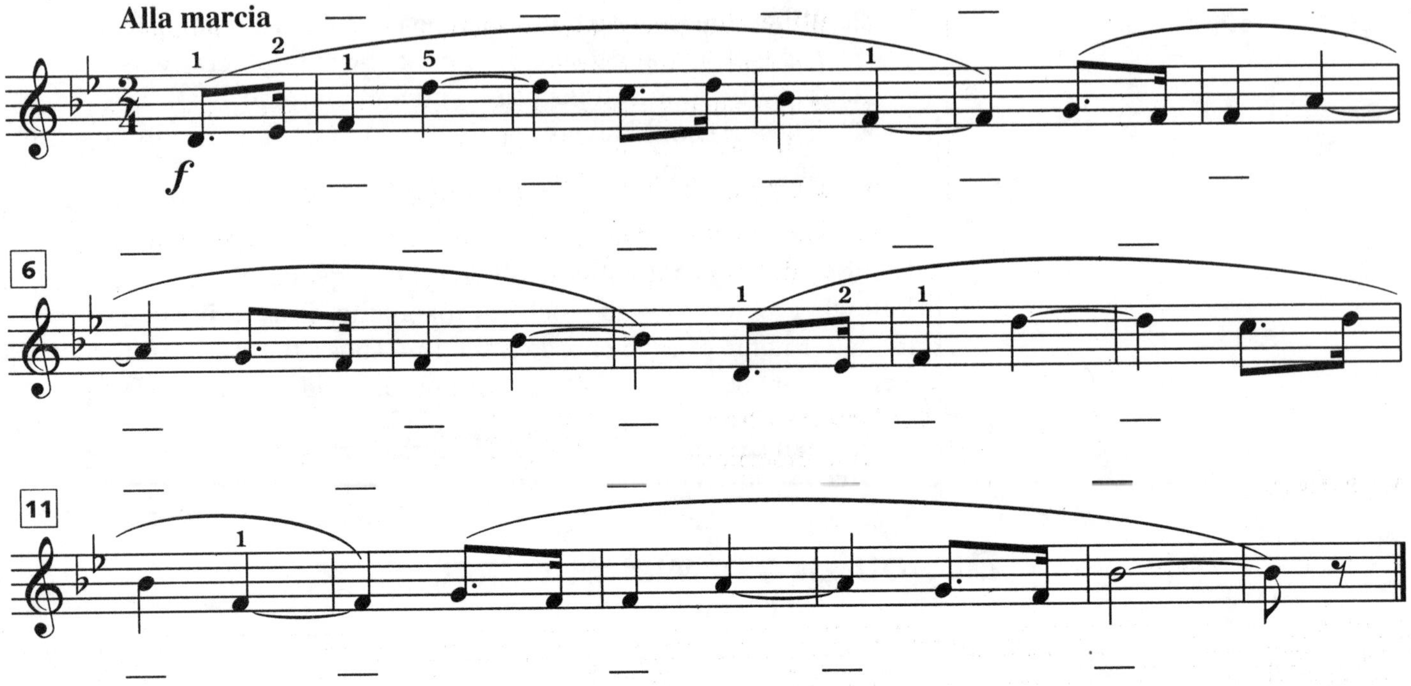

Harmonization with Two-Hand Accompaniment

Using the indicated chords, create a two-hand accompaniment for the following melody by continuing the pattern given in the first two measures.

Hush Little Baby

7-14 (48)

United States

Improvisation from Chord Symbols

Using the chord progressions below, improvise RH melodies while the LH plays the suggested accompaniment style. (First play the LH chord progression using the suggested accompaniment style and observing the indicated meter.) Notate your favorite improvisation.

Rules for improvisation:

1. When the tonic chord is used, play mostly scale tones 1, 3 and 5 in the melody.
2. When the dominant chord is used, play mostly scale tones 2, 4, 5 and 7 in the melody.
3. Most improvisations begin and end on tonic.
4. The ear should always be the final guide in determining which melody notes to play.

1. Broken Chord Accompaniment

7-15 (49)

Key of E♭ major

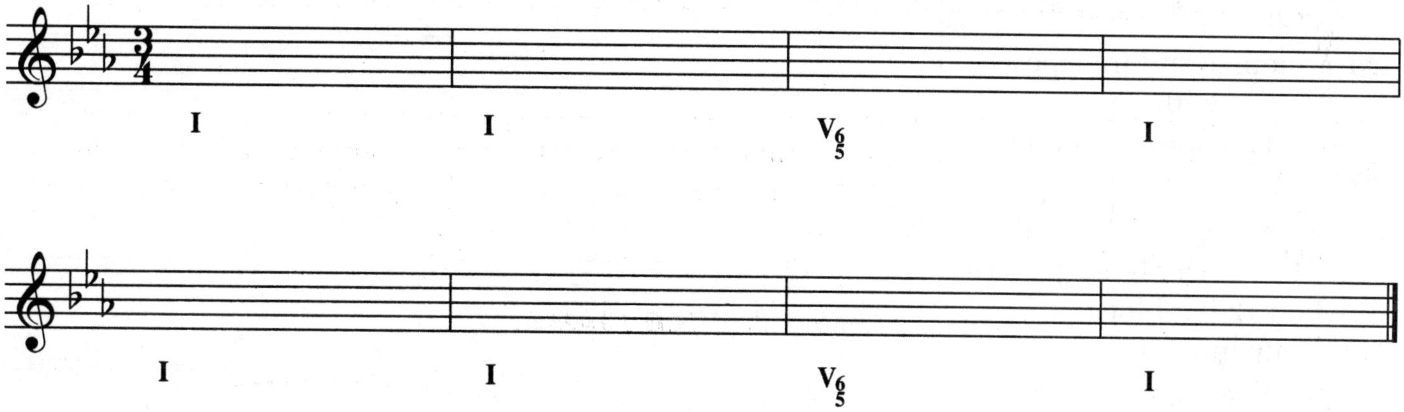

2. Block Chord Accompaniment

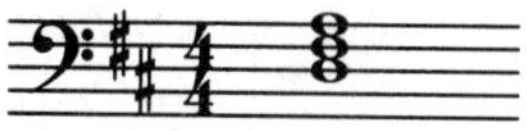

7-16 (50)

Key of D major

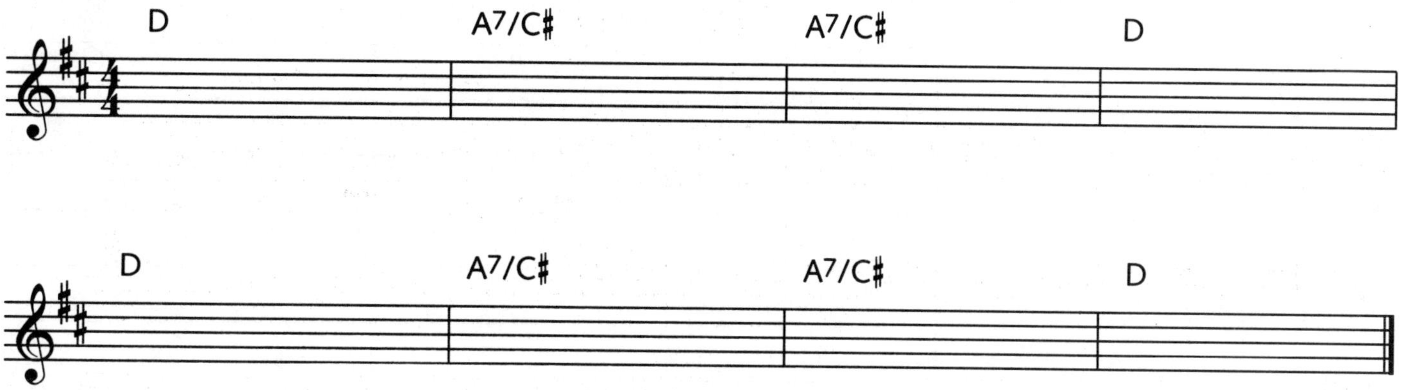

Unit 13

The Subdominant Chord

Objectives

Upon completion of this unit the student will be able to:

1. Play I–IV$^6_4$–I chord progressions in all major keys.
2. Perform solo repertoire that uses tonic, dominant and subdominant harmonies.
3. Sight-read and transpose music that uses tonic, dominant and subdominant chords.
4. Harmonize and transpose melodies with tonic, dominant and subdominant chords.
5. Improvise melodies with the five-finger blues pattern over a 12-bar blues accompaniment.
6. Create two-hand accompaniments from chord symbols.

Assignments

Week of ________

Write your assignments for the week in the space below.

Tonic and Subdominant

In the key of C, the **I** chord (tonic) is the C triad. The **IV** chord (subdominant) is the F triad.

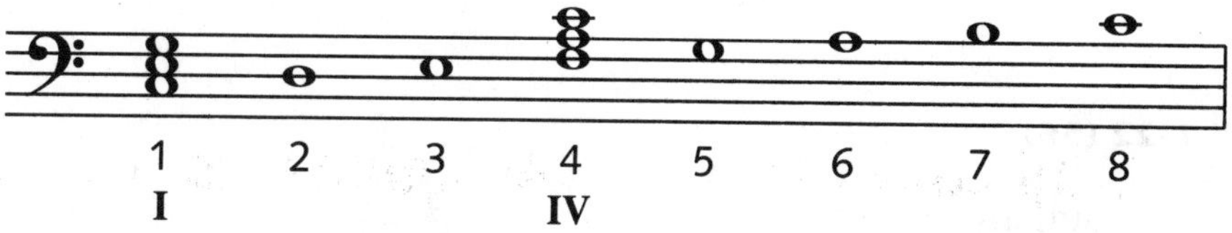

To make chord progressions easier to play and sound better, the **IV** chord may be played in the second inversion by moving the top note of the **IV** chord down an octave.

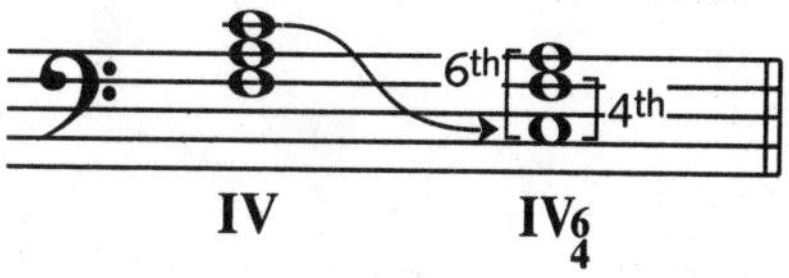

Playing the I–IV$^6_4$–I Chord Progression

Play the following chord progression:

▶ Transpose to all major keys.

Use the steps that follow to play the I–IV$^6_4$–I chord-progression exercise:

1. Top note moves up a whole step.
2. Middle note moves up a half step.
3. Bottom note remains the same.

🔊 **7-17 (51)**

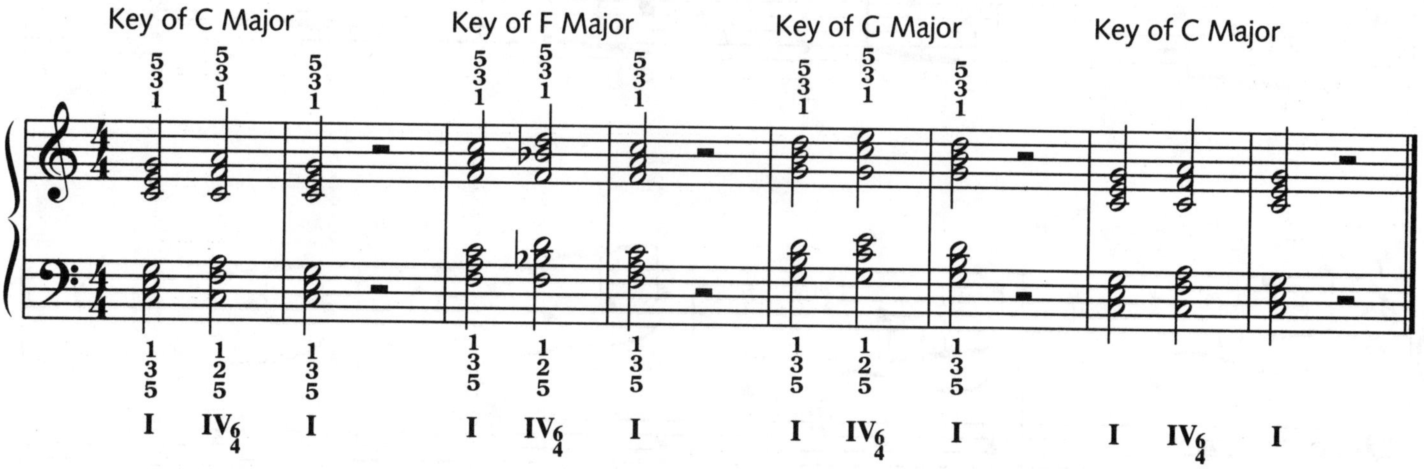

Practice the above exercise in the following major keys:

🔊 **7-18 (52)**	1. **D**	**G**	**A**	**D**
🔊 **7-19 (53)**	2. **E**	**A**	**B**	**E**
🔊 **7-20 (54)**	3. **D♭**	**G♭**	**A♭**	**D♭**
🔊 **7-21 (55)**	4. **E♭**	**A♭**	**B♭**	**E♭**

Technique

7-22 (56)

▶ Transpose to A♭ major and A major.

7-23 (57)

▶ Transpose to B major and D♭ major.

7-24 (58)

▶ Transpose to D major and G major.

Minuet in F Major

7-25 (59)

Leopold Mozart
(1719–1787)

Andante

Alberti Bass and Waltz Bass Accompaniment

Chords are often used as follows:

ALBERTI BASS

WALTZ BASS

Reading

Identify the key of each example. Use the indicated tempo, dynamics and articulation as you play these exercises.

Use the following practice directions:

1. Tap RH and count aloud; then LH.
2. Play hands separately and count aloud.
3. Tap hands together and count aloud.
4. Play hands together and count aloud.

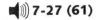

7-26 (60)

▶ Transpose to F major.

7-27 (61)

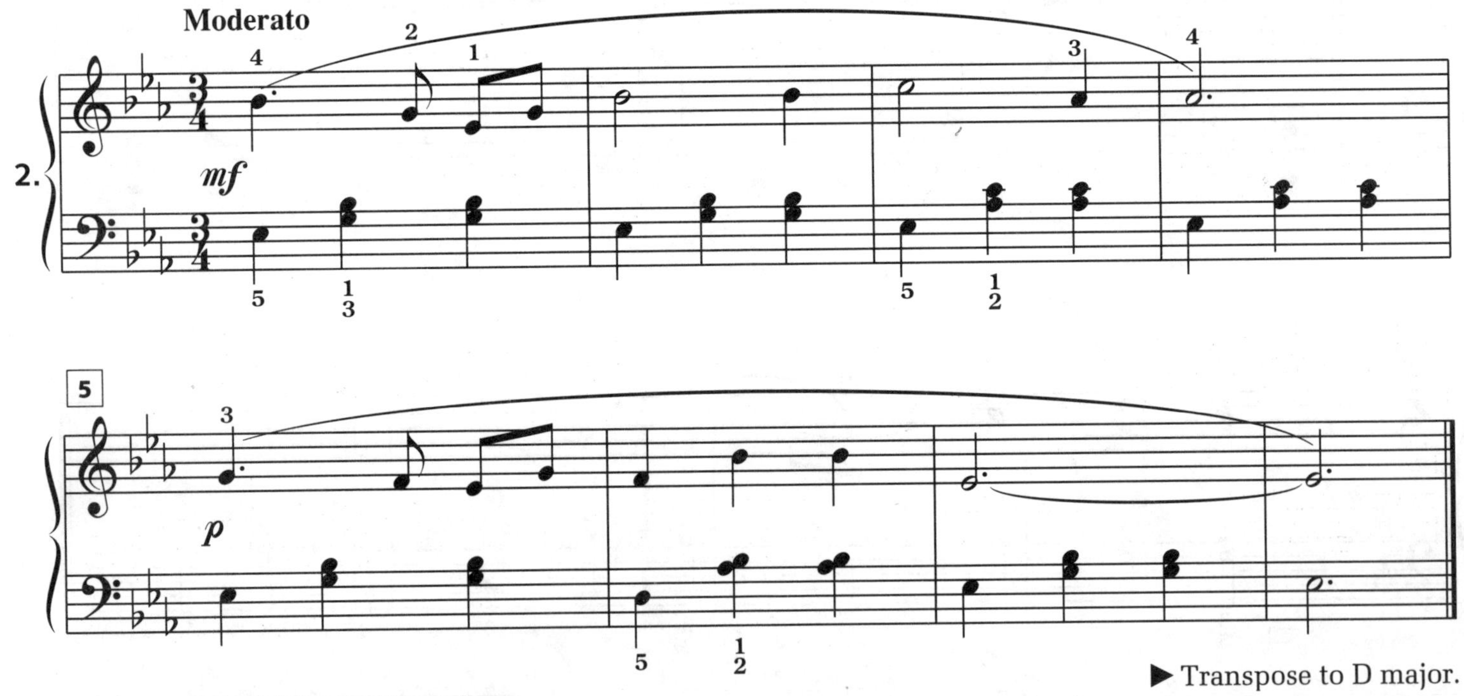

▶ Transpose to D major.

7-28 (62)

▶ Transpose to E major.

7-29 (63)

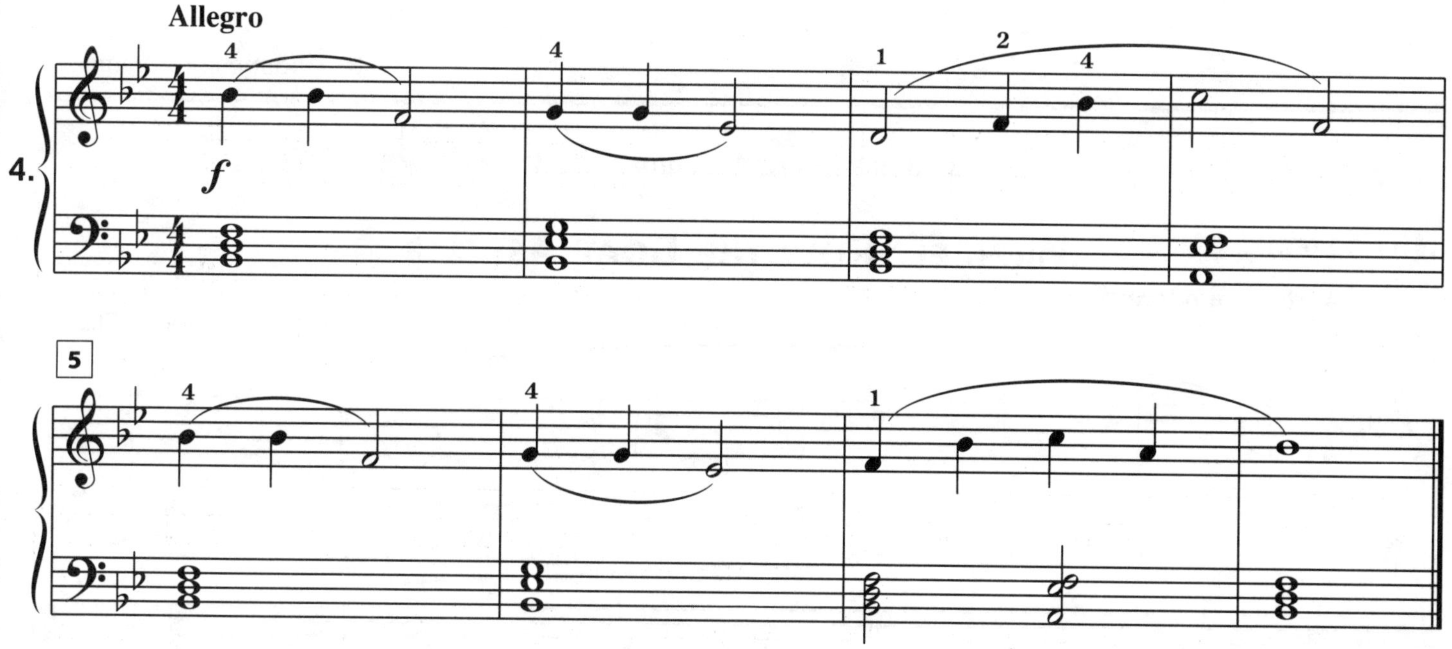

▶ Transpose to C major.

Harmonization

Using tonic (I), dominant (V7 or V$^6_5$) and subdominant (IV or IV$^6_4$) chords, harmonize the following melodies with the indicated accompaniment style. Write the letter name of each chord on the line above the staff and the Roman numeral name of each chord on the line below the staff.

1. Broken Chord Accompaniment

7-30 (64)

Sally Go Round

Allegretto

United States

▶ Transpose to F major.

---

2. Alberti Bass Accompaniment

7-31 (65)

Moderato

Germany

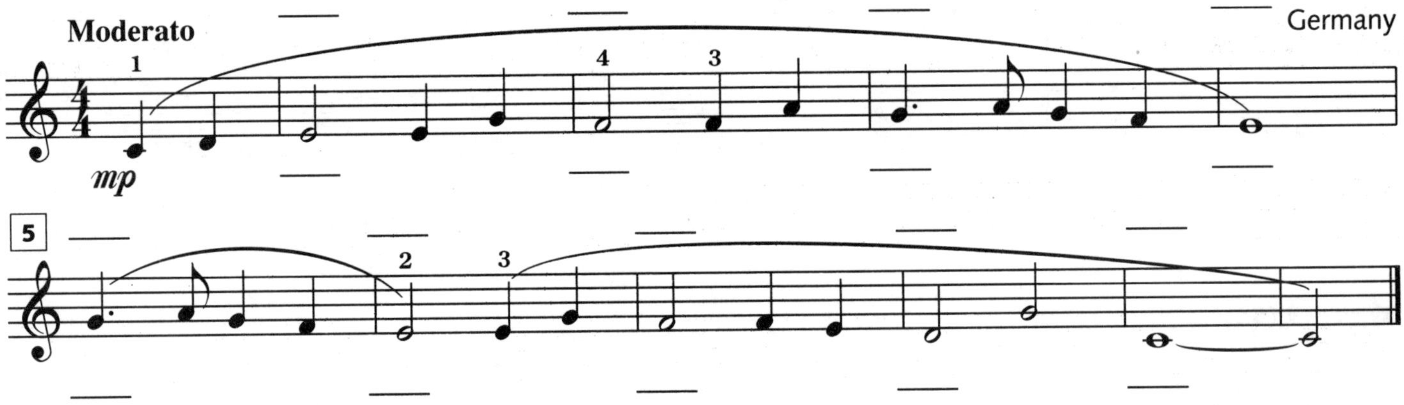

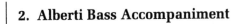

▶ Transpose to A major.

---

3. Block Chord Accompaniment

7-32 (66)

Michael, Row the Boat Ashore

Andante moderato

United States

▶ Transpose to E major.

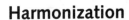

Harmonization with Two-Hand Accompaniment

Using the indicated chords, create a two-hand accompaniment for the following melody by continuing the pattern given in the first two measures.

The Streets of Laredo

🔊 7-33 (67)

United States

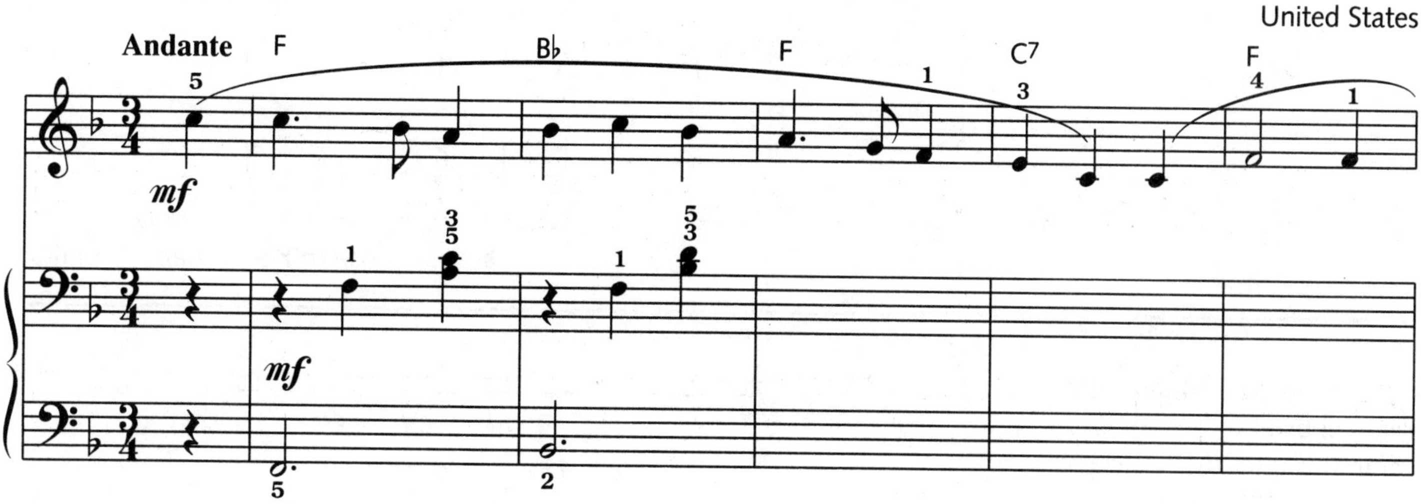

▶ Transpose to G major.

12-Bar Blues Improvisation

The blues accompaniment follows a strict 12-bar pattern. Using block chords, play the 12-bar blues pattern with the left hand.

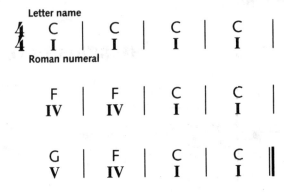

Letter name / Roman numeral ($\frac{4}{4}$)

C I	C I	C I	C I
F IV	F IV	C I	C I
G V	F IV	C I	C I

▶ Transpose to F major and G major.

This five-finger blues pattern may be used to improvise melodies over the blues pattern.

▶ Transpose to F major and G major.

Using the 12-bar blues progression, continue the RH melodic sequence, alternating ascending and descending five-finger blues patterns while the LH plays the root and fifth of the indicated chord.

7-34 (68)

Using the 12-bar blues progression, improvise other melodies with the five-finger blues pattern.

Unit 14

Primary Chords in Major Keys

Objectives

Upon completion of this unit the student will be able to:

1. Play I–IV$^6_4$–I–V$^6_5$–I chord progressions in all major keys.
2. Perform solo repertoire that uses tonic, dominant and subdominant harmonies.
3. Sight-read and transpose music that uses tonic, dominant and subdominant chords.
4. Harmonize and transpose melodies with tonic, dominant and subdominant chords.
5. Improvise melodies over tonic, dominant and subdominant chords.
6. Create two-hand accompaniments from chord symbols.
7. Create ensemble parts to accompany solo repertoire.

Assignments

Week of ________

Write your assignments for the week in the space below.

Playing the I–IV$^{6}_{4}$–I–V$^{6}_{5}$–I Chord Progression

Play the I–IV$^{6}_{4}$–I–V$^{6}_{5}$–I chord-progression exercise.

8-1 (37)

Key of C Major

Key of F Major

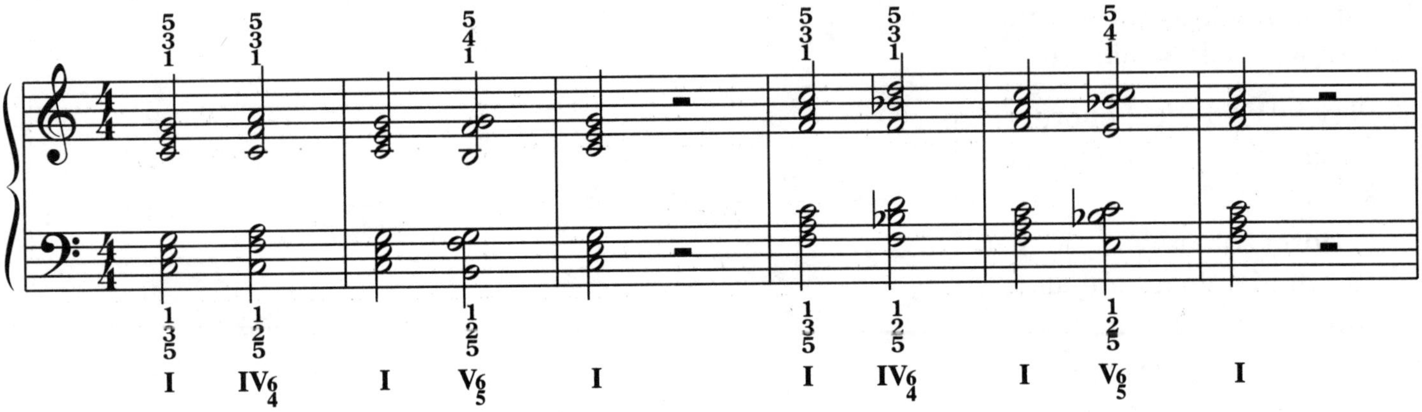

Key of G Major

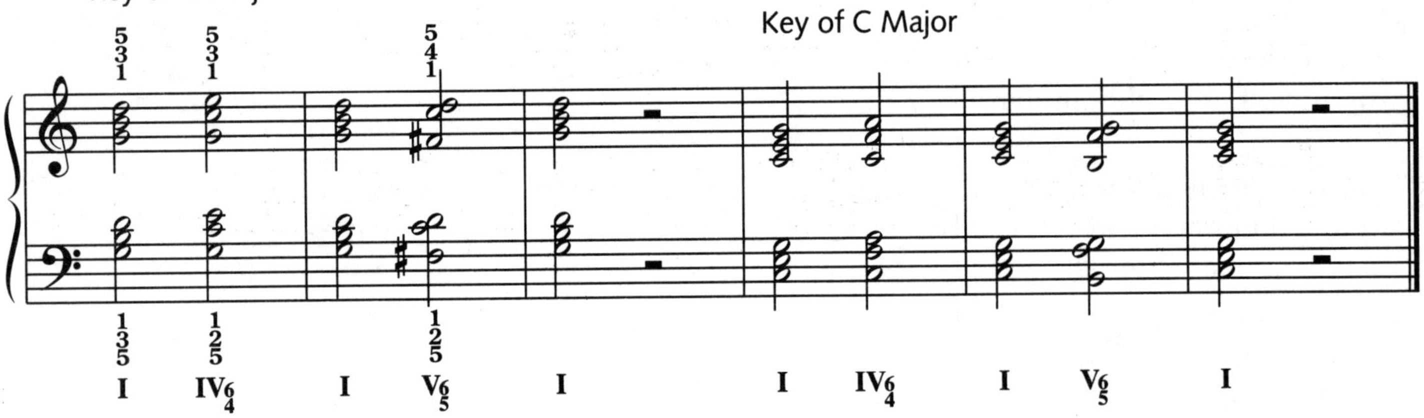

Practice the above exercise in the following major keys:

8-2 (38)	1.	D	G	A	D
8-3 (39)	2.	E	A	B	E
8-4 (40)	3.	D♭	G♭	A♭	D♭
8-5 (41)	4.	E♭	A♭	B♭	E♭

Funny Event

8-6 (42)

Dmitri Kabalevsky (1904–1987)
Op. 39, No. 7

Ensemble Repertoire

Play the three-part ensemble using the indicated chords to complete parts 2 and 3.

Part 1: Kabalevsky *Funny Event* (page 167)

Part 2: Descending broken chords (one octave higher than written throughout)

Part 3: Two-hand accompaniment

8-7 (43)

Reading

Identify the key of each example. Use the indicated tempo, dynamics and articulation as you play these exercises.
Use the following practice directions:

1. Tap RH and count aloud; then LH.
2. Play hands separately and count aloud.
3. Tap hands together and count aloud.
4. Play hands together and count aloud.

8-8 (44)

Kum-ba-yah!

Traditional

*Finger substitution: while holding the key down with finger 4, shift to finger 5.

▶ Transpose to E♭ major.

8-9 (45)

Vivace

Cornelius Gurlitt (1820–1901)
Op. 117, No. 8

▶ Transpose to D major.

Reading (continued)

8-10 (46)

3.

▶ Transpose to A major.

8-11 (47)

4.

▶ Transpose to G major.

Harmonization

Using tonic (I), dominant (V^7 or V^6_5) and subdominant (IV or IV^6_4) chords, harmonize the following melodies with the indicated accompaniment style. In the first example, write the Roman numeral name of each chord on the line below the staff.

1. Block Chord Accompaniment

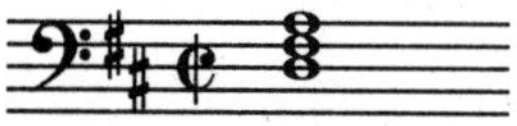

When the Saints Go Marching In

🔊 8-12 (48)

March time

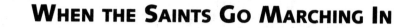

Traditional

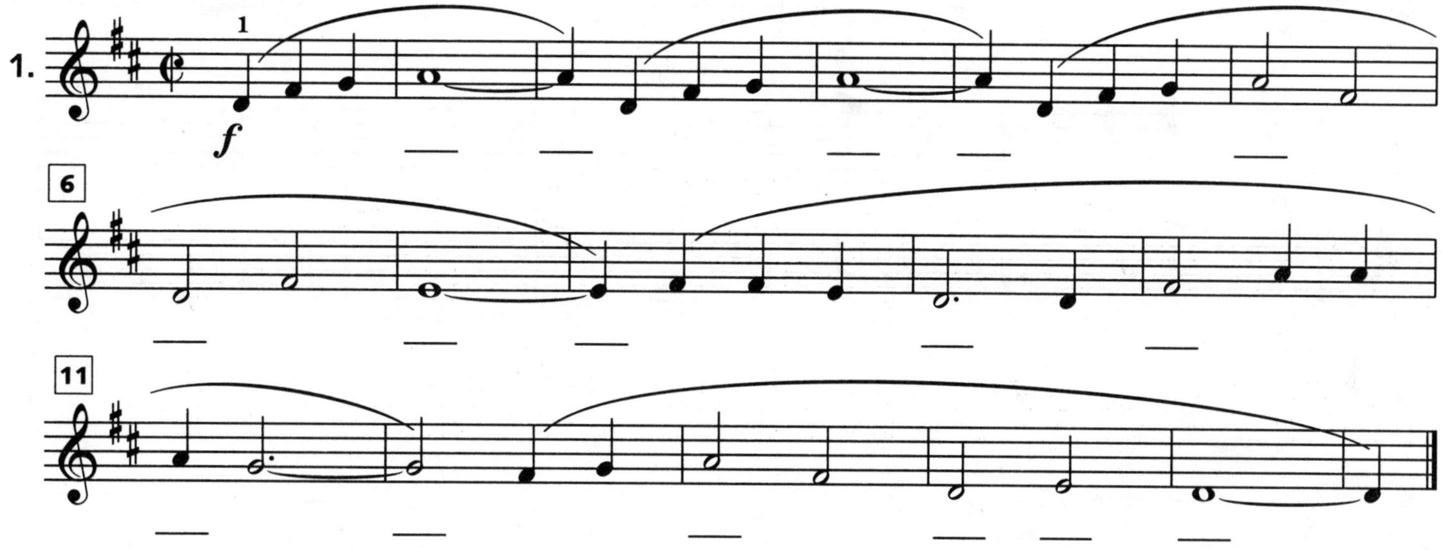

▶ Transpose to E major.

2. Waltz Style Accompaniment

Lullaby

🔊 8-13 (49)

Johannes Brahms (1833–1897)
Op. 49, No. 4

Moderato

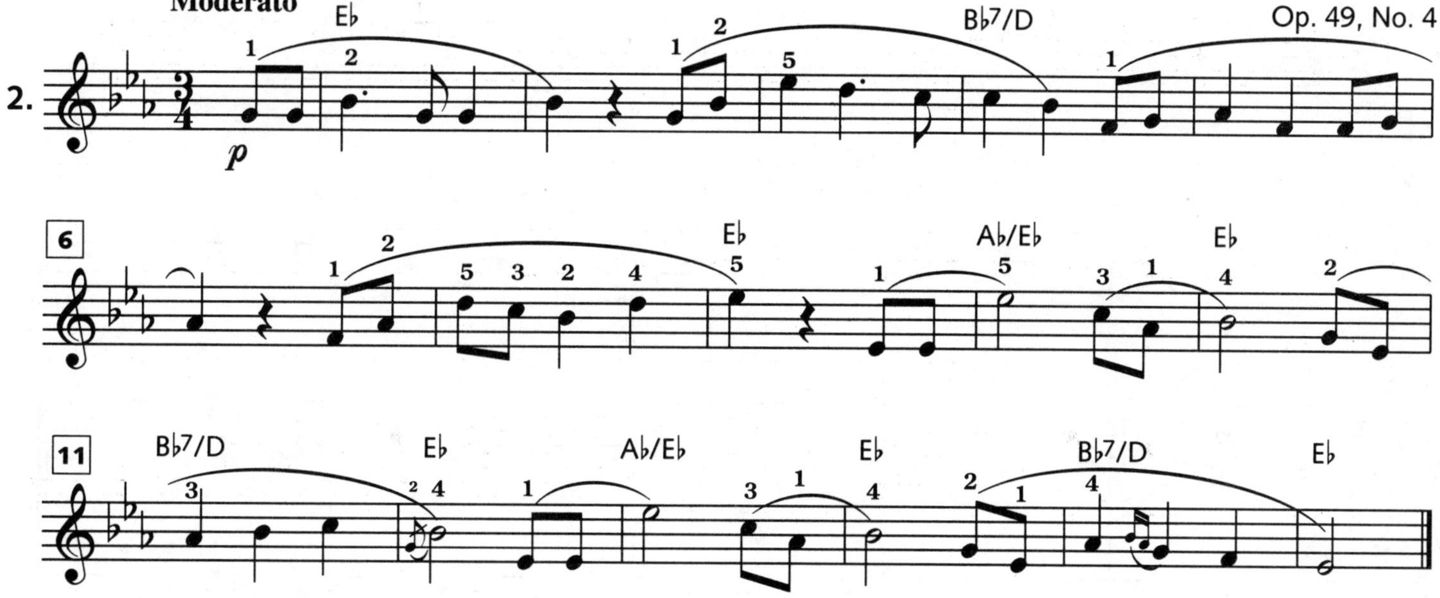

▶ Transpose to F major.

Harmonization with Two-Hand Accompaniment

Using the indicated chords, create a two-hand accompaniment for the following melody by continuing the pattern given in the first two measures.

Dona Nobis Pacem

8-14 (50)

Moderato

Anonymous

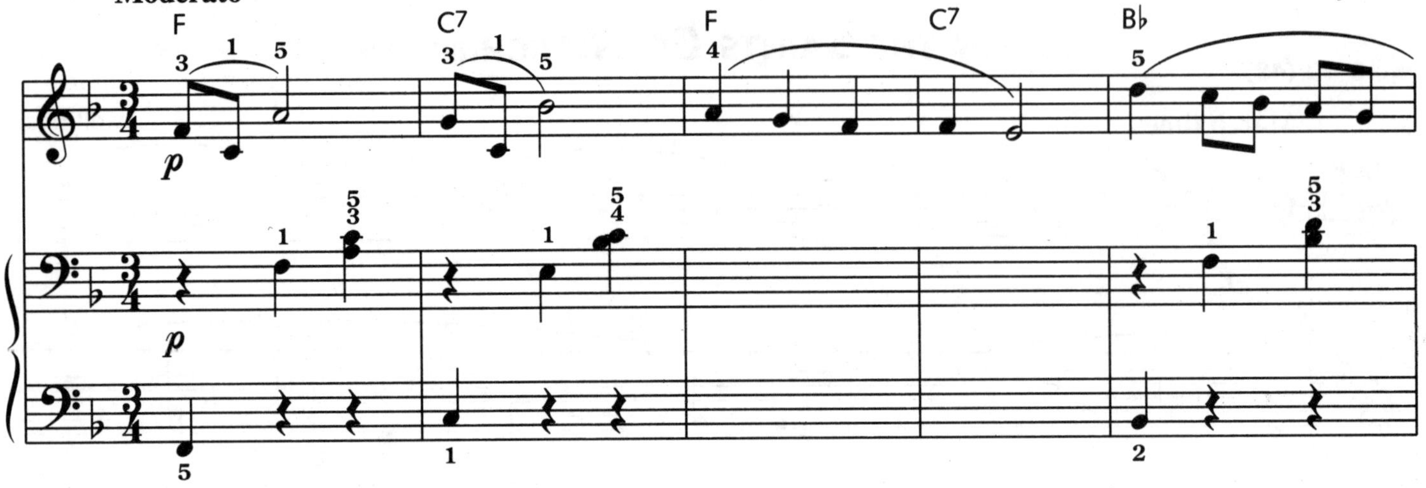

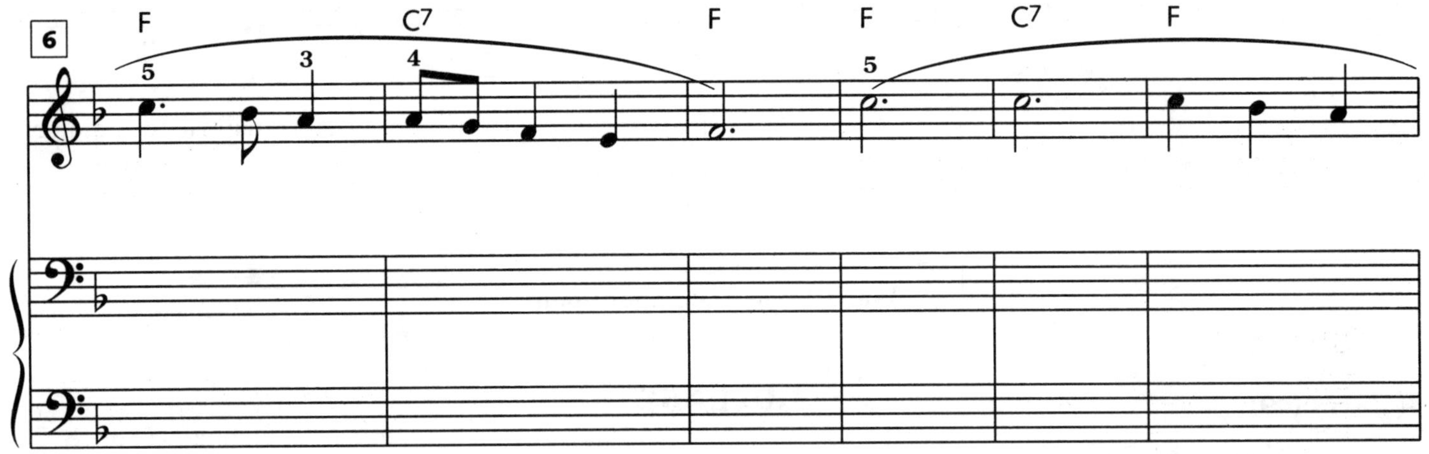

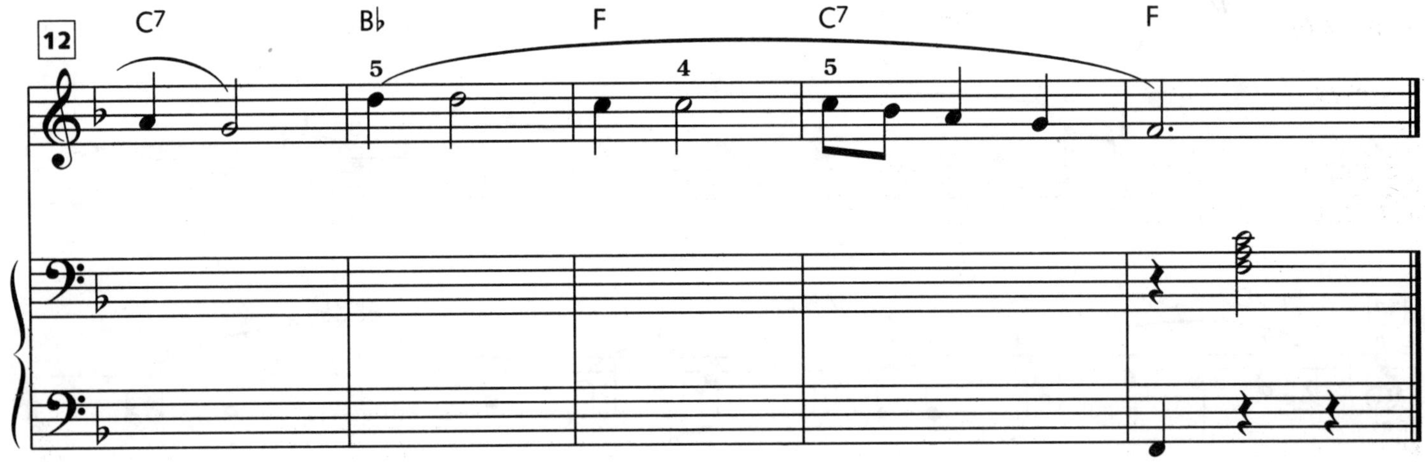

Improvisation from Chord Symbols

Using the chord progressions below, improvise RH melodies while the LH plays appropriate accompaniment styles. (First play the LH chord progression using the suggested accompaniment style and observing the indicated meter.) Notate your favorite improvisation.

Rules for improvisation:

1. When the tonic chord is used, play mostly scale tones 1, 3 and 5 in the melody.
2. When the dominant chord is used, play mostly scale tones 2, 4, 5 and 7 in the melody.
3. When the subdominant chord is used, play mostly scale tones 1, 4 and 6 in the melody.
4. Most improvisations begin and end on tonic.
5. The ear should always be the final guide in determining which melody notes to play.

8-15 (51)

1. Broken Chord Accompaniment

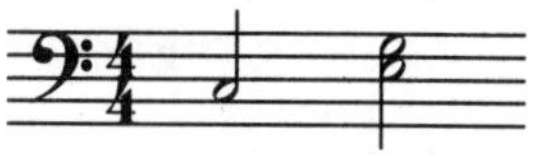

Key of C major

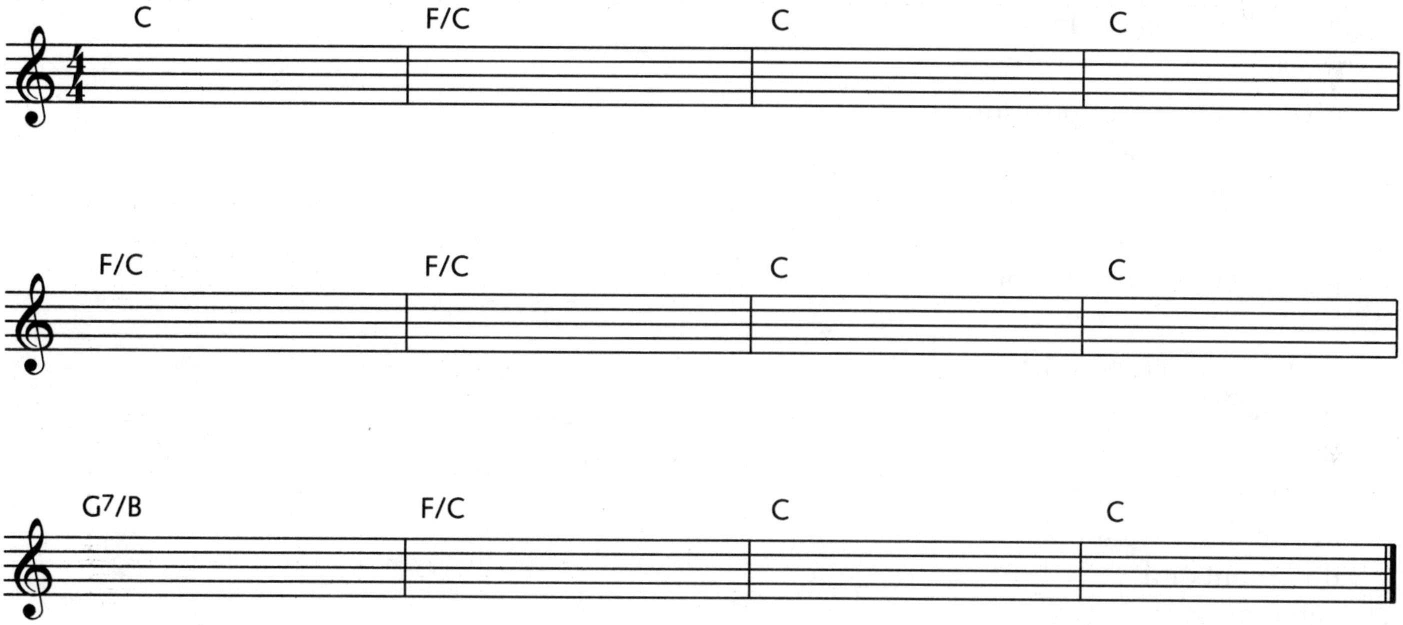

8-16 (52)

2. Broken Chord Accompaniment

Key of A major

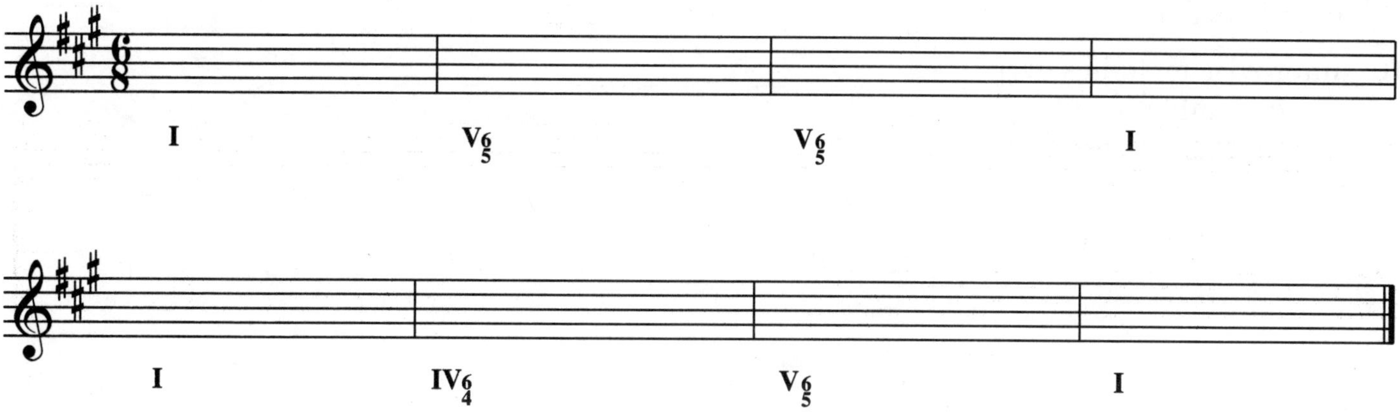

Unit 15 **Review**

Objectives

Upon completion of this unit the student will be able to:

1. Play exercises that utilize intervals up to an octave.
2. Play major, minor, augmented and diminished chords beginning on any key.
3. Play exercises that use major scales and triads of the key.
4. Play triads in root position, first inversion and second inversion.
5. Play I–IV–I–V^7–I chord progressions in all major keys.
6. Perform solo repertoire that uses scale patterns and chords.
7. Sight-read and transpose music that uses tonic, dominant and subdominant chords.
8. Harmonize and transpose melodies with tonic, dominant and subdominant chords.
9. Create two-hand accompaniments from chord symbols.
10. Improvise melodies over tonic, dominant and subdominant chords.

Assignments

Week of ________

Write your assignments for the week in the space below.

Playing Intervals

Play the following exercises that use intervals:

8-17 (53)

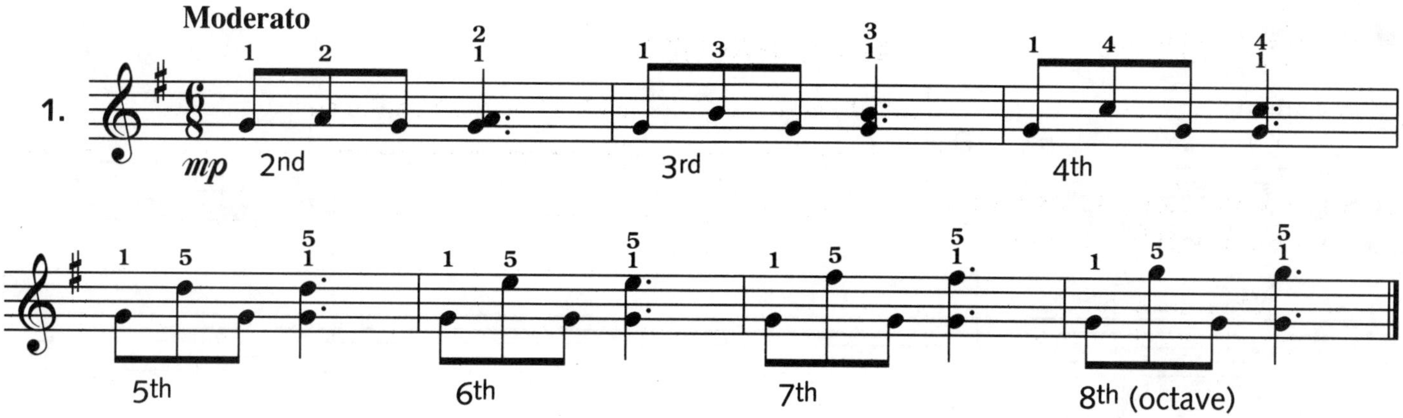

▶ Transpose to E major and B♭ major.

8-18 (54)

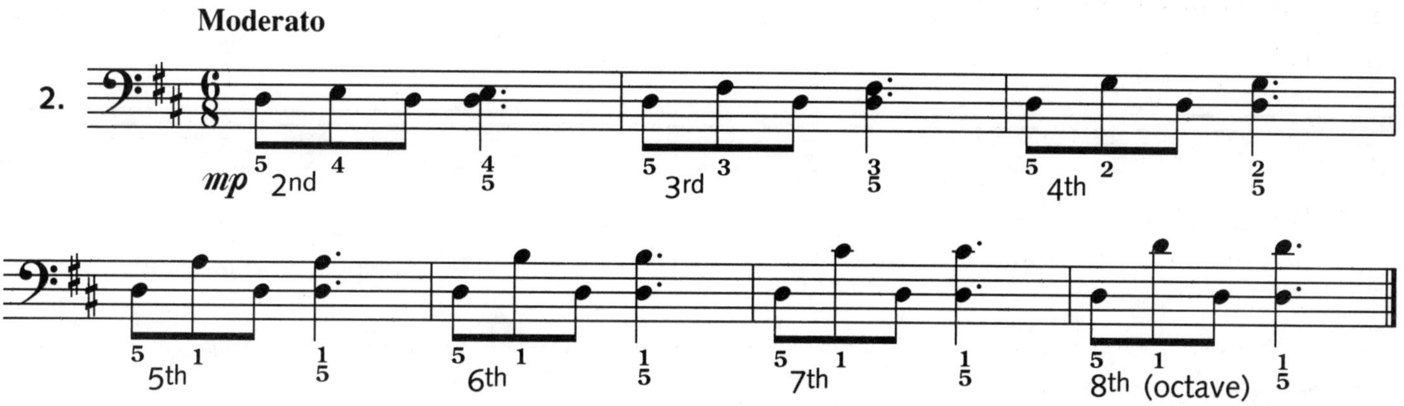

▶ Transpose to A major and F major.

Playing Major, Augmented, Minor and Diminished Chords

Play the following exercise that uses major, augmented, minor and diminished chords:

8-19 (55)

Playing Major Scales and Triads of the Key

Play the following exercises that use major scales and triads of the key:

8-20 (56)

▶ Transpose to D major and B major.

8-21 (57)

▶ Transpose to F major and A major.

Playing Chord Inversions

Play the following exercises that use chord inversions:

8-22 (58)

1.
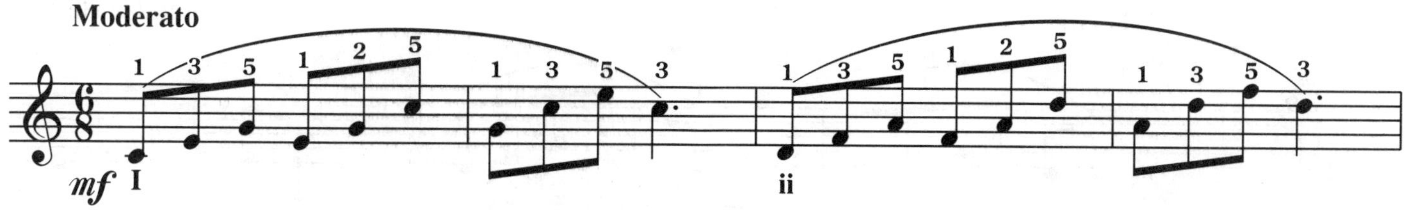

▶ Transpose to G major and A♭ major.

8-22 (58)

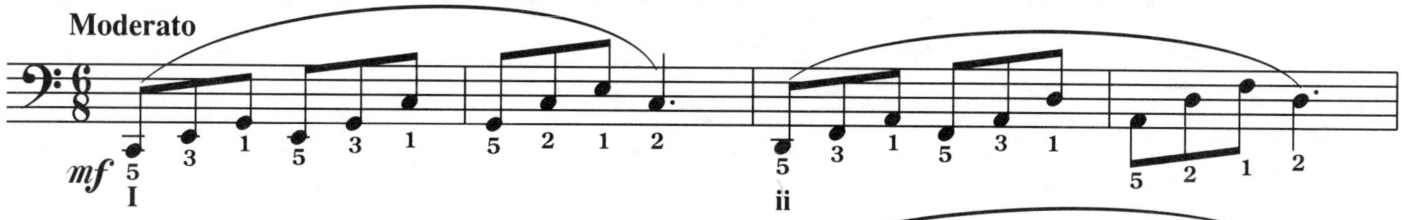

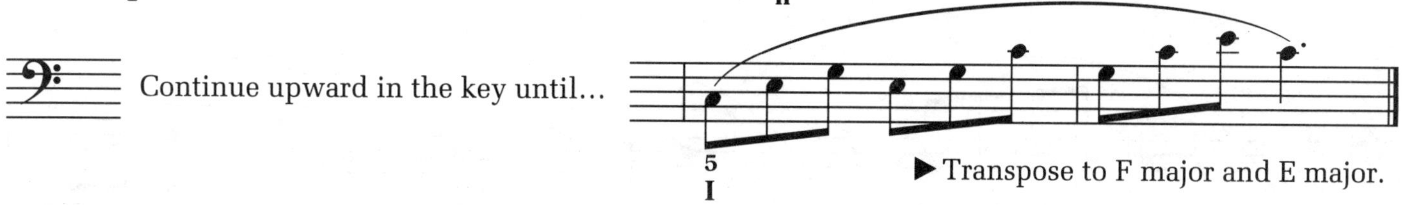

▶ Transpose to F major and E major.

Playing the I–IV–I–V7–I Chord Progression

Play the I–IV–I–V7–I chord progression exercise:

8-23 (59)

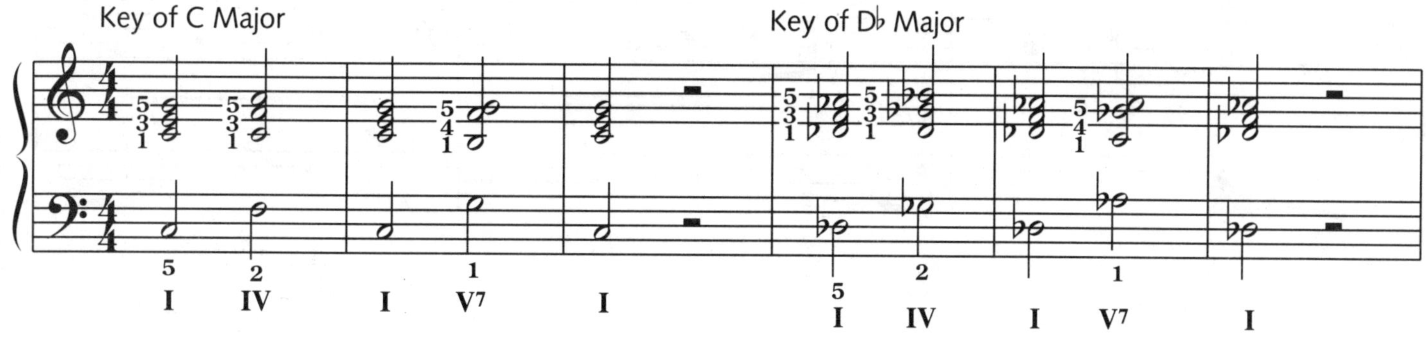

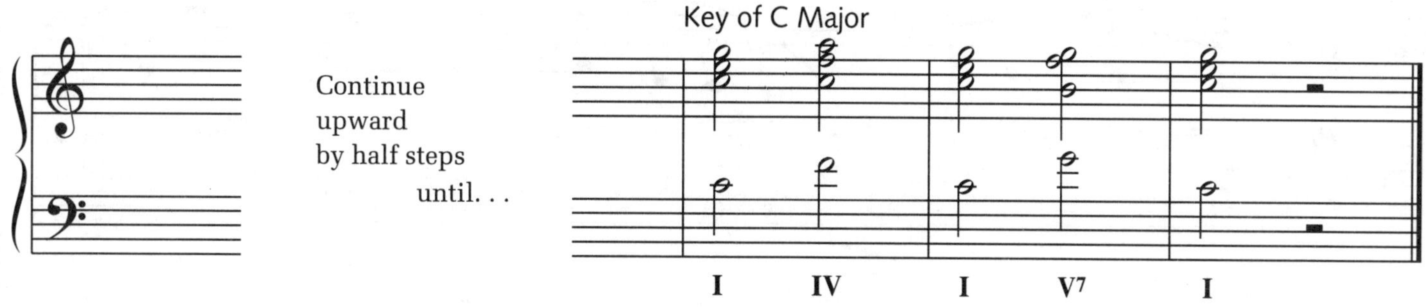

Moonlit Shores

8-24 (60)

Randall Hartsell

16
f
mp
f
5
19
mp
poco rit.
a tempo
mp
22
25
mp
mf
p
mp
1
RH
5
29
più (more)
p
poco rit.
LH
pp

Reading

Identify the key of each example. Use the indicated tempo, dynamics and articulation as you play these exercises.

Use the following practice directions:

1. Tap RH and count aloud; then LH.
2. Play hands separately and count aloud.
3. Tap hands together and count aloud.
4. Play hands together and count aloud.

MARCH

8-25 (61)

Daniel Gottlob Türk
(1756–1813)

Allegro moderato

MELODY

8-26 (62)

Louis Köhler (1820–1886)
Op. 218, No. 8

Moderato

▶ Transpose to A major.

🔊 8-27 (63)

Allegretto

▶ Transpose to F major.

🔊 8-28 (64)

Andante

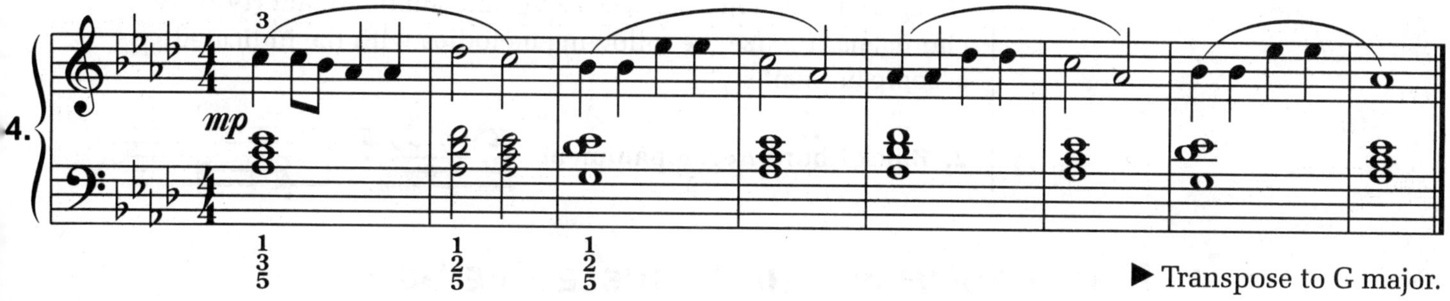

▶ Transpose to G major.

Ode to Joy

🔊 8-29 (65)

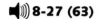

Ludwig van Beethoven
(1770–1827)

Moderato

▶ Transpose to C major.

Harmonization

1. Use the bottom note of each indicated chord to harmonize the following melody.

MINUET IN G MAJOR

8-30 (66)

(from the Notebook for Anna Magdalena)

Johann Sebastian Bach (1685–1750)

Using tonic (I), dominant (V^7 or V^6_5) and subdominant (IV or IV^6_4) chords, harmonize the following melodies with the indicated accompaniment style.

2. **Block Chord Accompaniment**

NOBODY KNOWS THE TROUBLE I'VE SEEN

8-31 (67)

United States

▶ Transpose to F major.

Write the Roman numeral name of each chord on the line below the staff.

3. Block Chord Accompaniment 

New River Train

8-32 (68)

Lively

United States

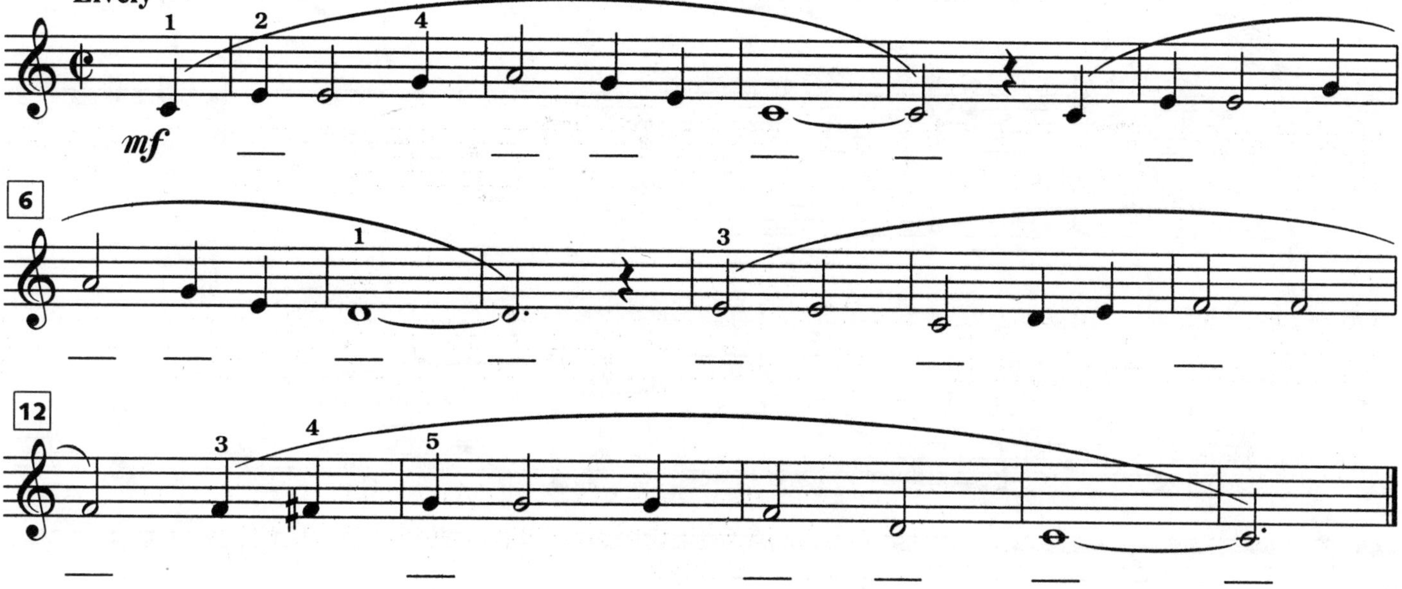

▶ Transpose to D major.

4. Broken Chord Accompaniment 

Silent Night

8-33 (69)

Gently, moderately slow

Franz Grüber
(1787–1863)

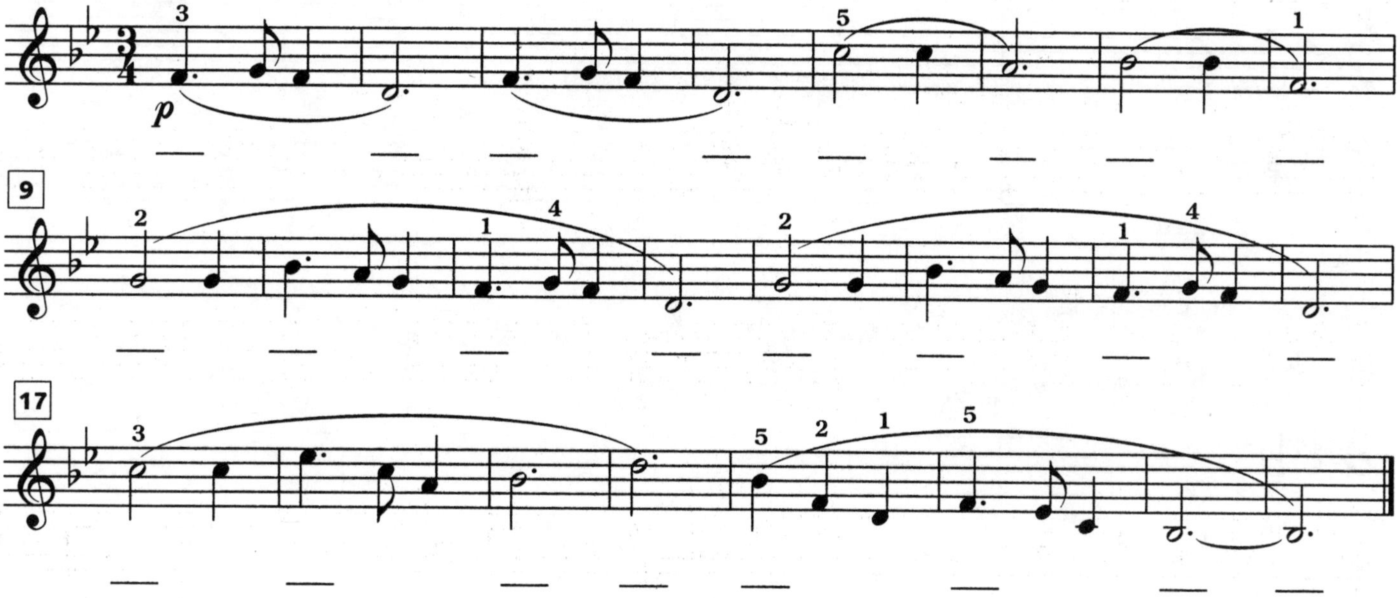

▶ Transpose to C major.

Harmonization with Two-Hand Accompaniment

Using the indicated chords, create a two-hand accompaniment for the following melody by continuing the pattern given in the first measure.

8-34 (70)

THE HAPPY FARMER

Robert Schumann
(1810–1856)

Allegro animato

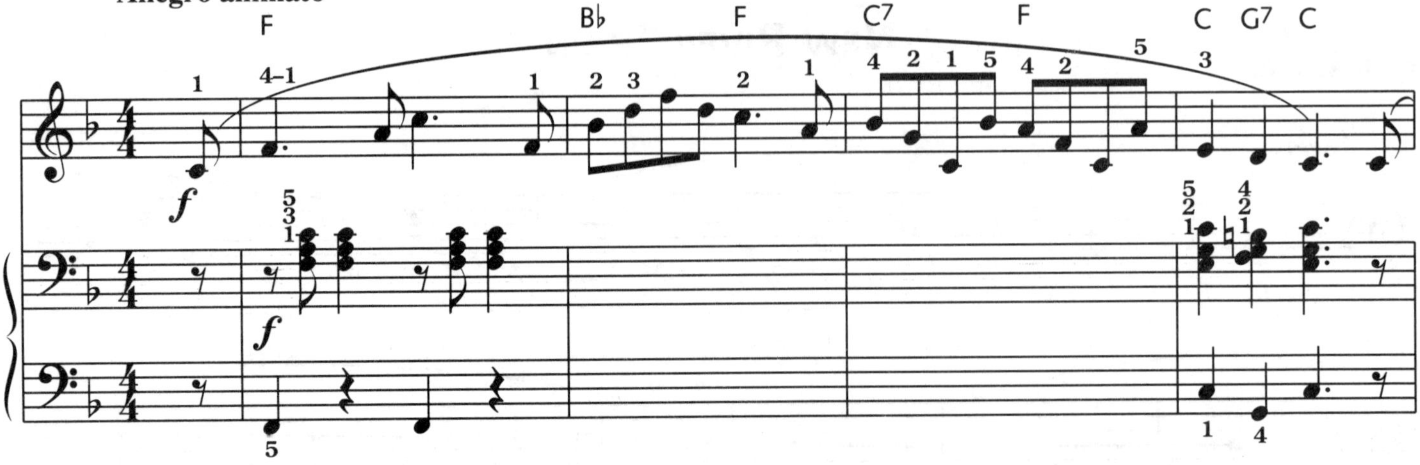

Improvisation from Chord Symbols

Using the chord progressions below, improvise RH melodies while the LH plays the suggested accompaniment style. See page 173 to review the rules for improvisation.

8-35 (71)

1. Block Chord Accompaniment

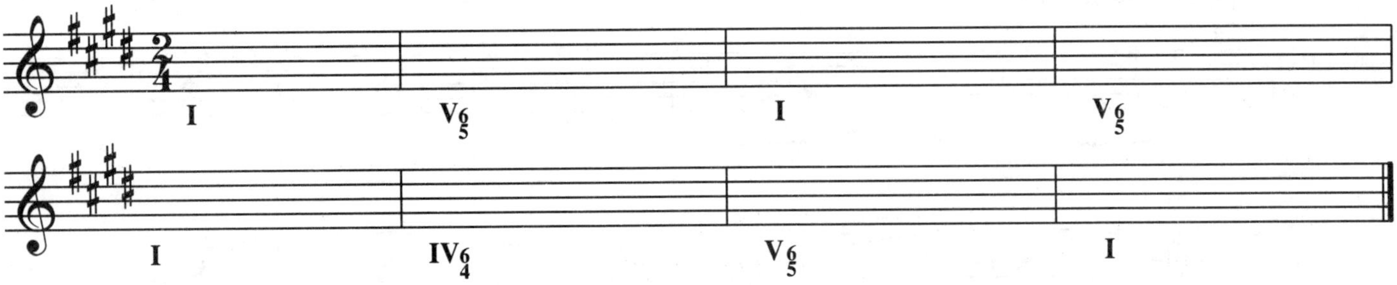

8-36 (72)

2. Waltz Style Accompaniment

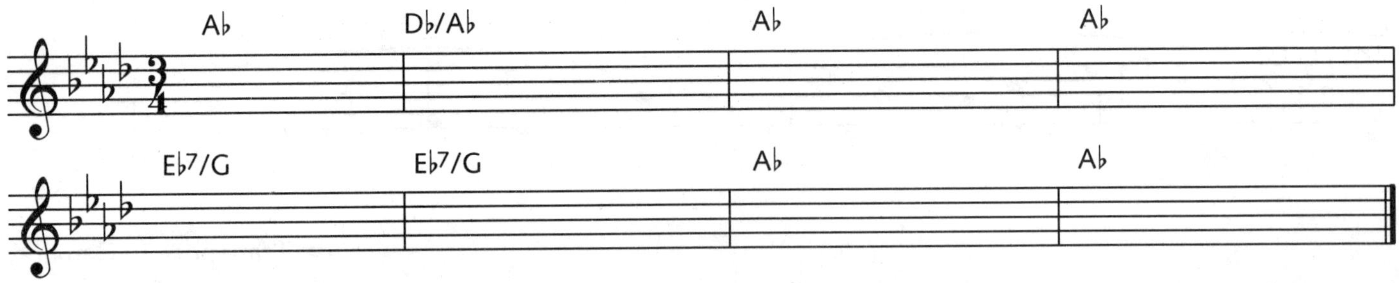

Unit 15

Review Worksheet

Name ______________________ *Date* ______________________

1. In each measure below, draw a whole note above the given note to make the indicated harmonic interval.

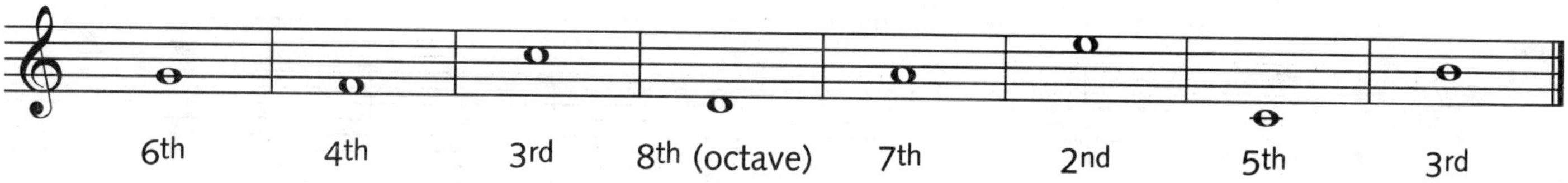

2. Identify the major and minor keys represented by each of the following key signatures by writing the major key and the minor key on the blanks between the staffs.

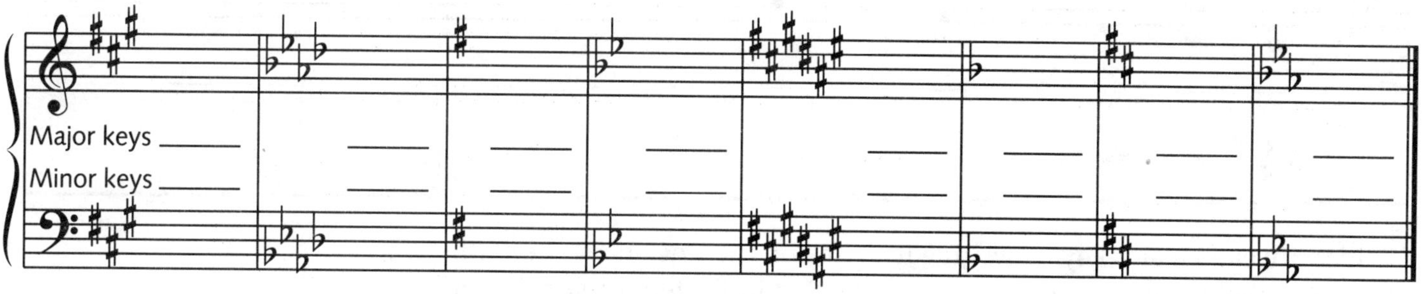

3. Identify the quality of each chord by writing M for major, A for augmented, m for minor or d for diminished on the lines below the staff.

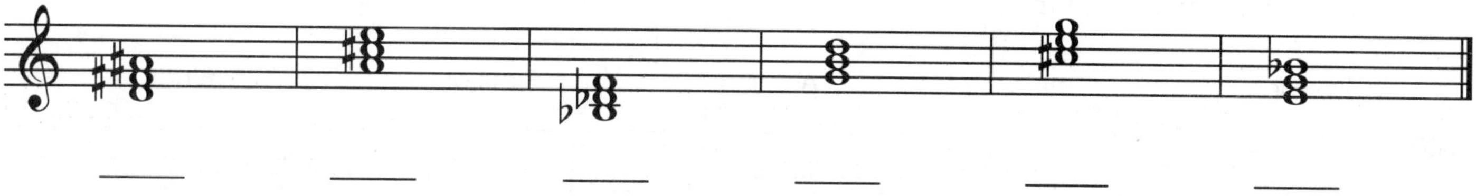

4. Identify each major scale below by writing its name on the indicated line. Write the correct RH fingering on the lines above the staff and the correct LH fingering on the lines below the staff.

___ major

___ major

___ major

___ major

5. Identify each major key by writing its name on the line above the staff. Using whole notes on the staff, write the triad indicated by each Roman numeral.

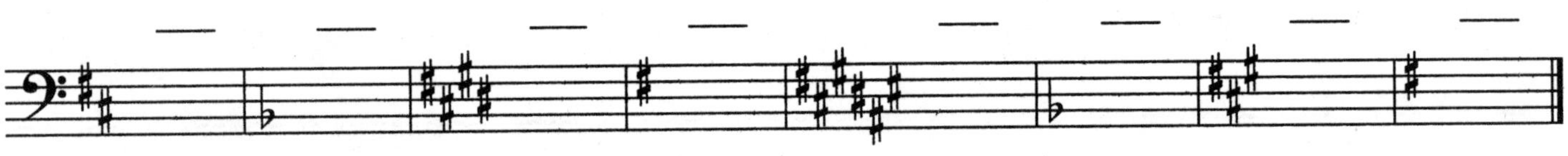

ii IV iii I vi vii° iii vi

6. Using whole notes, write the indicated chord in root position, first inversion and second inversion.

G major F minor A♭ minor E major C♯ minor

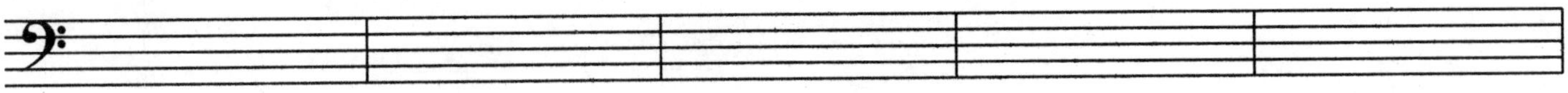

Root 1st 2nd Root 1st 2nd Root 1st 2nd Root 1st 2nd Root 1st 2nd

Unit 16

Primary Chords in Minor Keys

Objectives

Upon completion of this unit the student will be able to:

1. Play i–iv$^6_4$–i–V$^6_5$–i chord progressions in all minor keys.
2. Perform solo repertoire that uses tonic, dominant and subdominant harmonies in minor keys.
3. Sight-read and transpose music that uses tonic, dominant and subdominant chords in minor keys.
4. Harmonize and transpose melodies with tonic, dominant and subdominant chords in minor keys.
5. Improvise melodies over tonic, dominant and subdominant chords in minor keys.
6. Create two-hand accompaniments from chord symbols.
7. Create ensemble parts to accompany solo repertoire.

Assignments

Week of ________

Write your assignments for the week in the space below.

Playing the i–iv$^6_4$–i–V$^6_5$–i Chord Progression

Play the i–iv$^6_4$–i–V$^6_5$–i chord progression exercise:

9-1 (41)

Key of A Minor | Key of D Minor

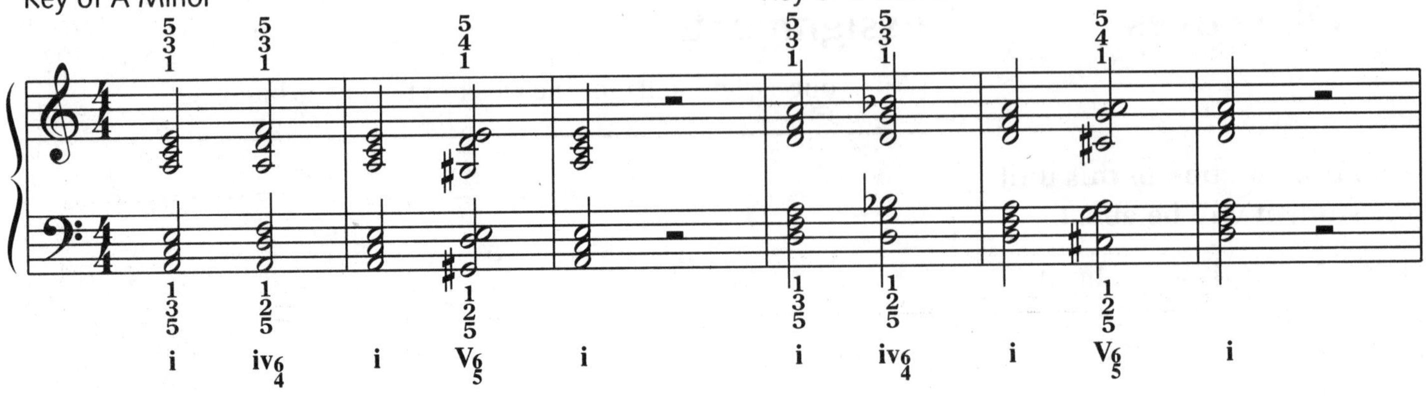

Key of E Minor | Key of A Minor

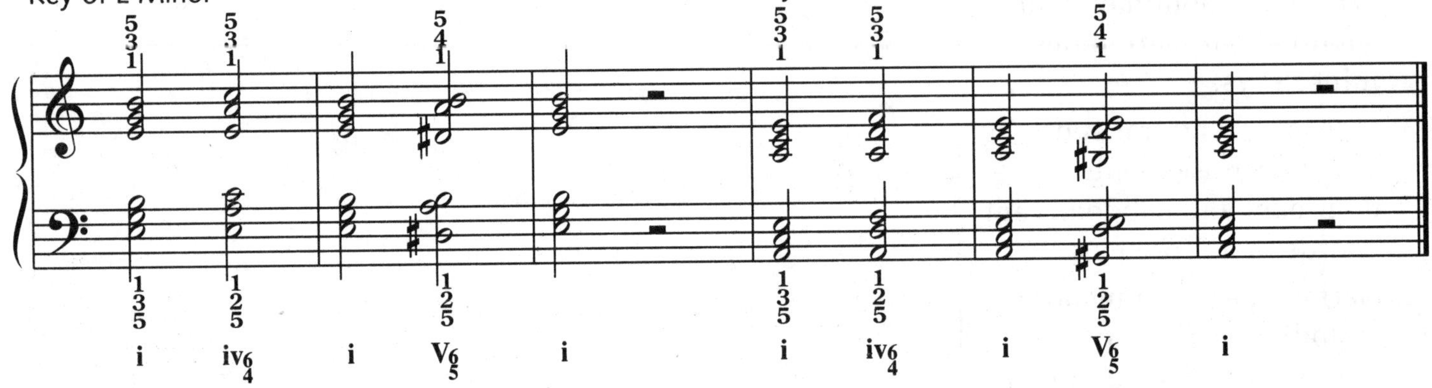

Practice the above exercise in the following minor keys:

9-2 (42) 1. B E F♯ B

9-3 (43) 2. C F G C

9-4 (44) 3. B♭ E♭ F B♭

9-5 (45) 4. C♯ F♯ G♯ C♯

Playing the i–iv–i–V7–i Chord Progression

Play the i–iv–i–V7–i chord progression exercise:

9-6 (46)

Key of A Minor | Key of B♭ Minor

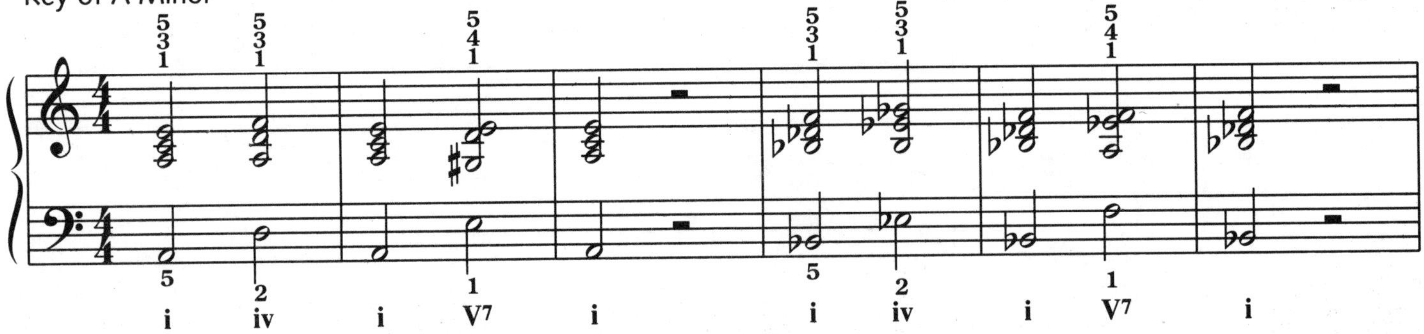

Continue upward by half steps until...

Key of A Minor

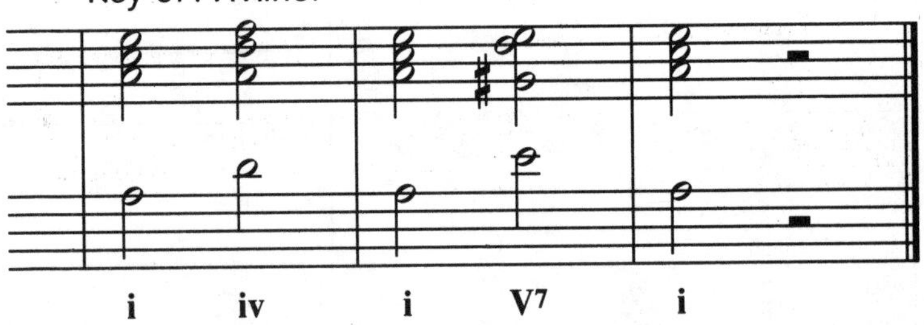

ETUDE

9-7 (47)

Ludvig Schytte
(1848–1909)

Moderato

Ensemble Repertoire

Play the four-part ensemble using the indicated chords to complete parts 2, 3 and 4.

Part 1: Schytte *Etude* (page 189)

Part 2: Descending five-finger patterns (one octave higher than written throughout)

Part 3: Broken chords

Part 4: Roots of chords (one octave lower than written throughout)

9-8 (48)

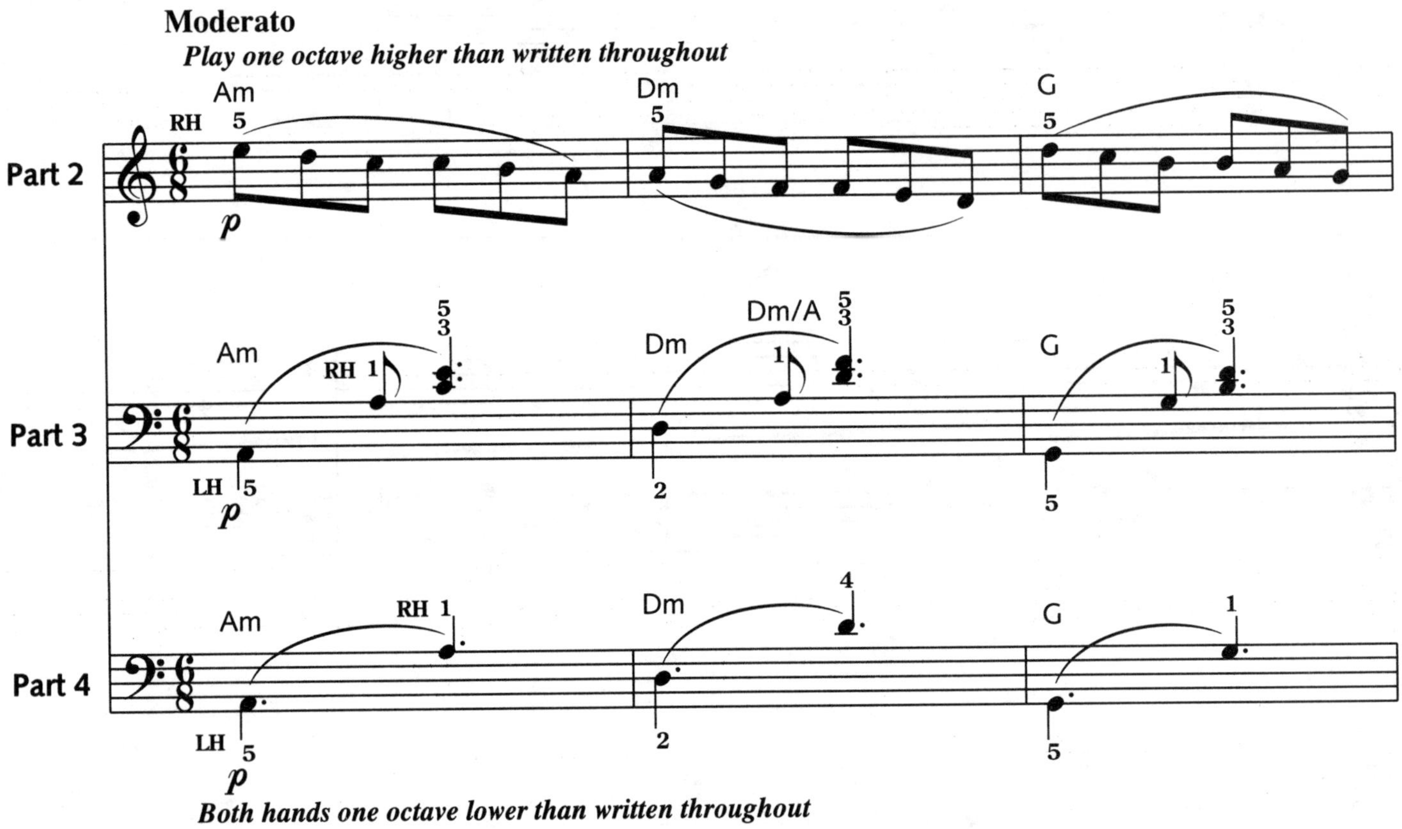

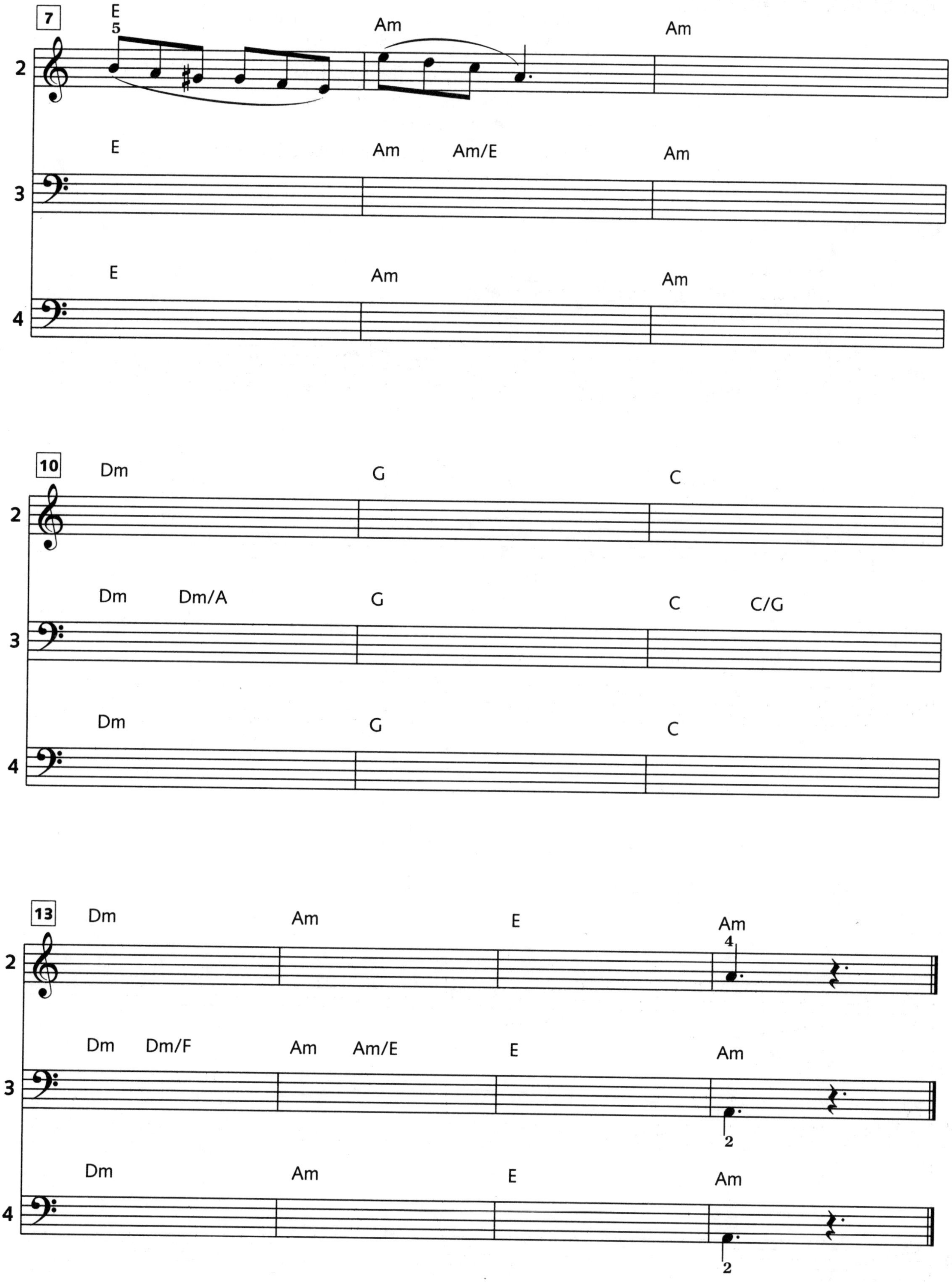
7
E
5
Am
Am
2
E
Am
Am/E
Am
3
E
Am
Am
4
10
Dm
G
C
2
Dm
Dm/A
G
C
C/G
3
Dm
G
C
4
13
Dm
Am
E
Am
4
2
Dm
Dm/F
Am
Am/E
E
Am
3
2
Dm
Am
E
Am
4
2

Reading

Identify the key of each example. Use the indicated tempo, dynamics and articulation as you play these exercises.

Use the following practice directions:

1. Tap RH and count aloud; then LH.
2. Play hands separately and count aloud.
3. Tap hands together and count aloud.
4. Play hands together and count aloud.

9-9 (49)

▶ Transpose to C minor.

9-10 (50)

▶ Transpose to A minor.

9-11 (51)

3.

▶ Transpose to B minor.

9-12 (52)

4.

▶ Transpose to F minor.

Harmonization

1. Harmonize with a broken chord accompaniment.

Broken Chord Accompaniment 

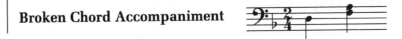

9-13 (53)

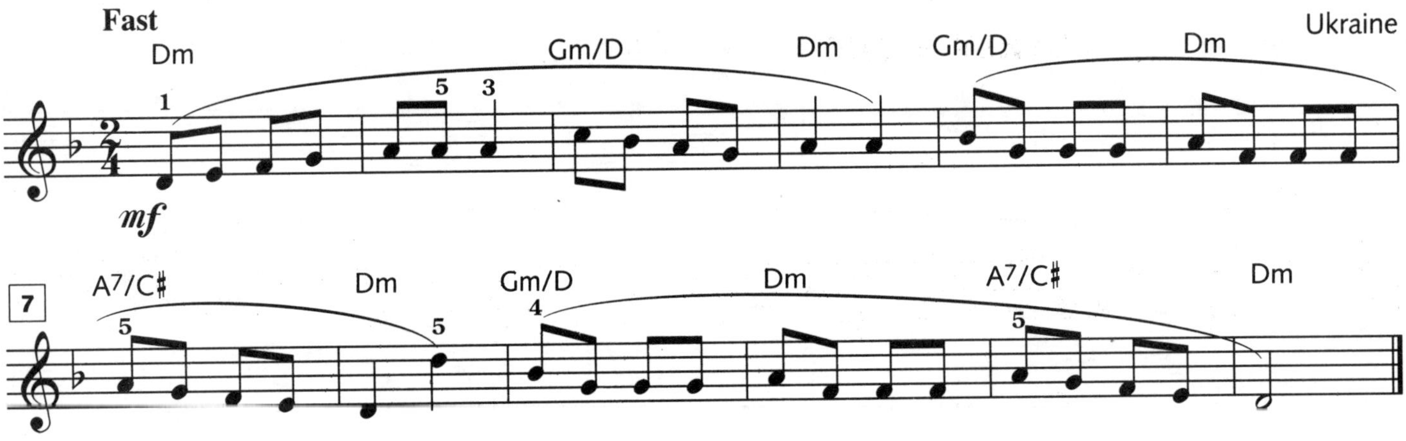

▶ Transpose to E minor.

2. Using i, iv$^6_4$ and V$^6_5$ chords, harmonize with a block chord accompaniment. Write the Roman numeral name of each chord on the line below the staff.

Block Chord Accompaniment 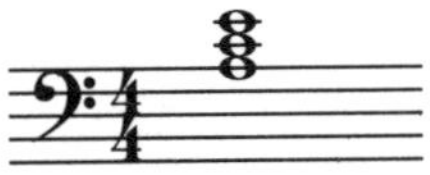

9-14 (54)

Go Down, Moses

▶ Transpose to G minor.

Harmonization with Two-Hand Accompaniment

Using the indicated chords, create a two-hand accompaniment for the following melody by continuing the pattern given in the first measure.

JOSHUA FOUGHT THE BATTLE OF JERICHO

9-15 (55)

Spiritual

Lively

▶ Transpose to D minor.

Improvisation from Chord Symbols

Using the chord progressions below, improvise RH melodies while the LH plays the suggested accompaniment style. (First play the LH chord progression using the suggested accompaniment style and observing the indicated meter.) Notate your favorite improvisation.

Rules for improvisation:

1. When the tonic chord is used, play mostly scale tones 1, 3 and 5 in the melody.
2. When the dominant chord is used, play mostly scale tones 2, 4, 5 and 7 in the melody.
3. When the subdominant chord is used, play mostly scale tones 1, 4 and 6 in the melody.
4. Most improvisations begin and end on tonic.
5. The ear should always be the final guide in determining which melody notes to play.

1. Broken Chord Accompaniment

9-16 (56)

Key of A minor

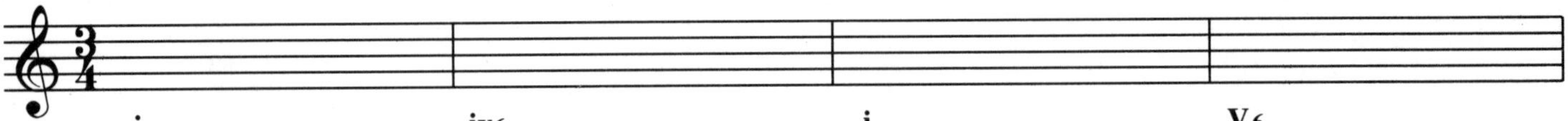

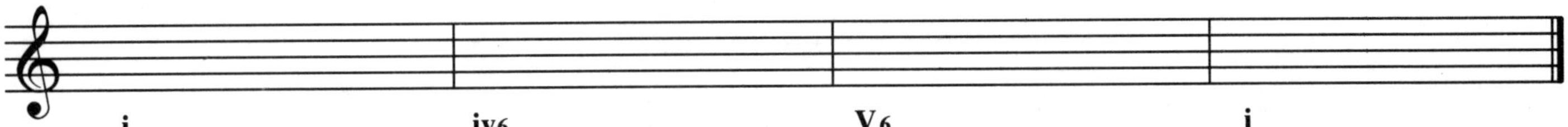

2. Block Chord Accompaniment

9-17 (57)

Key of C minor

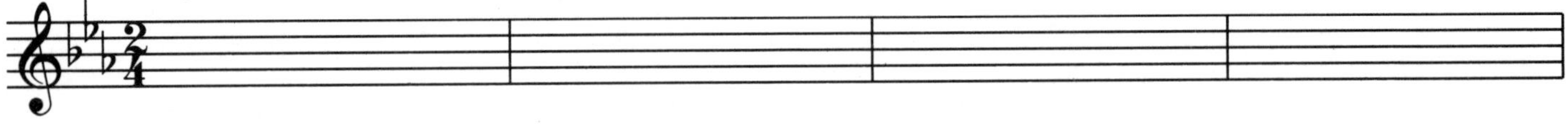

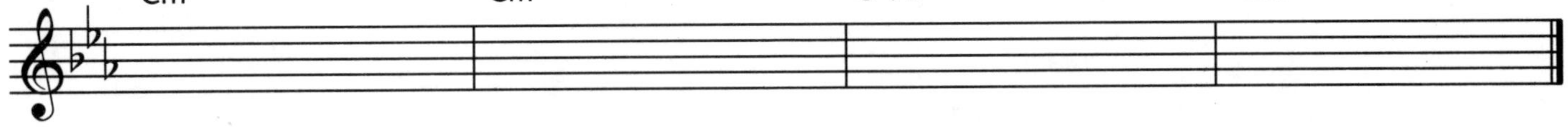

Unit 17

Minor Scales

Objectives

Upon completion of this unit the student will be able to:

1. Play natural, harmonic and melodic minor scales in tetrachord position.
2. Play harmonic minor scales and arpeggios beginning on white keys using traditional fingerings.
3. Perform solo repertoire that uses minor scale and arpeggio patterns.
4. Sight-read and transpose music that uses minor scale patterns.
5. Harmonize and transpose melodies with tonic, dominant and subdominant chords in minor keys.
6. Create two-hand accompaniments from chord symbols.

Assignments

Week of ________

Write your assignments for the week in the space below.

Minor Scales

Every major key has a **relative minor key** that has the same key signature. The relative minor begins on the 6th tone of the major scale.

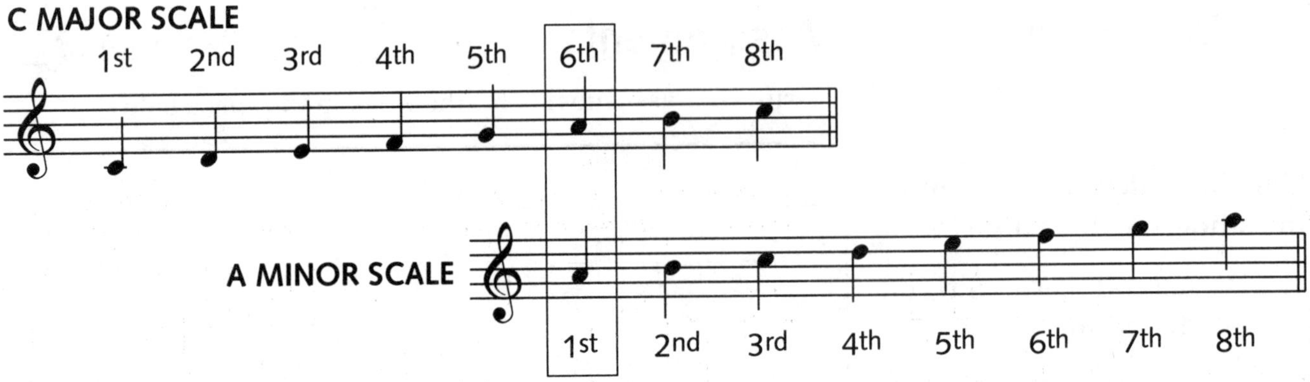

The Key of A Minor (Relative to C Major)

There are three kinds of minor scales: the **natural**, the **harmonic** and the **melodic.** The harmonic minor is the most frequently used of the three.

Practice each of the following scales using tetrachord position. Transpose to E, D, B and G minor.

1. The Natural Minor Scale

This scale uses *only* the tones of the relative major scale.

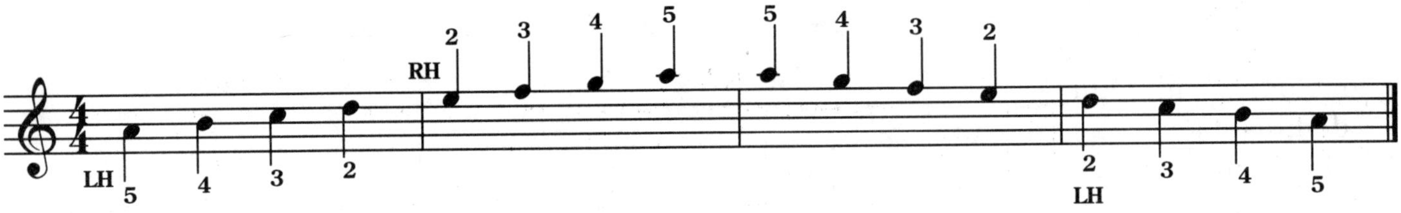

2. The Harmonic Minor Scale

The 7th tone (G) is raised one half step, ascending *and* descending.

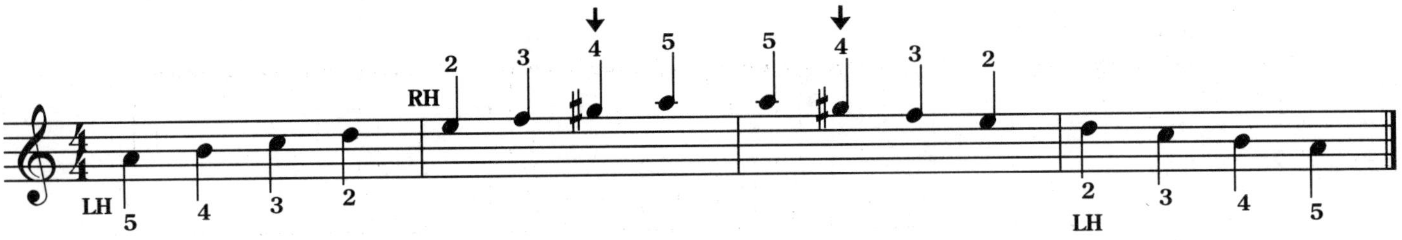

3. The Melodic Minor Scale

In the ascending scale, the 6th (F) and 7th (G) tones are raised one half step. The descending scale is the same as the natural minor.

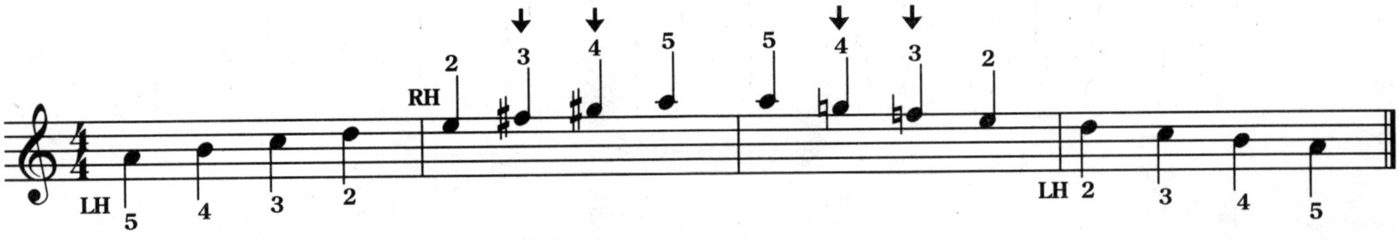

■ **Written Exercise:**
Write letter names on the correct keys to form each harmonic minor scale.

Then play using tetrachord position.

Example:

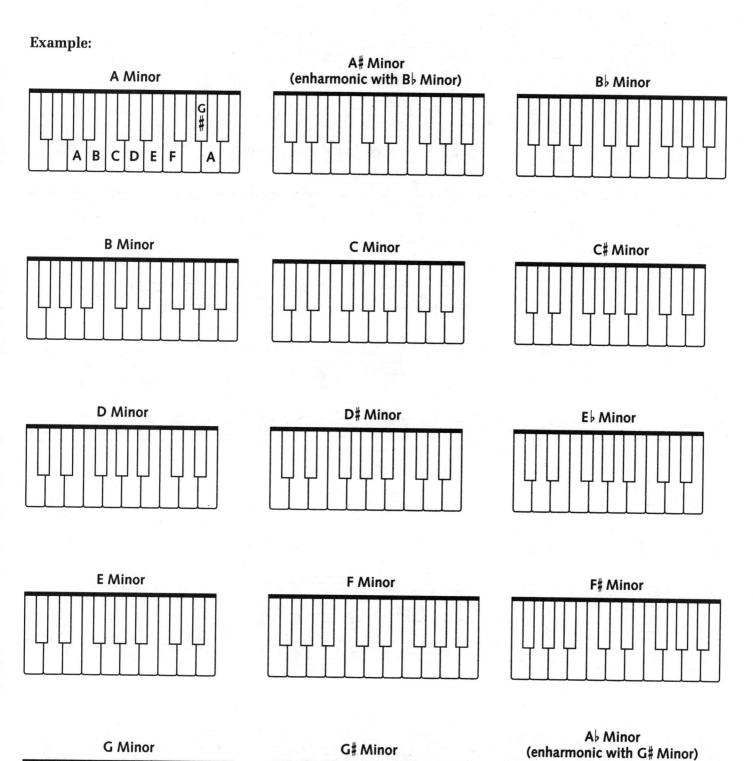

A Minor

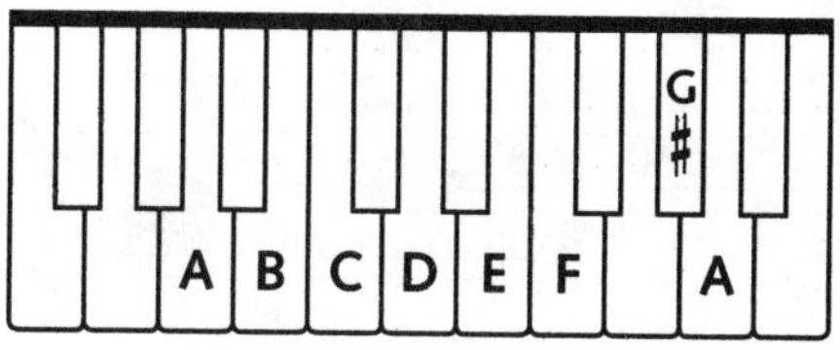

A♯ Minor
(enharmonic with B♭ Minor)

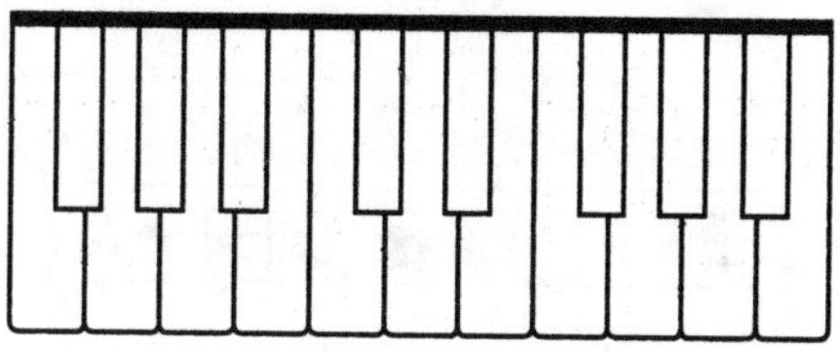

B♭ Minor

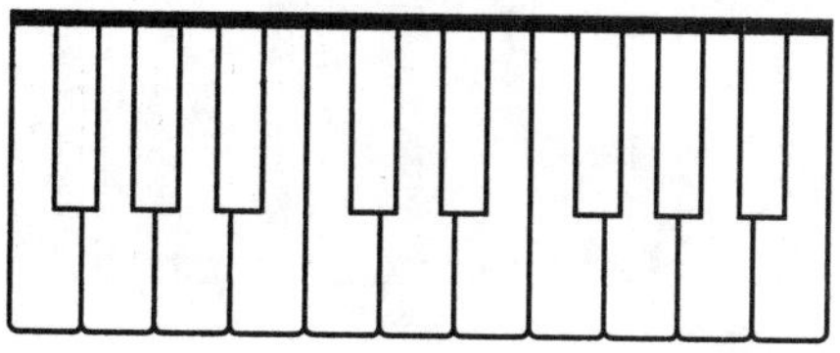

B Minor

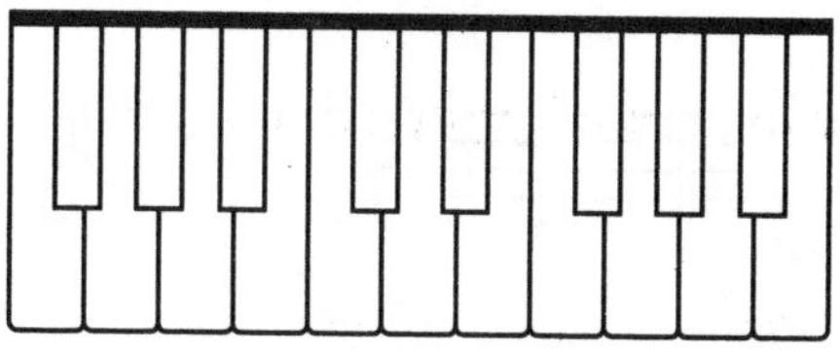

C Minor

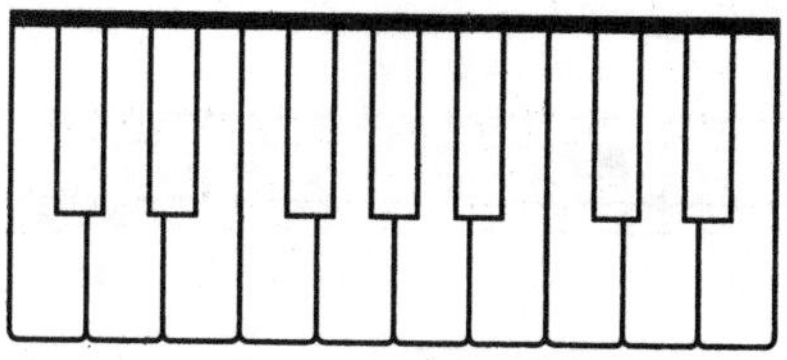

C♯ Minor

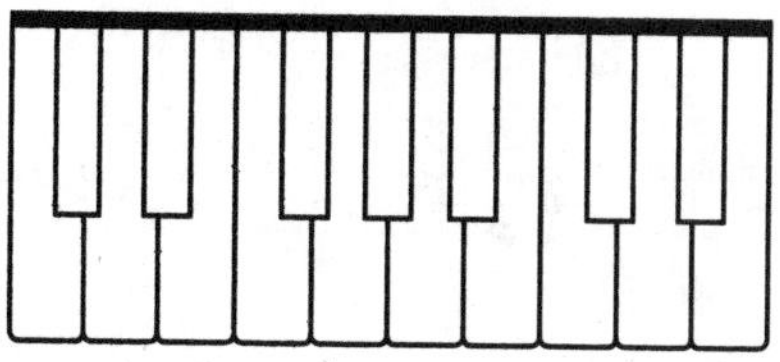

D Minor

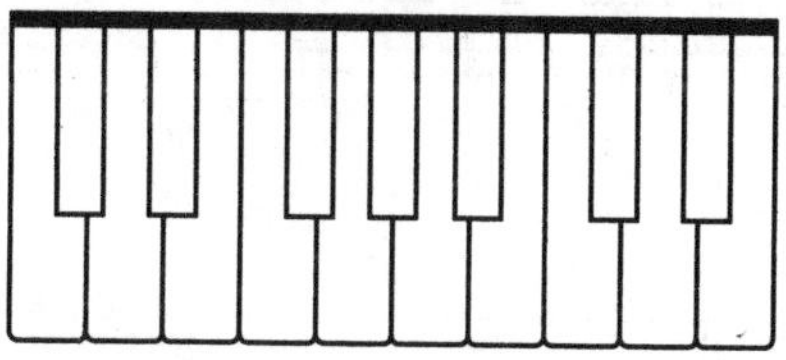

D♯ Minor

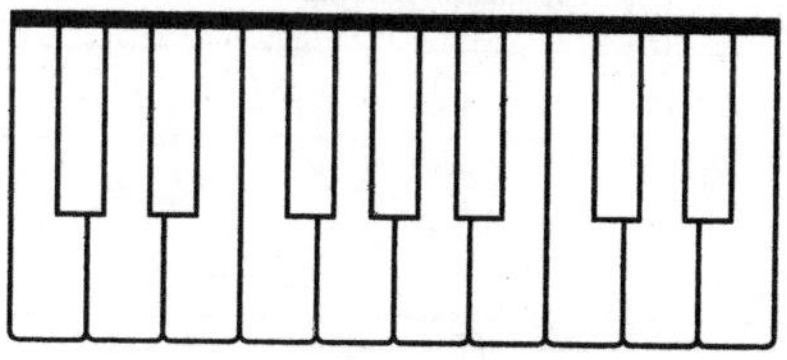

E♭ Minor

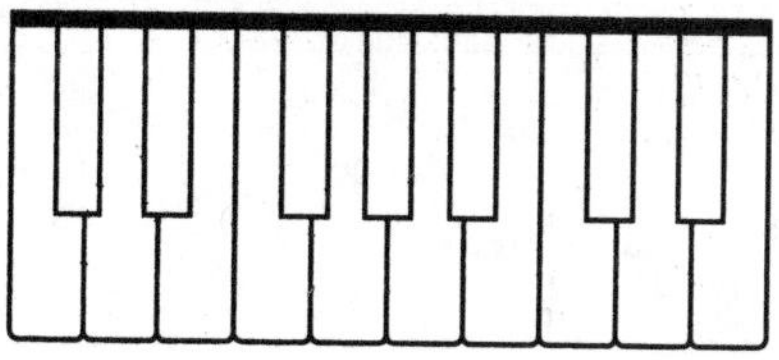

E Minor

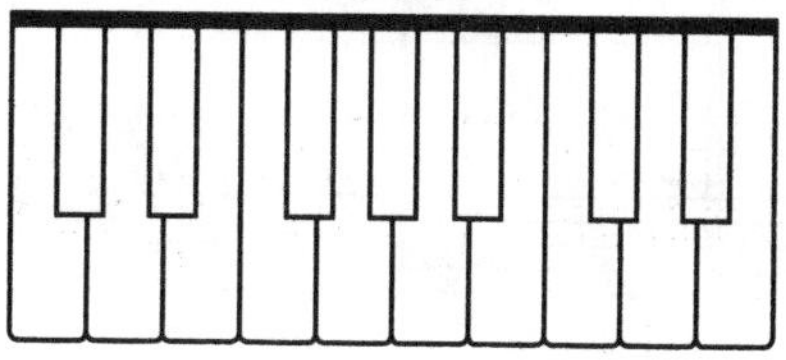

F Minor

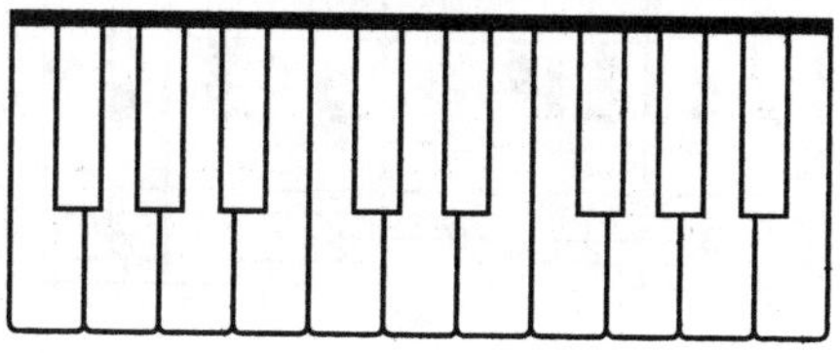

F♯ Minor

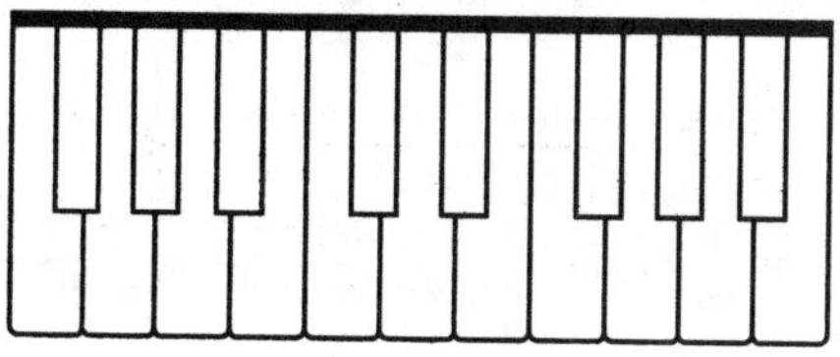

G Minor

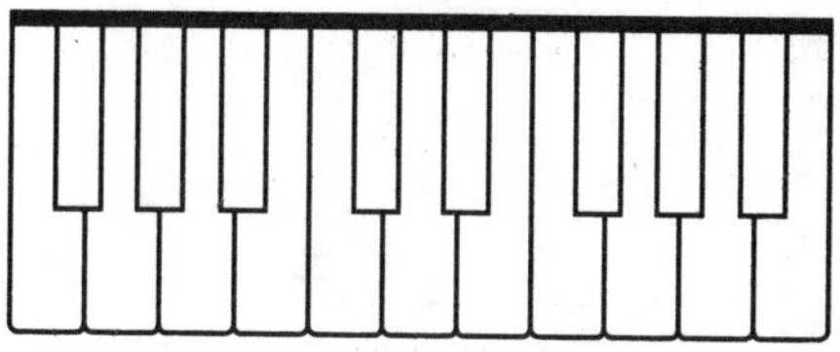

G♯ Minor

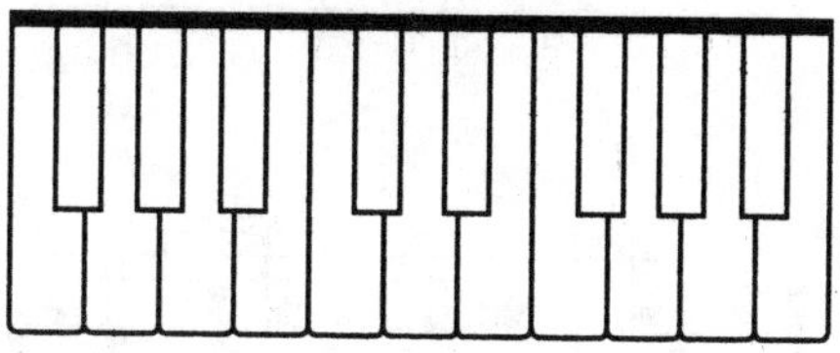

A♭ Minor
(enharmonic with G♯ Minor)

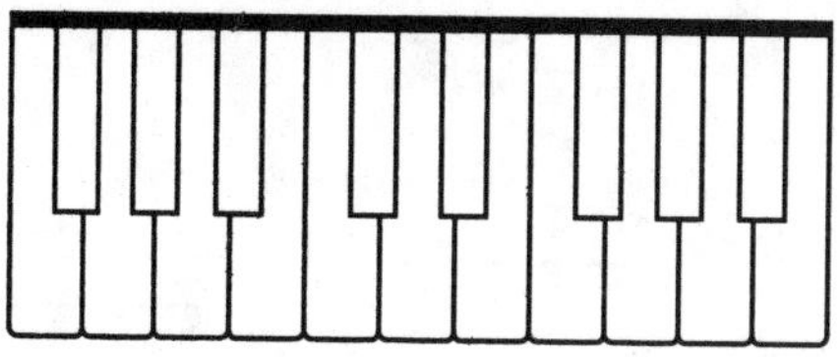

Playing Harmonic Minor Tetrachord Scales in Sharp Keys

Play the following harmonic minor scales in tetrachord position while the teacher plays an accompaniment.

🔊 **9-18 (58)**

Moderate waltz tempo

A Minor

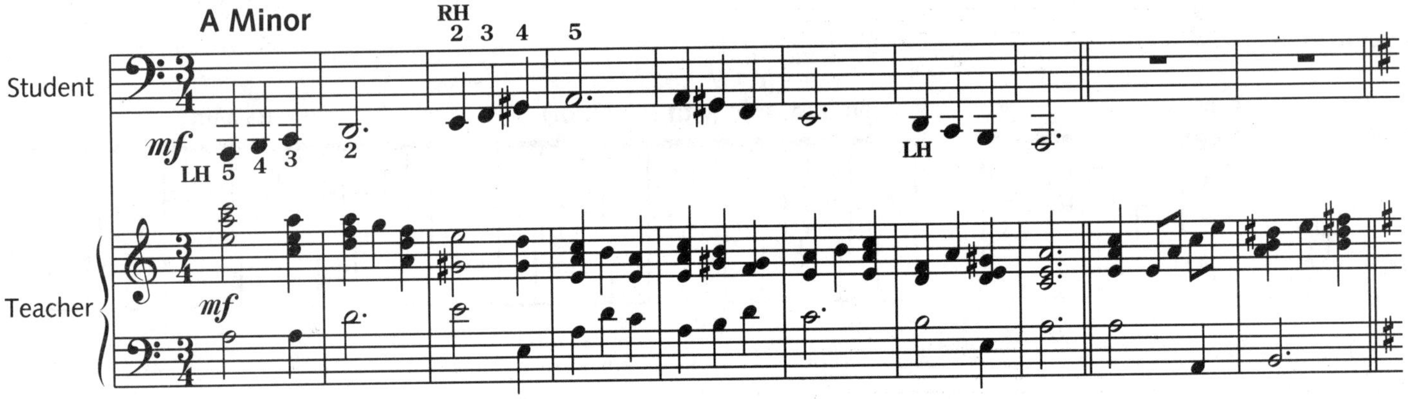

11 **E Minor**

21 **B Minor**

31 **F♯ Minor**

41 C♯ Minor

51 G♯ Minor

61 D♯ Minor

71 A♯ Minor

Playing Harmonic Minor Tetrachord Scales in Flat Keys

Play the following harmonic minor scales in tetrachord position while the teacher plays an accompaniment.

9-19 (59)

Moderate waltz tempo

A♭ Minor

11 E♭ Minor

21 B♭ Minor

31 F Minor

41 **C Minor**

51 **G Minor**

D Minor

61

A Minor

71

Playing Harmonic Minor Scales and Arpeggios

Build each scale in tetrachord position, then practice hands separately:

1. The blocked scale as written.
2. The scale as written.
3. The arpeggio as written.

A Minor

1.

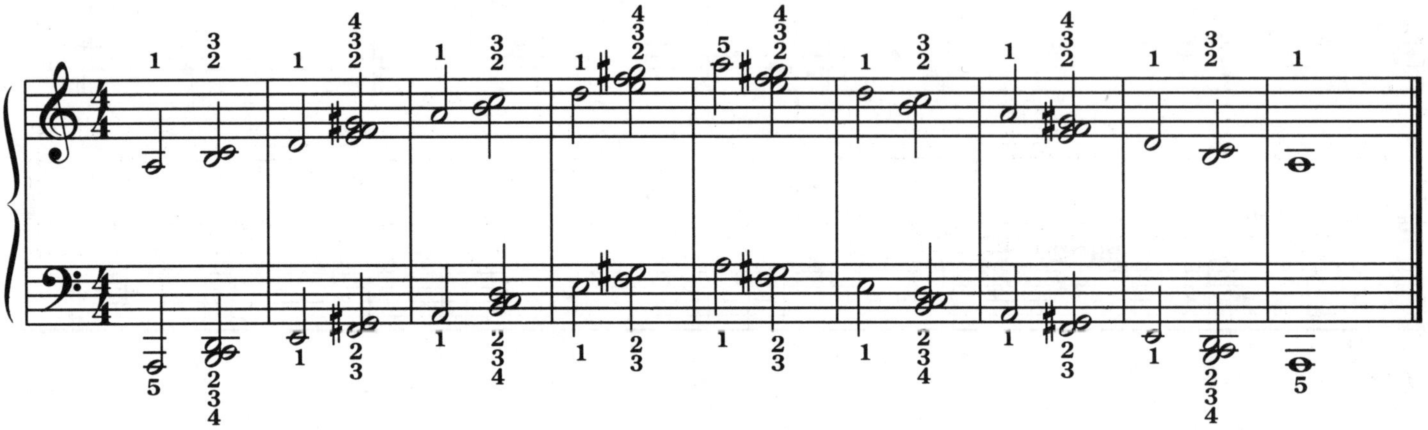

9-20 (60)

2.

9-21 (61)

3.

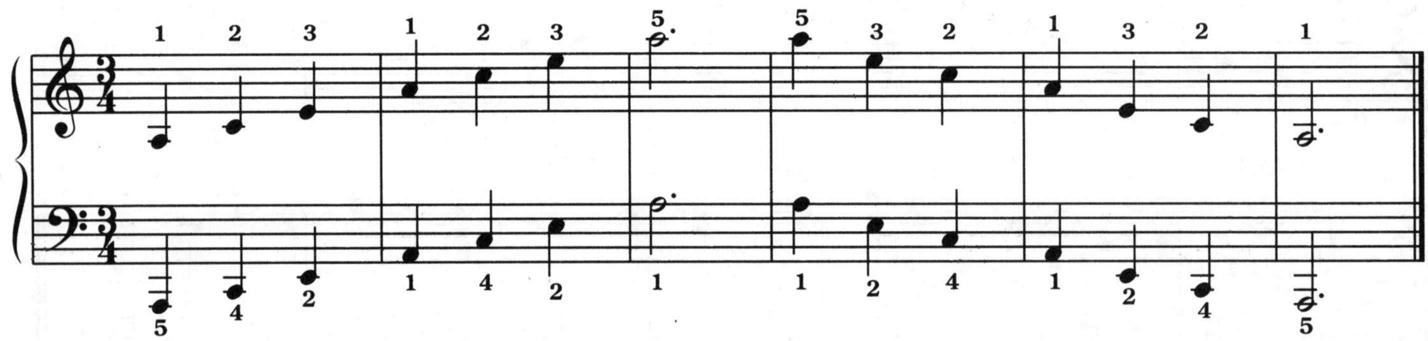

E Minor

🔊 9-22 (62)

🔊 9-23 (63)

B Minor

🔊 9-24 (64)

🔊 9-25 (65)

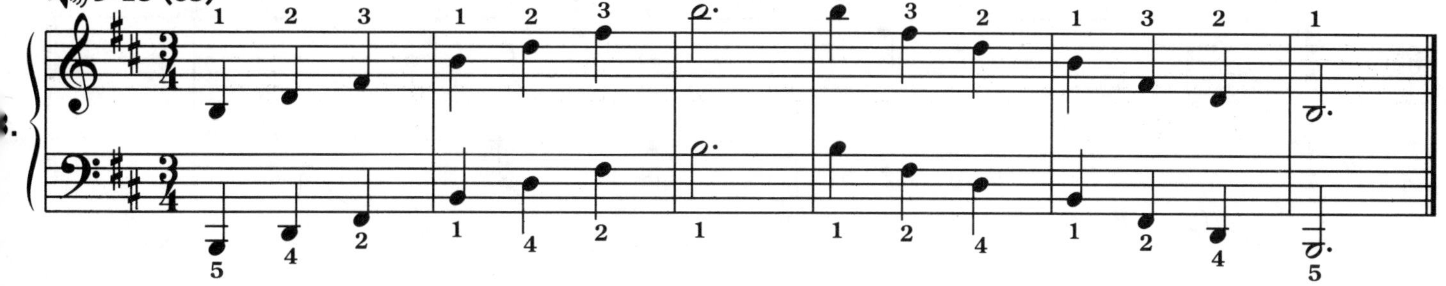

Playing Harmonic Minor Scales and Arpeggios (continued)

D Minor

1. 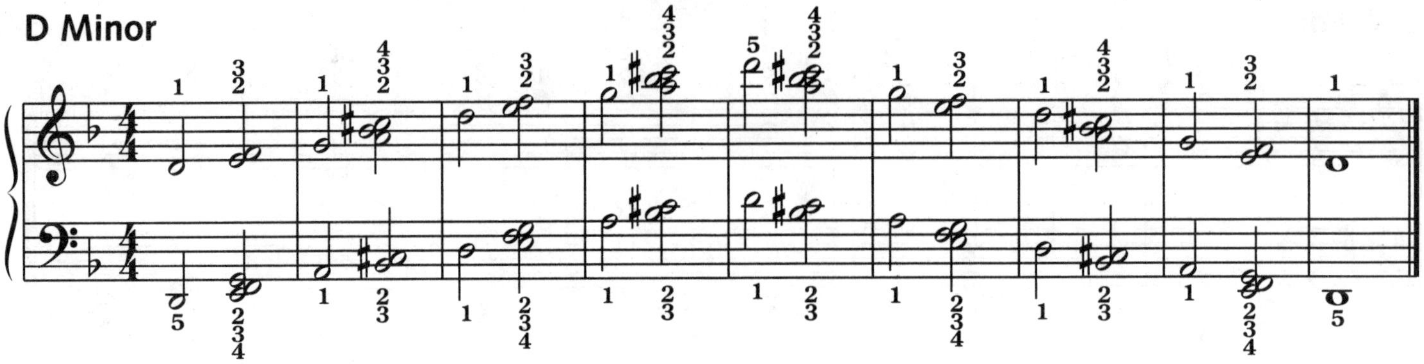

9-26 (66)

2. 

9-27 (67)

3. 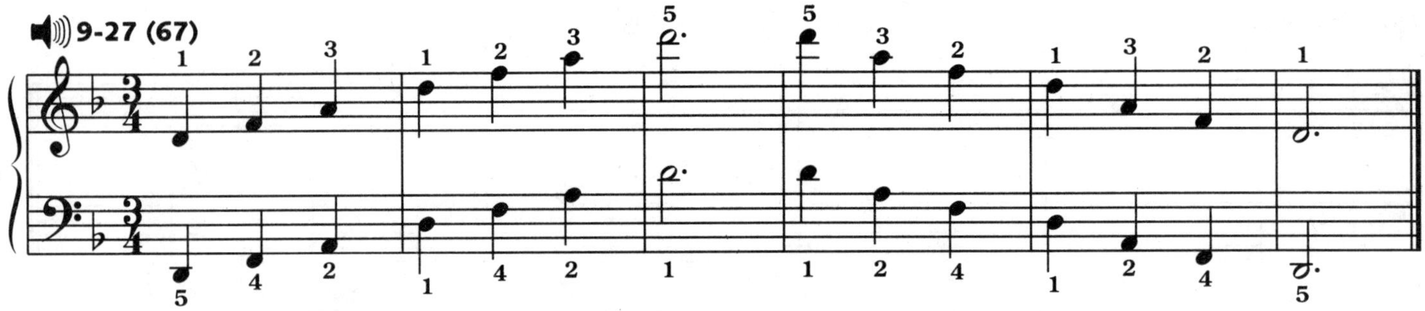

G Minor

1. 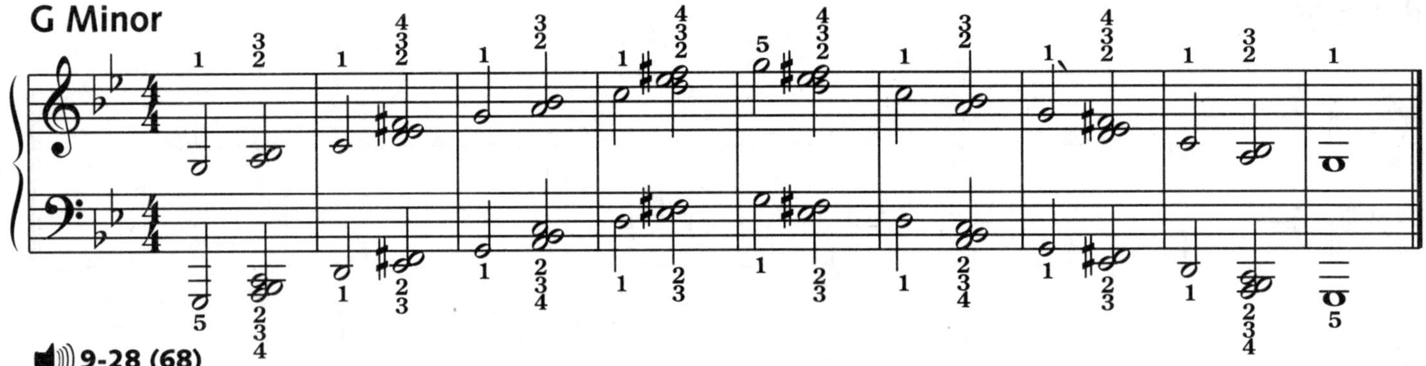

9-28 (68)

2. 

9-29 (69)

3. 

C Minor

1.

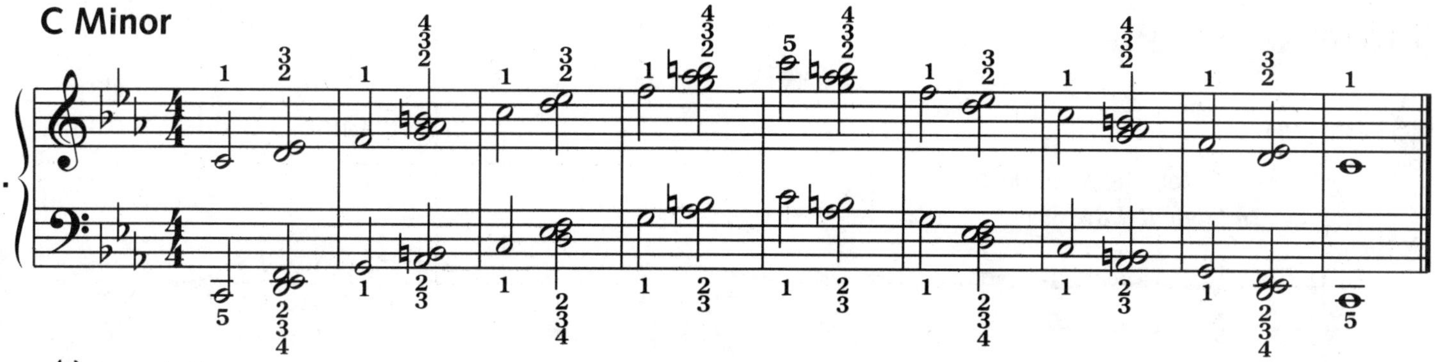

🔊 9-30 (70)

2.

🔊 9-31 (71)

3.

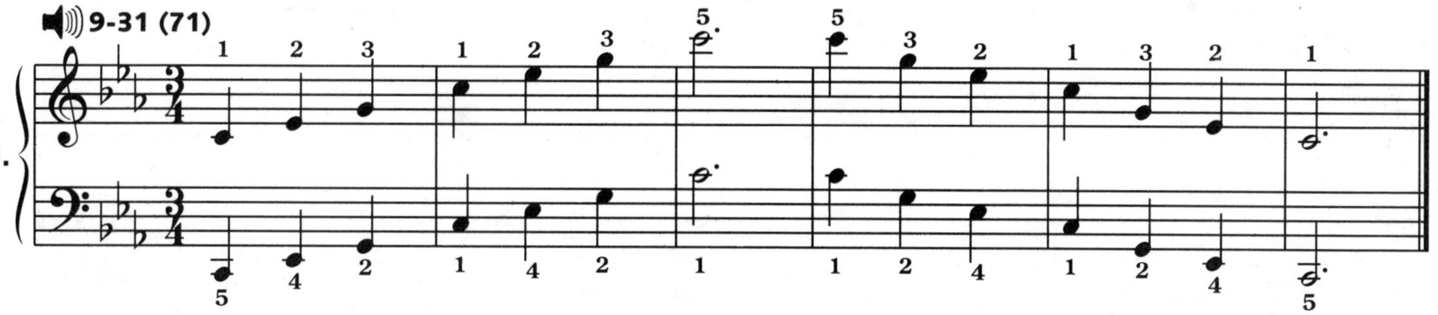

F Minor

1.

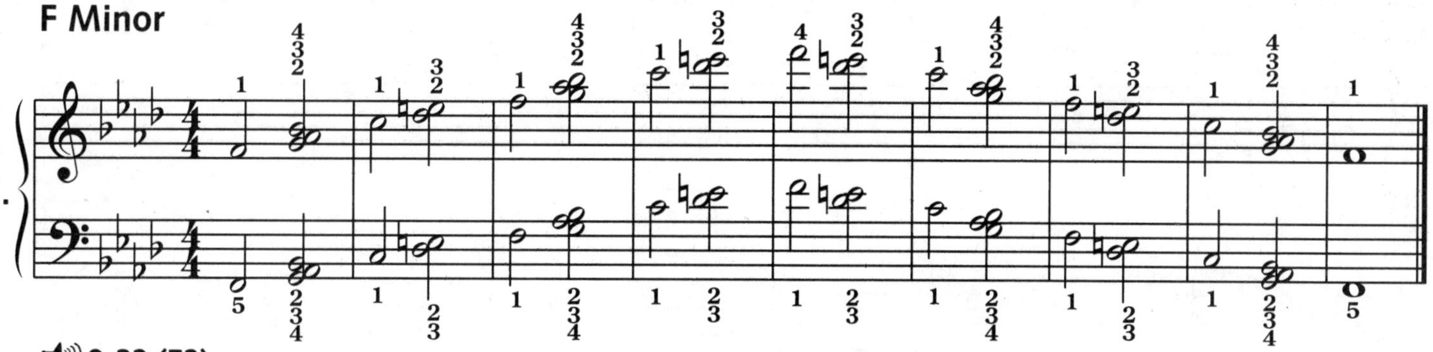

🔊 9-32 (72)

2.

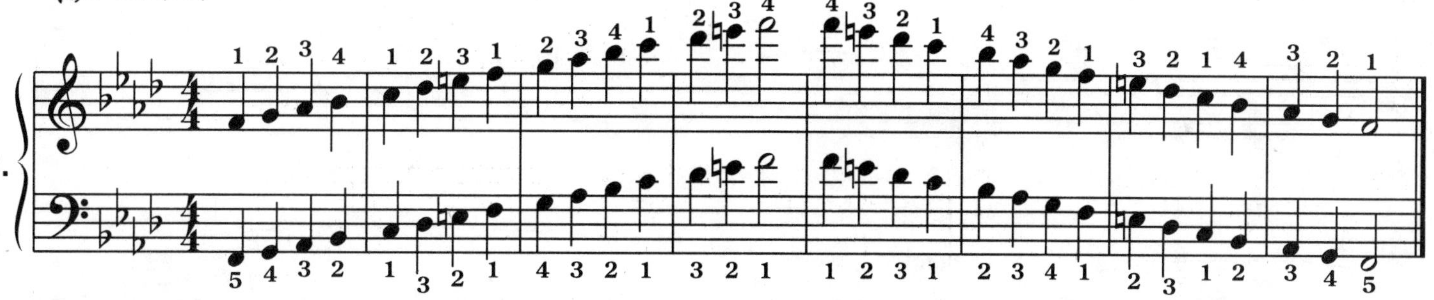

🔊 9-33 (73)

3.

Solo Repertoire

Bewildered

9-34 (74)

D.C. (da capo) al CODA means repeat from the beginning to ⊕, then skip to Coda (an added ending).

Margaret Goldston

"Bewildered" from MOODS, Book 1, by Margaret Goldston

Reading

Identify the key of each example. Use the indicated tempo, dynamics and articulation as you play these exercises.

Use the following practice directions:

1. Tap RH and count aloud; then LH.
2. Play hands separately and count aloud.
3. Tap hands together and count aloud.
4. Play hands together and count aloud.

9-35 (75)

Moderato

▶ Transpose to A minor.

9-36 (76)

Adagio

▶ Transpose to D minor.

9-37 (77)

Allegro

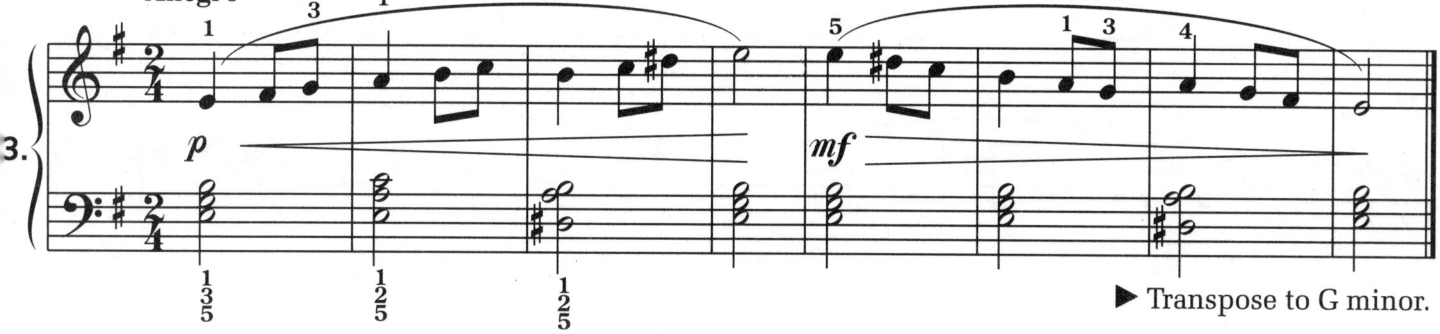

▶ Transpose to G minor.

Harmonization

1. Harmonize with a block chord accompaniment.

Block Chord Accompaniment 

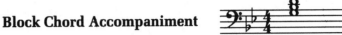

9-38 (78)

Russia

Moderato

▶ Transpose to F minor.

2. Using i, iv^6_4 and V^6_5 chords, harmonize with a waltz style accompaniment. Write the Roman numeral name of each chord on the line below the staff.

Waltz Style Accompaniment 

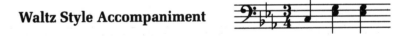

Raisins and Almonds

9-39 (79)

Israel

Allegro moderato

▶ Transpose to D minor.

Harmonization with Two-Hand Accompaniment

Using the indicated chords, create a two-hand accompaniment for the following melody by continuing the pattern given in the first two measures.

WAVES OF THE DANUBE

9-40 (80)

Ion Ivanovici
(1845–1902)

Unit 18

Triads of the Key in Minor

Objectives

Upon completion of this unit the student will be able to:

1. Build a triad of the key on any note of the harmonic minor scale.
2. Perform solo repertoire that uses triads of the key in minor keys.
3. Sight-read and transpose music that uses triads of the key in minor keys.
4. Harmonize minor melodies with roots of chords and root-position triads of the key.
5. Improvise scale melodies over roots of chords and root-position triads of the key in minor keys.
6. Create a four-part ensemble from chord symbols.

Assignments

Week of ________

Write your assignments for the week in the space below.

Playing Triads of the Key in Harmonic Minor

Triads may be built on any note of any scale. The sharps or flats in the key signature, as well as the raised seventh in harmonic minor, must be used when playing these triads. Triads of the key are identified by Roman numerals.

Play triads of the key in A harmonic minor. Note the quality of each chord.

Play with RH:

10-1 (35)

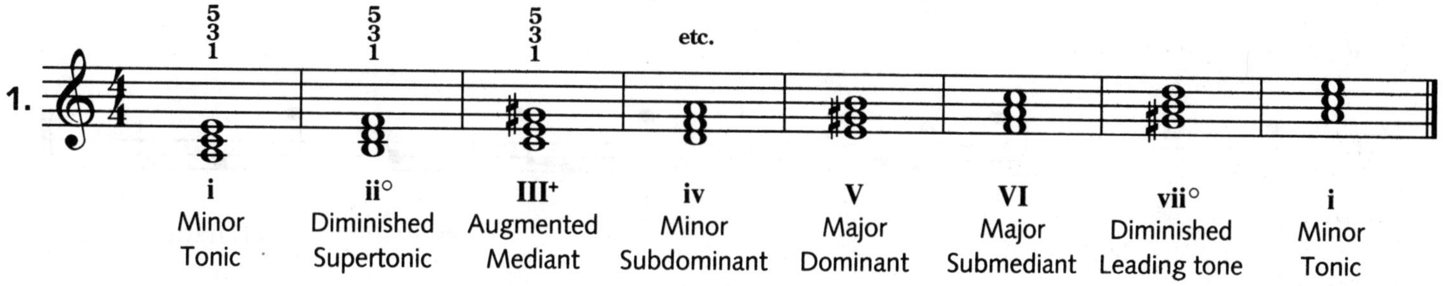

▶ Transpose to D harmonic minor and E harmonic minor.

Play with LH:

10-1 (35)

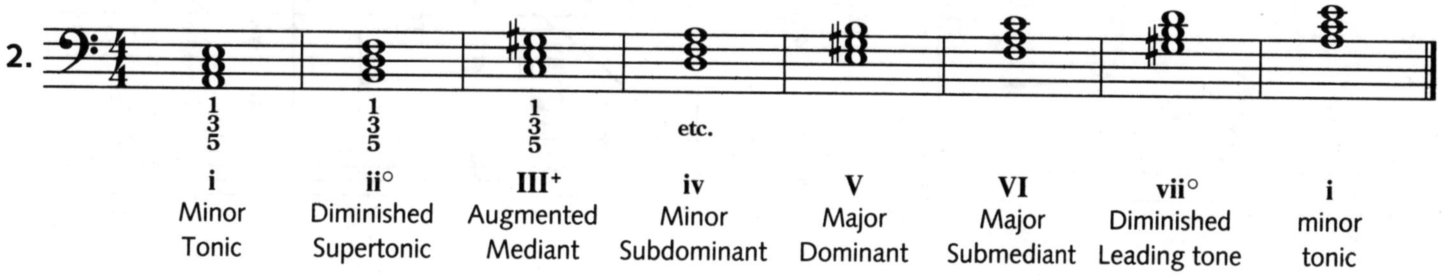

▶ Transpose to D harmonic minor and E harmonic minor.

Technique

10-2 (36)

Andante

1.

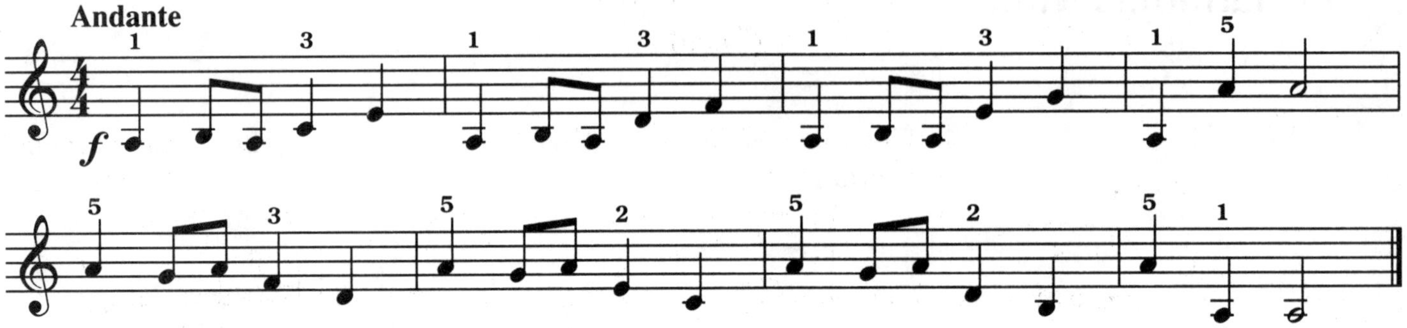

▶ Transpose to D natural minor.

10-2 (36)

Andante

2.

▶ Transpose to E natural minor.

10-3 (37)

Moderato

3.

▶ Transpose to A major.

10-4 (38)

Moderato

4.

▶ Transpose to G minor.

Solo Repertoire

Gypsy Dance
(Trio)

10-5 (39)

Franz Joseph Haydn
(1732–1809)

Reading

Identify the key of each example. Use the indicated tempo, dynamics and articulation as you play these exercises.
Use the following practice directions:

1. Tap RH and count aloud; then LH.
2. Play hands separately and count aloud.
3. Tap hands together and count aloud.
4. Play hands together and count aloud.

10-6 (40)

▶ Transpose to G minor.

10-7 (41)

▶ Transpose to E minor.

10-8 (42)

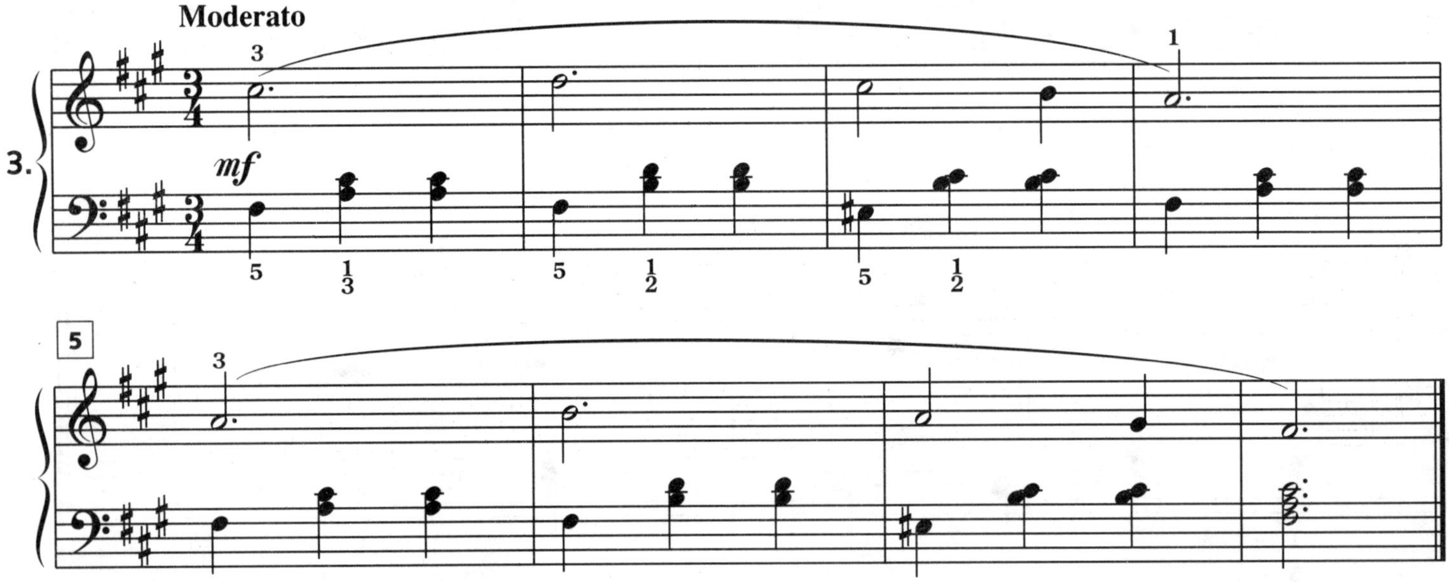

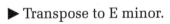

▶ Transpose to F minor.

Harmonization

Harmonize each melody below in two ways:

- Using the root of the indicated triads.
- Using the indicated root-position triads.

10-9 (43)

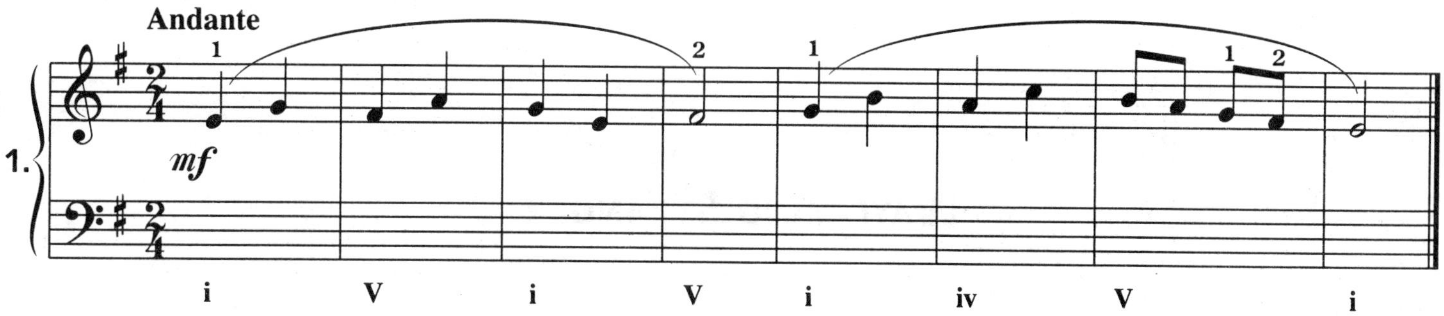

▶ Transpose to D minor.

10-10 (44)

▶ Transpose to B minor.

Harmonize the following melody using the indicated chords with a broken chord accompaniment style.

Broken Chord Accompaniment 

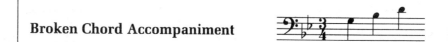

10-11 (45)

▶ Transpose to F minor.

Ensemble Repertoire

Play the four-part ensemble using the indicated chords to complete parts 2, 3 and 4.

Part 1: Melody
Part 2: Descending broken chords (one octave higher than written throughout)
Part 3: Two-Hand Accompaniment
Part 4: Roots of chords (one octave lower than written throughout)

WAYFARING STRANGER

10-12 (46)

United States

5
Dm Am F Dm

11
F Em C Am Dm Am

Improvisation from Chord Symbols

Improvise a RH melody in A natural minor for the chord progression below while the LH plays the root of the indicated chords. Begin and end each phrase with the given notes. Notate your favorite improvisation.

10-13 (47)

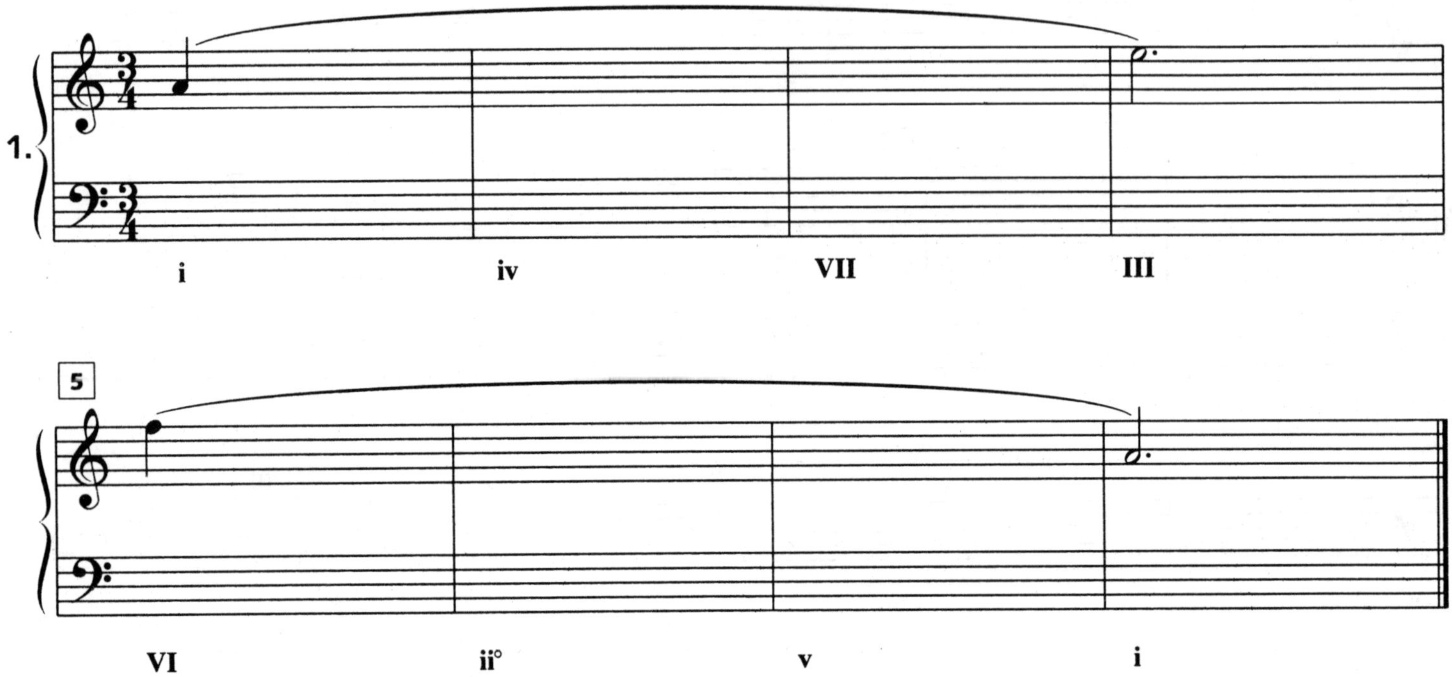

Continue the RH melodic sequence in A natural minor for the chord progression below while the LH plays the root-position chords.

10-14 (48)

Review Worksheet

Name ____________________ *Date* ____________________

1. Identify each harmonic minor scale below by writing its name on the indicated line. Write the correct RH fingering on the lines above the staff and the correct LH fingering on the lines below the staff.

____ Harmonic Minor Scale

____ Harmonic Minor Scale

____ Harmonic Minor Scale

____ Harmonic Minor Scale

2. Identify each minor key by writing its name on the line above the staff. Write the Roman numeral name for each triad in that key on the line below the staff.

3. Identify each minor key signature below by writing its name in the blank. Following the key signature, write the notes for each harmonic minor scale on the staff, using whole notes. Write the sharps or flats from the key signature in front of the appropriate notes.

____ Harmonic Minor Scale

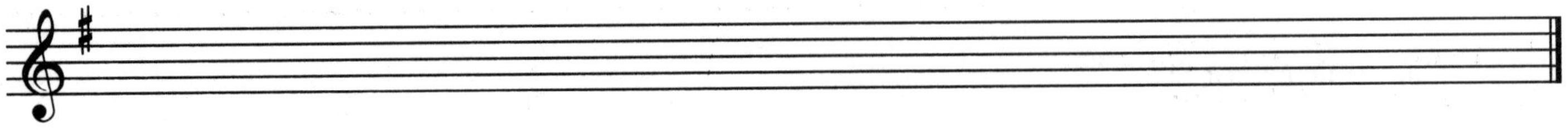

____ Harmonic Minor Scale

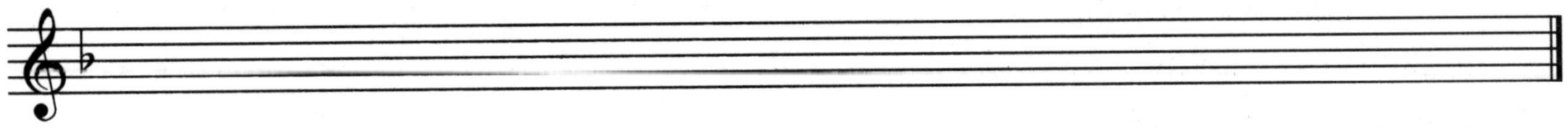

____ Harmonic Minor Scale

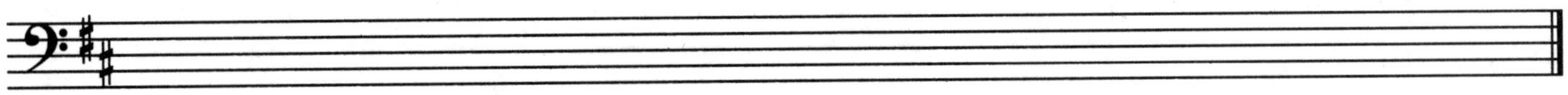

____ Harmonic Minor Scale

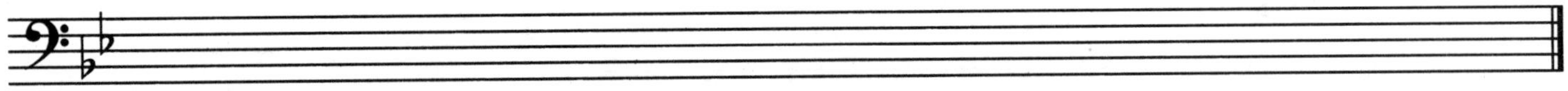

4. Identify each minor key by writing its name on the line above the staff. Using whole notes, write the triad in harmonic minor indicated by each Roman numeral.

Unit 19

The ii Chord

Objectives

Upon completion of this unit the student will be able to:

1. Play I–ii_6–$I_{6\atop 4}$–V^7–I chord progressions in all major and minor keys.
2. Perform solo repertoire that uses supertonic harmonies.
3. Sight-read and transpose music that uses supertonic chords.
4. Harmonize and transpose melodies with supertonic chords.
5. Create two-hand accompaniments from chord symbols.

Assignments

Week of ________

Write your assignments for the week in the space below.

The ii Chord

The ii chord (supertonic) is often substituted for the IV chord since they have two notes in common. It is frequently used in the first inversion (ii_6).

Key of C major:

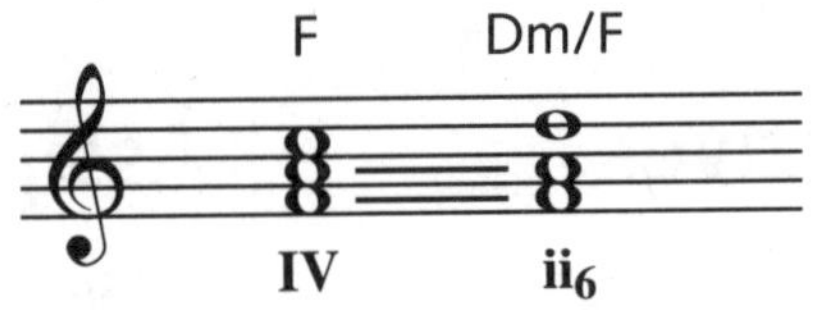

In major keys, the ii chord is a minor triad.

Key of C major:

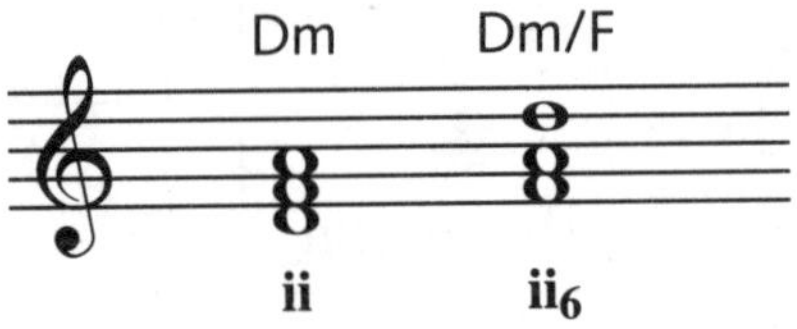

In natural and harmonic minor keys, the ii° chord is a diminished triad.

Key of A minor:

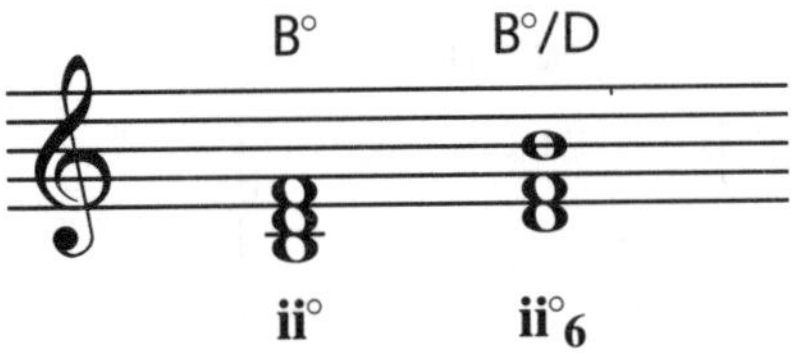

Play the following chord progressions hands separately.

1.

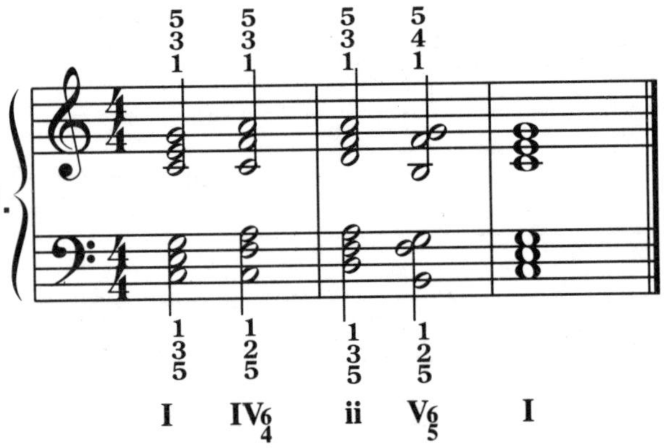

2.

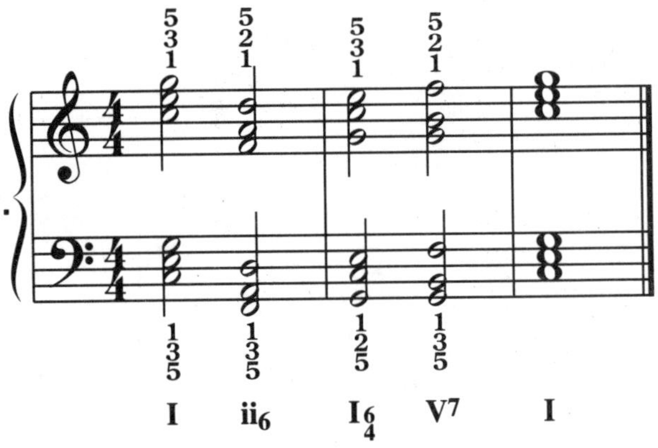

▶ Transpose each progression to G major, F major, A harmonic minor and C harmonic minor.

Playing the I–ii$_6$–I$^6_4$–V7–I Chord Progression

Play the **I–ii$_6$–I$^6_4$–V^7–I** chord progression exercise:

10-15 (49)

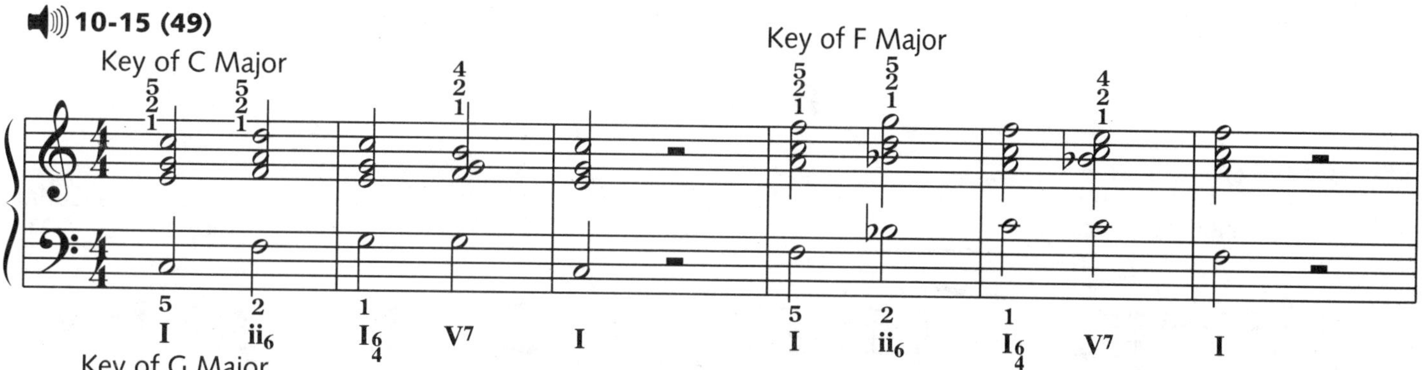

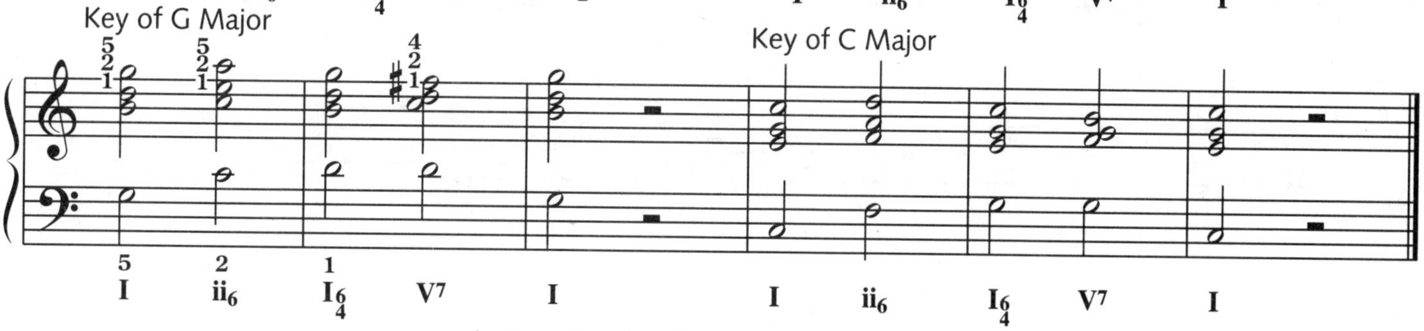

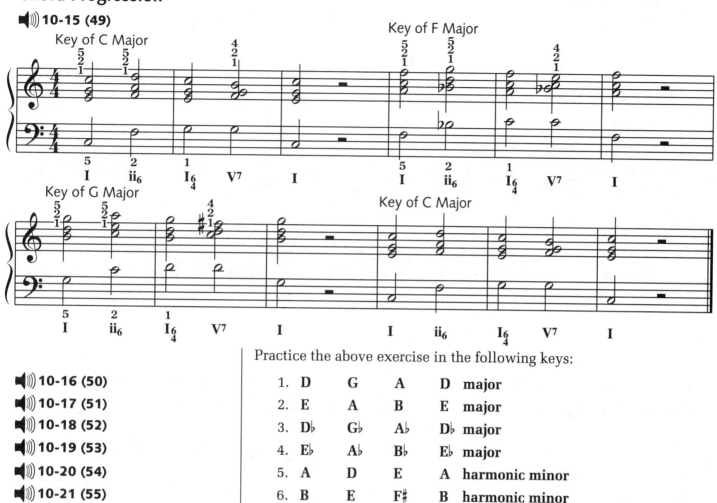

Practice the above exercise in the following keys:

10-16 (50)	1.	D	G	A	D	major
10-17 (51)	2.	E	A	B	E	major
10-18 (52)	3.	D♭	G♭	A♭	D♭	major
10-19 (53)	4.	E♭	A♭	B♭	E♭	major
10-20 (54)	5.	A	D	E	A	harmonic minor
10-21 (55)	6.	B	E	F♯	B	harmonic minor
10-22 (56)	7.	C	F	G	C	harmonic minor
10-23 (57)	8.	B♭	E♭	F	B♭	harmonic minor
10-24 (58)	9.	C♯	F♯	G♯	C♯	harmonic minor

Technique

10-25 (59)

1.

10-25 (59)

2.

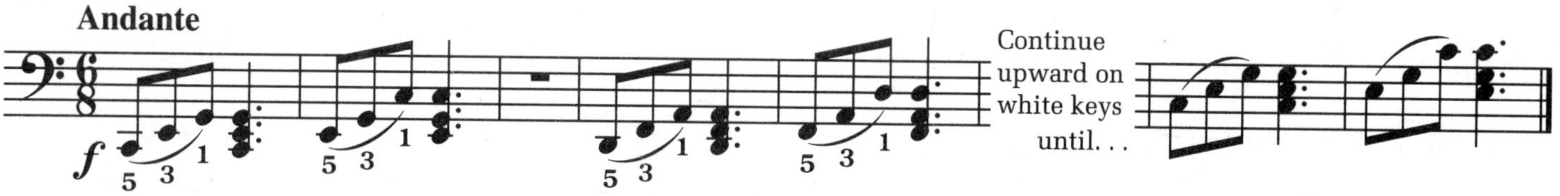

10-26 (60)

3.

▶ Transpose to G major, F major, C harmonic minor and A harmonic minor.

Solo Repertoire

The Chase

10-27 (61)

Cornelius Gurlitt
(1820–1901)

Grazioso *(gracefully)*

Reading

Identify the key of each example. Use the indicated tempo, dynamics and articulation as you play these exercises.

Use the following practice directions:

1. Tap RH and count aloud; then LH.
2. Play hands separately and count aloud.
3. Tap hands together and count aloud.
4. Play hands together and count aloud.

10-28 (62)

▶ Transpose to G major.

10-29 (63)

▶ Transpose to E minor.

Harmonization

1. Harmonize with a block chord accompaniment.

Block Chord Accompaniment

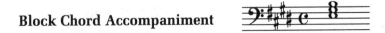

🔊 **10-30 (64)**

Allegro

Germany

▶ Transpose to F major.

2. Using i, i^6_4, iv^6_4, V^7 and ii_6 chords, harmonize with a broken chord accompaniment. Write the Roman numeral name of each chord on the line below the staff.

Broken Chord Accompaniment

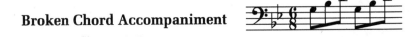

🔊 **10-31 (65)**

Andantino *(slightly faster than andante)*

Mexico

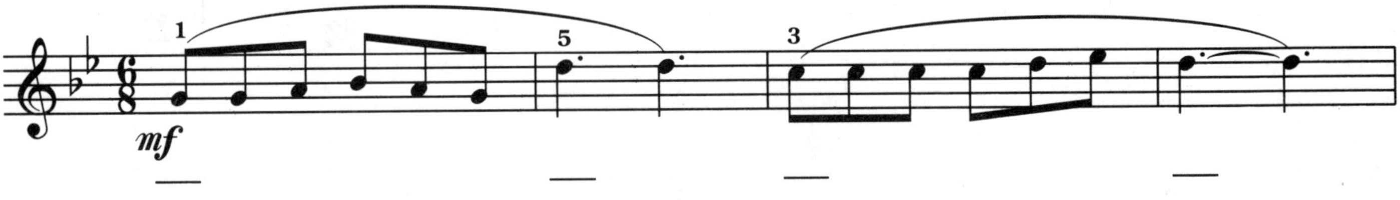

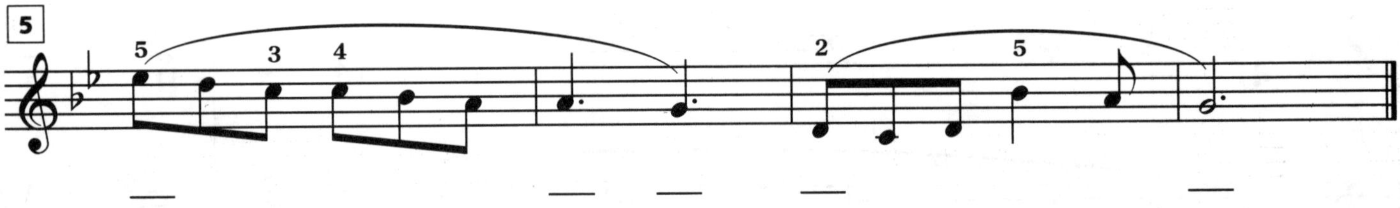

▶ Transpose to A minor.

Harmonization with Two-Hand Accompaniment

Using the indicated chords, create a two-hand accompaniment for the following melody by continuing the pattern given in the first two measures.

10-32 (66)

OVER THE WAVES

Jurentino Rosas
(1868–1894)

Moderato

Improvisation from Chord Symbols

Using the chord progressions below, improvise RH melodies while the LH plays the suggested accompaniment style. (First play the LH chord progressions using the suggested accompaniment style and observing the indicated meter.) Notate your favorite improvisation.

Rules for improvisation:

1. When the tonic chord is used, play mostly scale tones 1, 3 and 5 in the melody.
2. When the dominant chord is used, play mostly scale tones 2, 4, 5 and 7 in the melody.
3. When the subdominant chord is used, play mostly scale tones 1, 4 and 6 in the melody.
4. When the supertonic chord is used, play mostly scale tones 2, 4 and 6 in the melody.
5. Most improvisations begin and end on tonic.
6. The ear should always be the final guide in determining which melody notes to play.

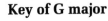

1. Waltz Style Accompaniment

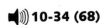

10-33 (67)

Key of G major

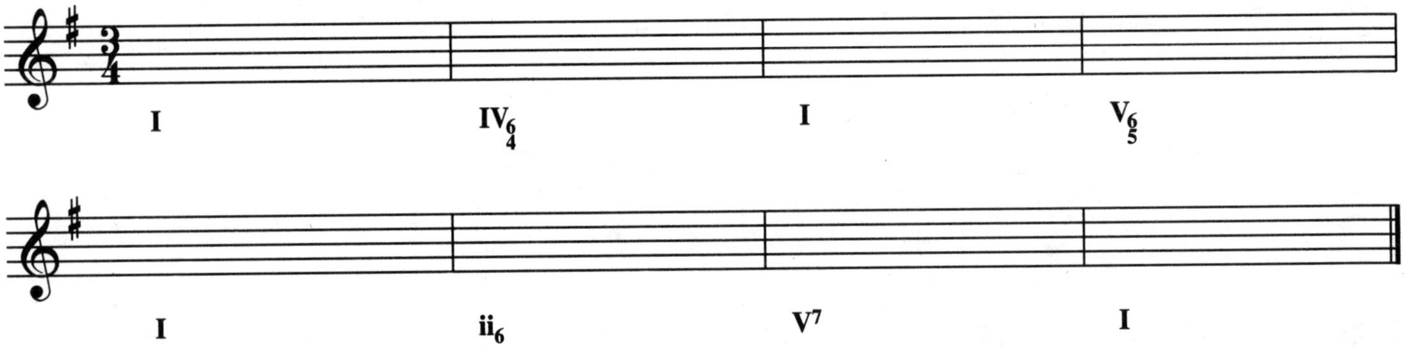

2. Broken Chord Accompaniment

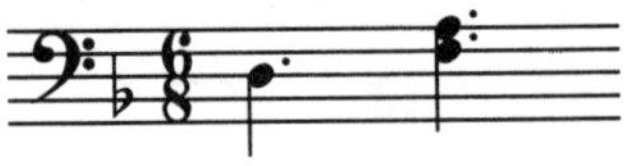

10-34 (68)

Key of D minor

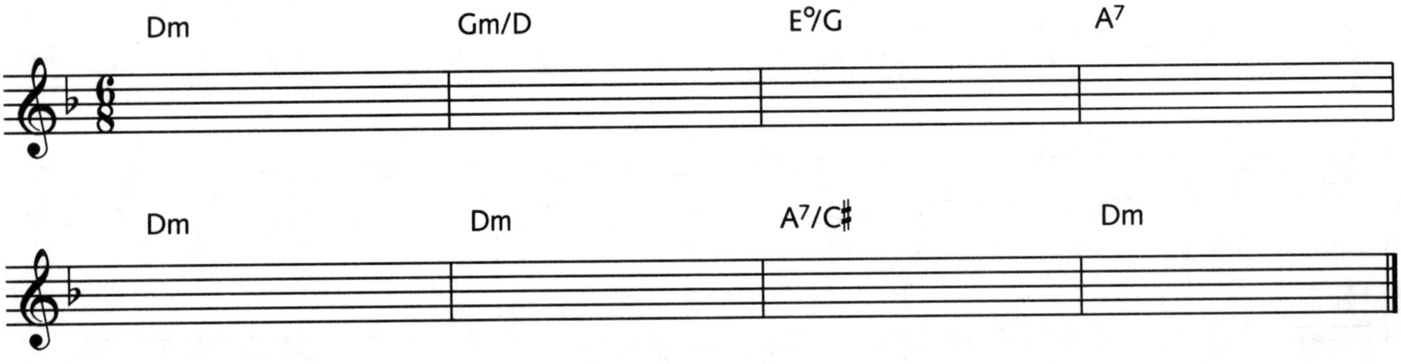

Unit 20

Major Scales Beginning on Black Keys

Objectives

Upon completion of this unit the student will be able to:

1. Play major scales and arpeggios beginning on black keys, using traditional fingerings.
2. Perform solo repertoire that uses supertonic harmonies.
3. Sight-read and transpose music that uses supertonic chords and major scales beginning on black keys.
4. Harmonize and transpose melodies with supertonic chords.
5. Create two-hand accompaniments from chord symbols.
6. Perform duet repertoire with a partner.

Assignments

Week of ________

Write your assignments for the week in the space below.

Playing Major Scales and Arpeggios

Build each scale in tetrachord position. Then practice hands separately:

1. The blocked scale as written.
2. The scale as written.
3. The arpeggio as written.

D♭ Major
(enharmonic to C♯ major)

1.

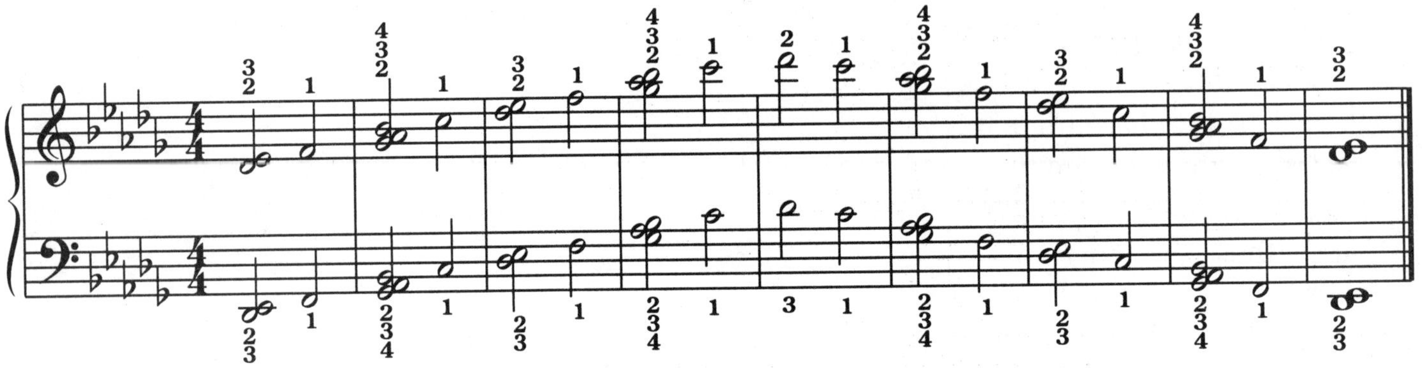

11-1 (33)

2.

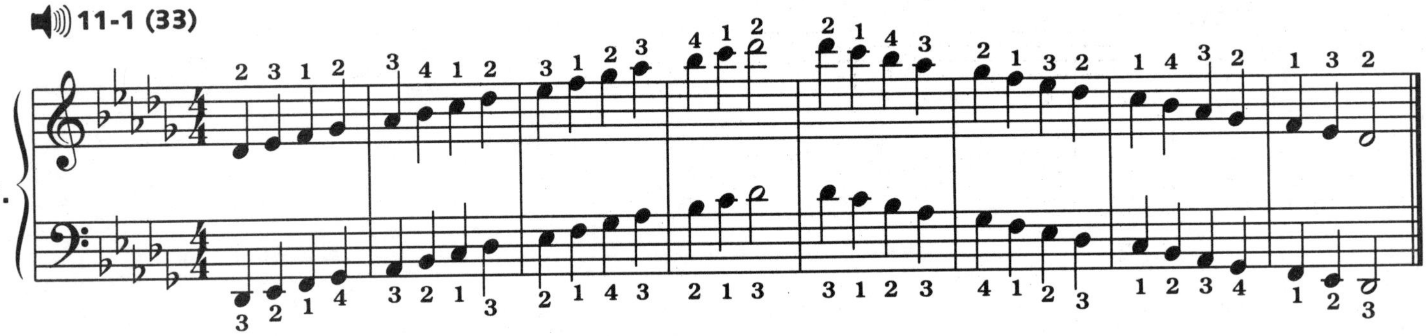

11-2 (34)

3.

Justin H.

Summer Night

Good

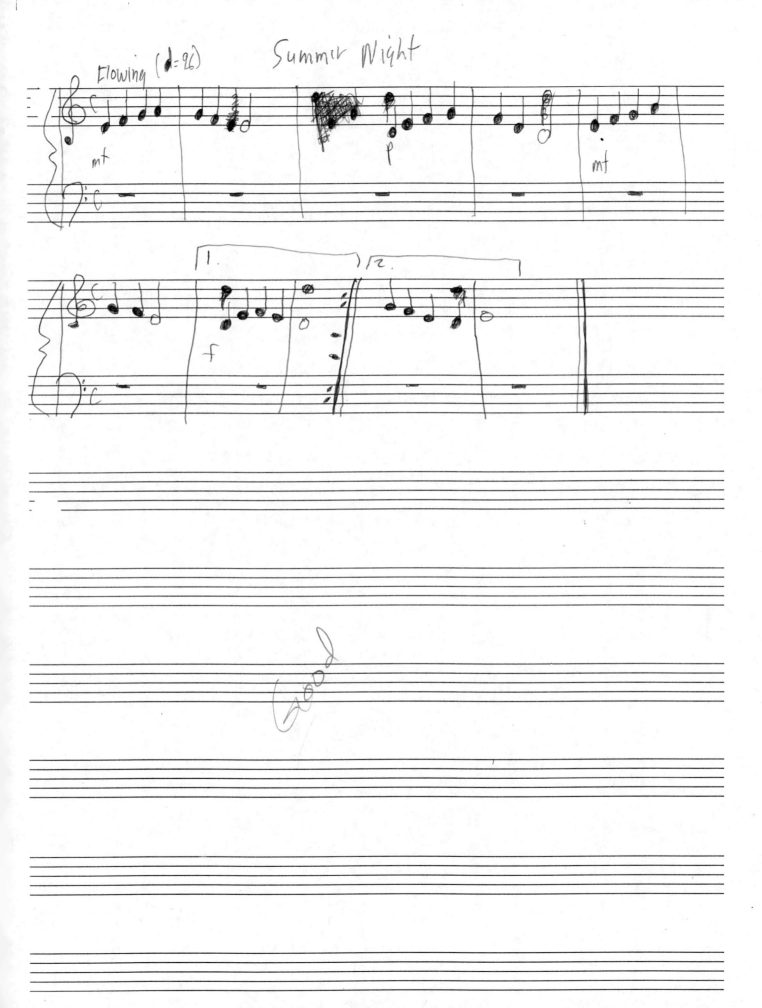

E♭ Major

🔊 11-3 (35)

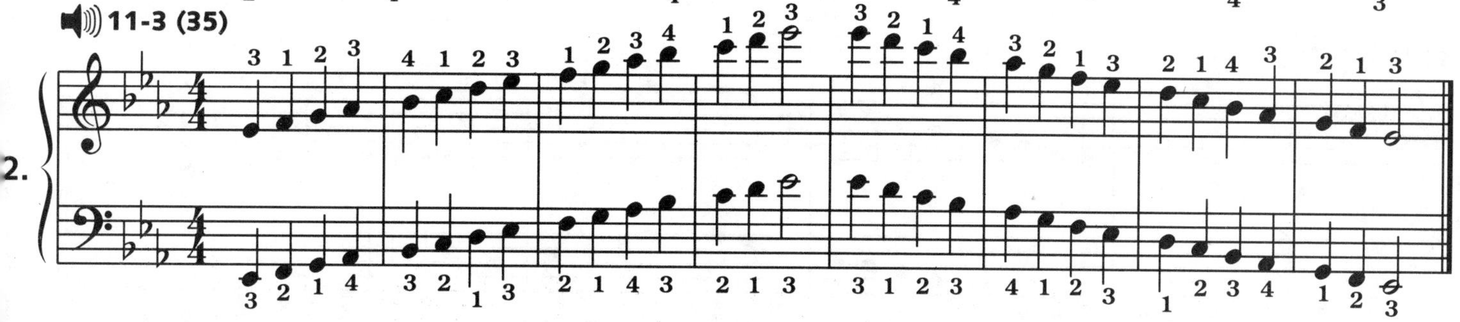

🔊 11-4 (36)

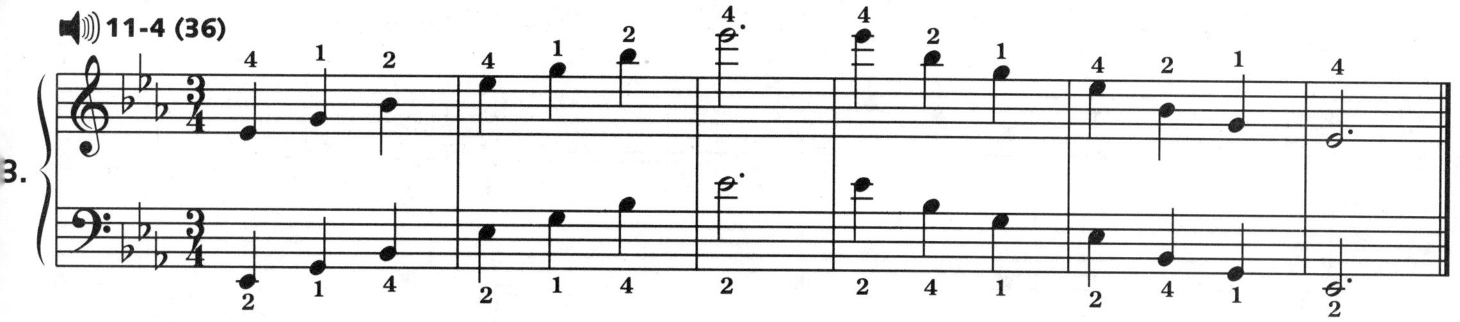

G♭ Major
(enharmonic to F♯ major)

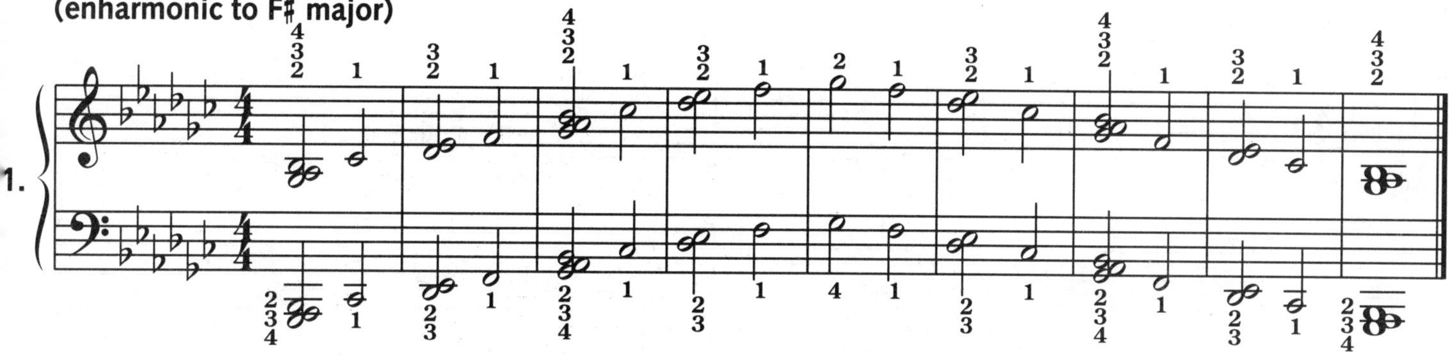

🔊 11-5 (37)

🔊 11-6 (38)

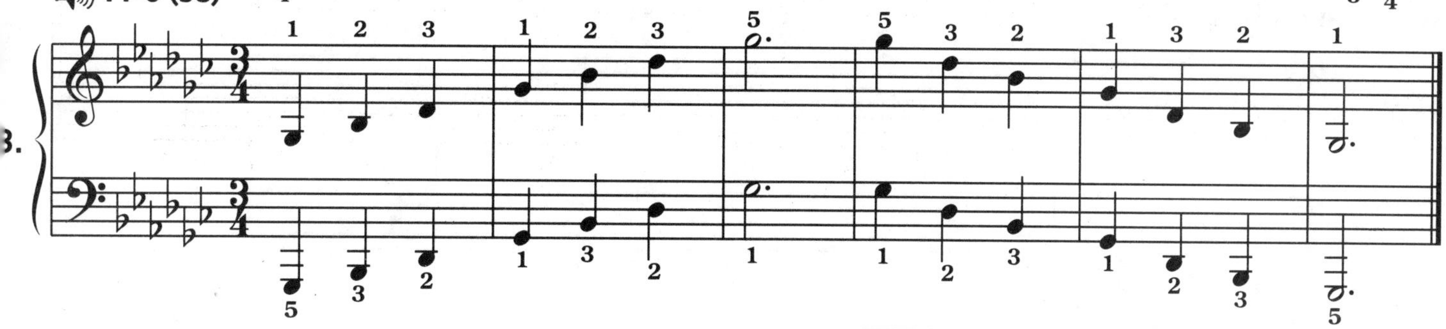

A♭ Major

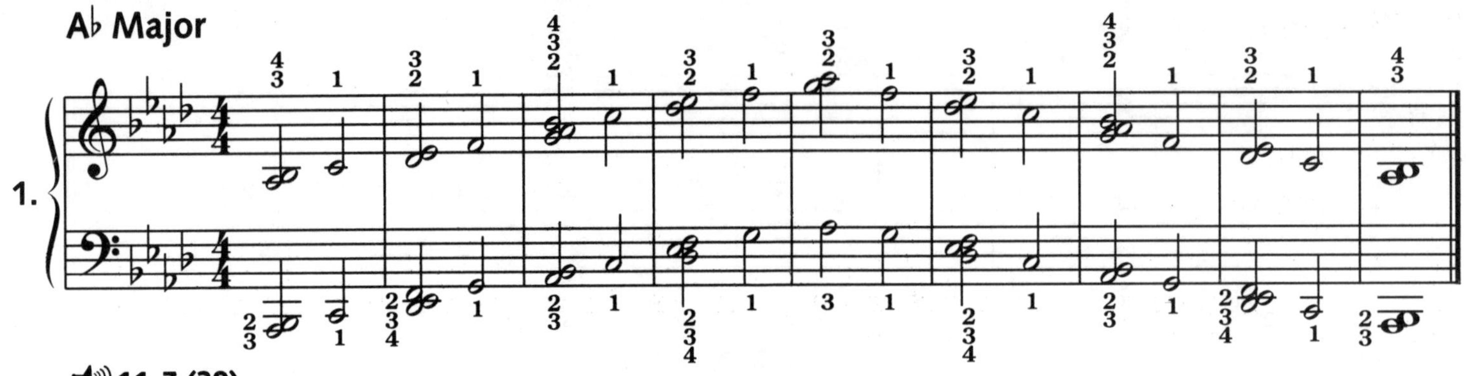

🔊 11-7 (39)

🔊 11-8 (40)

B♭ Major

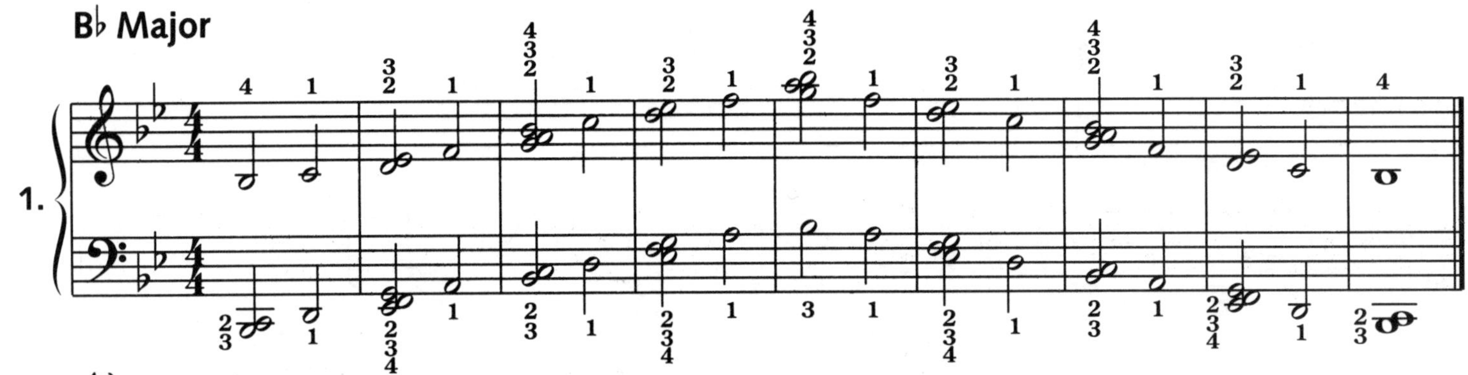

🔊 11-9 (41)

🔊 11-10 (42)

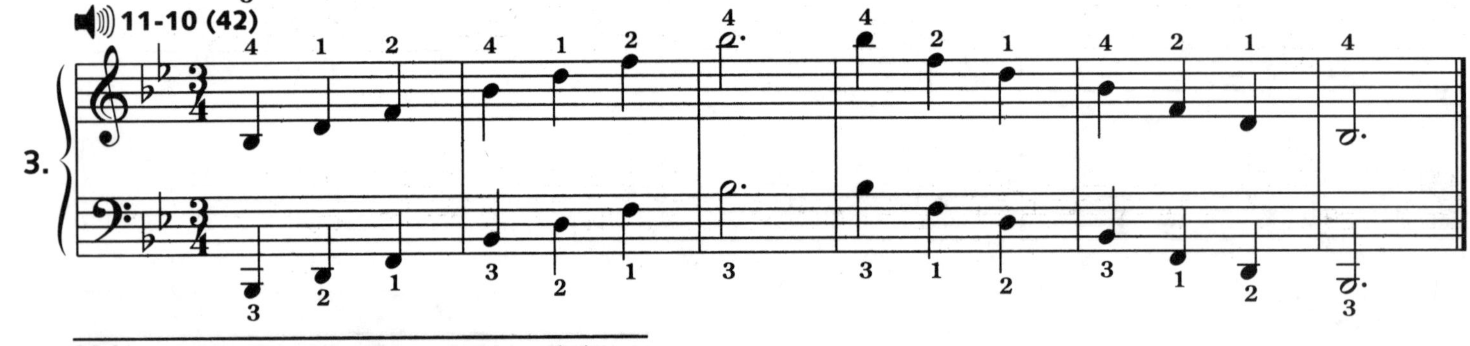

Technique

11-11 (43)

Moderato

1.

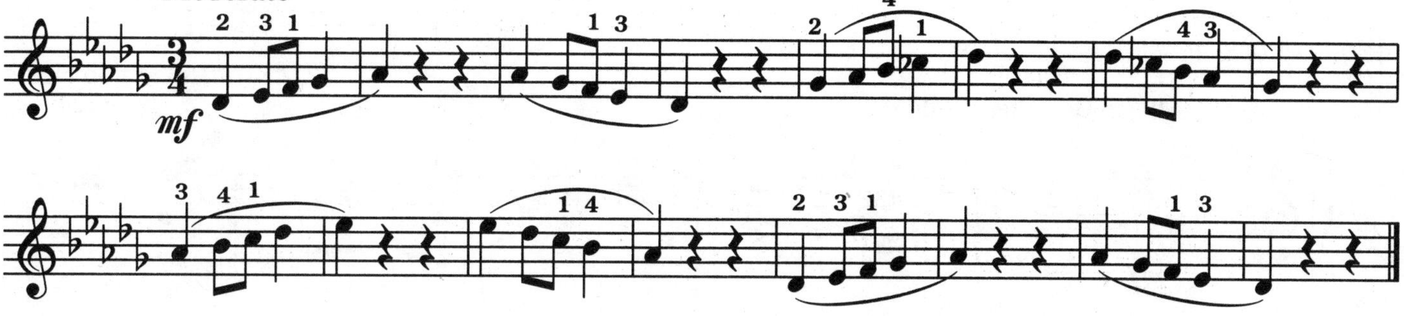

11-11 (43)

Moderato

2.

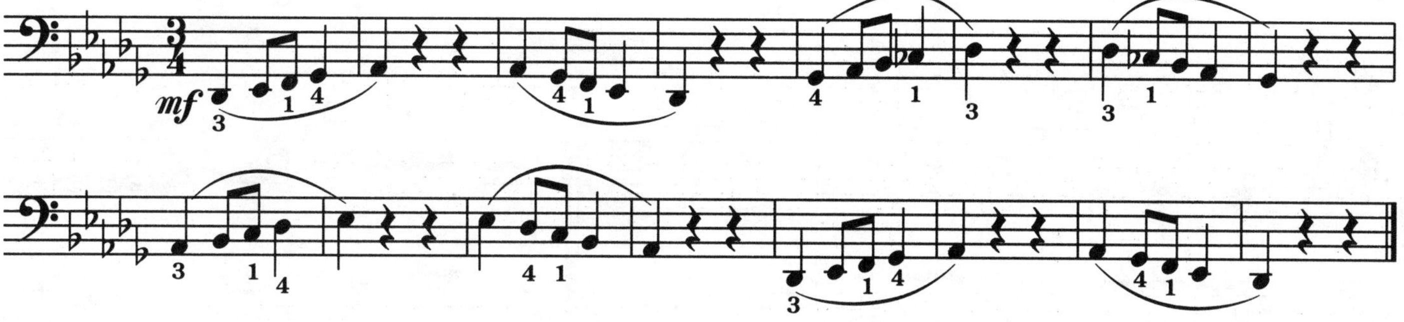

11-12 (44)

Moderato

3.

11-12 (44)

Moderato

4.

Solo Repertoire

Dance

11-13 (45)

Christian Gottlob Neefe
(1748–1798)

Allegretto scherzando

Reading

Identify the key of each example. Use the indicated tempo, dynamics and articulation as you play these exercises.

Use the following practice directions:

1. Tap RH and count aloud; then LH.
2. Play hands separately and count aloud.
3. Tap hands together and count aloud.
4. Play hands together and count aloud.

11-14 (46)

Largo

1.

▶ Transpose to D major.

11-15 (47)

Lively

2.

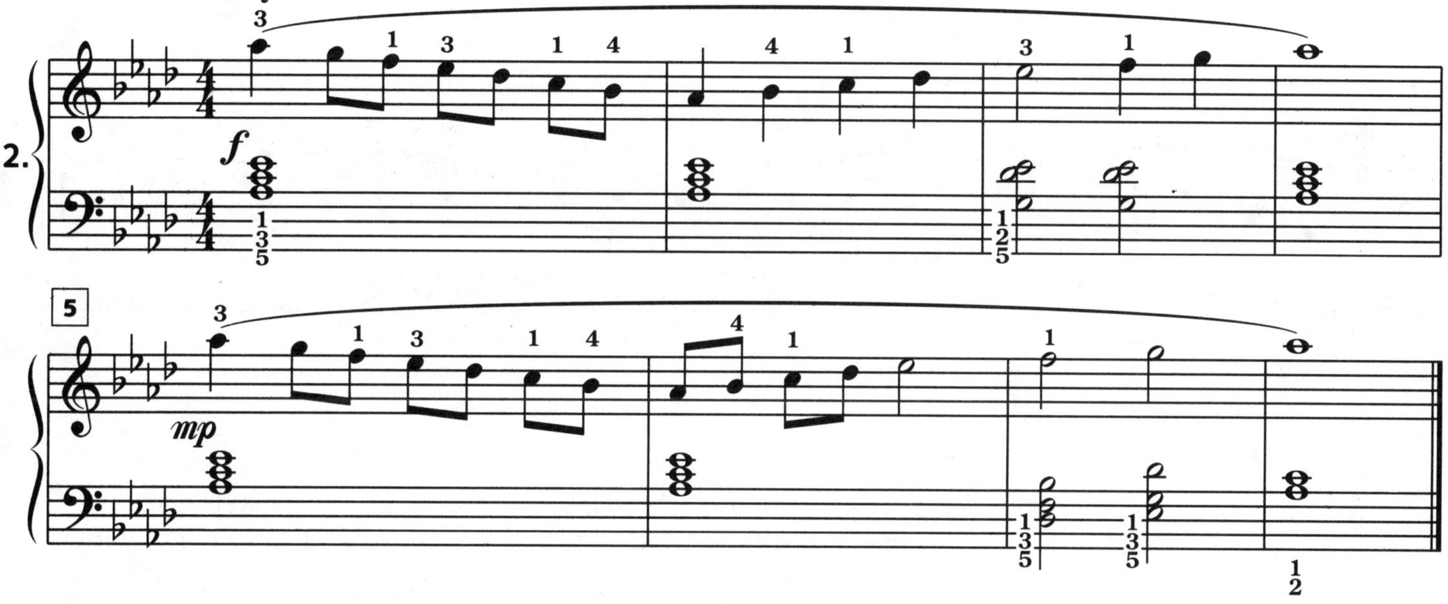

▶ Transpose to G major.

11-16 (48)

Largo

3.

▶ Transpose to C major.

Harmonization

1. Harmonize with a block chord accompaniment.

Block Chord Accompaniment

11-17 (49)

HANUKKAH

Moderately slow — Israel

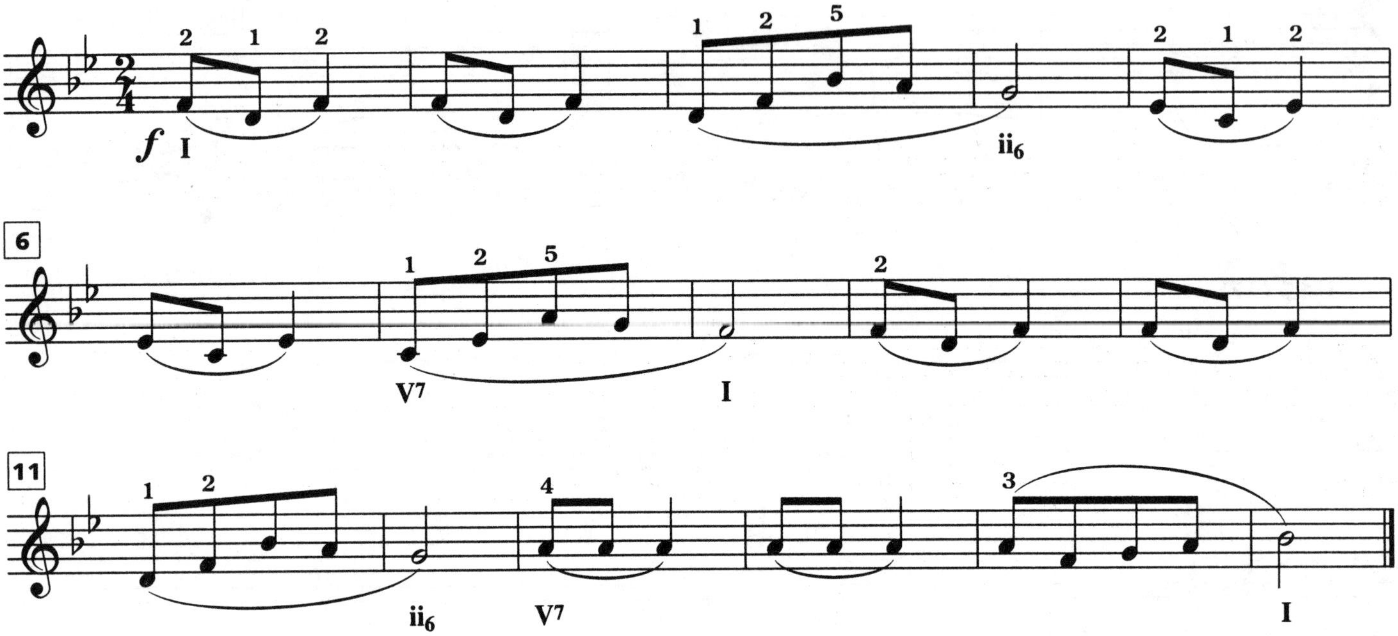

▶ Transpose to C major.

2. Using I, V^7 and ii_6 chords, harmonize with a waltz style accompaniment. Write the Roman numeral name of each chord on the line below the staff.

Waltz Style Accompaniment

11-18 (50)

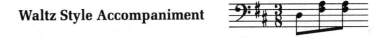

Andantino — Germany

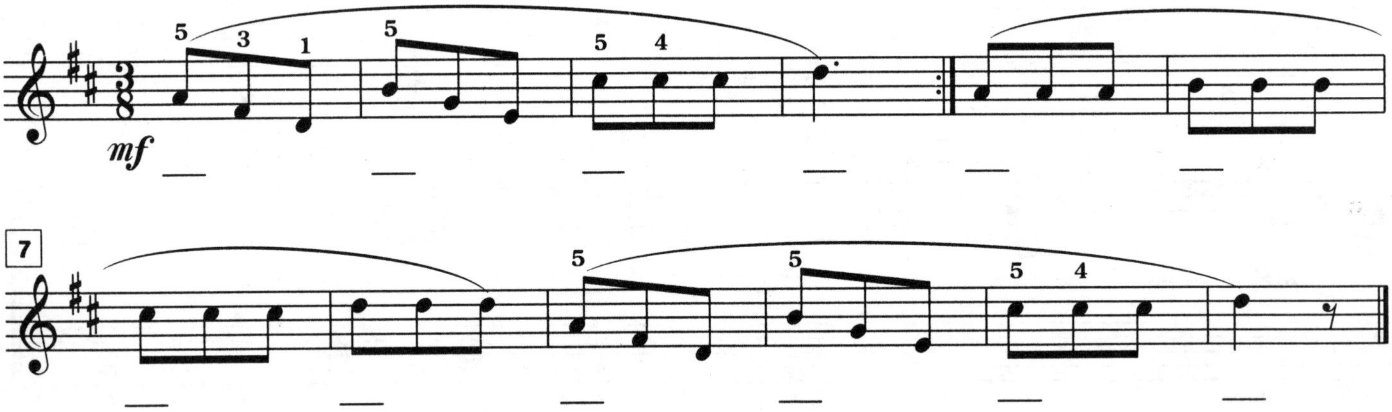

▶ Transpose to E♭ major.

Harmonization with Two-Hand Accompaniment

Using the indicated chords, create a two-hand accompaniment for the following melody by continuing the pattern given in the first two measures.

11-19 (51)

▶ Transpose to G major.

Duet Repertoire

DANCE

Secondo

Daniel Gottlob Türk
(1756–1813)

11-20 (52)

Dance

Primo

11-20 (52)

Daniel Gottlob Türk
(1756–1813)

Unit 21

Triads of the Key on Major Scales Beginning on Black Keys

Objectives

Upon completion of this unit the student will be able to:

1. Build a triad on any note of a major scale that begins on a black key.
2. Perform solo repertoire that uses triads and inversions.
3. Sight-read and transpose music that uses triads and inversions.
4. Harmonize and transpose melodies that use triads and inversions.
5. Create a three-part ensemble to accompany repertoire.

Assignments

Week of ________

Write your assignments for the week in the space below.

Playing Triads of the Key

Triads may be built on any note of any scale. The sharps or flats in the key signature must be used when playing these triads. Triads of the key are identified by Roman numerals.

Play triads of the key in D♭ major. Note the quality of each chord.

Play with RH:

🔊 11-21 (53)

1.
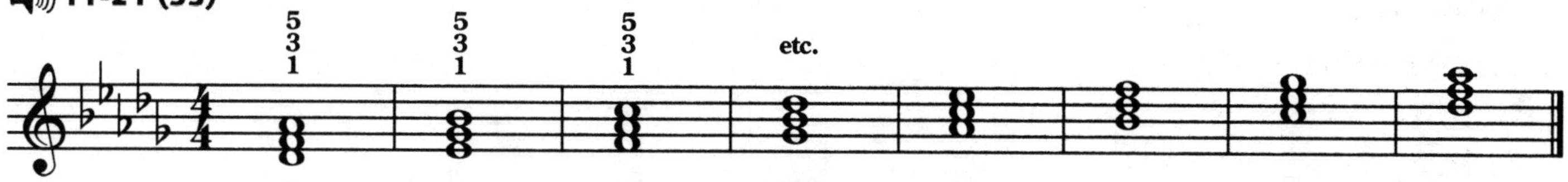

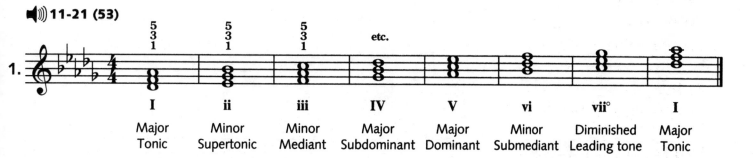

I	ii	iii	IV	V	vi	vii°	I
Major Tonic	Minor Supertonic	Minor Mediant	Major Subdominant	Major Dominant	Minor Submediant	Diminished Leading tone	Major Tonic

▶ Transpose to B♭ major and E♭ major.

Play with LH:

🔊 11-21 (53)

2.
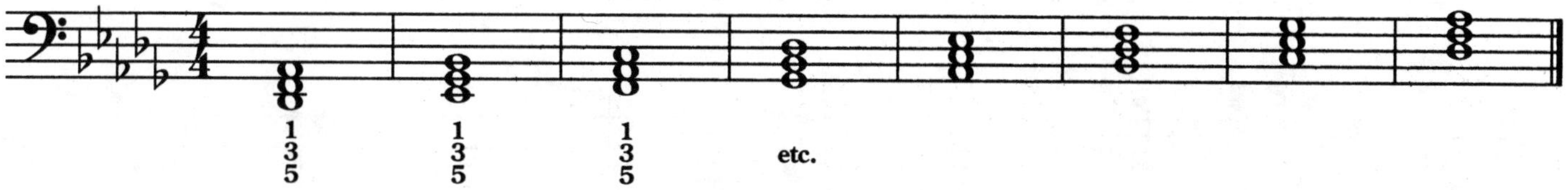

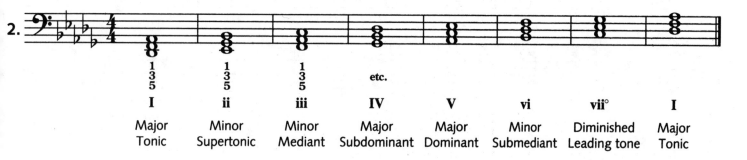

I	ii	iii	IV	V	vi	vii°	I
Major Tonic	Minor Supertonic	Minor Mediant	Major Subdominant	Major Dominant	Minor Submediant	Diminished Leading tone	Major Tonic

▶ Transpose to B♭ major and E♭ major.

Technique

11-22 (54)

1.

▶ Transpose to A♭ major.

11-22 (54)

2.

▶ Transpose to E♭ major.

11-23 (55)

3.

▶ Transpose to B♭ major.

11-23 (55)

4.

▶ Transpose to E♭ major.

Solo Repertoire

Waltz

11-24 (56)

Anton Diabelli
(1781–1858)

Ensemble Repertoire

Play the four-part ensemble using the indicated chords to complete parts 3 and 4.

Part 1: Diabelli *Waltz* (page 245)
Part 2: Countermelody
Part 3: Broken chords
Part 4: Waltz bass with bottom notes of triads and inversions in LH

11-25 (57)

Vivace

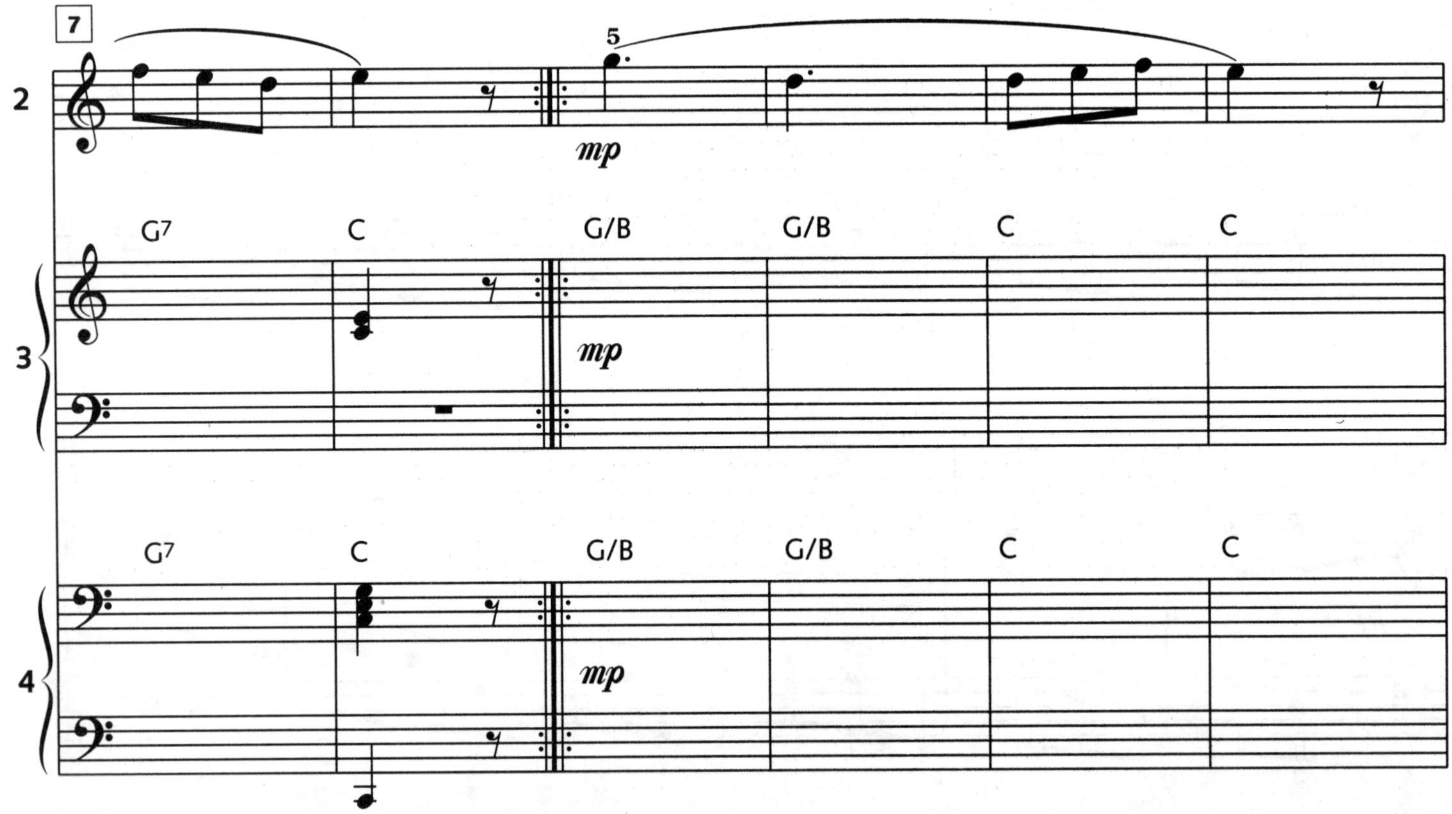

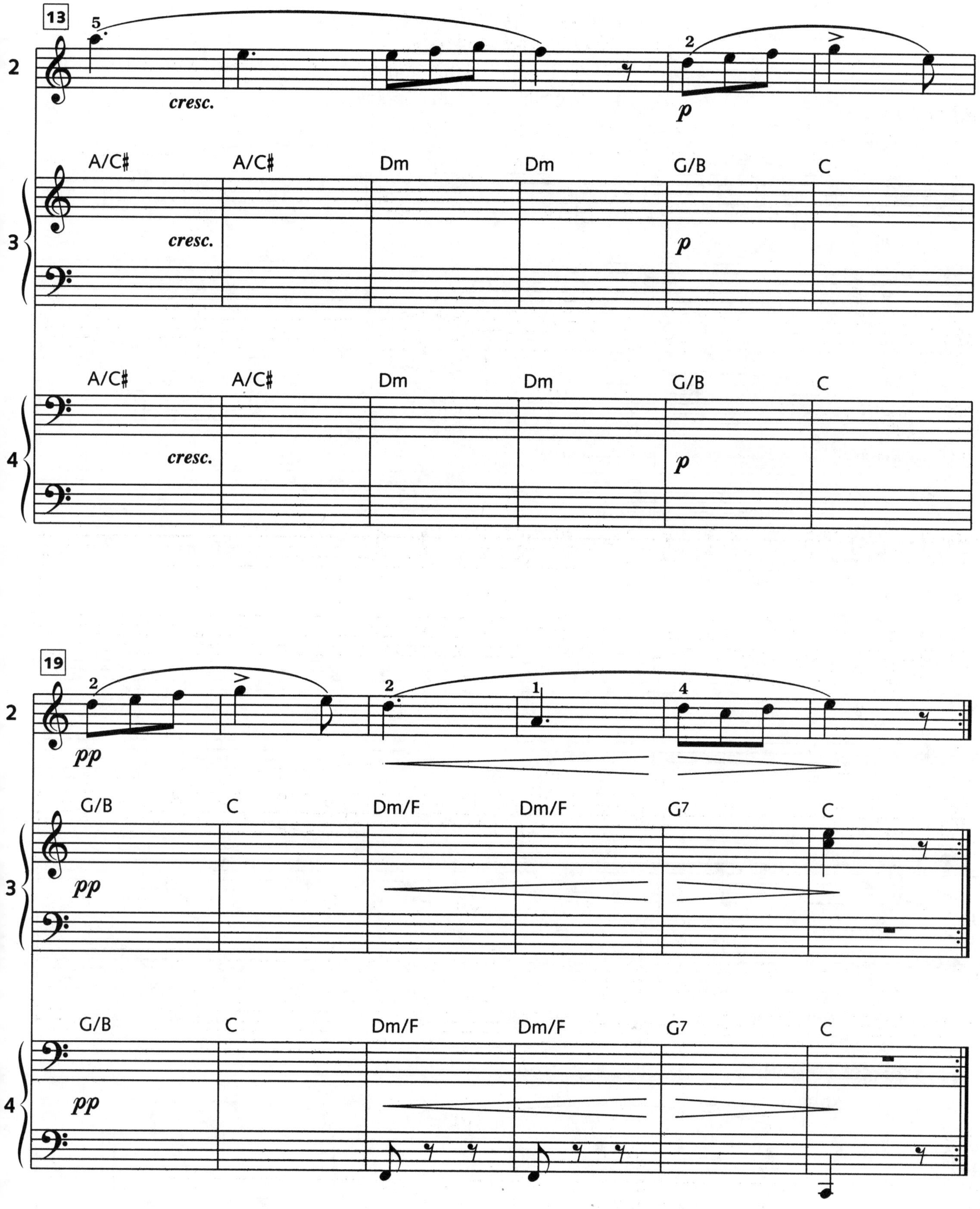
13
2
cresc.
p
3
A/C♯
A/C♯
Dm
Dm
G/B
C
cresc.
p
4
A/C♯
A/C♯
Dm
Dm
G/B
C
cresc.
p
19
2
pp
3
G/B
C
Dm/F
Dm/F
G7
C
pp
4
G/B
C
Dm/F
Dm/F
G7
C
pp

Reading

Identify the key of each example. Use the indicated tempo, dynamics and articulation as you play these exercises.

Use the following practice directions:

1. Tap RH and count aloud; then LH.
2. Play hands separately and count aloud.
3. Tap hands together and count aloud.
4. Play hands together and count aloud.

11-26 (58)

Allegretto

▶ Transpose to C major.

11-27 (59)

Andante

▶ Transpose to D major.

11-28 (60)

Animato

▶ Transpose to G major.

Harmonization

Harmonize each melody below in two ways:

- Using the bottom note of each triad and inversion.
- Using the indicated triads and inversions.

1. 11-29 (61)

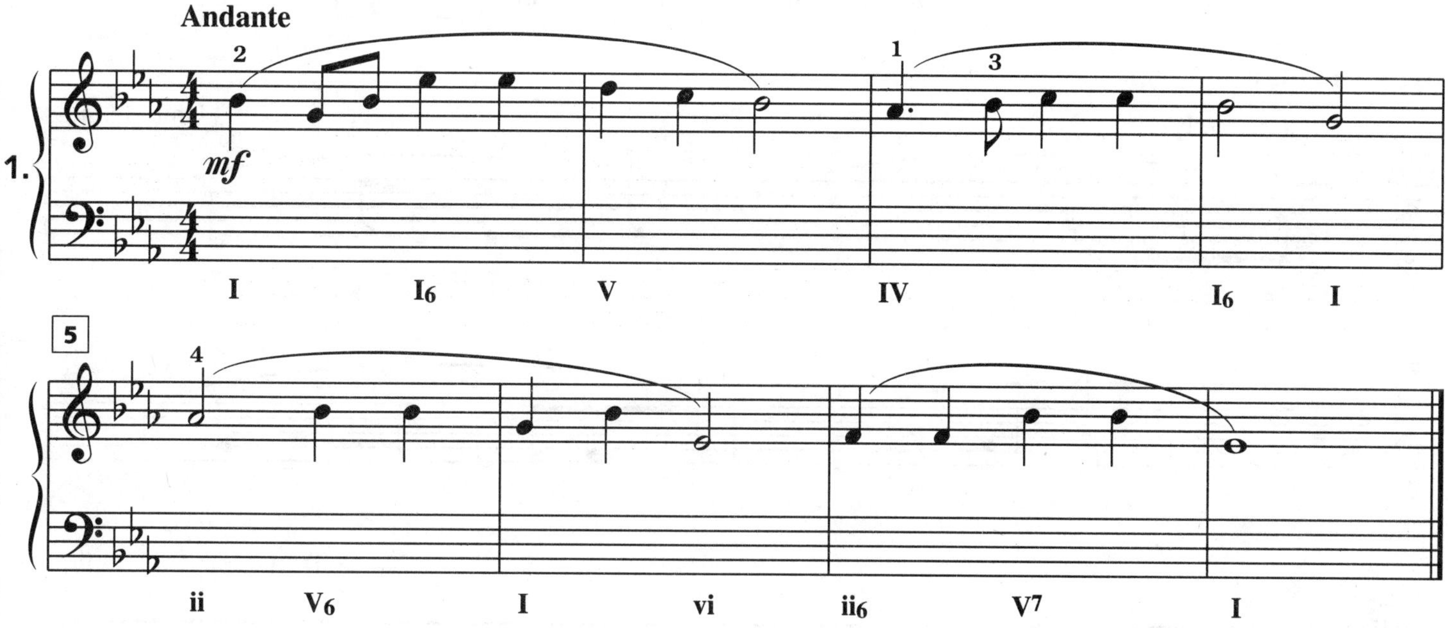

▶ Transpose to E major.

2. 11-30 (62)

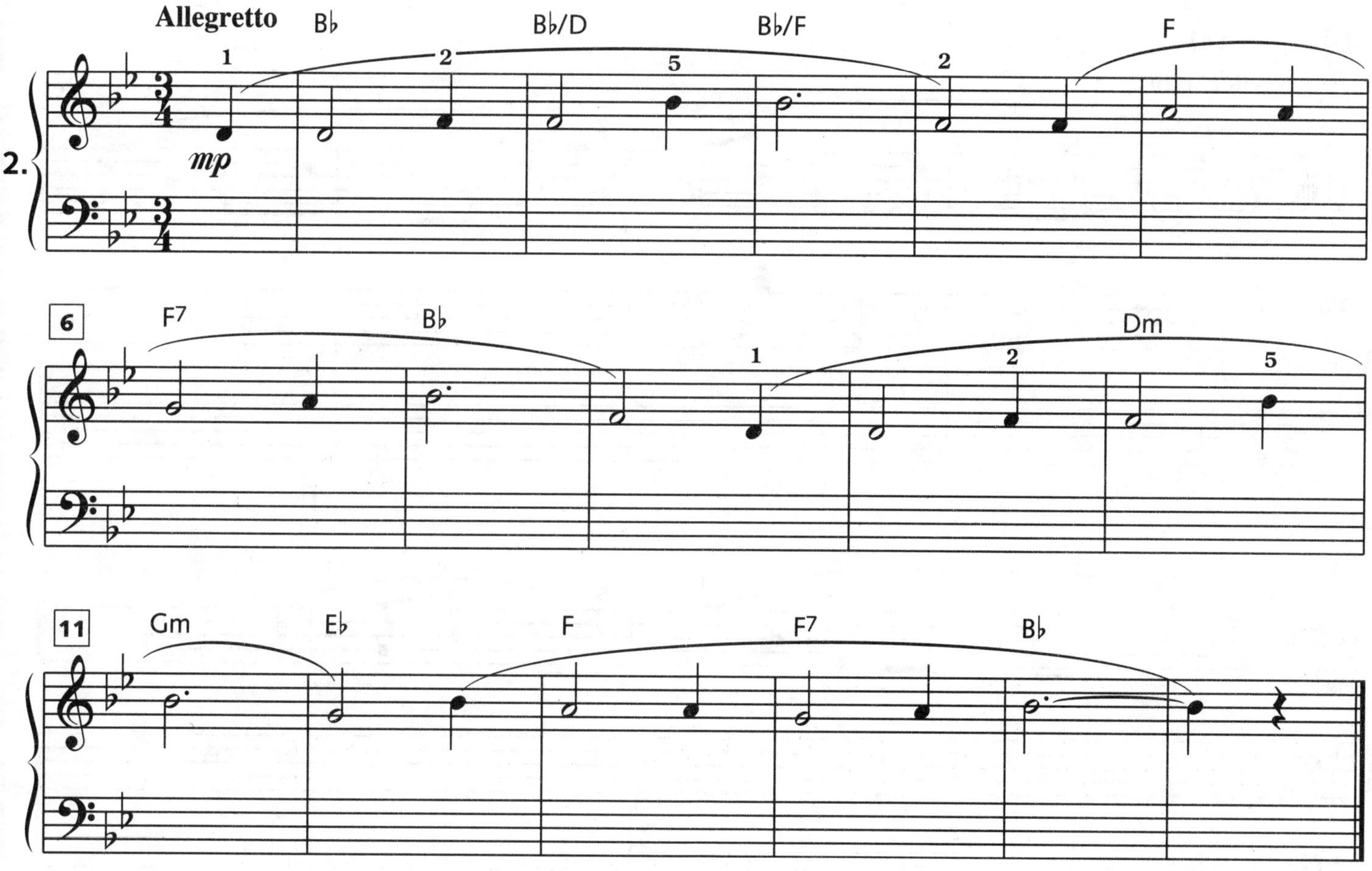

▶ Transpose to C major.

Harmonization (continued)

Using I, V^7 and ii_6 chords, harmonize with a broken chord accompaniment. Write the Roman numeral name of each chord on the line below the staff.

3. Broken Chord Accompaniment

11-31 (63)

Vivace (lively)

United States

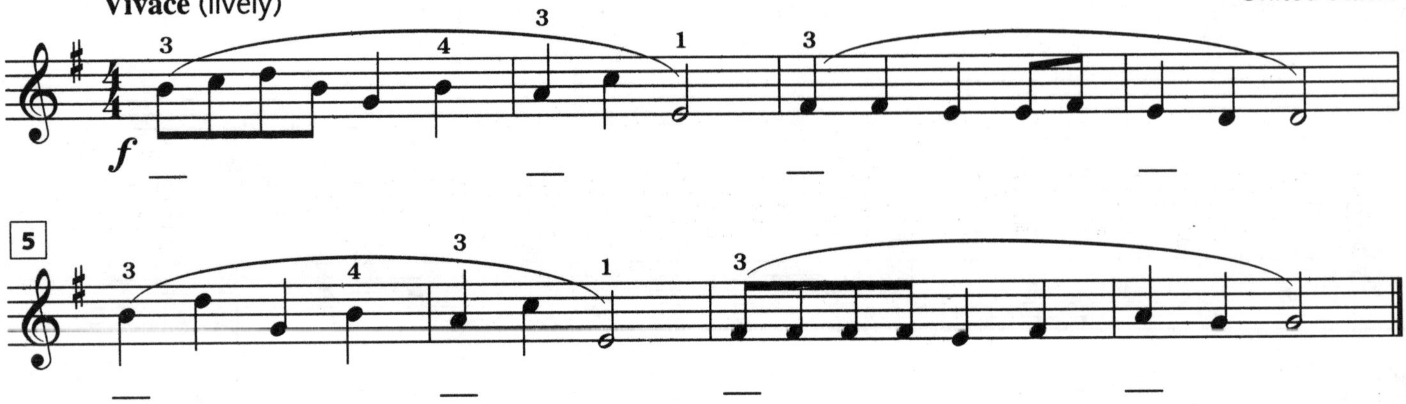

▶ Transpose to A major.

Harmonization with Two-Hand Accompaniment

Using the indicated chords, create a two-hand accompaniment for the following melody by continuing the pattern given in the first two measures.

11-32 (64)

Allegretto

United States

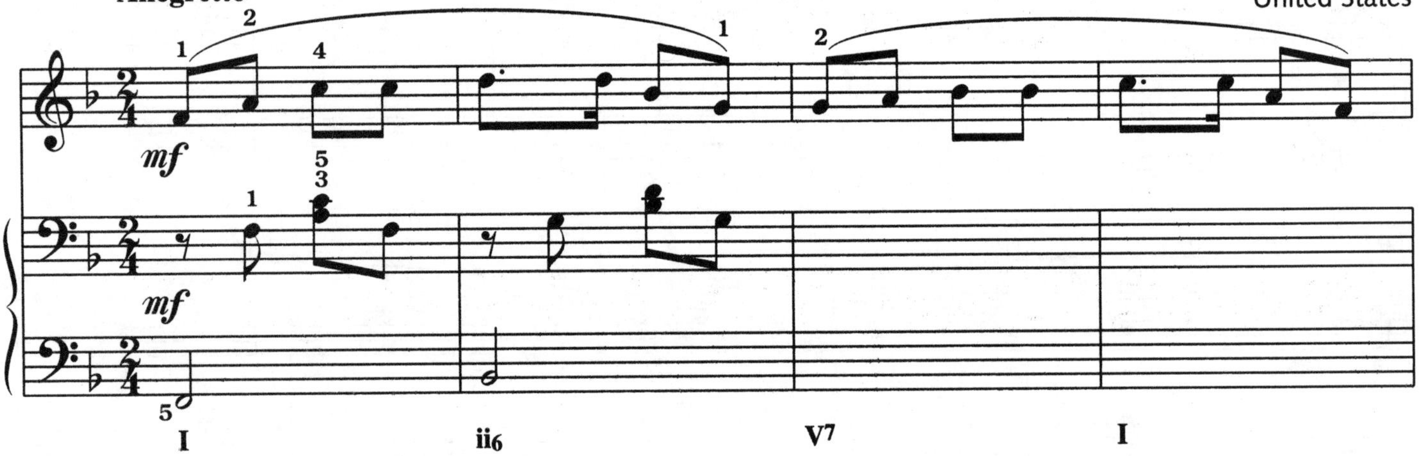

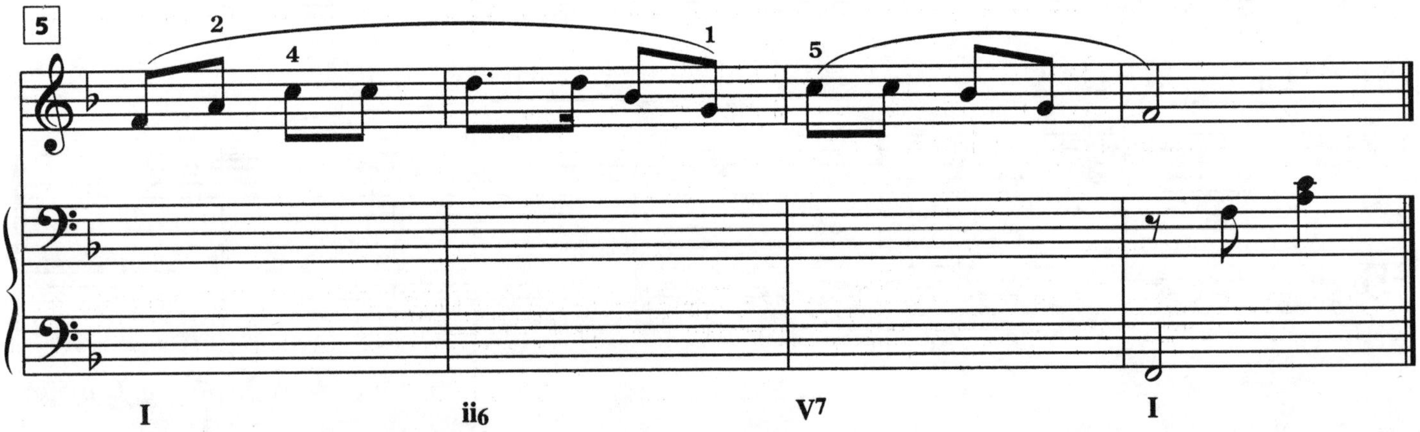

▶ Transpose to E major.

Review Worksheet

Name ____________________ *Date* ____________________

1. Identify each major scale below by writing its name on the indicated line. Write the correct RH fingering on the lines above the staff and the correct LH fingering on the lines below the staff.

____ Major Scale

____ Major Scale

____ Major Scale

____ Major Scale

2. Identify each major key by writing its name on the line above the staff. Using whole notes, write a ii_6 chord on the staff. Write the letter name for each chord on the line below the staff.

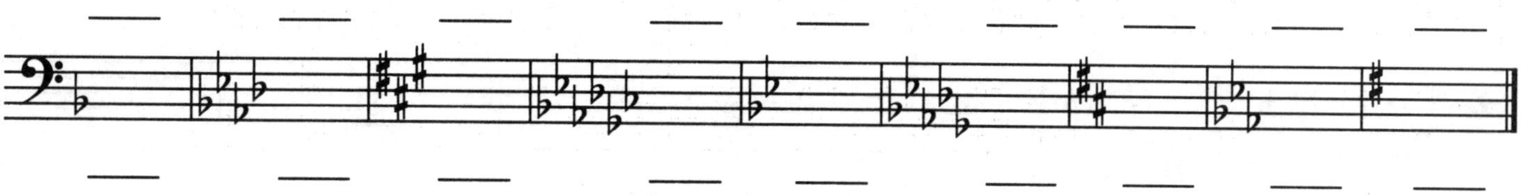

3. Identify each major arpeggio below by writing its name on the indicated line. Write the correct RH fingering on the lines above the staff and the correct LH fingering on the lines below the staff.

____ Major Arpeggio

____ Major Arpeggio

____ Major Arpeggio

____ Major Arpeggio

---

4. Identify each major key by writing its name on the line above the staff. Using whole notes on the staff, write the triad indicated by each Roman numeral.

Unit 22

The vi Chord

Objectives

Upon completion of this unit the student will be able to:

1. Play I–vi–IV–ii$_6$–I$^6_4$–V^7–I chord progressions in all major and minor keys.
2. Perform solo repertoire that uses submediant harmonies.
3. Sight-read and transpose music that uses submediant chords.
4. Harmonize and transpose melodies with submediant chords.
5. Create two-hand accompaniments from chord symbols.

Assignments

Week of ________

Write your assignments for the week in the space below.

The vi Chord

The vi chord (submediant) is often substituted for the I chord, since the chords have two notes in common.

Key of C Major:

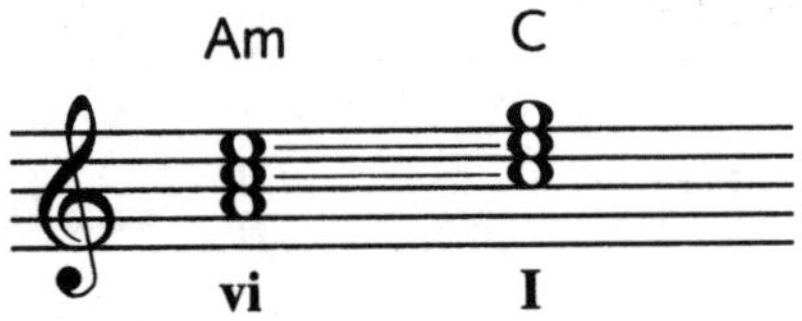

In major keys, the vi chord is a minor triad.

Key of C Major:

In natural and harmonic minor keys, the VI chord is a major triad.

Key of A Minor:

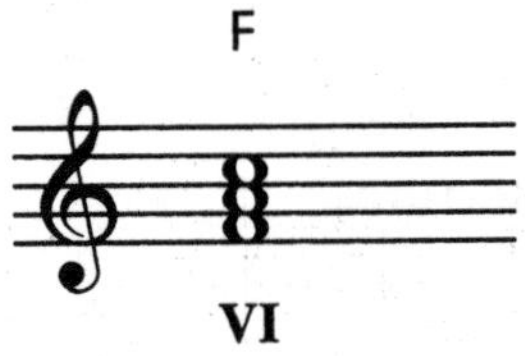

Play the following chord progression hands separately.

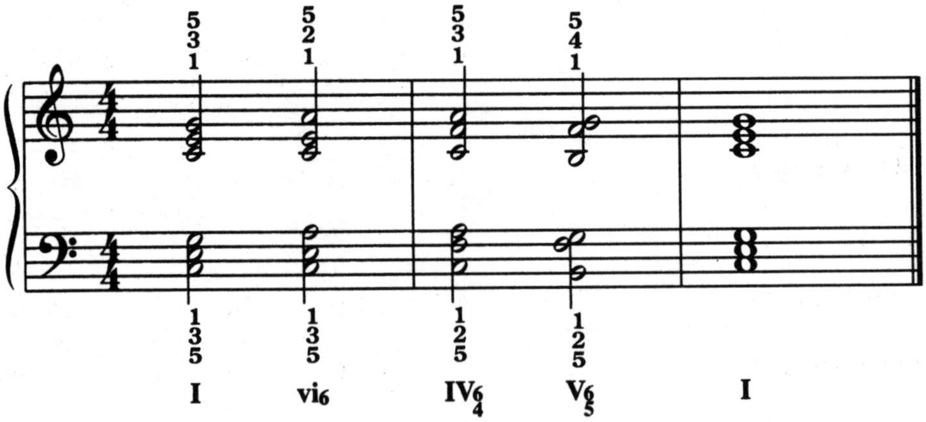

▶ Transpose to G major, F major, A harmonic minor and C harmonic minor.

Playing the I–vi–IV–ii$_6$–I$^6_4$–V^7–I Chord Progression

Play the I–vi–IV–ii$_6$–I$^6_4$–V^7–I chord progression exercise:

12-1 (32)

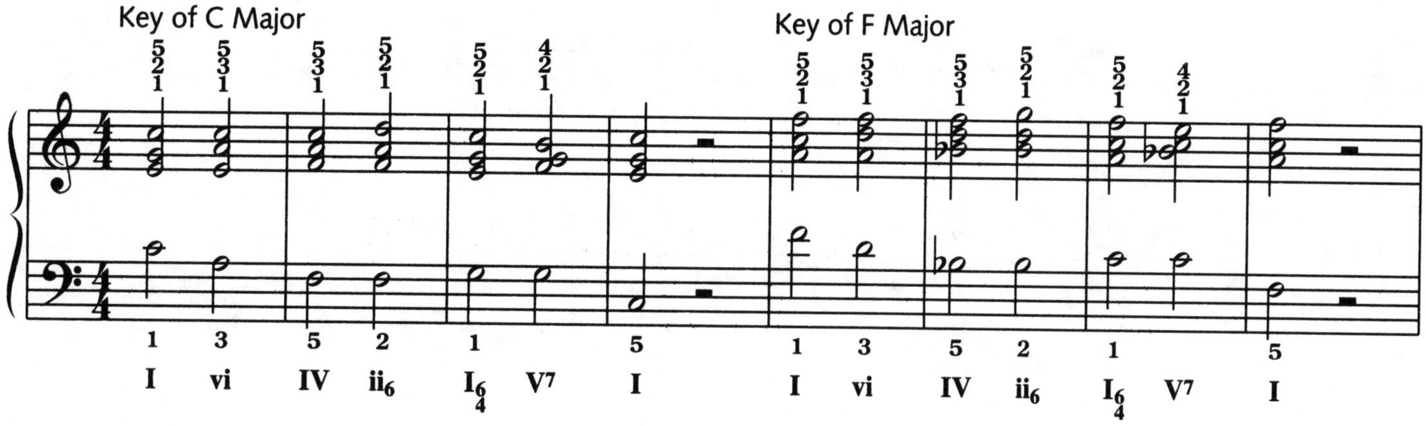

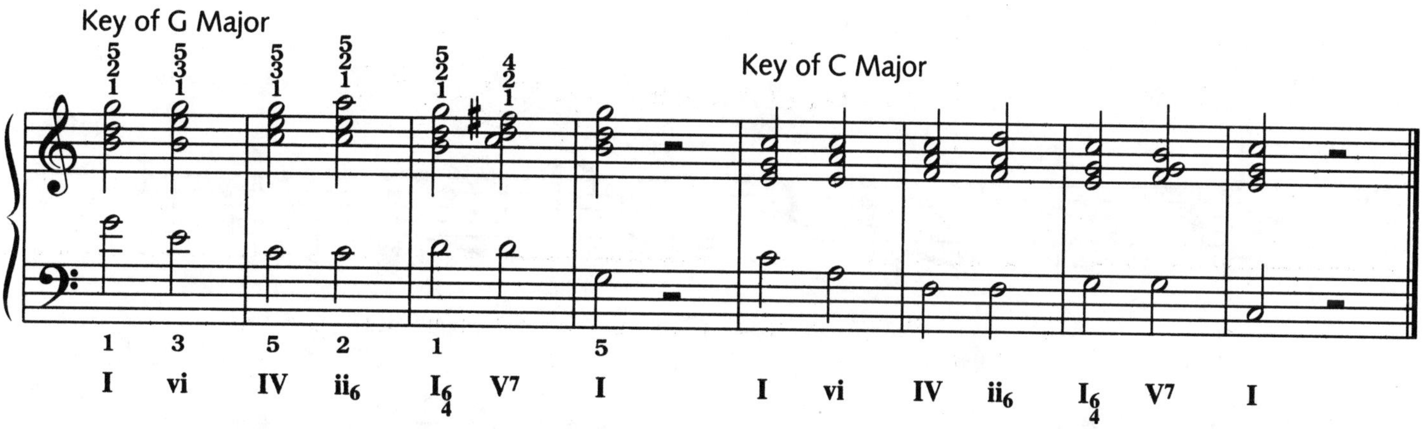

Practice the above exercise in the following keys:

12-2 (33)	1. D	G	A	D	major
12-3 (34)	2. E	A	B	E	major
12-4 (35)	3. D♭	G♭	A♭	D♭	major
12-5 (36)	4. E♭	A♭	B♭	E♭	major
12-6 (37)	5. A	D	E	A	harmonic minor
12-7 (38)	6. B	E	F♯	B	harmonic minor
12-8 (39)	7. C	F	G	C	harmonic minor
12-9 (40)	8. B♭	E♭	F	B♭	harmonic minor
12-10 (41)	9. C♯	F♯	G♯	C♯	harmonic minor

Technique

🔊 12-11 (42)

Andante

1.

🔊 12-11 (42)

Andante

2.

🔊 12-12 (43)

Moderato

3.

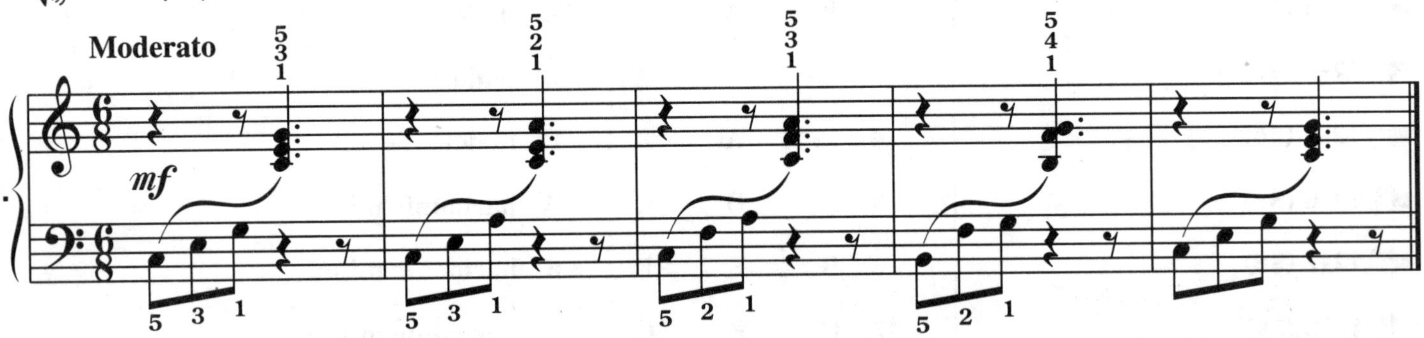

▶ Transpose to G major, F major, C harmonic minor and A harmonic minor.

Solo Repertoire

Ecossaise

12-13 (44)

Allegretto

Franz Schubert
(1797–1828)

Reading

Identify the key of each example. Use the indicated tempo, dynamics and articulation as you play these exercises.

Use the following practice directions:

1. Tap RH and count aloud; then LH.
2. Play hands separately and count aloud.
3. Tap hands together and count aloud.
4. Play hands together and count aloud.

12-14 (45)

▶ Transpose to C major.

12-15 (46)

▶ Transpose to G major.

Harmonization

1. Harmonize with a broken chord accompaniment.

Broken Chord Accompaniment 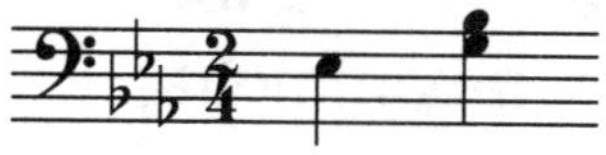

12-16 (47)

ECOSSAISE

Allegro con brio (quickly with vigor)

Ludwig van Beethoven (1770–1827)

▶ Transpose to D major.

2. Using I, V7, IV, vi and ii chords, harmonize with a block chord accompaniment. Use inversions to improve sound and for ease in performance. Write the Roman numeral name of each chord on the line below the staff.

Block Chord Accompaniment 

12-17 (48)

VIVE L'AMOUR

Allegro

France

▶ Transpose to C major.

Harmonization with Two-Hand Accompaniment

Using the indicated chords, create a two-hand accompaniment for the following melody by continuing the pattern given in the first two measures.

12-18 (49)

▶ Transpose to F major.

Improvisation from Chord Symbols

Using the chord progressions below, improvise RH melodies while the LH plays the suggested accompaniment style. (First play the LH chord progression using the suggested accompaniment style and observing the indicated meter.) Notate your favorite improvisation.

Rules for improvisation:

1. When the tonic chord is used, play mostly scale tones 1, 3 and 5 in the melody.
2. When the dominant chord is used, play mostly scale tones 2, 4, 5 and 7 in the melody.
3. When the subdominant chord is used, play mostly scale tones 1, 4 and 6 in the melody.
4. When the supertonic chord is used, play mostly scale tones 2, 4 and 6 in the melody.
5. When the submediant chord is used, play mostly scale tones 1, 3 and 6 in the melody.
6. Most improvisations begin and end on tonic.
7. The ear should always be the final guide in determining which melody notes to play.

1. Waltz Style Accompaniment

12-19 (50)

Key of E harmonic minor

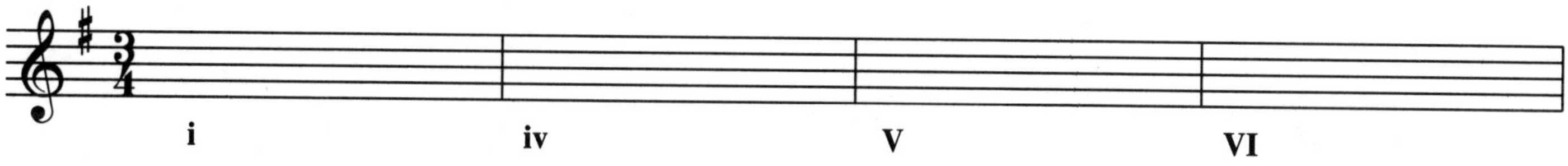

2. Alberti Bass Accompaniment

12-20 (51)

Key of F major

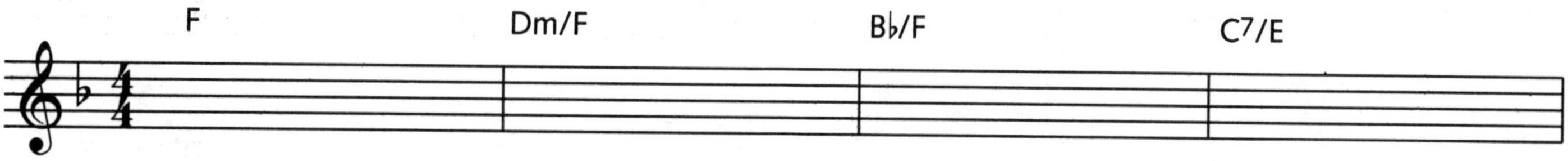

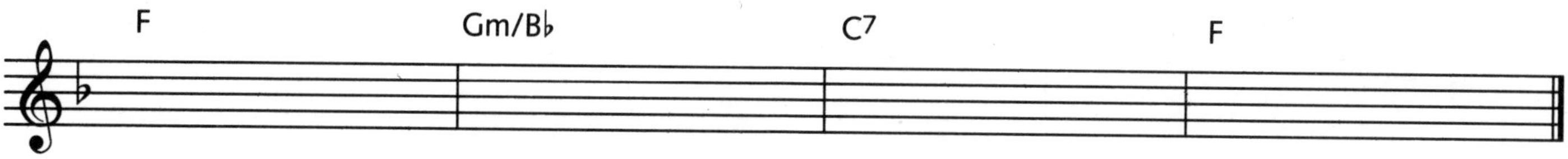

Unit 23

Seventh Chords

Objectives

Upon completion of this unit the student will be able to:

1. Play five types of seventh chords and inversions.
2. Perform solo repertoire that uses seventh chords.
3. Sight-read music that uses seventh chords.
4. Harmonize and transpose melodies with seventh chords.
5. Create two-hand accompaniments from chord symbols.

Assignments

Week of ________

Write your assignments for the week in the space below.

Seventh-Chord Review

A seventh chord may be formed by adding to the root position triad a note that is a seventh above the root. Seventh chords in root position look like this:

There are five types of seventh chords:

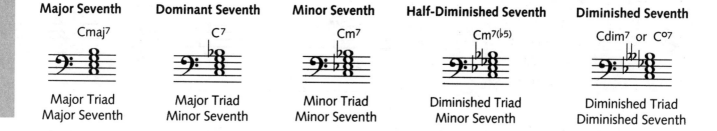

Major Seventh

Cmaj7

Major Triad
Major Seventh

Dominant Seventh

C7

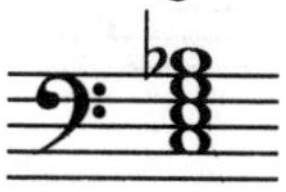

Major Triad
Minor Seventh

Minor Seventh

Cm7

Minor Triad
Minor Seventh

Half-Diminished Seventh

Cm7(♭5)

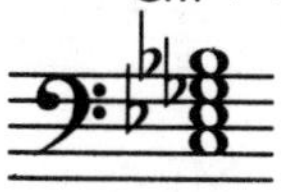

Diminished Triad
Minor Seventh

Diminished Seventh

Cdim7 or C°7

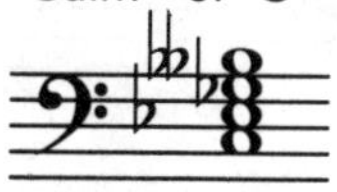

Diminished Triad
Diminished Seventh

Playing Seventh Chords

Play the following seventh chord exercise hands separately.
Use fingers 5 3 2 1 for the LH.
Use fingers 1 2 3 5 for the RH and play one octave higher than written.

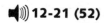

12-21 (52)

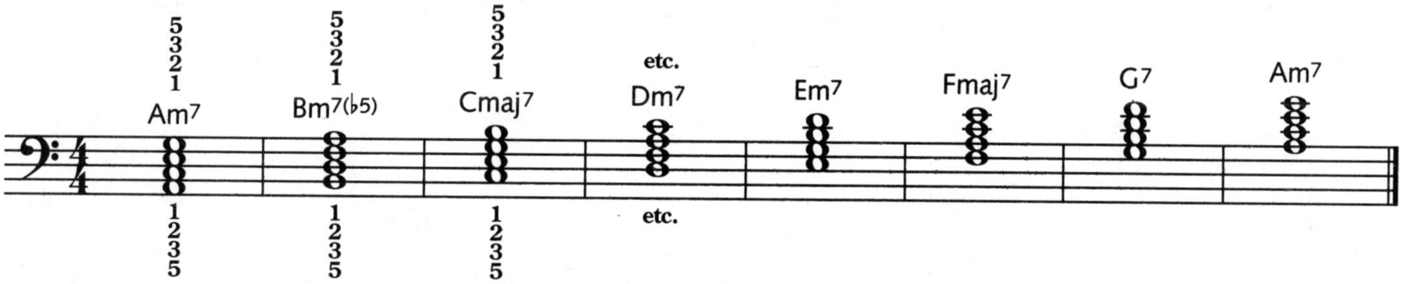

The 5th is often omitted from the seventh chord. This makes it simple to play with one hand. Play the following exercise with the LH.

12-21 (52)

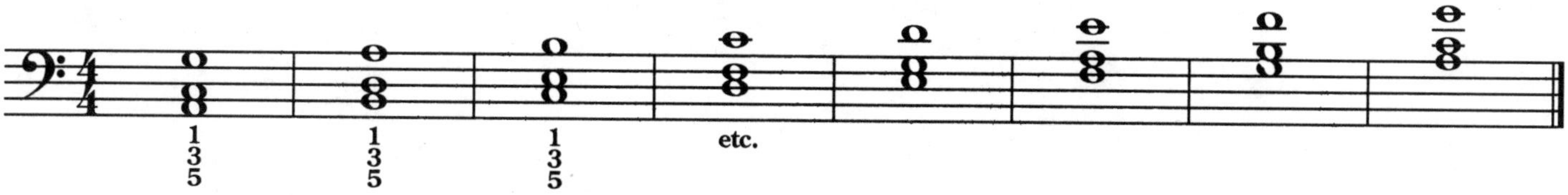

The 3rd is sometimes omitted from the seventh chord.
Play the following exercise with the LH.

12-21 (52)

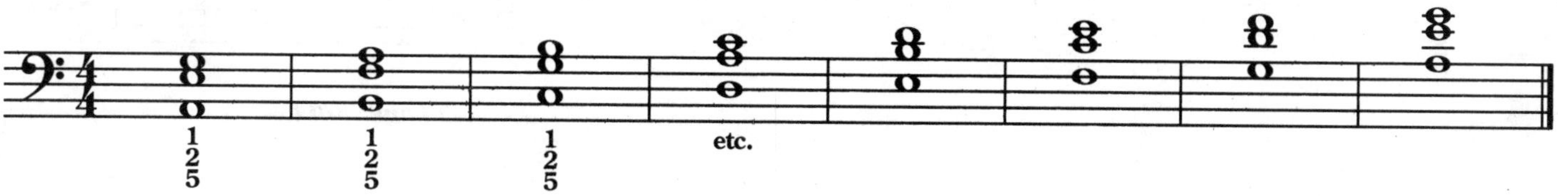

Playing Five Types of Seventh Chords

Play the following seventh chord exercise hands separately. Use fingers 1 2 3 5 for the RH and fingers 5 3 2 1 for the LH.

12-22 (53)

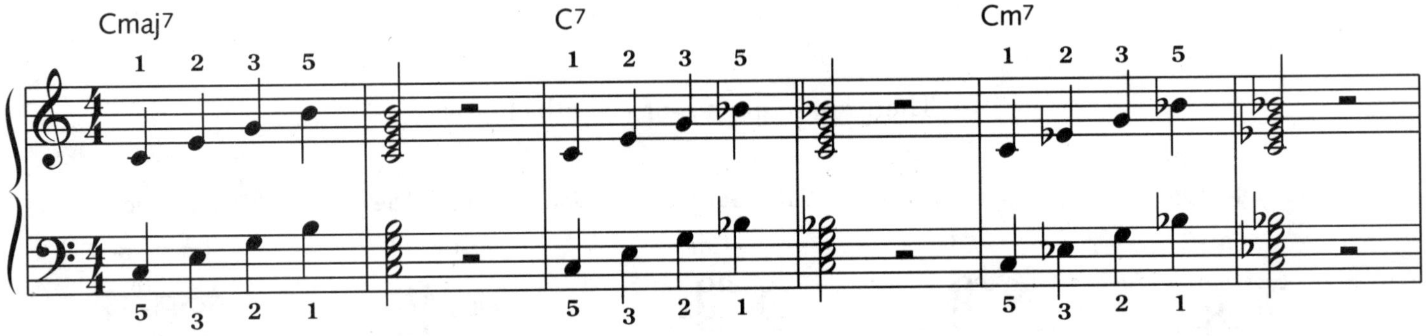

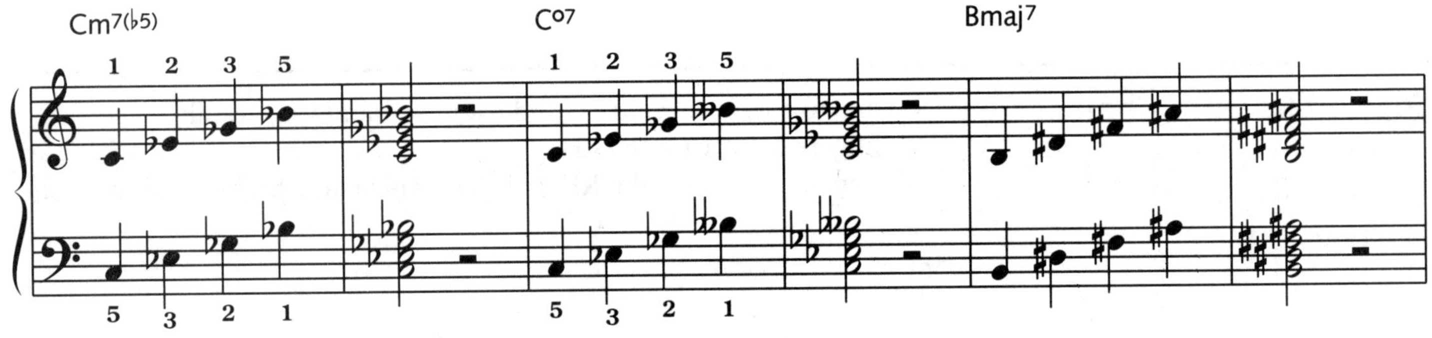

Continue downward by half steps until. . .

Inversions of Seventh Chords

Four-note seventh chords may be played in the following positions. All note names are the same in each position, but in a different order!

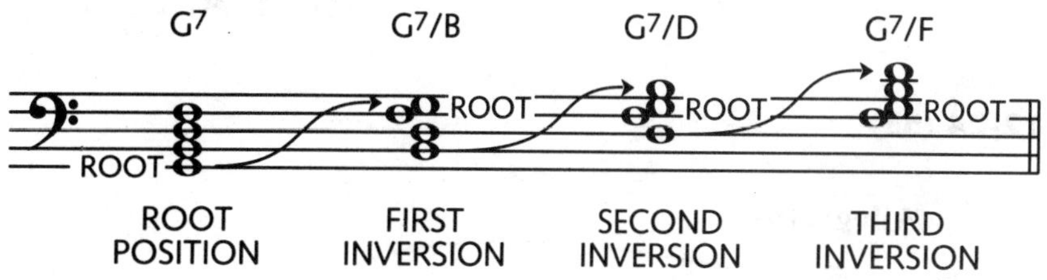

The first, second and third inversions are easily recognized by the interval of a 2nd in each chord. The top note of the 2nd is always the root!

Play the G7 chord and its inversions.

12-23 (54)

1.

12-23 (54)

2.

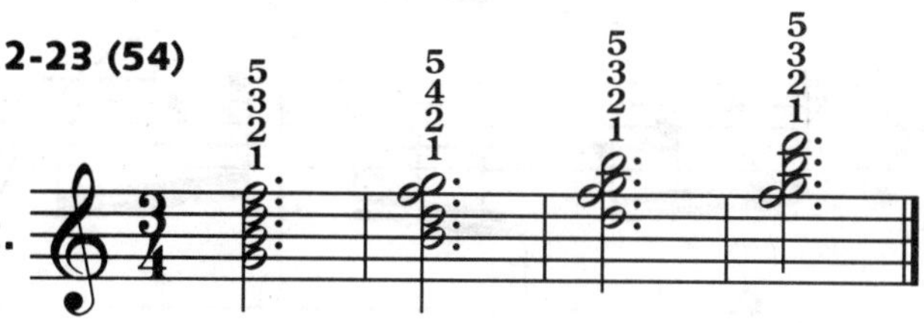

12-23 (54)

3.

12-23 (54)

4.

12-23 (54)

5.

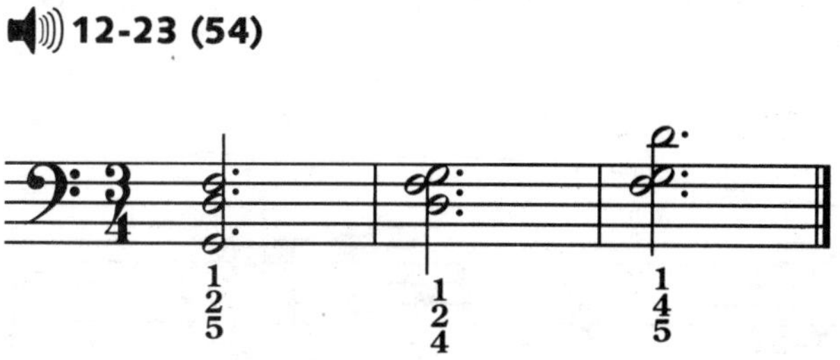

12-23 (54)

6.

▶ Play each example above using a D7 chord and C7 chord.

The Harpist

🔊 12-24 (55)

Dmitri Kabalevsky (1904–1987)
Op. 89, No. 24

Reading

Identify the key of each example. Use the indicated tempo, dynamics and articulation as you play these exercises.

Use the following practice directions:

1. Tap RH and count aloud; then LH.
2. Play hands separately and count aloud.
3. Tap hands together and count aloud.
4. Play hands together and count aloud.

12-25 (56)

Freely

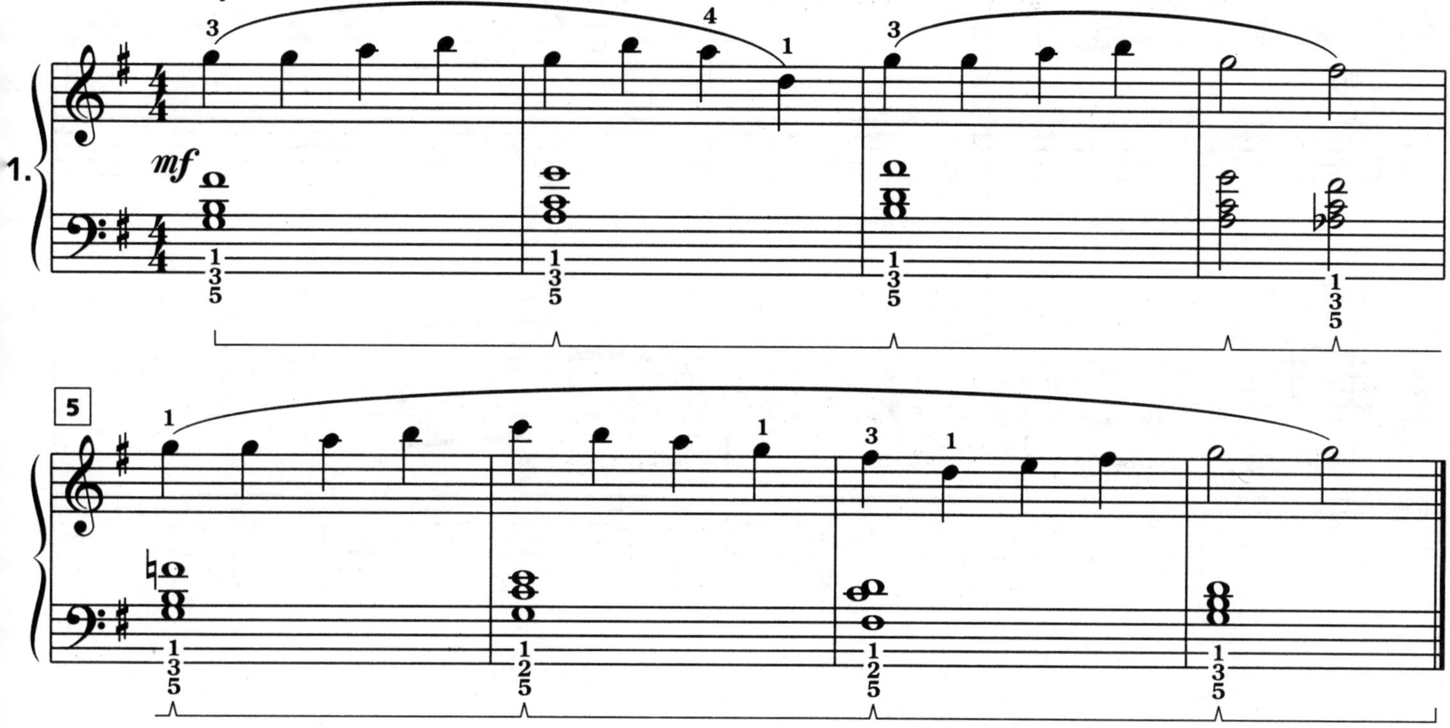

12-26 (57)

Misterioso *(mysteriously)*

Harmonization

Harmonize each melody below in two ways:

- Using the bottom note of each indicated seventh chord.
- Using the indicated root-position seventh chords.

12-27 (58)

12-28 (59)

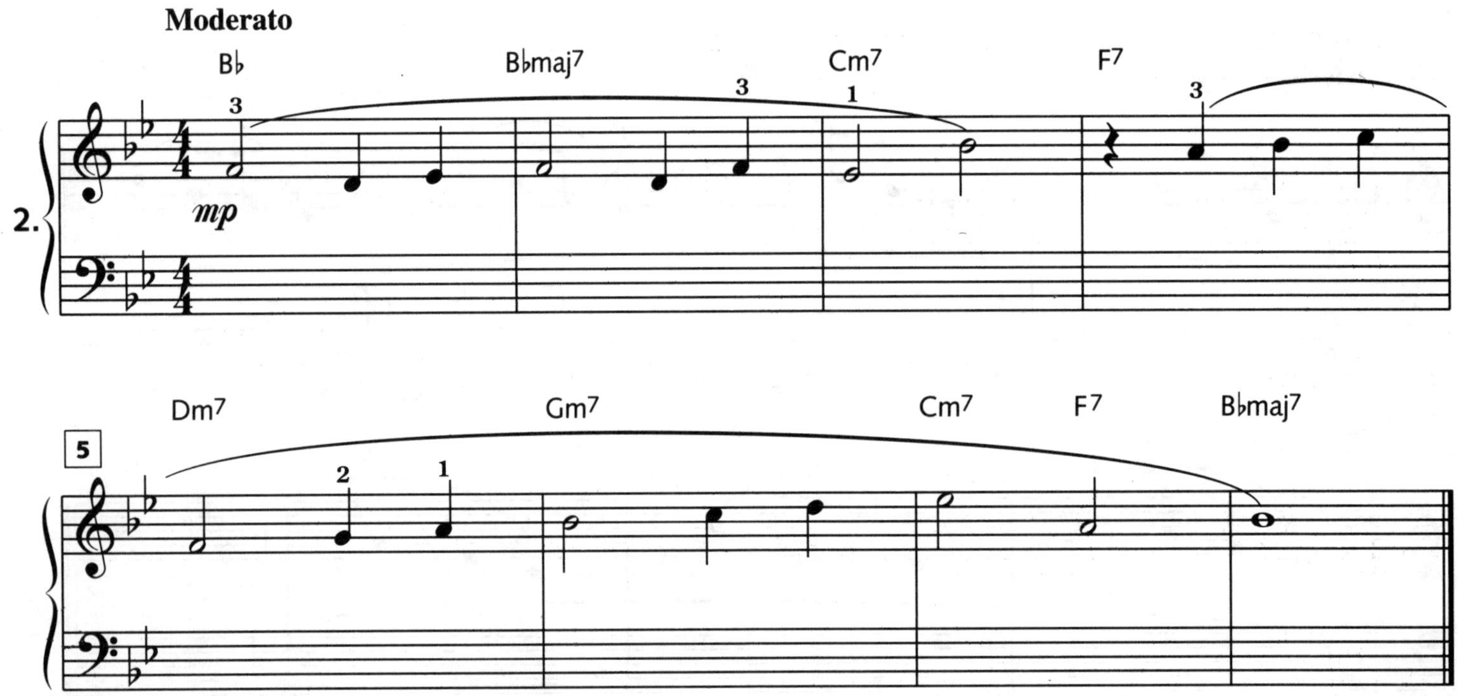

Using I, V^7, vi and ii chords, harmonize with a broken chord accompaniment. Use inversions to improve sound and for ease in performance. Write the Roman numeral name of each chord on the line below the staff.

3. Broken Chord Accompaniment

🔊 **12-29 (60)**

Moderato Denmark

▶ Transpose to G major.

Improvisation from Chord Symbols

Using the chord progressions below, improvise RH melodies while the LH plays the suggested accompaniment style. (First play the LH chord progressions using the suggested accompaniment style and observing the indicated meter.) Notate your favorite improvisation.

Rules for improvisation:

1. Use mostly chord tones and passing tones in the melody.
2. Most improvisations begin and end on tonic.
3. The ear should always be the final guide in determining which melody notes to play.

1. Broken Chord Accompaniment

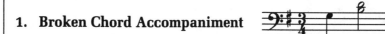

🔊 **12-30 (61)**

Key of G major

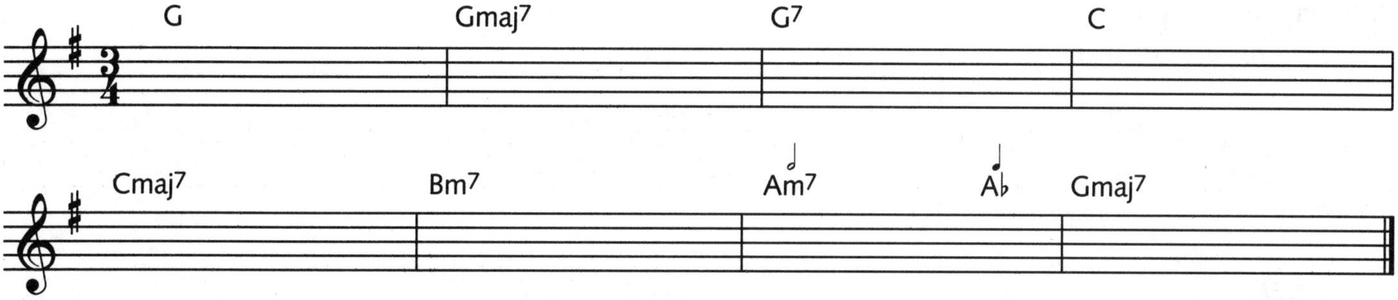

🔊 **12-31 (62)**

2. Block Chord Accompaniment

Key of C major

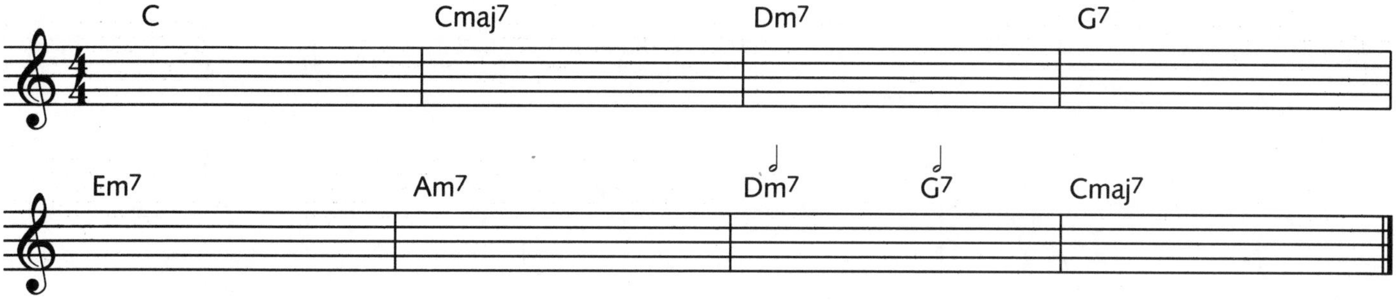

Unit 24

Minor Scales Beginning on Black Keys

Objectives

Upon completion of this unit the student will be able to:

1. Play harmonic minor scales and arpeggios beginning on black keys, using traditional fingerings.
2. Perform solo repertoire that uses primary and secondary chords in minor keys.
3. Sight-read and transpose music that uses primary chords, secondary chords and seventh chords in minor keys.
4. Harmonize and transpose melodies with primary chords, secondary chords and seventh chords.
5. Create two-hand accompaniments from chord symbols.
6. Create a four-part ensemble from chord symbols.

Assignments

Week of ________

Write your assignments for the week in the space below.

Playing Harmonic Minor Scales and Arpeggios

Build each scale in tetrachord position. Then practice hands separately:

1. The blocked scale as written.
2. The scale as written.
3. The arpeggio as written.

F♯ Minor

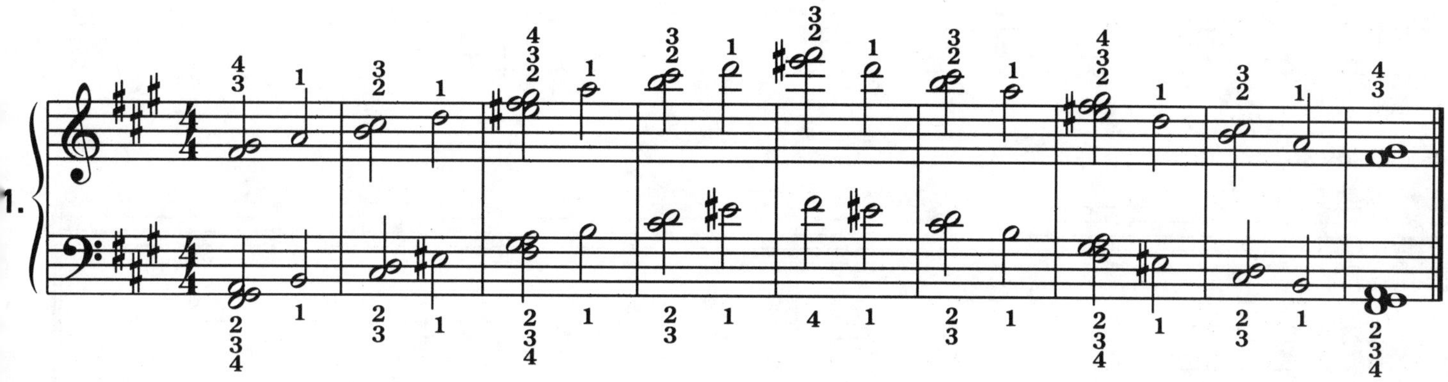

13-1 (33)

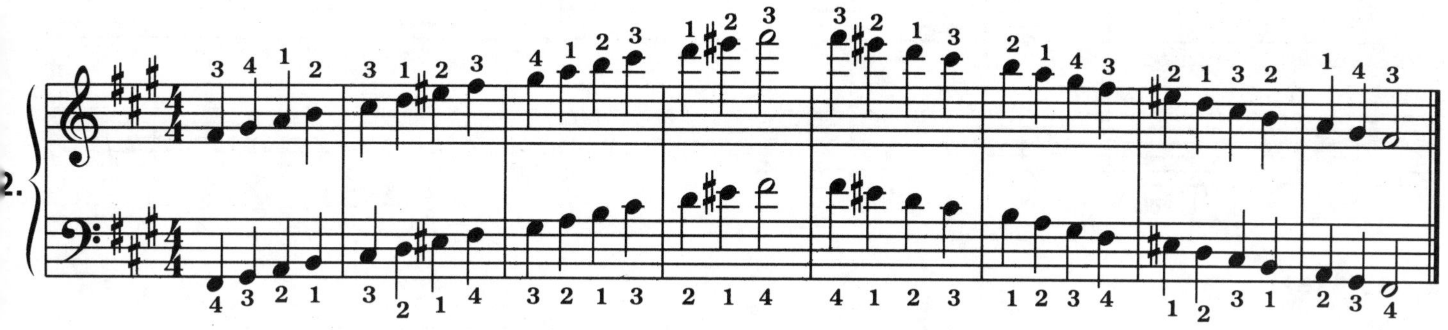

13-2 (34)

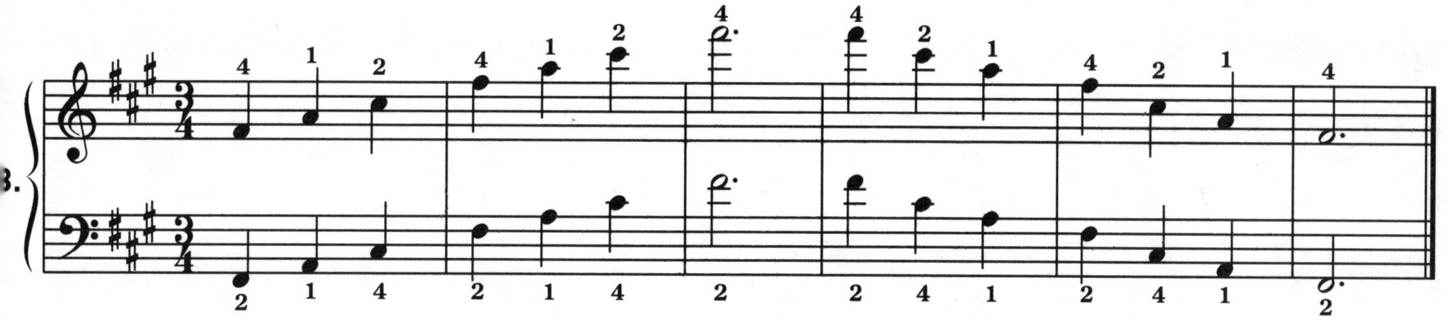

Playing Harmonic Minor Scales and Arpeggios (continued)

C♯ Minor

1.

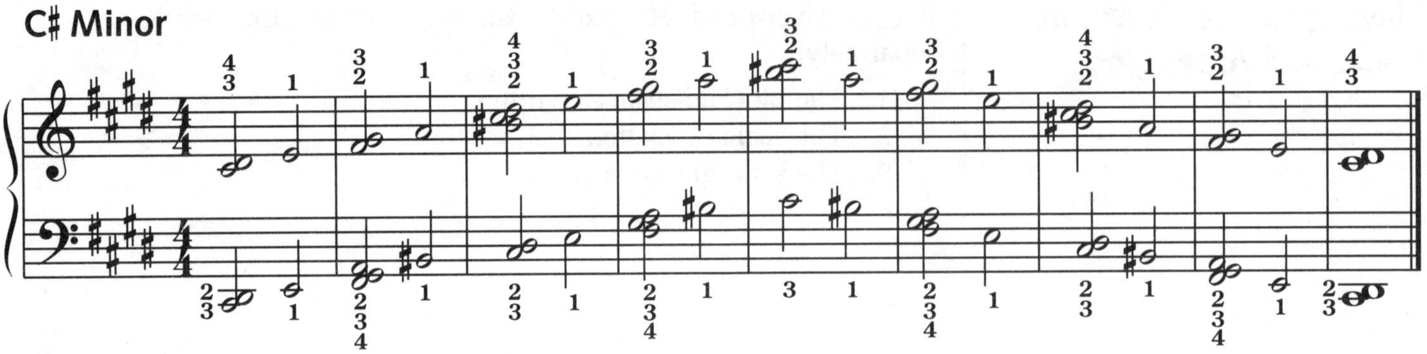

13-3 (35)

2.

13-4 (36)

3.

G♯ Minor

1.

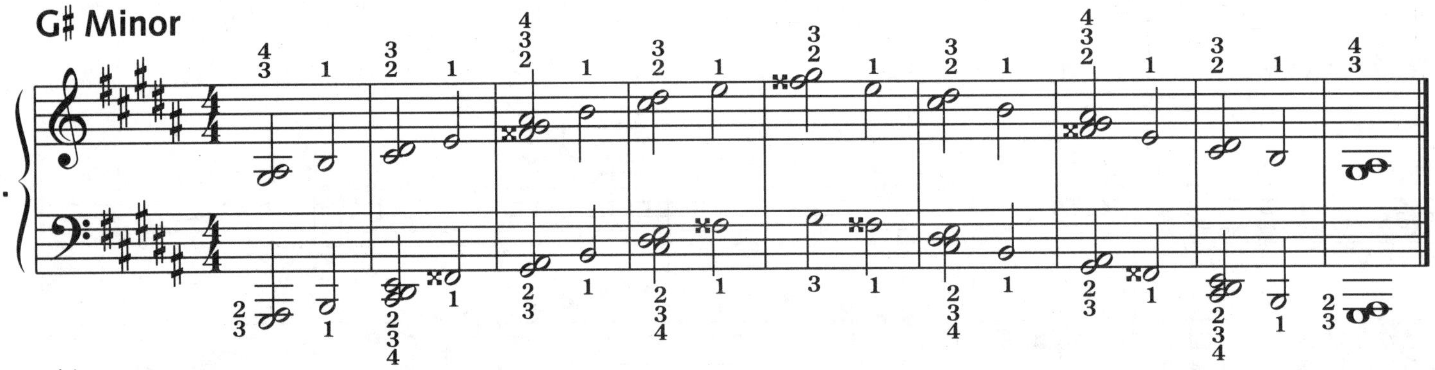

13-5 (37)

2.

13-6 (38)

3.

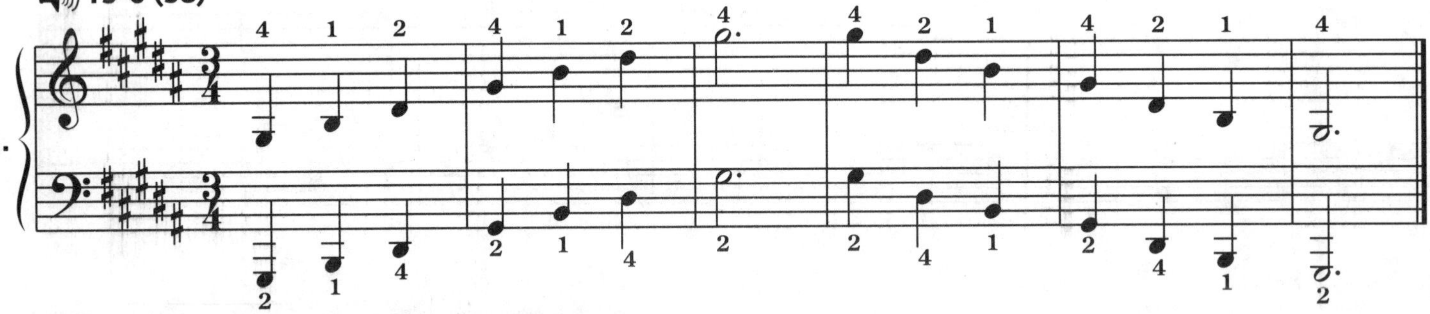

B♭ Minor

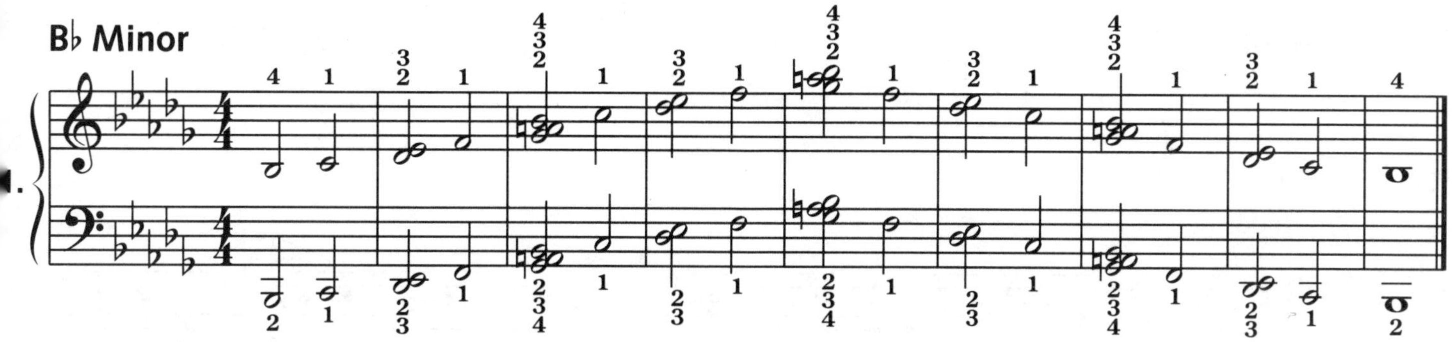

🔊 13-7 (39)

🔊 13-8 (40)

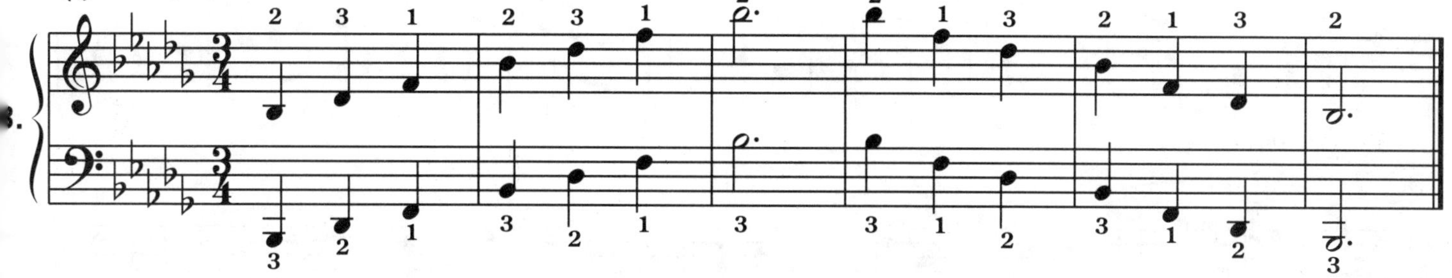

E♭ Minor

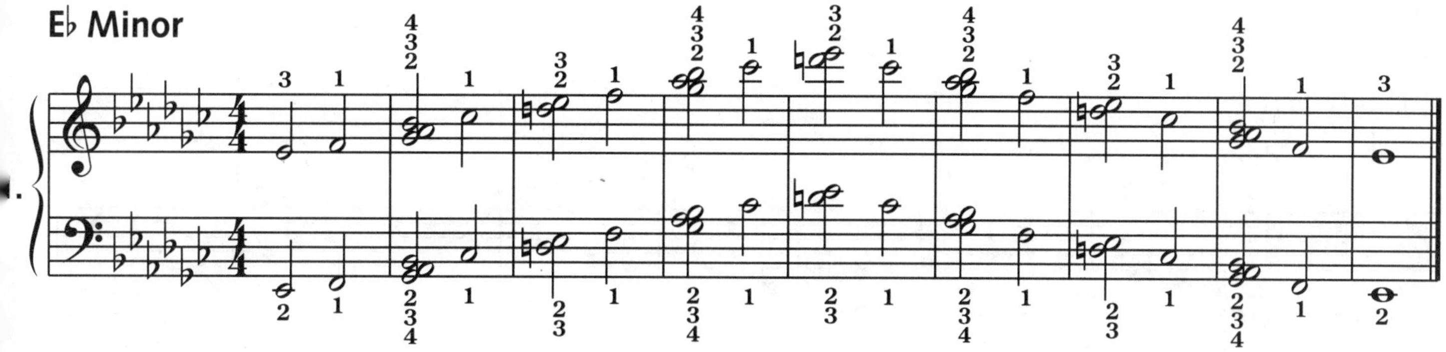

🔊 13-9 (41)

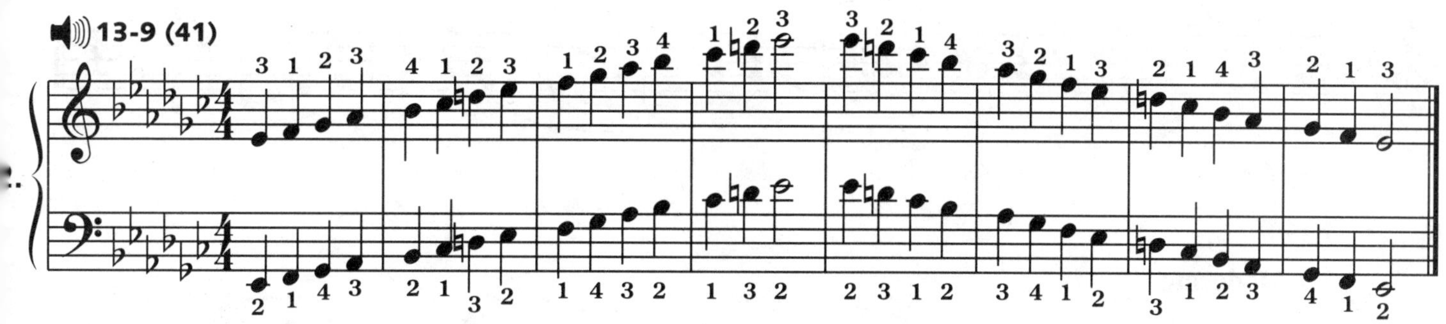

🔊 13-10 (42)

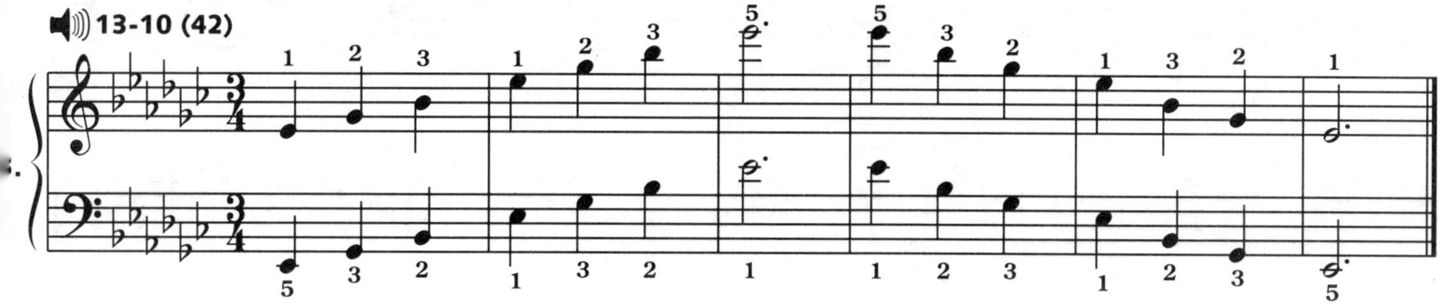

Technique

13-11 (43)

1.

13-11 (43)

2.

13-12 (44)

3.

13-12 (44)

4.

Solo Repertoire

PRELUDE NO. 1

13-13 (45)

Flowing forward

Catherine Rollin

Reading

Identify the key of each example. Use the indicated tempo, dynamics and articulation as you play these exercises.

Use the following practice directions:

1. Tap RH and count aloud; then LH.
2. Play hands separately and count aloud.
3. Tap hands together and count aloud.
4. Play hands together and count aloud.

13-14 (46)

Adagio

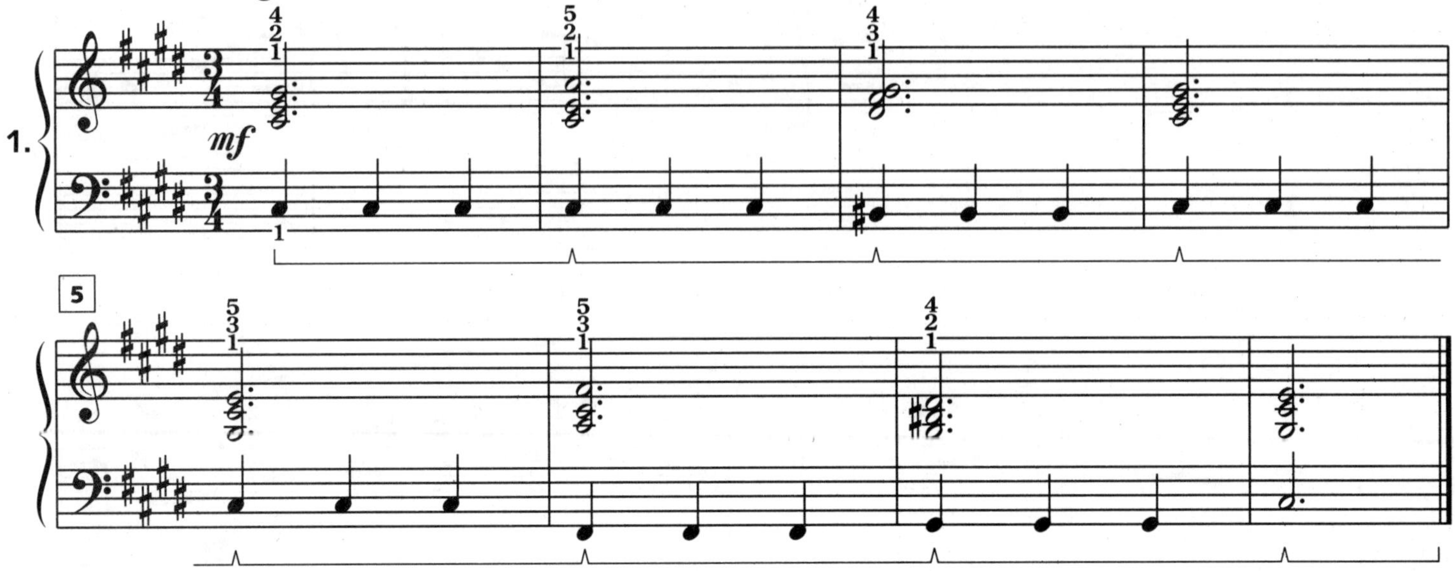

13-15 (47)

Andante

13-16 (48)

Allegretto

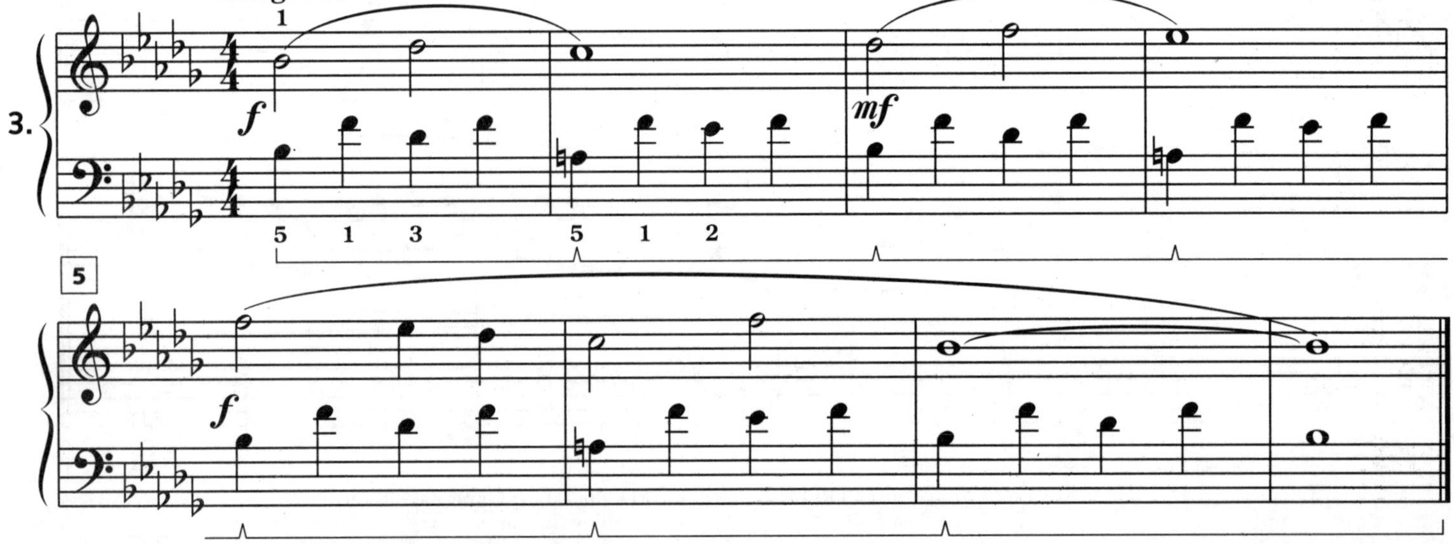

▶ Transpose to A minor.

Harmonization

1. Harmonize with a block chord accompaniment.

Block Chord Accompaniment

13-17 (49)

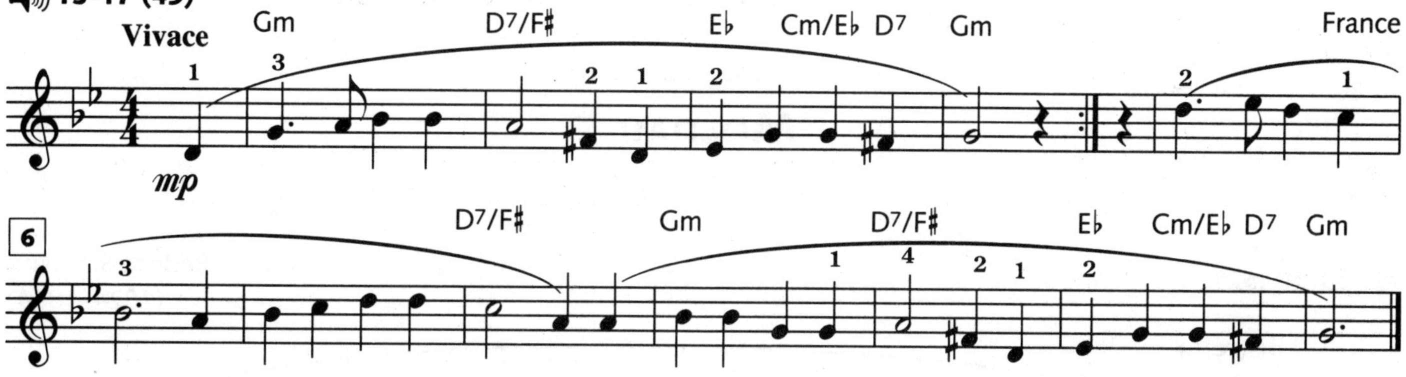

2. Using i, V7, iv and VI chords, harmonize with a waltz style accompaniment. Use inversions to improve the sound and for ease in performance.

Write the Roman numeral name of each chord on the line below the staff.

Waltz Style Accompaniment

13-18 (50)

▶ Transpose to G minor.

3. Harmonize the melody below in two ways:
   - Using the bottom note of each indicated seventh chord.
   - Using the indicated root-position seventh chords.

13-19 (51)

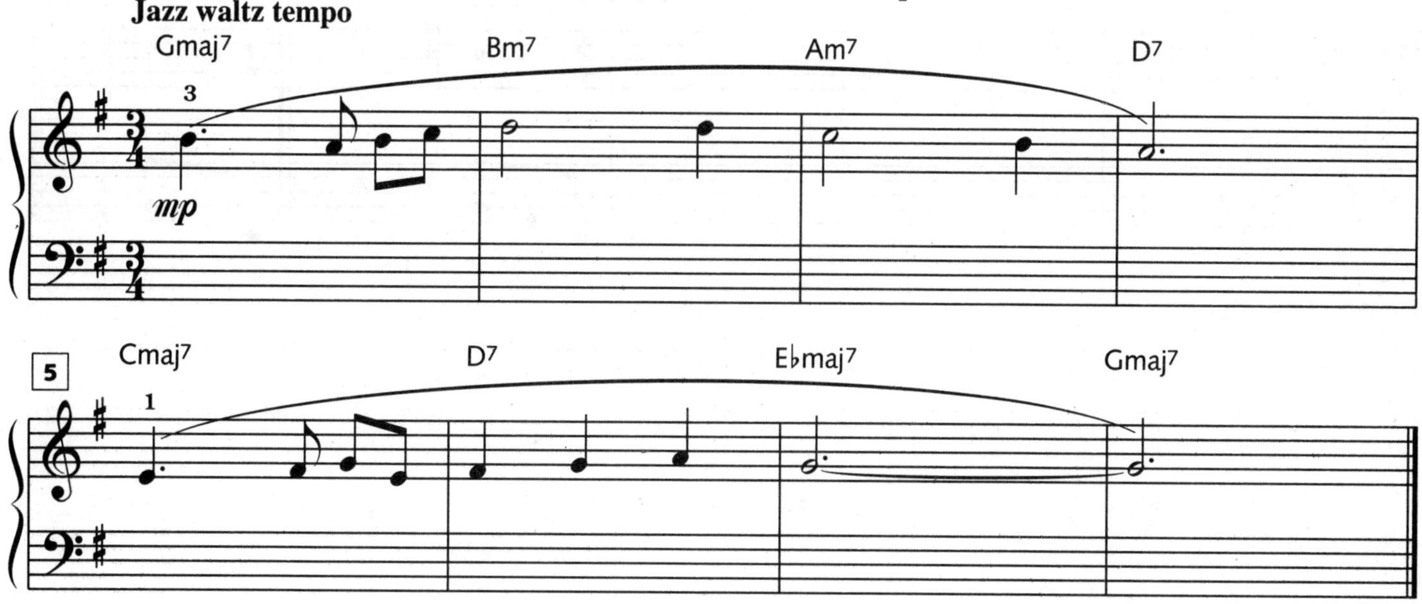

Harmonization with Two-Hand Accompaniment

Using the indicated chords, create a two-hand accompaniment for the following melody by continuing the pattern given in the first measure.

MOLDAU

13-20 (52)

Bedrich Smetana
(1824–1884)

Ensemble Repertoire

Play the four-part ensemble using the indicated chords to complete parts 3 and 4.

Part 1: Melody
Part 2: Countermelody
Part 3: Two-hand accompaniment
Part 4: Bass line (root–5th–root)

13-21 (53)

PRELUDE IN SEVENTHS

Flowing

E. L. Lancaster

Unit 25

Triads of the Key on Minor Scales Beginning on Black Keys

Objectives

Upon completion of this unit the student will be able to:

1. Build a triad on any note of a harmonic minor scale that begins on a black key.
2. Perform solo repertoire that uses triads of the key, scale and arpeggio patterns in minor.
3. Sight-read and transpose music that uses primary chords in minor keys.
4. Harmonize and transpose melodies with primary chords, secondary chords and their inversions.
5. Perform duet repertoire with a partner.

Assignments

Week of ________

Write your assignments for the week in the space below.

Playing Triads of the Key in Harmonic Minor

Play triads of the key in C♯ harmonic minor. Note the quality of each chord.

Play with RH:

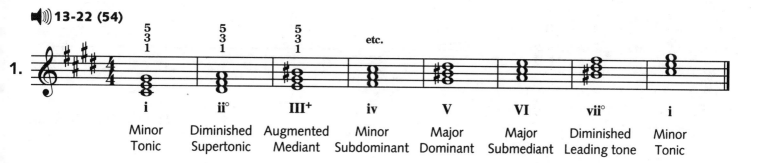

🔊 13-22 (54)

1. 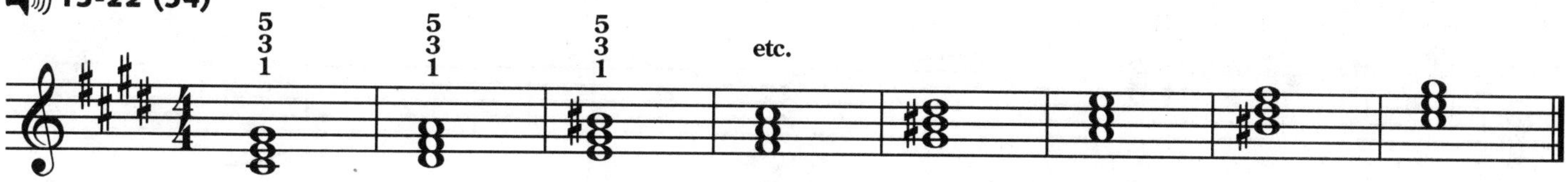

i	ii°	III+	iv	V	VI	vii°	i
Minor Tonic	Diminished Supertonic	Augmented Mediant	Minor Subdominant	Major Dominant	Major Submediant	Diminished Leading tone	Minor Tonic

▶ Transpose to F♯ harmonic minor and B♭ harmonic minor.

Play with LH:

🔊 13-22 (54)

2. 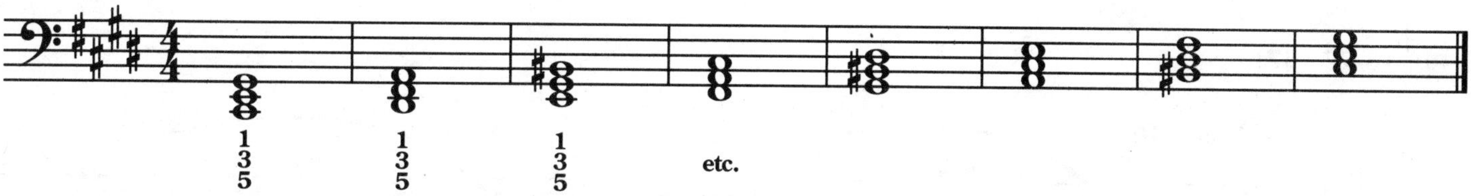

i	ii°	III+	iv	V	VI	vii°	i
Minor Tonic	Diminished Supertonic	Augmented Mediant	Minor Subdominant	Major Dominant	Major Submediant	Diminished Leading tone	Minor Tonic

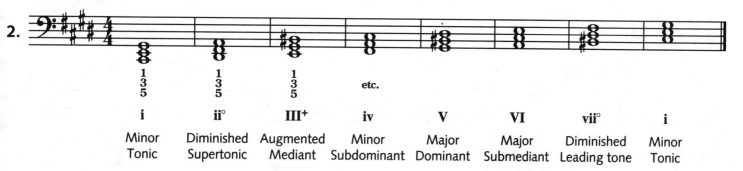

▶ Transpose to F♯ harmonic minor and B♭ harmonic minor.

Technique

13-23 (55)

1.

▶ Transpose to F♯ minor.

13-24 (56)

2.

▶ Transpose to G♯ minor.

13-25 (57)

3.

▶ Transpose to B♭ minor.

Solo Repertoire

Menuet in D Minor

13-26 (58)

Jean-Baptiste Lully
(1632–1687)

Reading

Identify the key of each example. Use the indicated tempo, dynamics and articulation as you play these exercises.

Use the following practice directions:

1. Tap RH and count aloud; then LH.
2. Play hands separately and count aloud.
3. Tap hands together and count aloud.
4. Play hands together and count aloud.

13-27 (59)

▶ Transpose to G minor.

13-28 (60)

▶ Transpose to E minor.

Harmonization

Harmonize each melody below in two ways:

- Using the bottom note of each indicated triad and inversion.
- Using the indicated triads and inversions.

13-29 (61)

▶ Transpose to G minor.

13-30 (62)

Concerto for Horn

13-31 (63)

Allegro

Wolfgang Amadeus Mozart (1756–1791)

K. 417

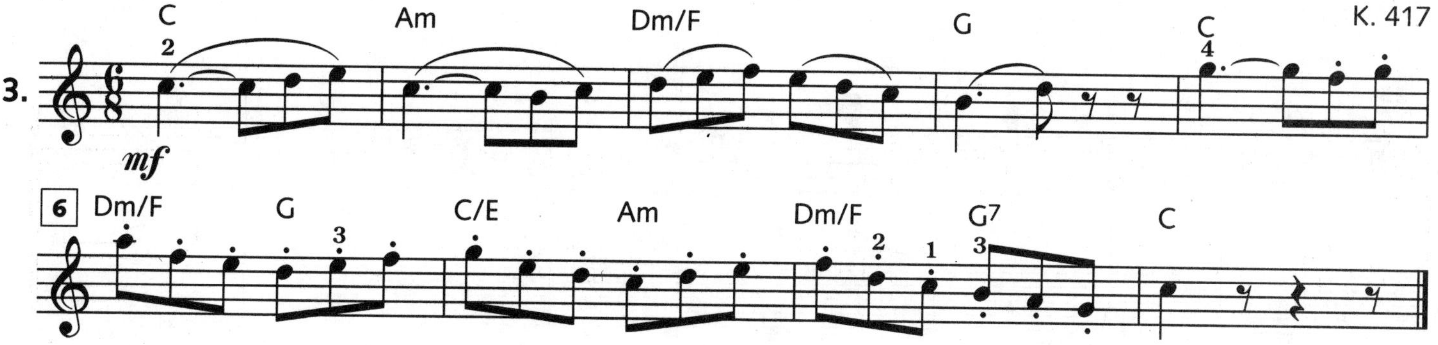

▶ Transpose to D major.

Duet Repertoire

Dance

from The Children's Musical Friend

Secondo

Heinrich Wohlfahrt (1797–1883)
Op. 87, No. 49

13-32 (64)

Dance
from The Children's Musical Friend
Primo

Heinrich Wohlfahrt (1797–1883)
Op. 87, No. 49

13-32 (64)

Unit 26

The iii Chord

Objectives

Upon completion of this unit the student will be able to:

1. Play I–IV–vii°–iii–vi–ii–V–I chord progressions in all major and minor keys.
2. Perform solo repertoire that uses mediant harmonies.
3. Sight-read and transpose music that uses mediant chords.
4. Harmonize and transpose melodies with mediant chords.
5. Improvise melodies from chord symbols.

Assignments

Week of ________

Write your assignments for the week in the space below.

The iii Chord

The iii chord (mediant) is sometimes substituted for the V chord since the chords have two notes in common.

Key of C Major

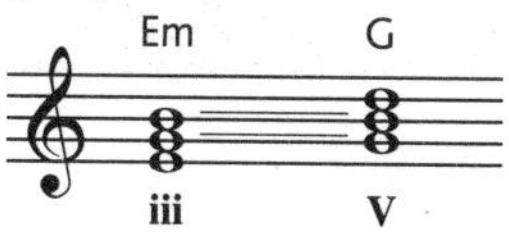

In major keys, the iii chord is a minor triad.

Key of C Major

In natural minor keys, the III chord is a major triad.

Key of A Natural Minor

In harmonic minor keys, the III chord is an augmented triad.

Key of A Harmonic Minor

Play the following chord progression hands separately.

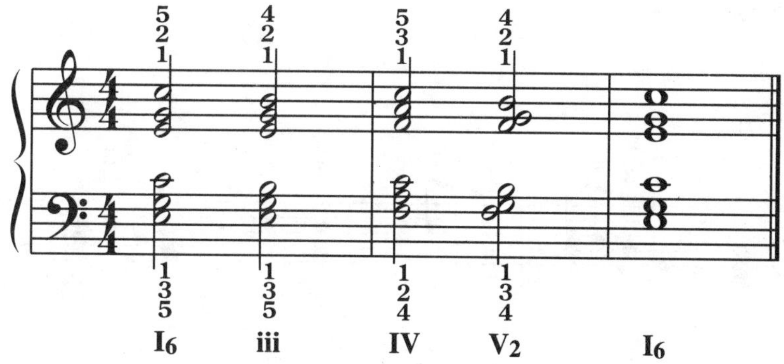

▶ Transpose to G major, F major, A harmonic minor and C harmonic minor.

Playing the I–IV–vii°–iii–vi–ii–V–I Chord Progression

14-1 (34)

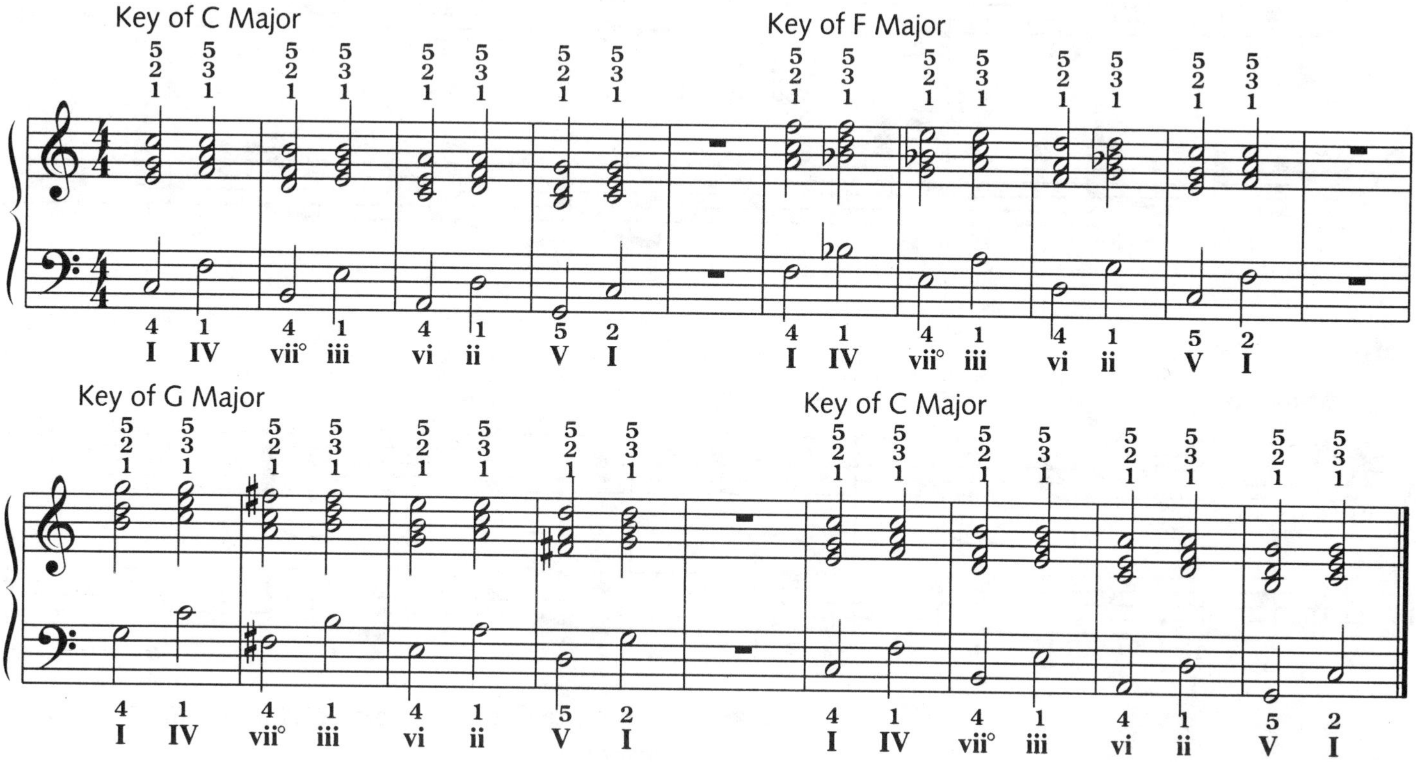

Practice the preceding example in the following keys:

14-2 (35)	1. D	G	A	D	major
14-3 (36)	2. E	A	B	E	major
14-4 (37)	3. D♭	G♭	A♭	D♭	major
14-5 (38)	4. E♭	A♭	B♭	E♭	major
14-6 (39)	5. A	D	E	A	natural minor
14-7 (40)	6. B	E	F♯	B	natural minor
14-8 (41)	7. C	F	G	C	natural minor
14-9 (42)	8. B♭	E♭	F	B♭	natural minor
14-10 (43)	9. C♯	F♯	G♯	C♯	natural minor

Technique

14-11 (44)

Andante

1.

14-11 (44)

Andante

2.

14-12 (45)

Moderato

3.

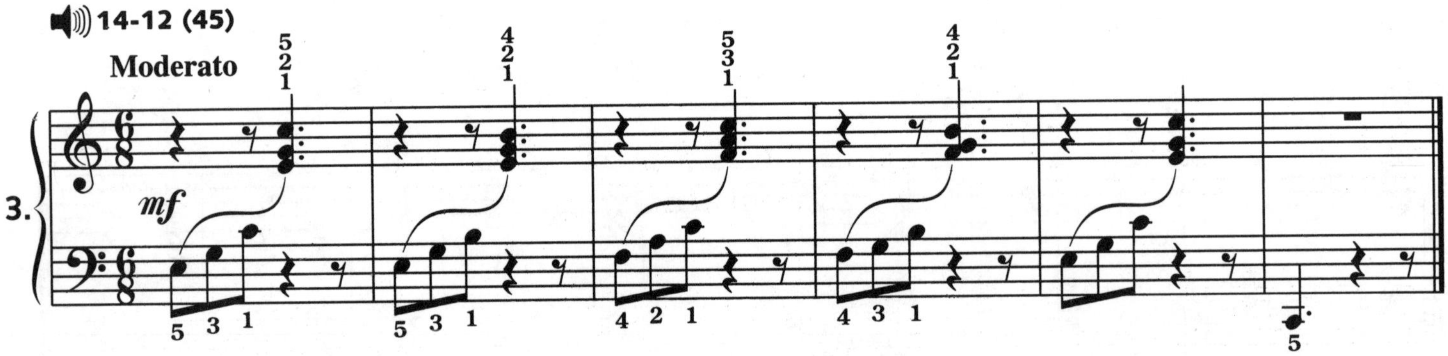

▶ Transpose to G major, F major, A harmonic minor and C harmonic minor.

Solo Repertoire

German Dance

14-13 (46)

Franz Joseph Haydn
(1732–1809)

Reading

Identify the key of each example. Use the indicated tempo, dynamics and articulation as you play these exercises.

Use the following practice directions:

1. Tap RH and count aloud; then LH.
2. Play hands separately and count aloud.
3. Tap hands together and count aloud.
4. Play hands together and count aloud.

14-14 (47)

▶ Transpose to G major.

14-15 (48)

▶ Transpose to A minor.

Harmonization

1. Harmonize with a broken chord accompaniment.

Broken Chord Accompaniment 

14-16 (49)

REUBEN, RACHEL

Traditional

Allegretto

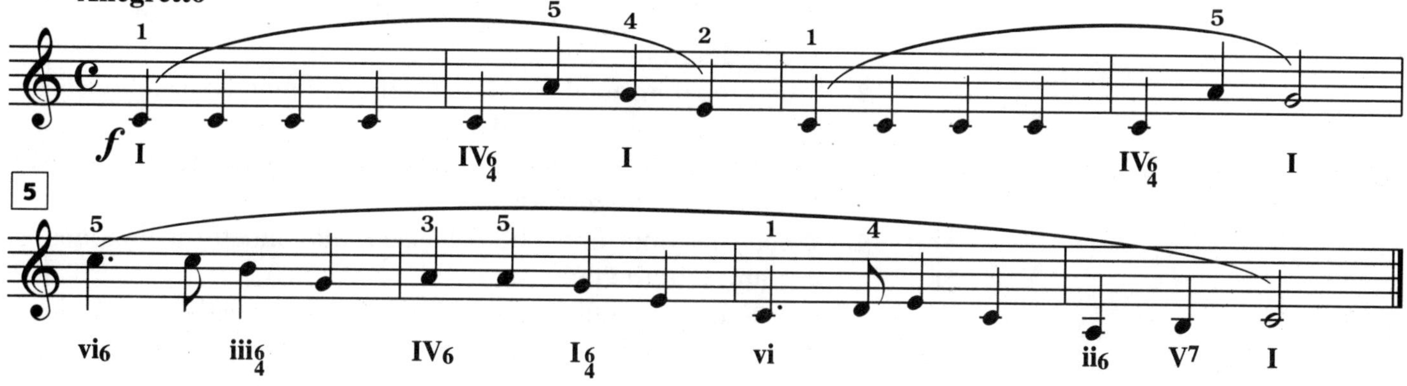

▶ Transpose to D major.

2. Using i, V7, and III chords, harmonize with a block chord accompaniment. Use inversions to improve sound and for ease in performance. Write the Roman numeral name of each chord on the line below the staff.

Block Chord Accompaniment 

14-17 (50)

Ukraine

Allegro

▶ Transpose to F major.

3. Harmonize the melody below in two ways:
   - Using the bottom note of each indicated triad and inversion.
   - Using the indicated triads and inversions.

14-18 (51)

SHENANDOAH

United States

Slowly

Improvisation from Chord Symbols

Using the chord progressions below, improvise RH melodies while the LH plays the suggested accompaniment style. (First play the LH chord progression using the suggested accompaniment style and observing the indicated meter.) Notate your favorite improvisation.

Rules for improvisation:

1. When the tonic chord is used, play mostly scale tones 1, 3 and 5 in the melody.
2. When the dominant chord is used, play mostly scale tones 2, 4, 5 and 7 in the melody.
3. When the subdominant chord is used, play mostly scale tones 1, 4 and 6 in the melody.
4. When the supertonic chord is used, play mostly scale tones 2, 4 and 6 in the melody.
5. When the submediant chord is used, play mostly scale tones 1, 3 and 6 in the melody.
6. When the mediant chord is used, play mostly scale tones 3, 5 and 7 in the melody.
7. Most improvisations begin and end on tonic.
8. The ear should always be the final guide in determining which melody notes to play.

1. Broken Chord Accompaniment

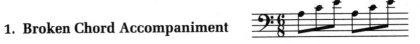

14-19 (52)

Key of A harmonic minor

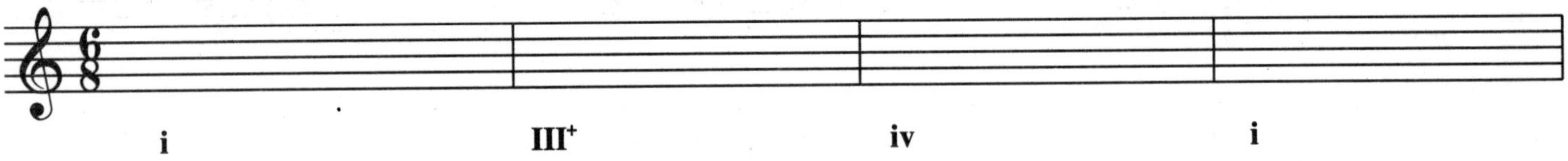

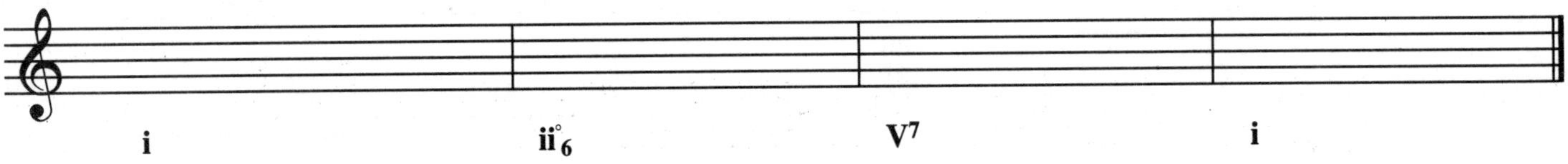

2. Alberti Bass Accompaniment

14-20 (53)

Key of G major

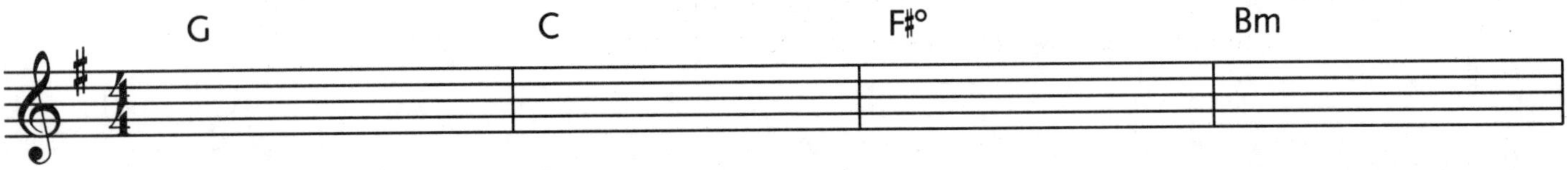

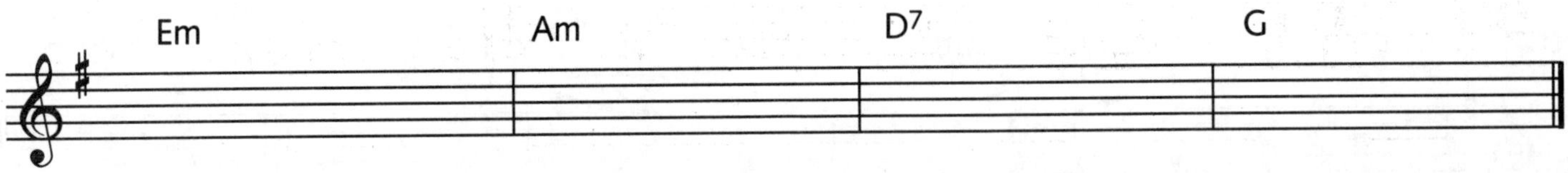

Unit 26 **Review Worksheet**

Name ____________________ *Date* ____________________

1. Identify each harmonic minor scale below by writing its name on the indicated line. Write the correct RH fingering on the lines above the staff and the correct LH fingering on the lines below the staff.

____ harmonic minor scale

____ harmonic minor scale

____ harmonic minor scale

____ harmonic minor scale

2. Identify each harmonic minor key by writing its name on the line above the staff. Using whole notes, write a VI chord on the staff. Write the letter name for each chord on the line below the staff.

3. Draw a line to connect the seventh chord on the left with its name on the right.

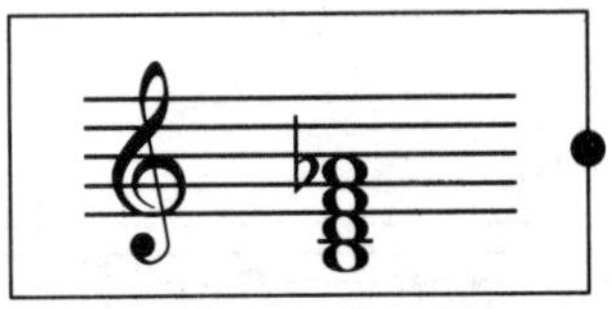

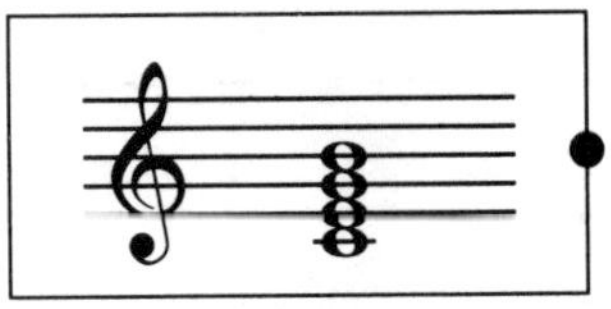

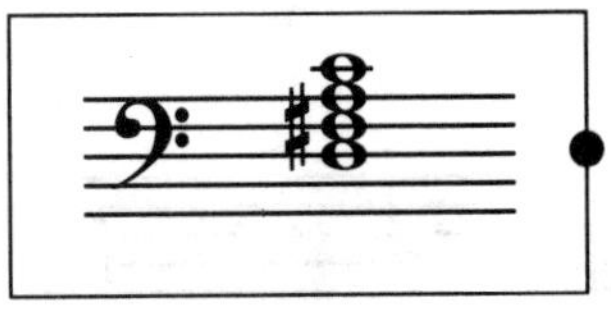

- Cmaj⁷
- D⁷
- Fm⁷⁽♭⁵⁾
- F♯m⁷
- B°⁷
- A♭⁷

---

4. Identify each harmonic minor key by writing its name on the line above the staff. Using whole notes, write the triad indicated by each Roman numeral on the staff.

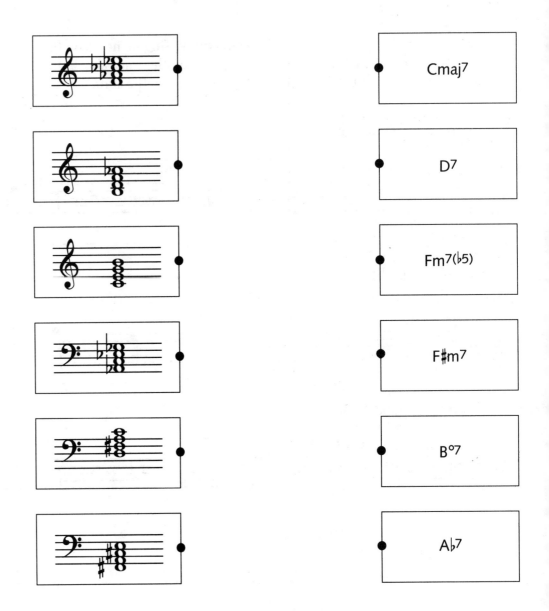

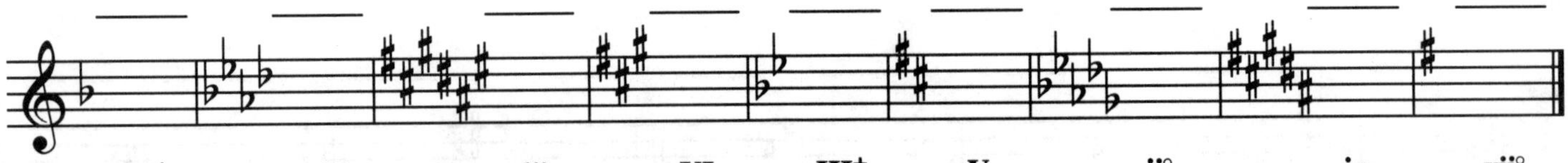

III⁺   vii°   ii°   VI   III⁺   V   ii°   iv   vii°

Unit 27

Modes Related to Major

Objectives

Upon completion of this unit the student will be able to:

1. Play Lydian and Mixolydian scales built on any note.
2. Play triads of the key in Lydian and Mixolydian modes.
3. Sight-read music in Lydian and Mixolydian modes.
4. Harmonize melodies in Lydian and Mixolydian modes.
5. Improvise melodies in Lydian and Mixolydian modes as the teacher plays an accompaniment.

Assignments

Week of ________

Write your assignments for the week in the space below.

Ionian Mode

In ancient Greece, the early church used a system of music based on modes. Almost all music written before the 1500s was based on the various modes. Many well-known folk songs are modal. Recently, modal music has become more popular and modern composers use modal melodies and harmonies in their compositions.

Any scale of eight neighboring white keys is a **modal scale.** The scale using eight white keys beginning and ending on C, which we call the C major scale, may also be called the **Ionian scale.**

Play *Yankee Doodle* in the Ionian mode (major).

IONIAN YANKEE DOODLE

🔊 **14-21 (54)**

Lydian Mode

The scale using eight white keys, beginning and ending on F, is called the **Lydian scale.** The Lydian scale is like a major scale with the 4th tone raised one half-step.

Using tetrachord position, play the Lydian scale.

▶ Transpose to C Lydian, G Lydian, B♭ Lydian and E♭ Lydian.

Play triads of the key in F Lydian.

14-22 (55)

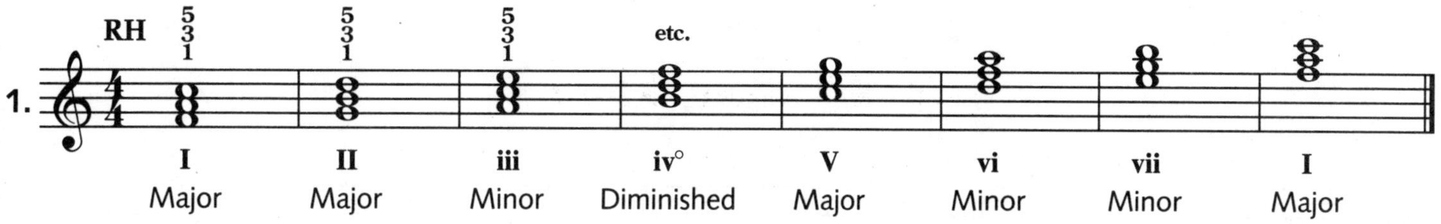

▶ Transpose to C Lydian and B♭ Lydian.

14-22 (55)

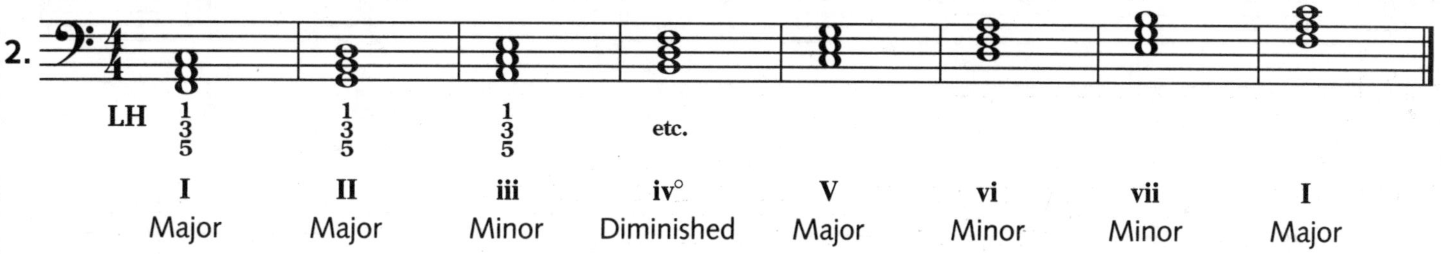

▶ Transpose to C Lydian and B♭ Lydian.

Play *Yankee Doodle* in the Lydian mode.

LYDIAN YANKEE DOODLE

14-23 (56)

Allegro

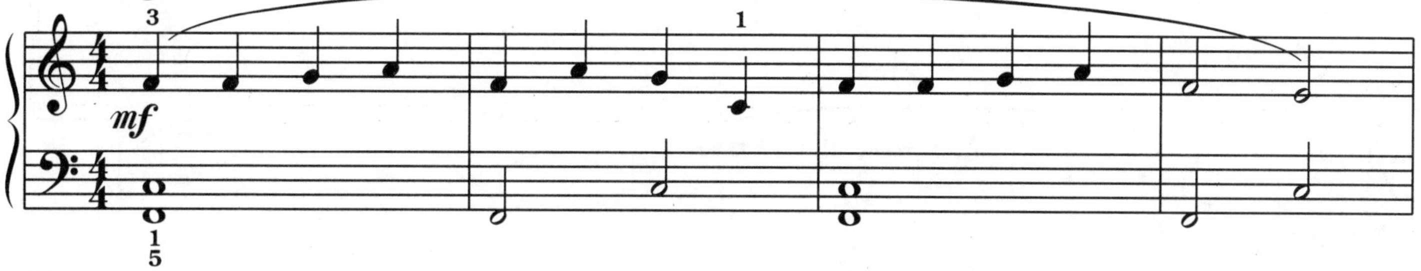

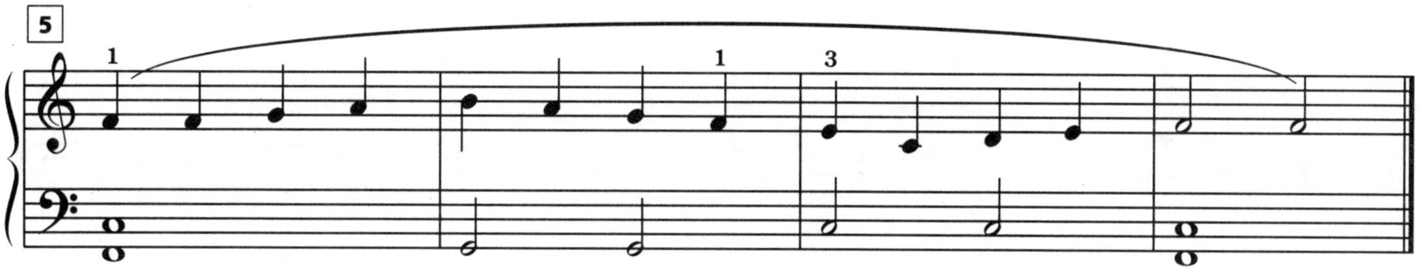

Reading in Lydian Mode

Use the indicated tempo, dynamics and articulation as you play the exercise. Use the following practice directions:

1. Tap RH and count aloud; then LH.
2. Play hands separately and count aloud.
3. Tap hands together and count aloud.
4. Play hands together and count aloud.

14-24 (57)

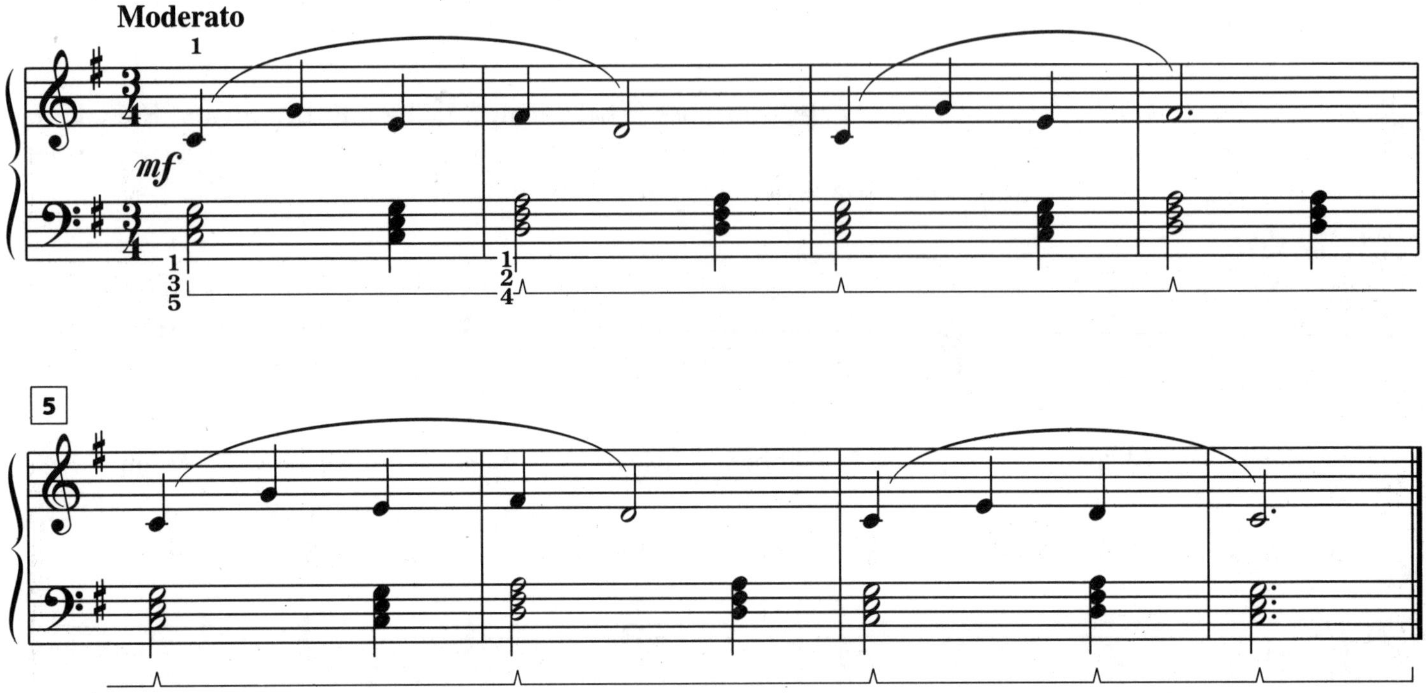

Harmonization in Lydian Mode

Harmonize with a broken chord accompaniment.

Broken Chord Accompaniment

14-25 (58)

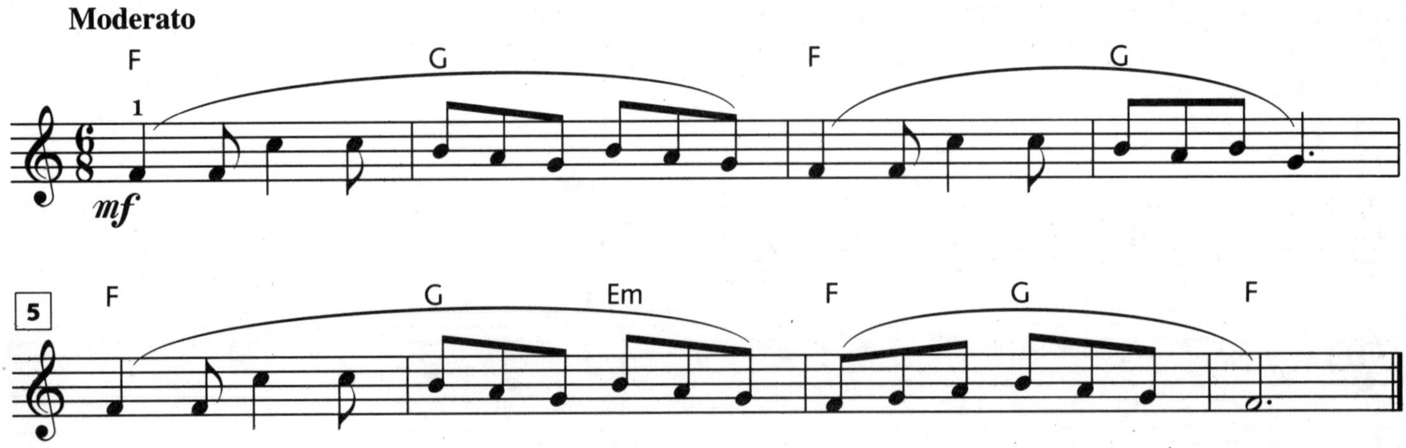

Improvisation in Lydian Mode

Improvise an 8-measure melody using the appropriate Lydian scale in tetrachord position as your teacher plays each accompaniment. Listen to the 4-measure introduction to establish the tempo, mood and style before beginning the melody.

14-26 (59)

TEACHER ACCOMPANIMENT

1. **F Lydian:** Begin and end your melody on F.

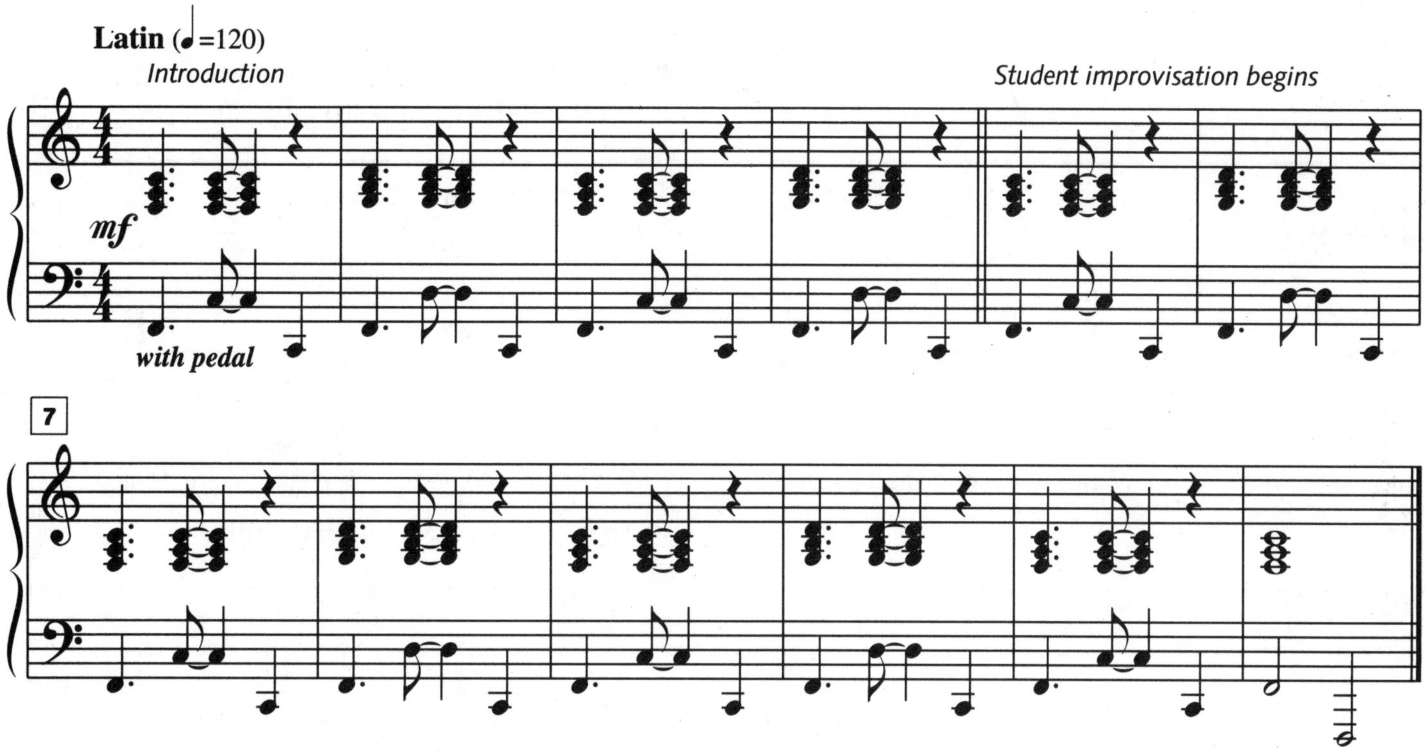

14-27 (60)

TEACHER ACCOMPANIMENT

2. **C Lydian:** Begin and end your melody on C.

Mixolydian Mode

The scale using eight white keys, beginning and ending on G, is called the **Mixolydian scale.** The Mixolydian scale is like a major scale with the 7th tone lowered one half-step.

Using tetrachord position, play the Mixolydian scale.

▶ Transpose to C Mixolydian, F Mixolydian, D Mixolydian and A Mixolydian.

Play triads of the key in G Mixolydian.

14-28 (61)

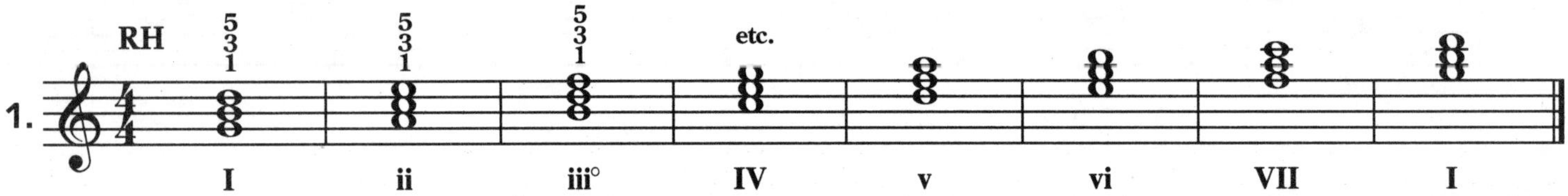

I	ii	iii°	IV	v	vi	VII	I
Major	Minor	Diminished	Major	Minor	Minor	Major	Major

▶ Transpose to C Mixolydian and D Mixolydian.

14-28 (61)

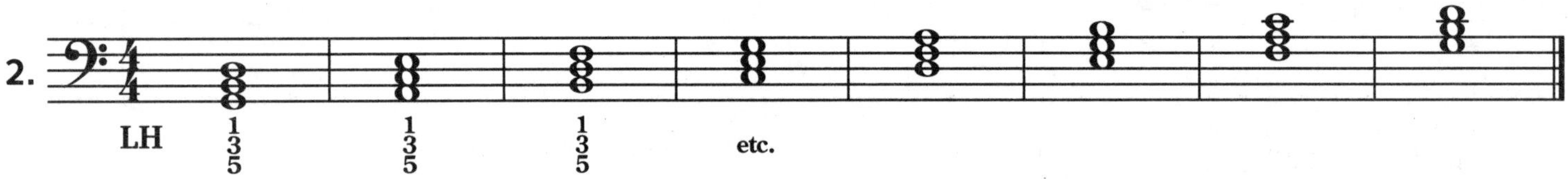

I	ii	iii°	IV	v	vi	VII	I
Major	Minor	Diminished	Major	Minor	Minor	Major	Major

▶ Transpose to C Mixolydian and D Mixolydian.

Play *Yankee Doodle* in the Mixolydian mode.

14-29 (62)

MIXOLYDIAN YANKEE DOODLE

Reading in Mixolydian Mode

Use the indicated tempo, dynamics and articulation as you play the exercise. Use the following practice directions:

1. Tap RH and count aloud; then LH.
2. Play hands separately and count aloud.
3. Tap hands together and count aloud.
4. Play hands together and count aloud.

🔊 **14-30 (63)**

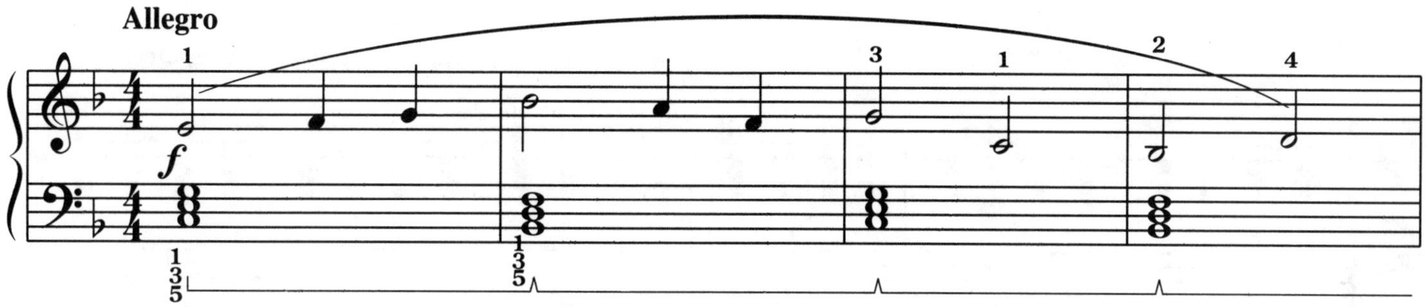

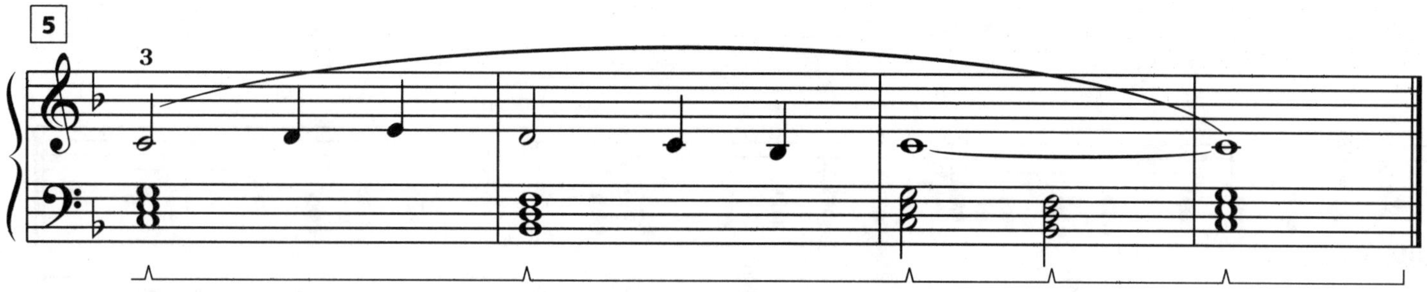

Harmonization in Mixolydian Mode

Harmonize with a waltz style accompaniment.

Waltz Style Accompaniment

🔊 **14-31 (64)**

Improvisation in Mixolydian Mode

Improvise an 8-measure melody using the appropriate Mixolydian scale in tetrachord position as your teacher plays each accompaniment. Listen to the 4-measure introduction to establish the tempo, mood and style before beginning the melody.

1. **G Mixolydian:** Begin and end your melody on G.

14-32 (65)

TEACHER ACCOMPANIMENT

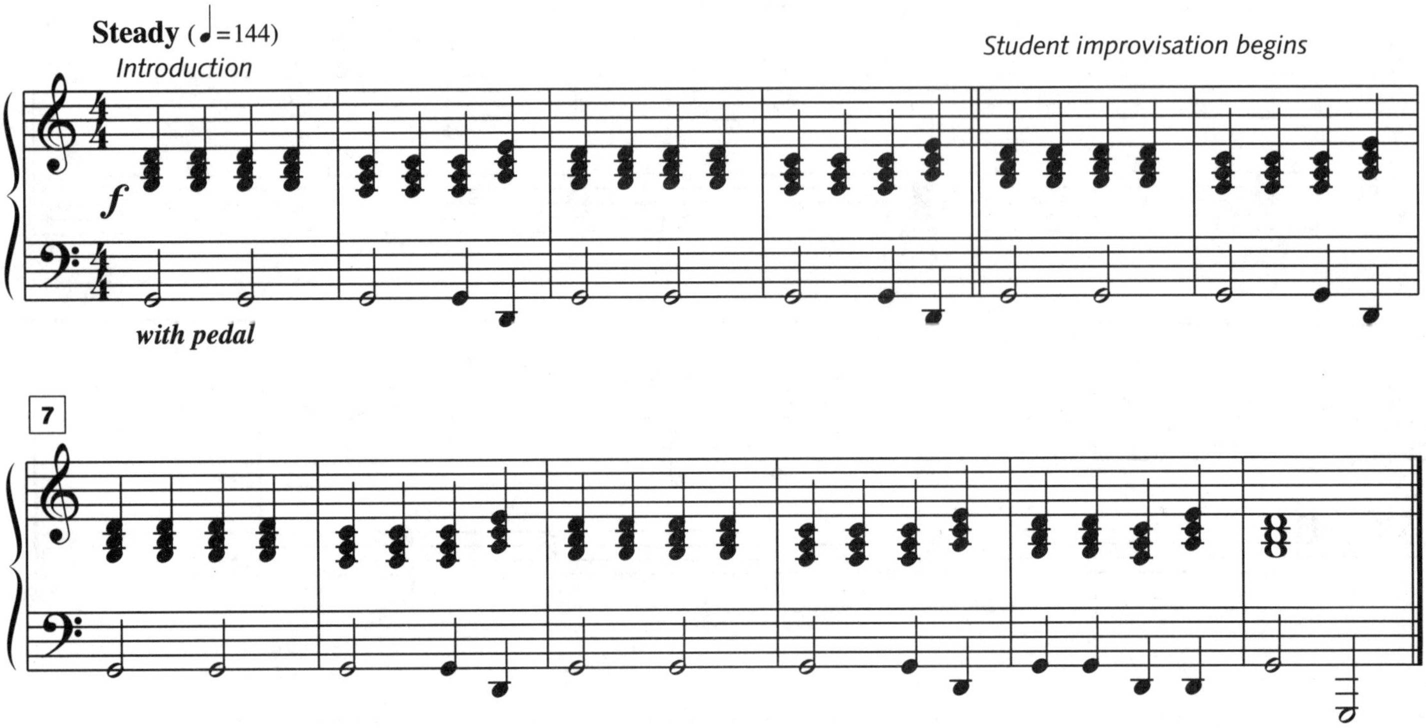

2. **C Mixolydian:** Begin and end your melody on C.

14-33 (66)

TEACHER ACCOMPANIMENT

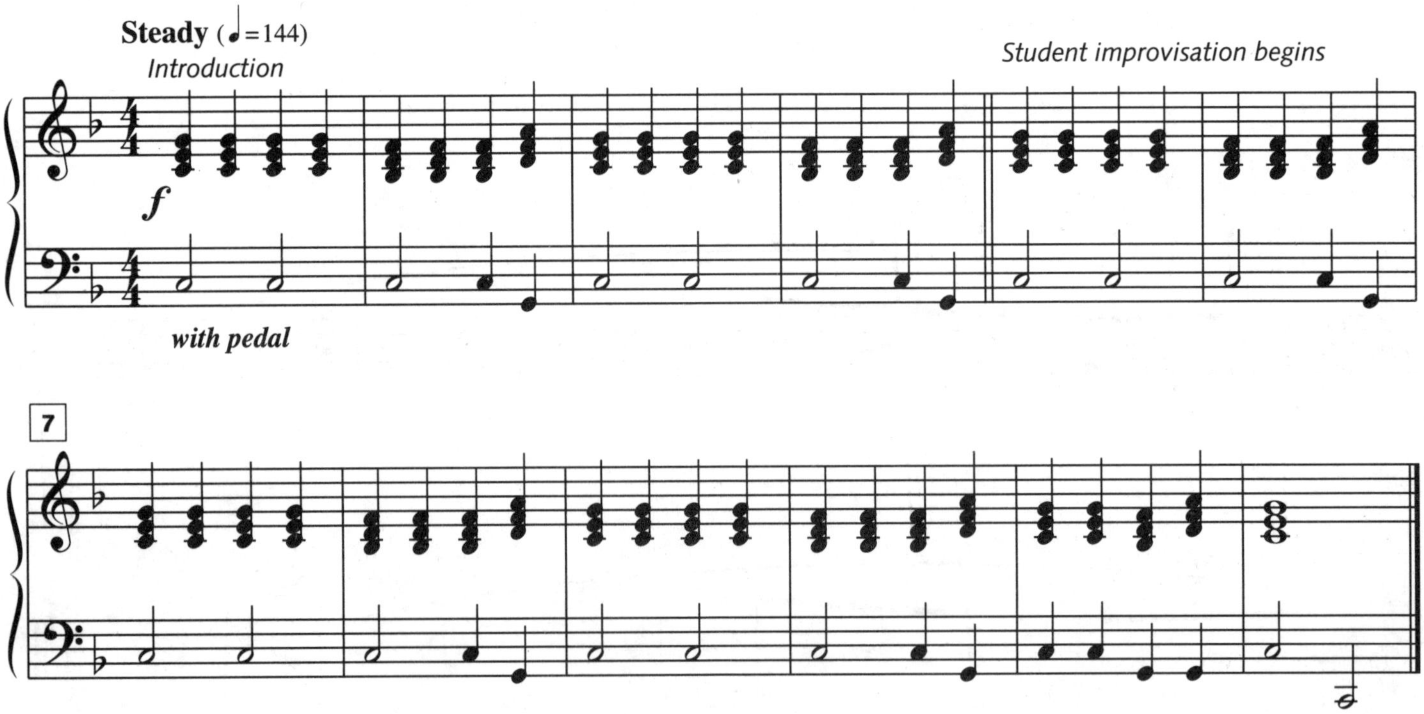

Unit 28

Modes Related to Minor

Objectives

Upon completion of this unit the student will be able to:

1. Play Dorian and Phrygian scales built on any note.
2. Play triads of the key in Dorian and Phrygian modes.
3. Sight-read music in Dorian and Phrygian modes.
4. Harmonize melodies in Dorian and Phrygian modes.
5. Improvise melodies in Dorian and Phrygian modes as the teacher plays an accompaniment.
6. Perform solo repertoire in Dorian mode.
7. Create a four-part ensemble from chord symbols.

Assignments

Week of ________

Write your assignments for the week in the space below.

Aeolian Mode

The scale using eight white keys beginning and ending on A, which we call the A natural minor scale, may also be called the **Aeolian scale.**

Play *Yankee Doodle* in the Aeolian mode (natural minor).

AEOLIAN YANKEE DOODLE

15-1 (29)

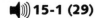

Allegro

Reading in Aeolian Mode

Use the indicated tempo, dynamics and articulation as you play the exercise. Use the following practice directions:

1. Tap RH and count aloud; then LH.
2. Play hands separately and count aloud.
3. Tap hands together and count aloud.
4. Play hands together and count aloud.

15-2 (30)

Lively

Ensemble Repertoire

Play the four-part ensemble using the indicated chords to complete parts 2, 3 and 4.

Part 1: Melody
Part 2: Broken chords
Part 3: Two-hand accompaniment
Part 4: Roots of chords

JOHNNY HAS GONE FOR A SOLDIER

15-3 (31)

United States

Dorian Mode

The scale using eight white keys, beginning and ending on D, is called the **Dorian scale.** The Dorian scale is like a natural minor scale with the 6th tone raised one half-step.

Using tetrachord position, play the Dorian scale.

▶ Transpose to A Dorian, E Dorian, G Dorian and C Dorian.

Play triads of the key in D Dorian.

15-4 (32)

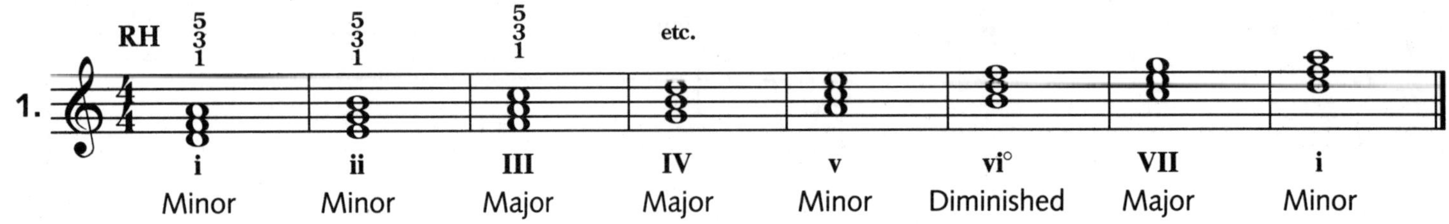

▶ Transpose to A Dorian and G Dorian.

15-4 (32)

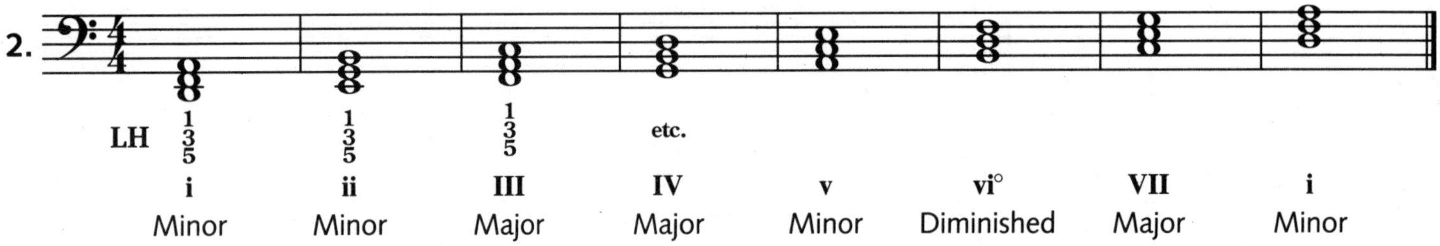

▶ Transpose to A dorian and G Dorian.

Play *Yankee Doodle* in the Dorian mode.

Dorian Yankee Doodle

15-5 (33)

Allegro

Reading in Dorian Mode

Use the indicated tempo, dynamics and articulation as you play the exercise. Use the following practice directions:

1. Tap RH and count aloud; then LH.
2. Play hands separately and count aloud.
3. Tap hands together and count aloud.
4. Play hands together and count aloud.

Scarborough Fair

15-6 (34)

Andante moderato

England

Harmonization in Dorian Mode

Harmonize with a broken chord accompaniment.

Broken Chord Accompaniment

15-7 (35)

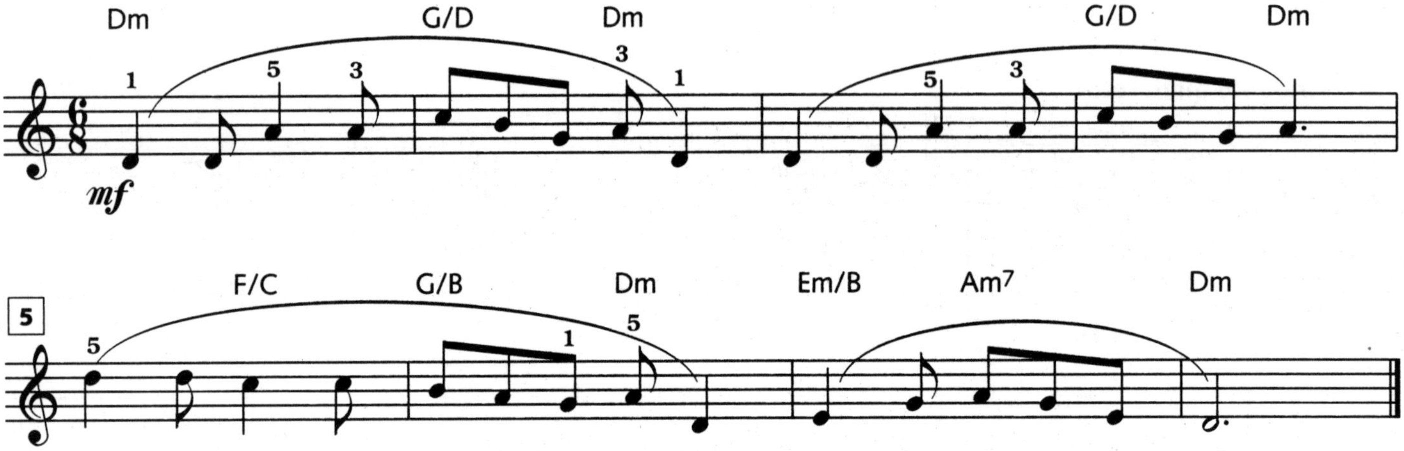

Harmonization

Using i, V7, iv and III chords, harmonize with a block chord accompaniment. Use inversions to improve sound and for ease in performance. Write the Roman numeral name of each chord on the line below the staff.

Block Chord Accompaniment

15-8 (36)

▶ Transpose to A minor.

Improvisation in Dorian Mode

Improvise an 8-measure melody using the appropriate Dorian scale in tetrachord position as your teacher plays each accompaniment. Listen to the 4-measure introduction to establish the tempo, mood and style before beginning the melody.

15-9 (37)

TEACHER ACCOMPANIMENT

1. **D Dorian:** Begin and end your melody on D.

15-10 (38)

TEACHER ACCOMPANIMENT

2. **A Dorian:** Begin and end your melody on A.

Phrygian Mode

The scale using eight white keys, beginning and ending on E, is called the **Phrygian scale.** The Phrygian scale is like a natural minor scale with the 2nd tone lowered one half-step.

Using tetrachord position, play the Phrygian scale.

▶ Transpose to A Phrygian, D Phrygian, B Phrygian and F♯ Phrygian.

Play triads of the key in E Phrygian.

15-11 (39)

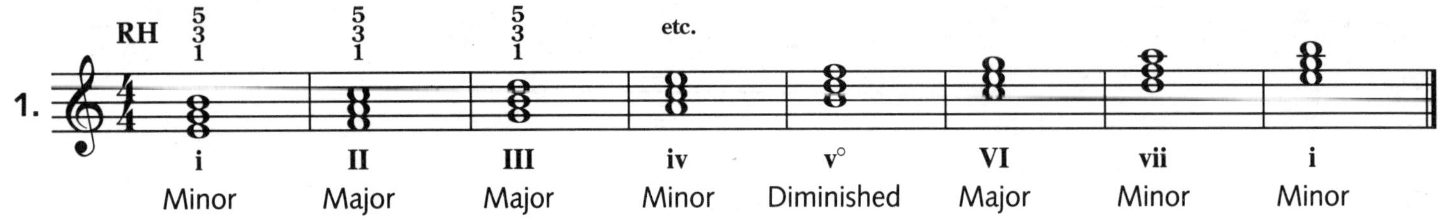

15-11 (39)

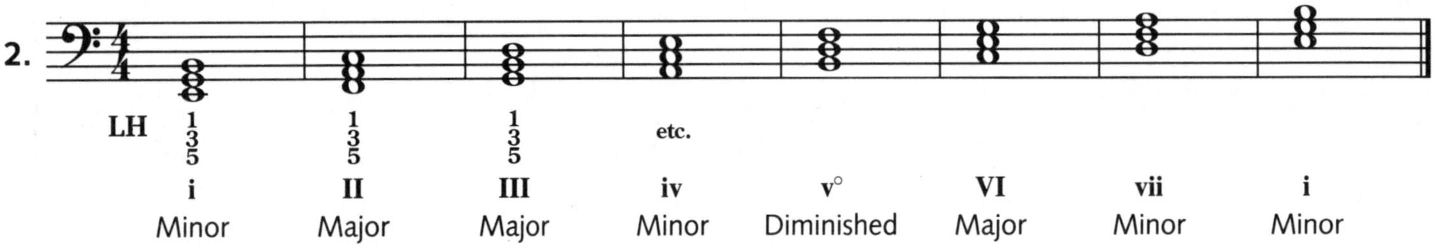

▶ Transpose to A Phrygian and B Phrygian.

Play *Yankee Doodle* in the Phrygian mode.

Phrygian Yankee Doodle

15-12 (40)

Reading in Phrygian Mode

Use the indicated tempo, dynamics and articulation as you play the exercise. Use the following practice directions:

1. Tap RH and count aloud; then LH.
2. Play hands separately and count aloud.
3. Tap hands together and count aloud.
4. Play hands together and count aloud.

15-13 (41)

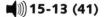

Harmonization in Phrygian Mode

Harmonize with a broken chord accompaniment.

Broken Chord Accompaniment

15-14 (42)

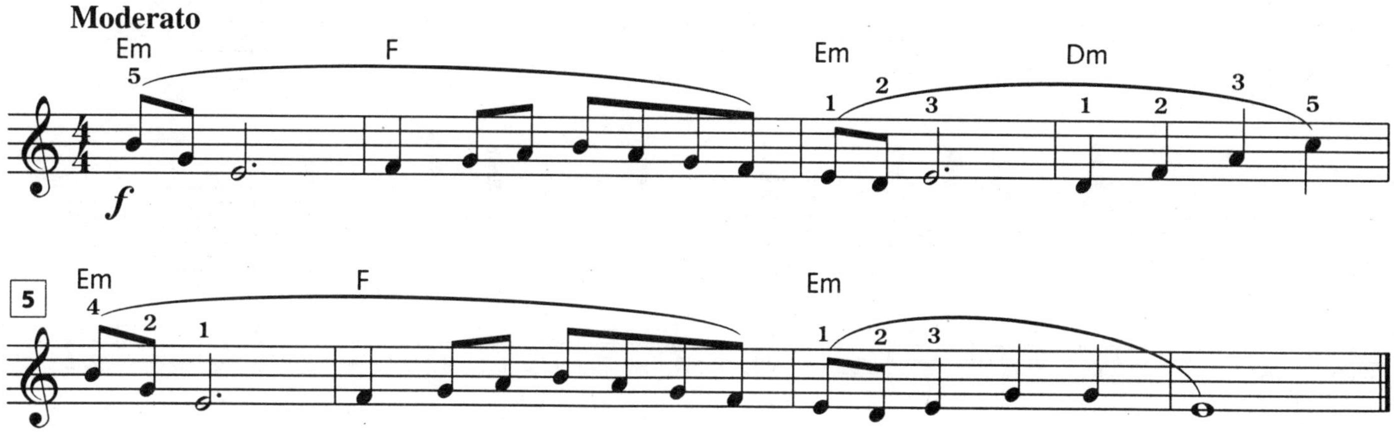

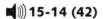

Improvisation in Phrygian Mode

Improvise an 8-measure melody using the appropriate Phrygian scale in tetrachord position as your teacher plays an accompaniment. Listen to the 4-measure introduction to establish the tempo, mood and style before beginning the melody.

15-15 (43)

1. E Phrygian: Begin and end your melody on E.

TEACHER ACCOMPANIMENT

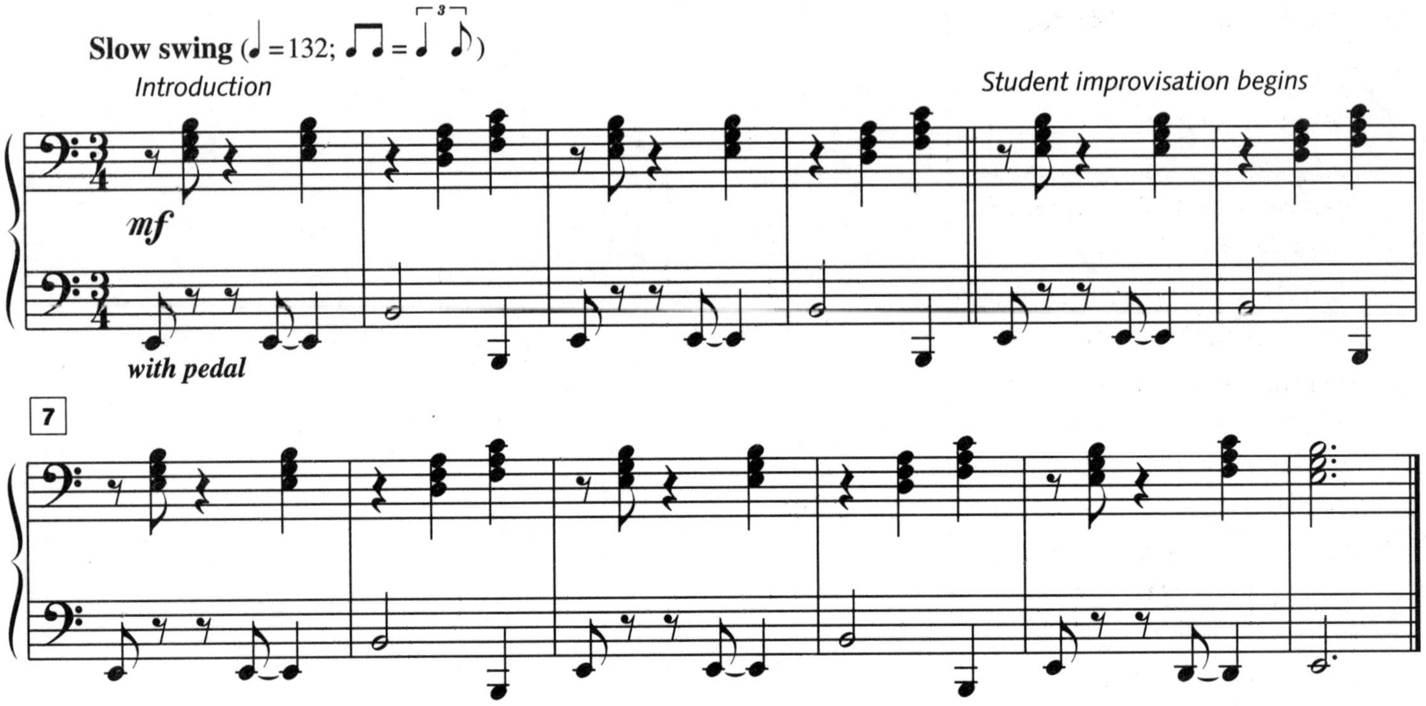

15-16 (44)

2. A Phrygian: Begin and end your melody on A.

TEACHER ACCOMPANIMENT

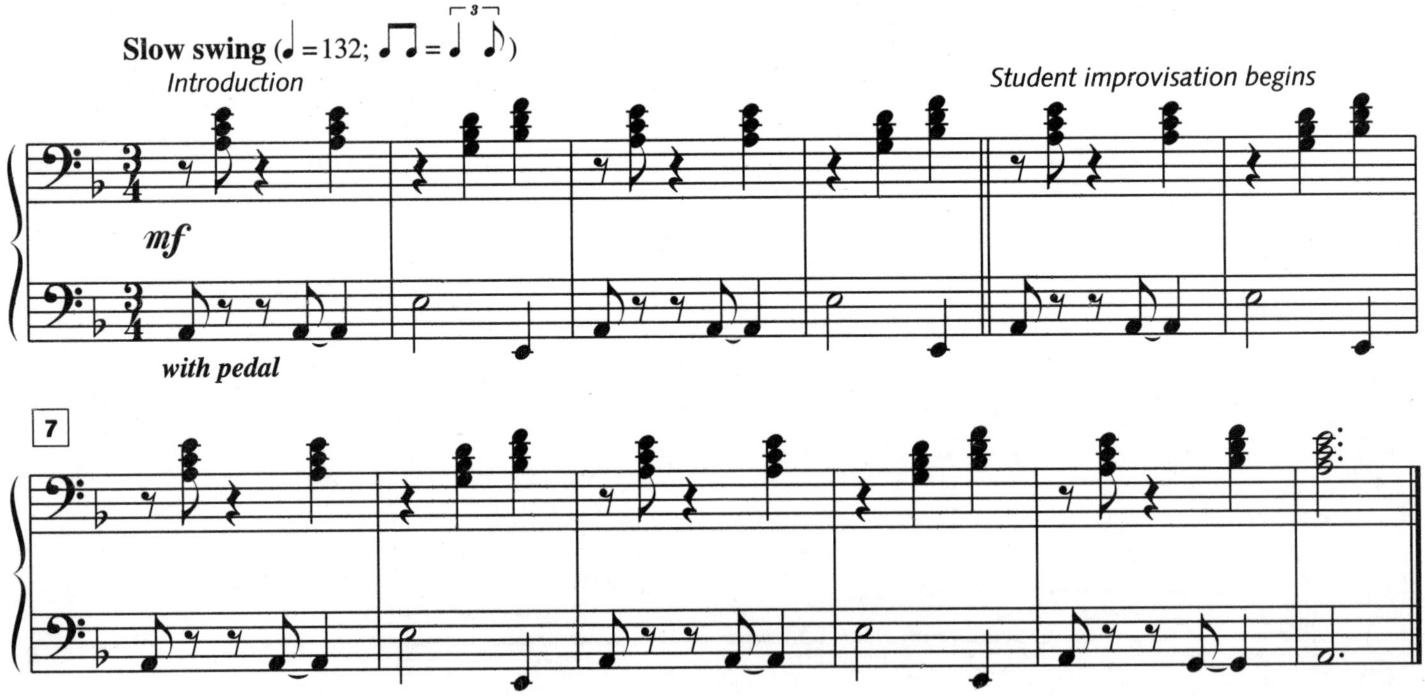

Unit 29

Other Scale Structures

Objectives

Upon completion of this unit the student will be able to:

1. Play chromatic, whole tone and blues scales.
2. Sight-read music that uses chromatic, whole tone and blues scales.
3. Perform solo repertoire that uses chromatic scales.
4. Harmonize and transpose melodies with primary, secondary and seventh chords.
5. Create two-hand accompaniments from chord symbols.
6. Improvise melodies over a 12-bar blues accompaniment.

Assignments

Week of ________

Write your assignments for the week in the space below.

The Chromatic Scale

The **chromatic scale** is made up entirely of half steps. It goes up and down, using every key, black and white. It may begin on any note.

The fingering rules are:

- Use 3 on each black key.
- Use 1 on each white key, except when two white keys are together (no black key between), then use 1 2, or 2 1.

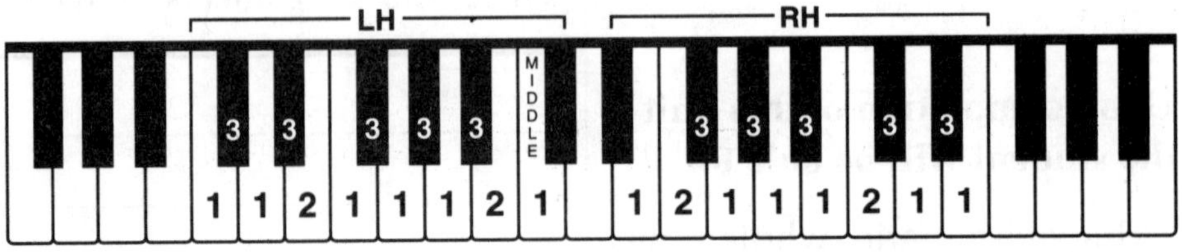

Play the one-octave chromatic scale hands separately. Then play hands together in contrary motion.

Reading

Use the indicated tempo, dynamics and articulation as you play the exercise. Use the following practice directions:

1. Tap RH and count aloud; then LH.
2. Play hands separately and count aloud.
3. Tap hands together and count aloud.
4. Play hands together and count aloud.

15-17 (45)

Not fast!

The Whole-Tone Scale

The **whole-tone scale** is made up entirely of whole steps. From the twelve tones of the chromatic scale, two whole tone scales can be built, each consisting of six whole tones within an octave. Usually, the ascending scale is written with sharps and the descending scale is written with flats.

Play the one-octave whole-tone scales hands separately.

1. 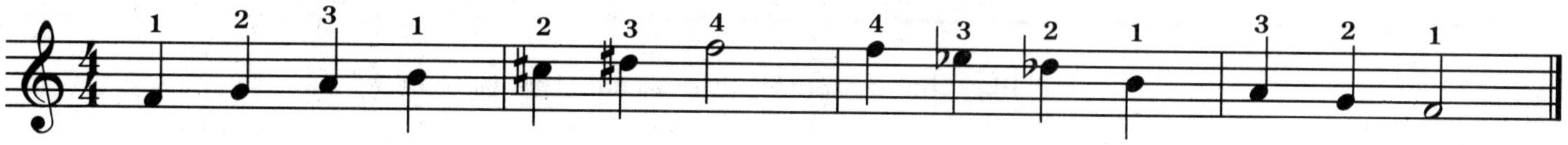

2. 

3. 

4. 

Reading

Use the indicated tempo, dynamics and articulation as you play the exercise. Use the following practice directions:

1. Tap RH and count aloud; then LH.
2. Play hands separately and count aloud.
3. Tap hands together and count aloud.
4. Play hands together and count aloud.

🔊 15-18 (46)

Adagio

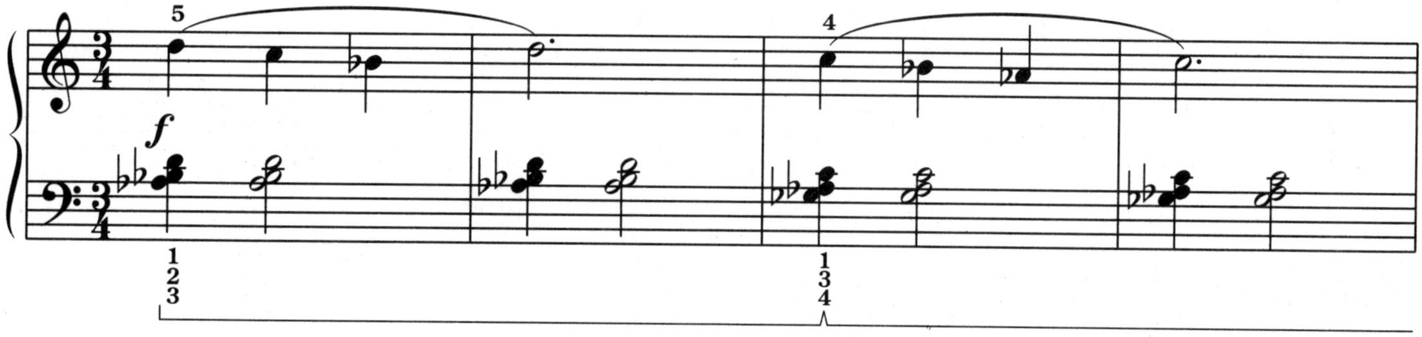

The Blues Scale

The **blues scale** contains seven tones in the following order:

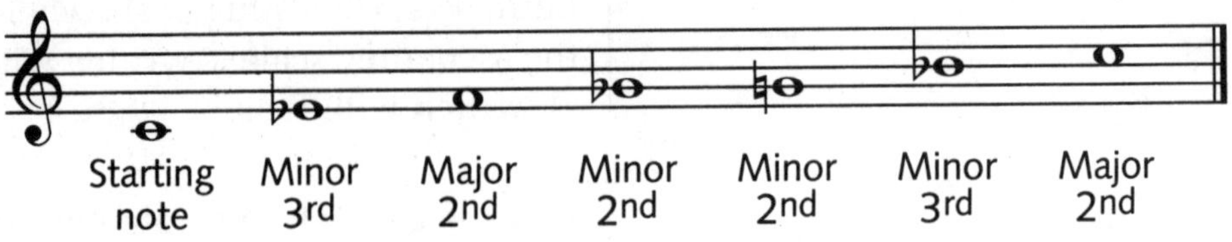

Play the one-octave blues scales on C, G and F hands separately.

C Blues Scale

G Blues Scale

F Blues Scale

Reading

Use the indicated tempo, dynamics and articulation as you play the exercise. Use the following practice directions:

1. Tap RH and count aloud; then LH.
2. Play hands separately and count aloud.
3. Tap hands together and count aloud.
4. Play hands together and count aloud.

15-19 (47)

Chromatic Rag

Willard A. Palmer
Morton Manus
Amanda Vick Lethco

15-20 (48)

"Chromatic Rag" from Alfred's Basic Piano Library FUN BOOK, Level 3, by Willard Palmer, Morton Manus and Amanda Vick Lethco

13
Fine
17
20
23
1.
2.
D. C. al Fine

Technique

15-21 (49)

Moderato

1.

15-22 (50)

Moderato

2.

15-23 (51)

Allegro

3.

15-23 (51)

Allegro

4.

Harmonization

1. Harmonize with a block chord accompaniment.

Block Chord Accompaniment 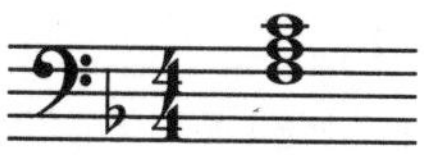

SIMPLE GIFTS

🔊 15-24 (52)

Shaker Hymn

Andante

▶ Transpose to G major.

2. Using I, V7, IV, vi and ii chords, harmonize with a block chord accompaniment. Use inversions to improve sound and for ease in performance. Write the Roman numeral name of each chord on the line below the staff.

Block Chord Accompaniment 

BINGO

🔊 15-25 (53)

Scotland

Moderato

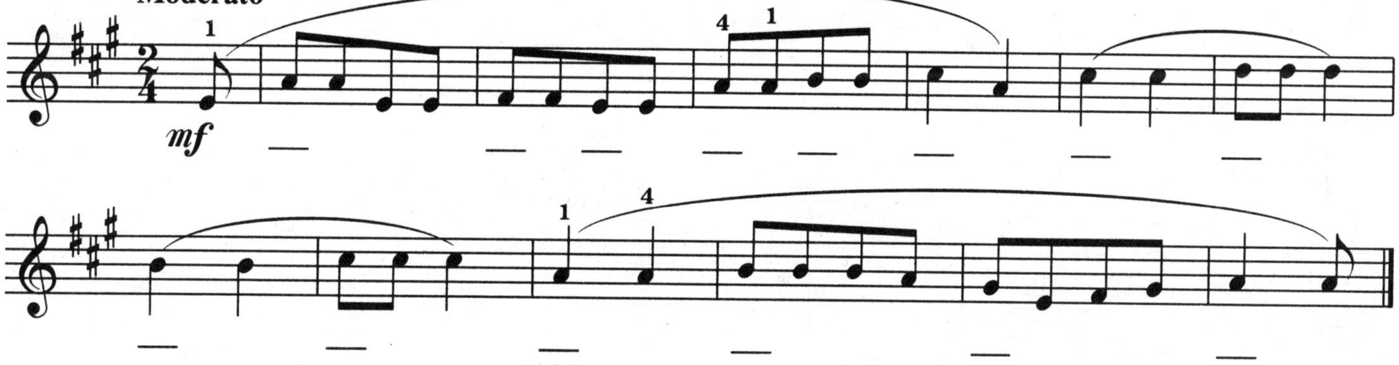

▶ Transpose to F major.

3. Harmonize the melody below in two ways:
   - Using the bottom note of each indicated seventh chord.
   - Using the indicated root position seventh chords.

🔊 15-26 (54)

Jazz waltz tempo

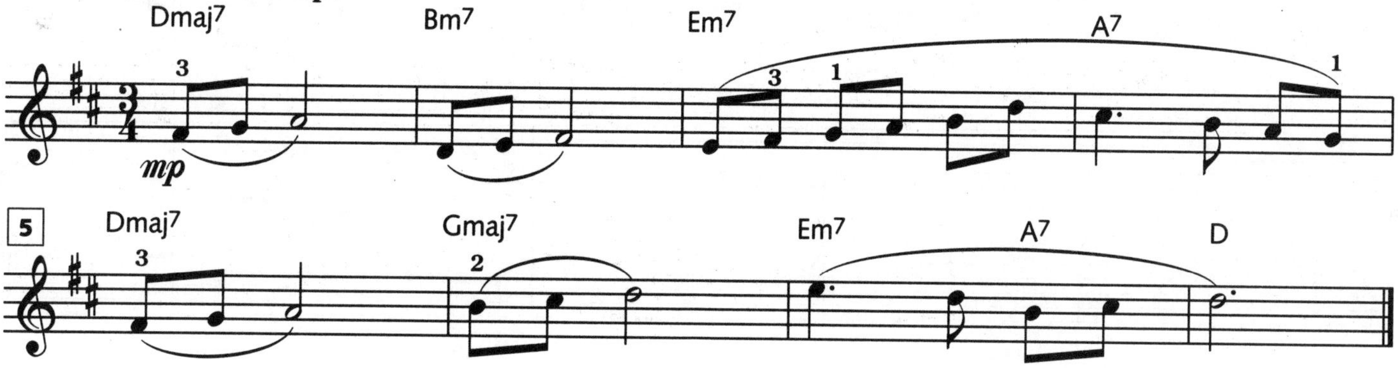

Harmonization with Two-Hand Accompaniment

Using the indicated chords, create a two-hand accompaniment for the following melody by continuing the pattern given in the first two measures.

GREENSLEEVES

15-27 (55)

12-Bar Blues Improvisation

Improvise a 12-measure melody using the appropriate blues scale as your teacher plays each accompaniment. Listen to the 4-measure introduction to establish the tempo, mood and style before beginning the melody.

C, F and G Blues Scales: Begin and end your melody on C.

15-28 (56)

TEACHER ACCOMPANIMENT

Unit 30

Review

Objectives

Upon completion of this unit the student will be able to:

1. Play I–vi–IV–ii_6–I^6_4–V^7–I chord progressions in all major keys.
2. Play five types of seventh chords.
3. Play exercises that use harmonic minor scales and triads of the key.
4. Perform solo repertoire that uses scale patterns and primary and secondary chords.
5. Sight-read and transpose music that uses primary and secondary chords.
6. Harmonize and transpose melodies with primary and secondary chords.
7. Create two-hand accompaniments from chord symbols.
8. Improvise melodies over primary, secondary and seventh chords.

Assignments

Week of ________

Write your assignments for the week in the space below.

Playing the I–vi–IV–ii6–I6/4–V7–I Chord Progression

Play the I–vi–IV–ii$_6$–I$^6_4$–V7–I chord-progression exercise.

16-1 (36)

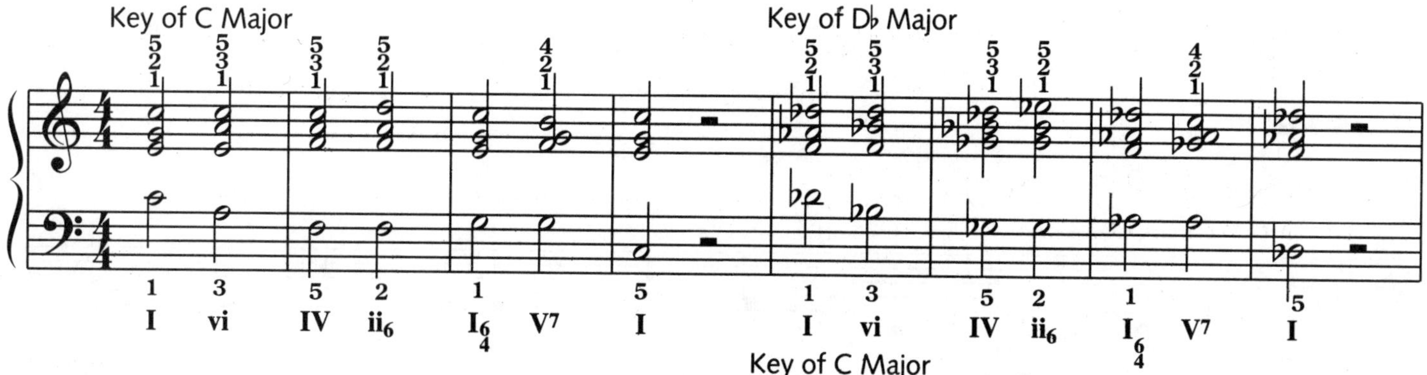

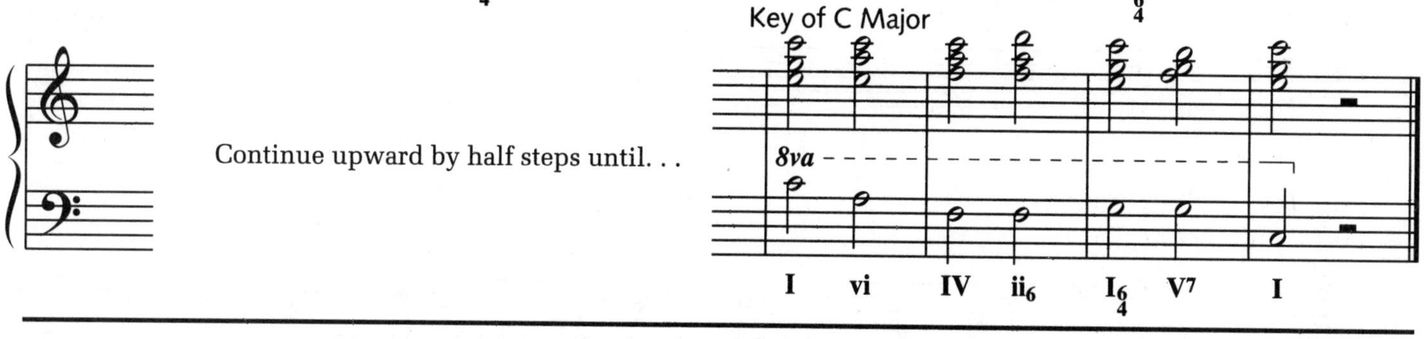

Playing Seventh Chords

Play the seventh-chord exercises with the RH as written. Then play with LH one octave lower than written.

16-2 (37)

16-3 (38)

16-4 (39)

16-5 (40)

16-6 (41)

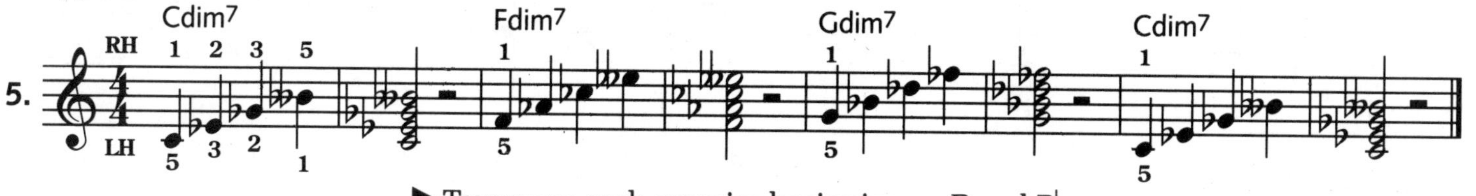

▶ Transpose each exercise beginning on D and B♭.

Playing Harmonic Minor Scales and Triads of the Key

Play the following exercises that use harmonic minor scales and triads of the key.

16-7 (42)

1.

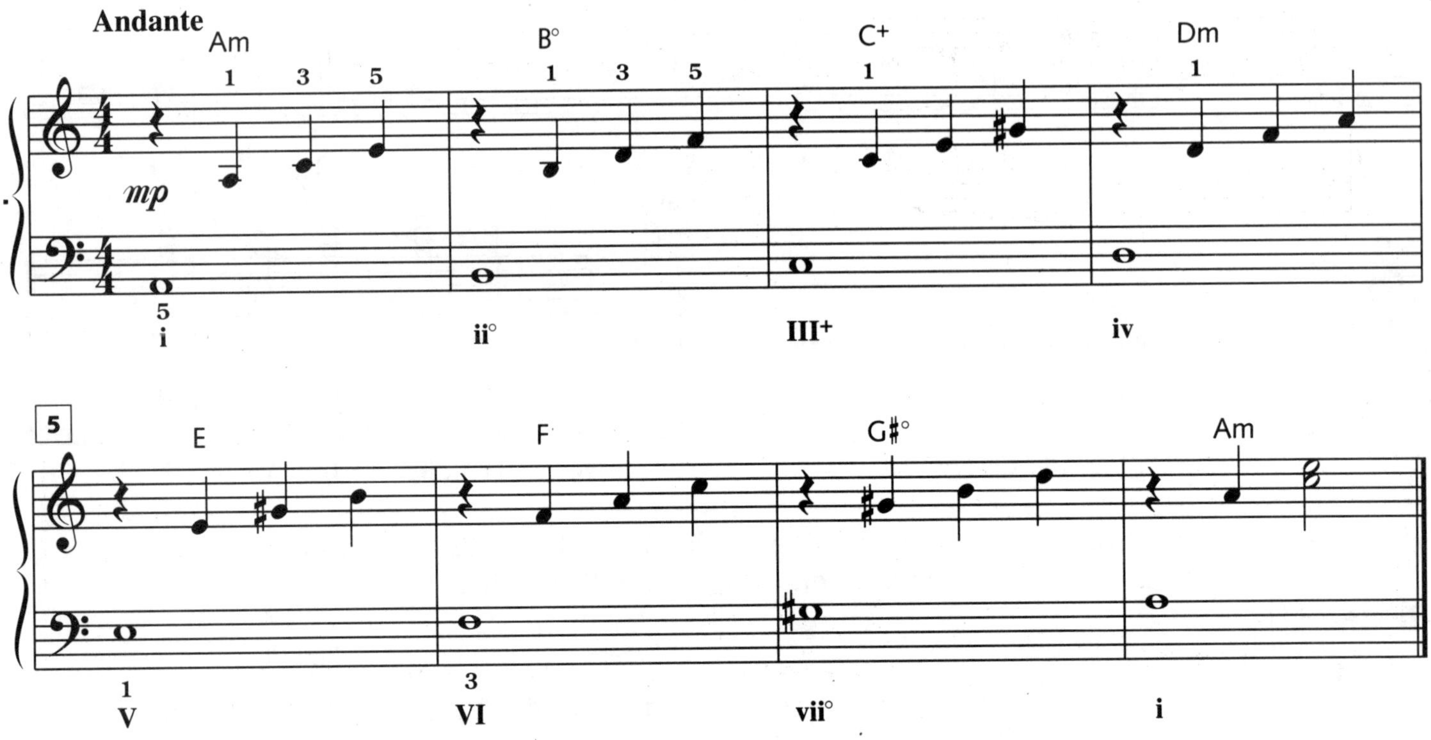

▶ Transpose to D harmonic minor and G harmonic minor.

16-8 (43)

2.

▶ Transpose to E harmonic minor and G harmonic minor.

Solo Repertoire

Ecossaise

16-9 (44)

Ludwig van Beethoven
(1770–1827)

Reading

Identify the key of each example. Use the indicated tempo, dynamics and articulation as you play these exercises.
Use the following practice directions:

1. Tap RH and count aloud; then LH.
2. Play hands separately and count aloud.
3. Tap hands together and count aloud.
4. Play hands together and count aloud.

16-10 (45)

▶ Transpose to D minor.

16-11 (46)

▶ Transpose to C minor.

16-12 (47)

3.

▶ Transpose to D♭ major.

Dance

16-13 (48)

Ludvig Schytte (1848–1909)
from Op. 108, No. 1

4.

▶ Transpose to D major.

Harmonization

1. Harmonize with a block chord accompaniment.

Block Chord Accompaniment

Eine Kleine Nachtmusik

16-14 (49)

Wolfgang Amadeus Mozart (1756–1791)
K. 525

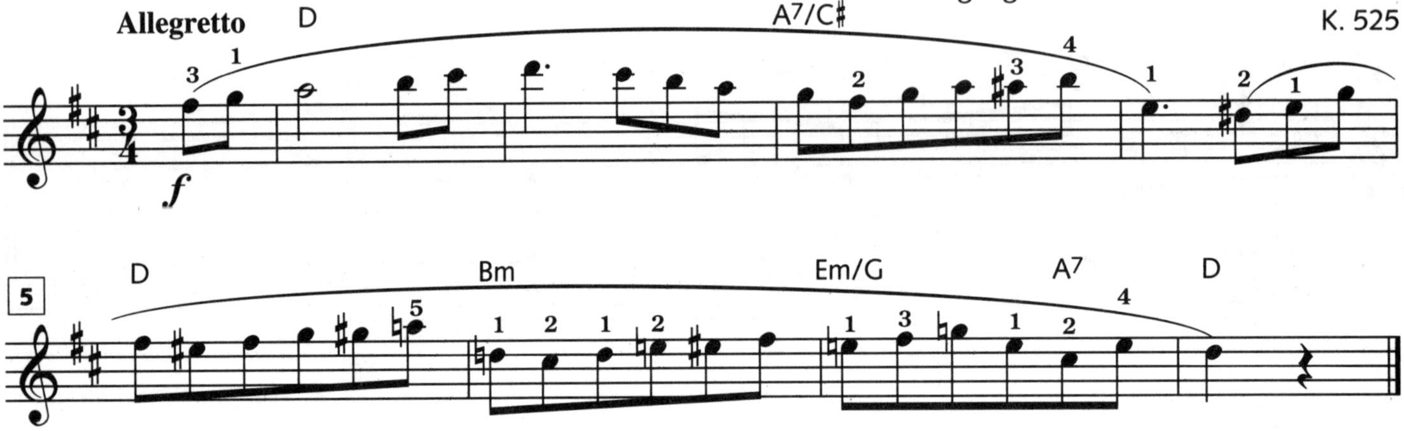

2. Using I, V7, IV, vi and ii chords, harmonize with a waltz style accompaniment. Use inversions to improve sound and for ease in performance. Write the Roman numeral name of each chord on the line below the staff.

Waltz Style Accompaniment

16-15 (50)

Germany

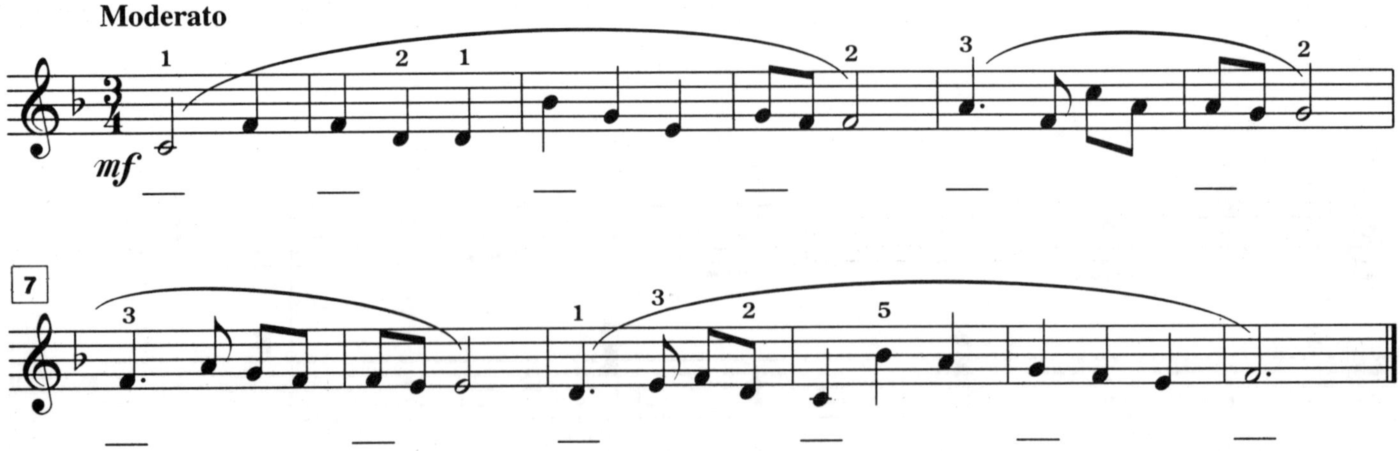

▶ Transpose to G major.

3. Harmonize the melody below in two ways:
   - Using the bottom note of each indicated seventh chord.
   - Using the indicated root-position seventh chords.

16-16 (51)

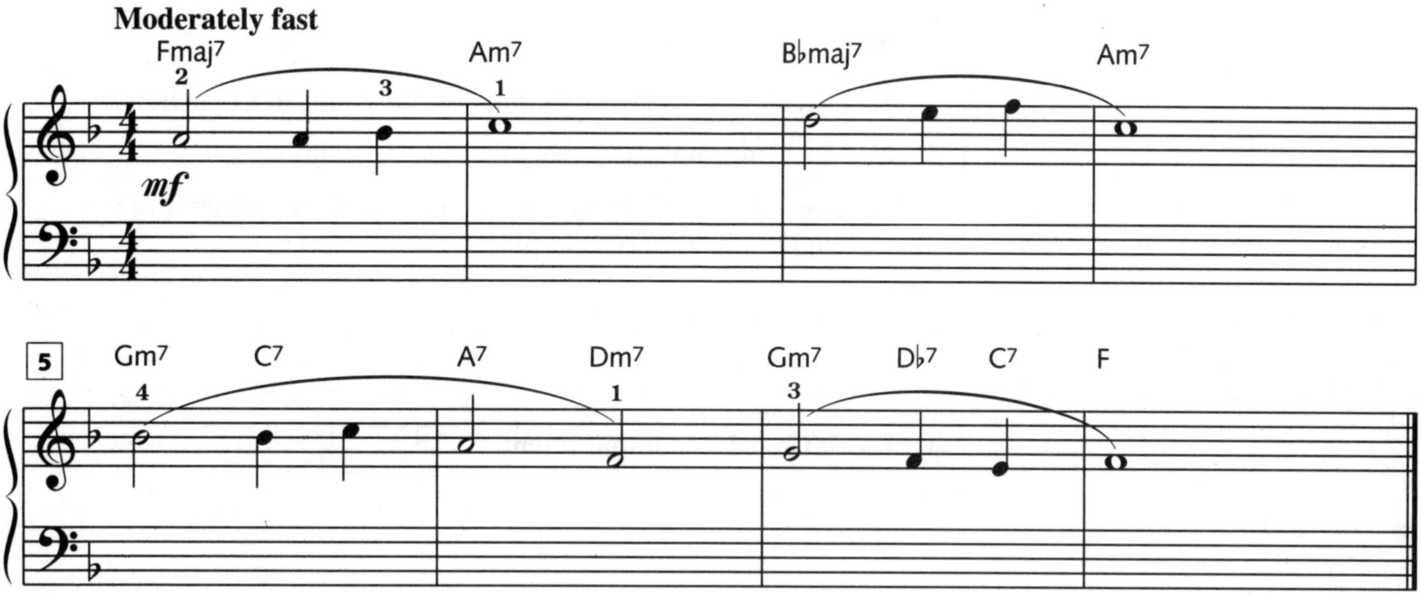

Harmonization with Two-Hand Accompaniment

Using the indicated chords, create a two-hand accompaniment for the following melody by continuing the pattern given in the first measure.

16-17 (52)

STILL, STILL, STILL

Austria

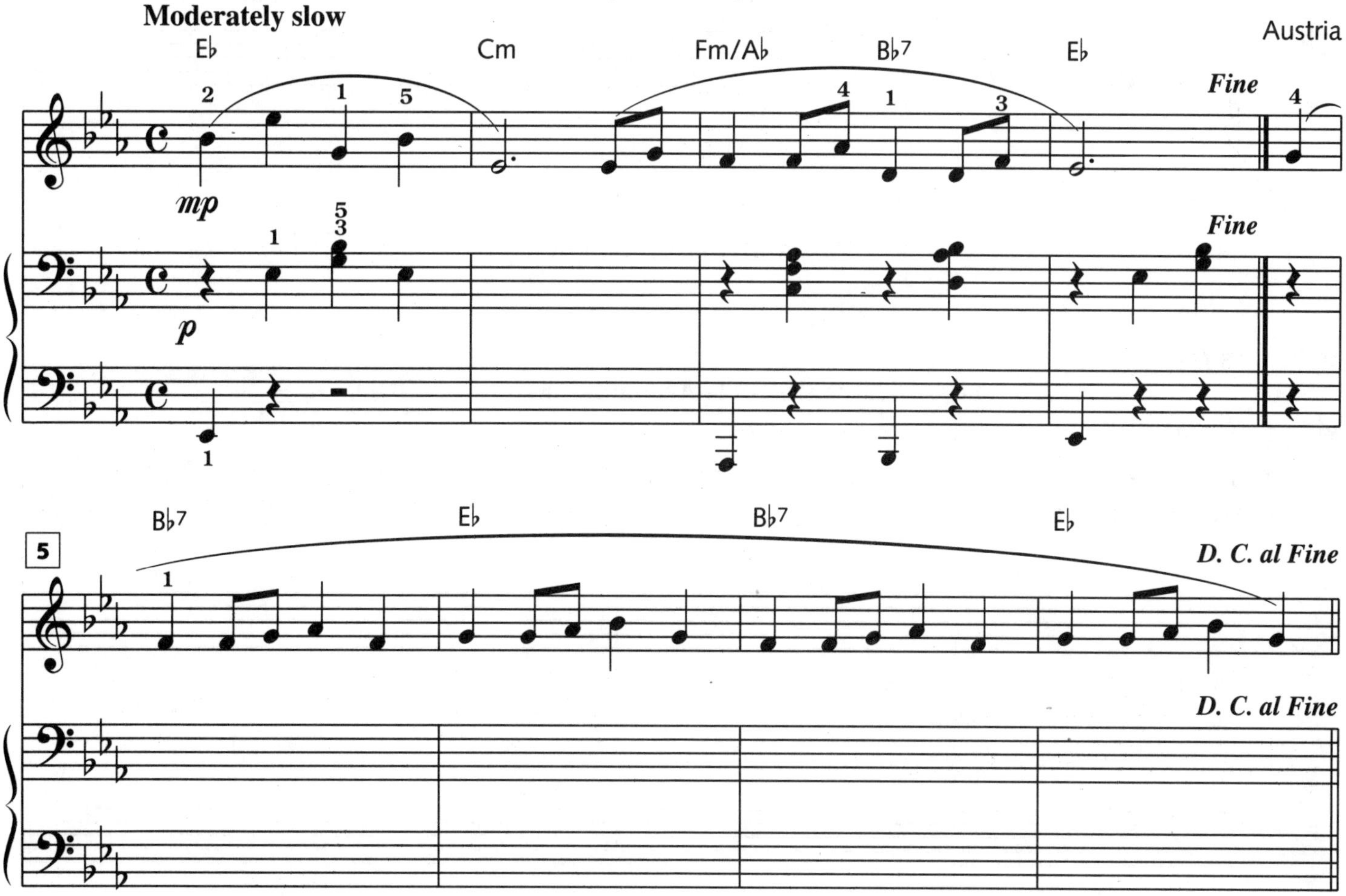

▶ Transpose to D major.

Improvisation from Chord Symbols

Using the chord progressions below, improvise RH melodies while the LH plays the suggested accompaniment style. (First play the LH chord progressions using the suggested accompaniment style and observing the indicated meter.) Notate your favorite improvisation.

Rules for improvisation:

1. Use mostly chord tones and passing tones in the melody.
2. Most improvisations begin and end on tonic.
3. The ear should always be the final guide in determining which melody notes to play.

1. Block Chord Accompaniment

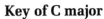

16-18 (53)

Key of C major

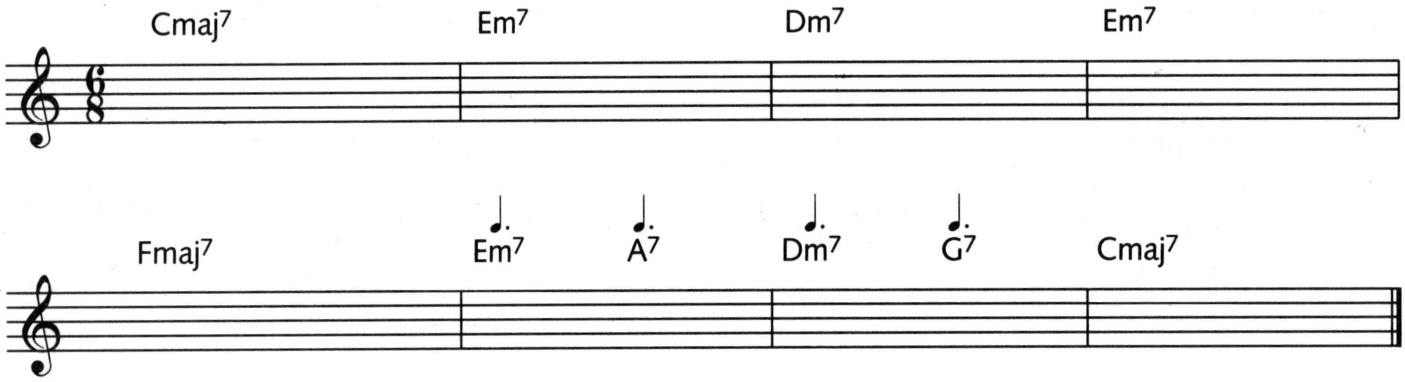

2. Waltz Style Accompaniment

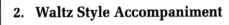

16-19 (54)

Key of D harmonic minor

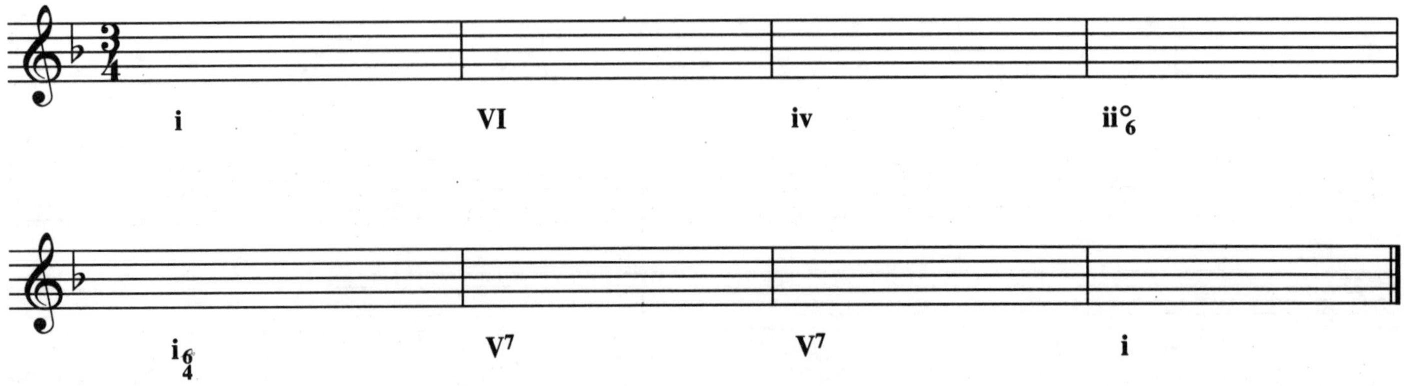

Unit 30

Review Worksheet

Name ____________________ *Date* ____________________

1. Identify each scale below by writing its name (Aeolian, Dorian, Phrygian, Lydian, Mixolydian, whole tone, chromatic or blues) on the line.

a. 

____

b. 

____

c. 

____

d. 

____

e. 

____

f. 

____

g. 

____

h. 

____

2. Using whole notes, write each seventh chord on the staff in root position.

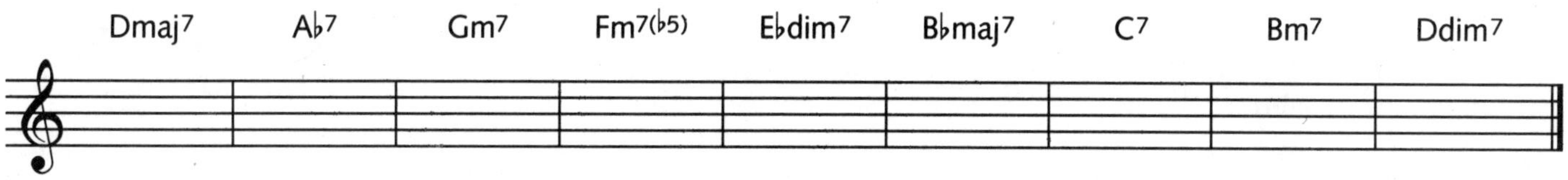

3. Draw a line to connect the chord on the right with its key and Roman numeral on the left.

Key of D Major: **ii**

Key of B Harmonic Minor: **VI**

Key of C♯ Harmonic Minor: **iv**

Key of B♭ Major: **IV**

Key of G Major: **iii**

Key of C Harmonic Minor: **vii°**

Key of F Harmonic Minor: **ii°**

Key of F Major: **V**

Key of G Harmonic Minor: **V**

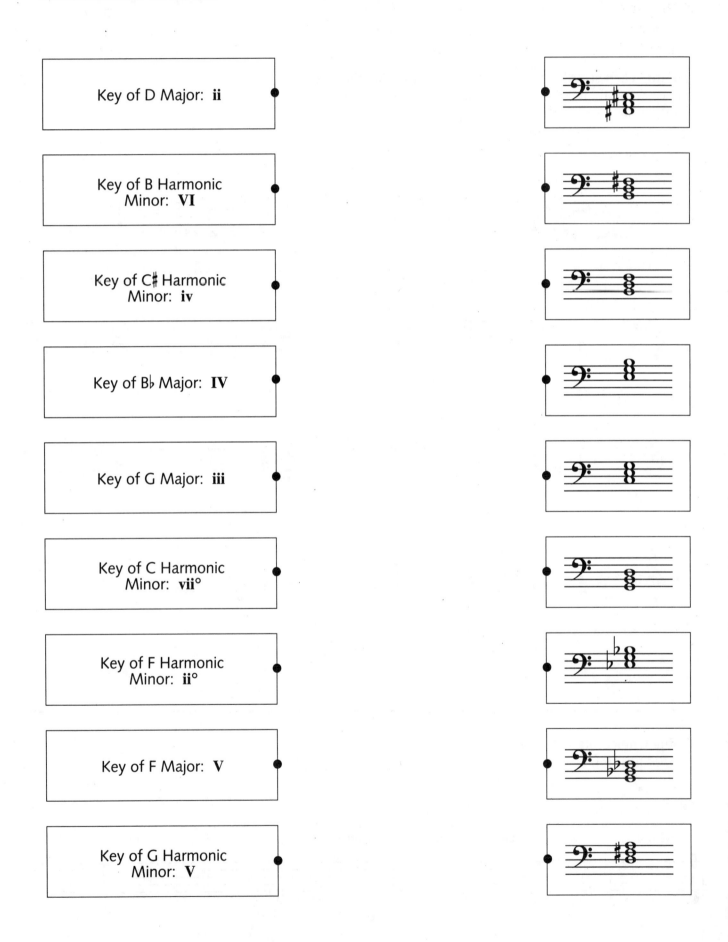

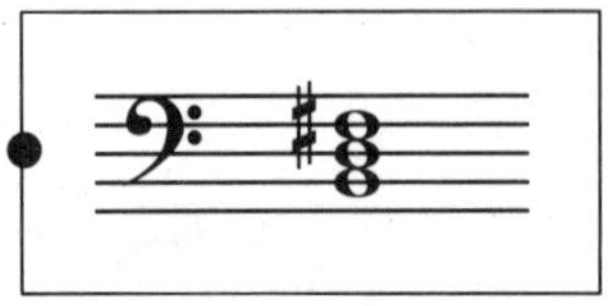

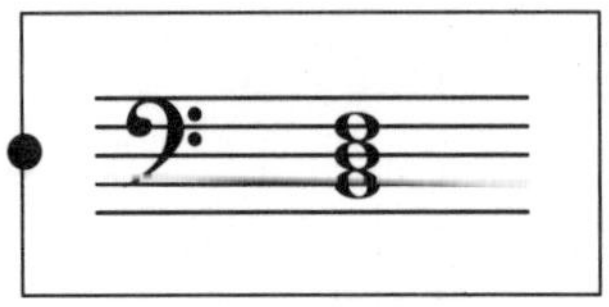

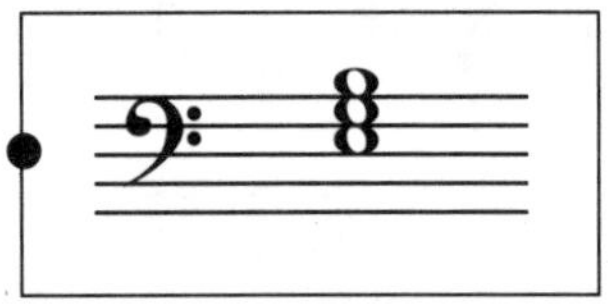

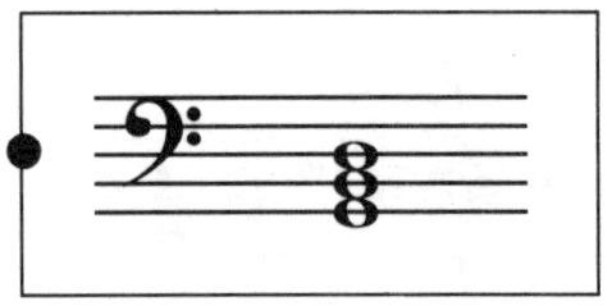

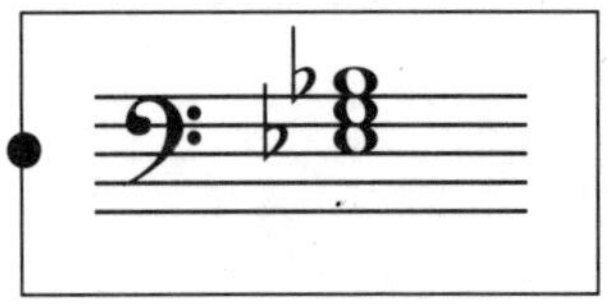

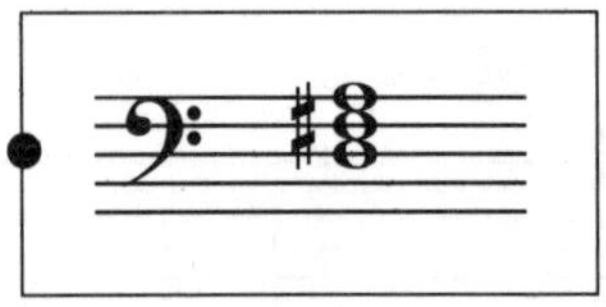

Supplementary Solo Repertoire

THE CHASE

16-20 (55)

Cornelius Gurlitt (1820–1901)
Op. 117, No. 15

Allegro molto

ETUDE

16-21 (56)

Felix LeCouppey (1811–1887)
Op. 17, No. 6

Allegretto

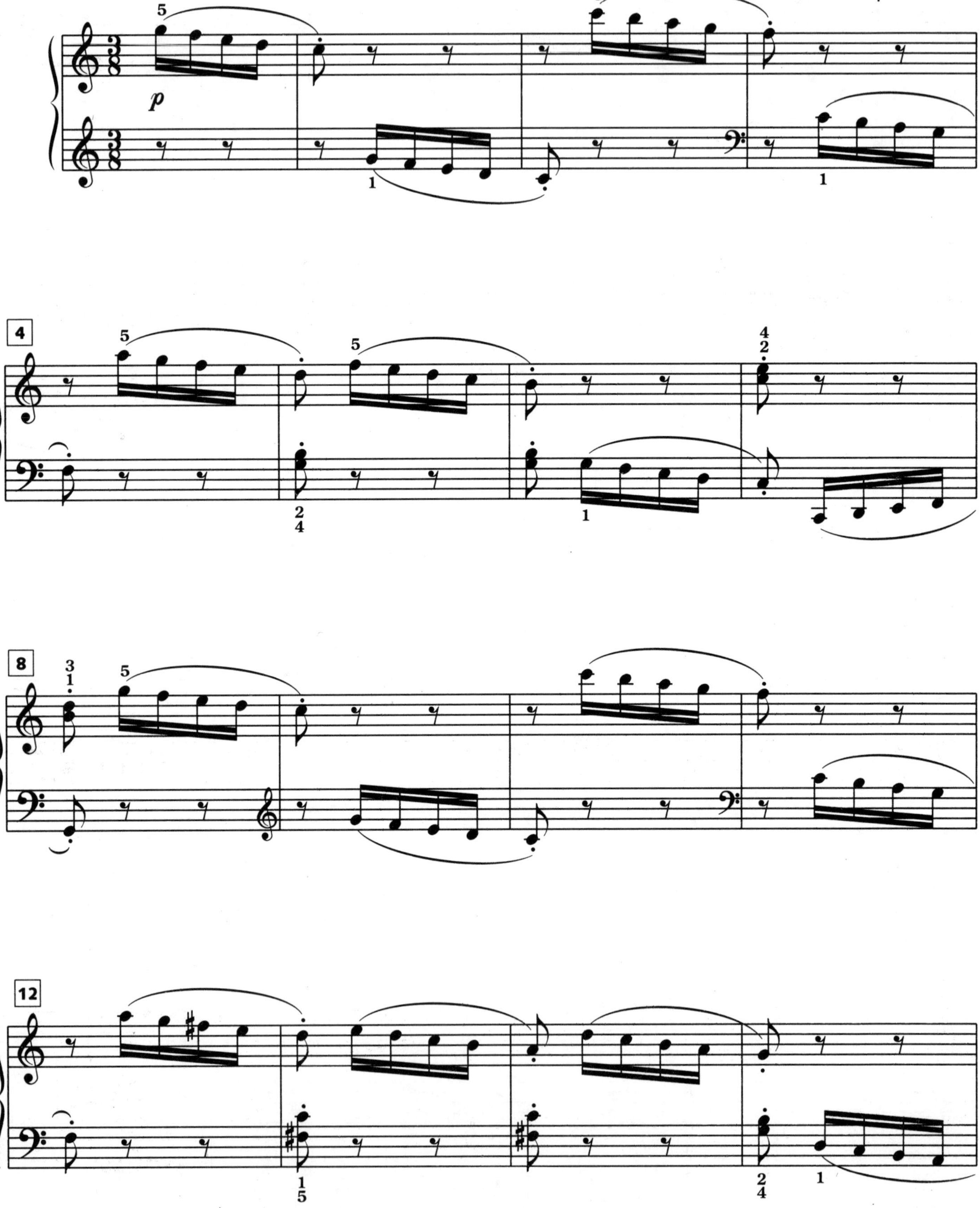

16
20
poco cresc.
mp
24
p
28

BAGATELLE

16-22 (57)

Anton Diabelli
(1781–1858)

Study in Triplets

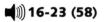

🔊 **16-23 (58)**

Cornelius Gurlitt
(1820–1901)

Moderato

The Entertainer

🔊 16-24 (59)

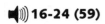

Scott Joplin (1868–1917)
Arr. E. L. Lancaster
Kenon D. Renfrow

10
13
16
cresc.
19
1.
2.

BURLESKE

16-25 (60)

Leopold Mozart
(1719–1787)

The Little Beggar

16-26 (61)

Alexander Gretchaninoff (1864–1956)

Op. 123, No. 2

Popcorn

16-27 (62)

Lynn Freeman Olson
(1938–1987)

17
mf
f
21
mf
f
25
mf
30

Just Struttin' Along

16-28 (63)

Moderate blues swing (♫ = ♩ ♪ with 3 over the eighth note)

Martha Mier

"Just Struttin' Along" from JAZZ, RAGS 'N' BLUES, Book 1, by Martha Mier

13
mf
16
f
19
8va
mp
22
p
8va
mp
(no rit.)
LH
pp

German Dance

16-29 (64)

Franz Joseph Haydn
(1732–1809)

Attention All Students!

We strongly suggest that you DO NOT purchase **OPTIONAL TEXTS** until you have attended class. We do not refund textbooks without a drop slip, therefore, attending class is very important prior to purchasing **OPTIONAL** texts.

"**REQUIRED**" on the shelf tag means that you will need the textbook to take the class. You should check the used book bulletin boards in the Student Center, your friends, and the school library before purchasing. You will NOT receive a refund without a drop slip.

"**OPTIONAL**" on the shelf tag means that you will NOT need the textbook to take the class. It is **OPTIONAL**. If you purchase the book, you will NOT receive a refund without a drop slip. **GO TO CLASS PRIOR TO PURCHASING OPTIONAL BOOKS**.

WARNING !!!

Be a good consumer, check your used books carefully before buying!! There are no warranties on used books. We do not have the staff to check each book purchased from the students to make sure that they are complete and undamaged. Used books are sold at a 25% discount from new. **Buy at your own risk.** After a textbook has been bought and sold several times the condition deteriorates, and the bookstore cannot continue to purchase the book. There is no guarantee that any book will be bought back at the end of the term even if it is going to be used in the following term.

ALLAN HANCOCK
COLLEGE BOOKSTORE
NO REFUND OR EXCHANGE
WITHOUT RECEIPT

LANCASTER GF	29.95
9780882846538	
SBTL	32.27
TAX1	2.32
TOTL	32.27
CASH	32.27
TS	299
ITEM	1
A101	8010001
0156 14:18	8/22/97

AVE THIS RECEIPT!!!!

D OR EXCHANGE ANY PURCHASE, YOU MUST HAVE THIS RECEIPT!

EIVE A TEXTBOOK REFUND DURING REE WEEKS OF THE TERM IF YOU:

register receipt.
slip (or the class must be canceled). No refunds on classes in which you are in WAIT status.
handise in exactly the same condition in which it nk wrap unbroken, software unopened, book intact).

eceive a textbook refund if:

istered in the class.
2. You do not have your receipt.
3. Your materials have been opened or damaged, or bar codes are removed.
4. It is past the first three weeks of the term.

Fast Track Classes

1. NO refunds are allowed for fast track textbooks if you attended the class
2. All other refund rules apply.

Returned checks are immediately turned over to either the San Luis Obispo/Santa Barbara credit bureaus or to the Office of the Santa Barbara District Attorney for collection. A $25.00 service charge will be assessed on all bad checks. Failure to pay bad checks will result in a hold on grades/transcripts and you will not be able to register for future classes. You may have your credit rating damaged and/or charges may be filed against you by the District Attorney. We aggressively pursue collection on EVERY bad check.

TAKE YOUR FINAL - SELL YOUR BOOK

At the end of the term, we make every effort to buy as many texts as possible. Buy Back is based on the instructors order for the following term and the number of books needed by the bookstore. We do not buy back old editions, workbooks, or study guides. We do not buy back books which contain software. If the book was a part of a set, all parts must be returned. We do not buy books with water damage, torn pages, loose spines, or any other type of damage. A receipt is not necessary. We always buy back during finals week. We never buy back at the beginning of the term.

SANTA MARIA CAMPUS
922-2391

LOMPOC BOOKSTORE
736-8610

VAFB BOOKSTORE
734-3360

C:PM6\SAVREC2.97

Song without Words

16-30 (65)

Louis Köhler
(1820–1886)

Andantino

Full Moon Rising

16-31 (66)

Dennis Alexander

"Full Moon Rising" from SIMPLY SENSATIONAL, Book 1, by Dennis Alexander

15
19
f
22
mp
25

The Bear

🔊 16-32 (67)

Vladimir Rebikov
(1866–1920)

RONDINO

16-33 (68)

Jean-Philippe Rameau
(1683–1764)

Distant Bells

16-34 (69)

J. L. Streabbog (1835–1886)
Op. 63, No. 6

14
pp
p
18
simile
21
24
poco rit.

GALOP

16-35 (70)

Dmitri Kabalevsky (1904–1987)
Op. 39, No. 18

Animato

Appendix B

Glossary

Accent sign (>) . . . . placed over or under a note that gets special emphasis; play that note louder.
Adagio . . . . slowly.
Alla breve (𝄵). . . . . cut time or $\frac{2}{2}$ time.
Alla marcia . . . . . . in march style.
Allegretto . . . . moderately fast.
Allegro . . . . quickly, happily.
Allegro non troppo . . quickly, but not too much.
Andante. . . . . moving along (the word actually means "walking").
Andantino . . . . . . slightly faster than andante.
Animato. . . . . animated; lively.
A tempo. . . . . resume original speed.
Cantabile . . . . in a singing style.
Chromatic scale . . . made up entirely of half steps; it goes up and down, using every key, black and white.
Coda. . . . . an added ending.
Coda sign (𝄌). . . . . indication to proceed to coda.
Common time (𝄴) . . same as $\frac{4}{4}$ time.
Crescendo (<) . . . gradually louder.
Cut time (𝄵). . . . . . same as $\frac{2}{2}$ time; alla breve.
D. C. al Coda . . . . . repeat from the beginning to 𝄌, then skip to Coda.
D. C. al Fine. . . . . . repeat from the beginning to the word "Fine."
Decrescendo (>) . . gradually softer.
Diatonic. . . . . using only notes in the given key, with no alterations.
Diminuendo (>) . . gradually softer.
Dominant . . . . the fifth scale degree.
Double flat (𝄫) . . . . lowers a flatted note another half step or a natural note one whole step.
Double sharp (×) . . . raises a sharped note another half step, or a natural note one whole step.
Enharmonic. . . . . . notes that are spelled (written) differently but are identical in sound.
Fermata (𝄐) . . . . . hold the note under the sign longer than its full value.
Fine . . . . the end.
First ending (1.) . play first time only.
Flat sign (♭). . . . . . lowers a note one half step; play the next key to the left, whether black or white.
Forte (*f*) . . . . loud.
Fortissimo (*ff*). . . . very loud.
Giocoso . . . . humorous.
Grand staff . . . . . . the bass staff and the treble staff joined together by a brace.
Grazioso . . . . gracefully.
Harmonic intervals. . distances between notes or keys that are played together.
Incomplete measure . a measure at the beginning of a piece with fewer counts than indicated in the time signature. The missing beats are usually found in the last measure.
Intervals . . . . distances between notes or keys.
Key signature . . . . . the number of sharps or flats in any key, written at the beginning of each line.
Largo . . . . very slow.
Leading tone . . . . . the seventh scale degree.
Legato. . . . . smoothly connected.
Leger line . . . . used above or below the staff to extend its range.
Leggiero. . . . . lightly.
Lento . . . . slow.
Maestoso . . . . majestically.

Glossary (continued)

Marcato . . . . marked, stressed.
Mediant . . . . the third scale degree.
Melodic intervals . . . distance between notes or keys that are played separately.
Mezzo forte (*mf*) . . . moderately loud.
Mezzo piano (*mp*) . . . moderately soft.
Misterioso . . . . mysteriously.
Moderato . . . . moderately.
Molto . . . . much.
Natural sign (♮) . . . . cancels a sharp or flat.
Non troppo . . . . . . not too much.
Octave . . . . the distance from one key on the keyboard to the next key (lower or higher) with the same letter name.
Octave sign (*8va*) . . . play eight scale tones (one octave) higher when the sign is above the notes; eight scale tones lower when the sign is below the notes.
Pedal mark (└───┘) . press the damper, hold it, and release it.
Pesante . . . . heavy, with emphasis.
Phrase . . . . musical thought or sentence.
Pianissimo (*pp*) . . . . very soft.
Piano (*p*) . . . . soft.
Poco . . . . little.
Repeat sign (:‖) . . . . repeat from the beginning, or from the first repeat (‖:).
Rests . . . . signs for silence.
Ritardando (*rit.* or *ritard.*) . . . . . gradually slowing.
Scherzando . . . . . . playful.
Second ending (2. ──┐) play second time only.
Sequence . . . . a short musical motive stated successively, beginning on different pitches.
Sharp sign (♯) . . . . . raises a note one half step; play the next key to the right, whether black or white.
Simile . . . . continue in the same manner.
Slur . . . . curved line over or under notes on different lines or spaces. Slurs mean to play legato.
Staccato . . . . dots over or under notes meaning to play short, detached.
Subdominant . . . . . the fourth scale degree.
Subito (*sub.*) . . . . . . suddenly.
Submediant . . . . . . the sixth scale degree.
Supertonic . . . . . . the second scale degree.
Syncopated notes . . . notes played between the main beats of a measure and held across the beat.
Tempo . . . . rate of speed.
Tenuto (–) . . . . hold the note for its full value.
Tetrachord . . . . . . a series of four notes having a pattern of whole step, whole step, half step.
Tied notes . . . . notes on the same line or space joined by a curved line and held for the combined values of both notes.
Time signatures ($\frac{2}{4}$, $\frac{3}{4}$, $\frac{4}{4}$, $\frac{6}{8}$, $\frac{3}{8}$) . . . numbers found at the beginning of a piece or section of a piece. The top number shows the number of beats in each measure. The bottom number shows the kind of note that gets one beat.
Tonic . . . . the first scale degree.
Tranquillo . . . . tranquil, calm.
Transpose . . . . perform in a key other than the original. Each pitch must be raised or lowered by precisely the same interval, which results in the change of key.
Triad . . . . three-note chord.
Vivace . . . . lively.
Vivo . . . . lively.
Whole step . . . . . . equal to two half steps; skip one key (black or white).

Appendix C

List of Compositions
(Alphabetical by Composer)

Solo Repertoire

Duet Repertoire

List of Compositions (Alphabetical by Composer), continued

Ensemble Repertoire

Harmonizations (Titled)

Reading (Titled)

List of Compositions
(Alphabetical by Title)

Solo Repertoire

Duet Repertoire

Ensemble Repertoire

Harmonizations (Titled)

Reading (Titled)

Index

Index (continued)